QUEEN OF THE MAPLE LEAF

Sexuality Studies Series

This series focuses on original, provocative, scholarly research examining from a range of perspectives the complexity of human sexual practice, identity, community, and desire. Books in the series explore how sexuality interacts with other aspects of society, such as law, education, feminism, racial diversity, the family, policing, sport, government, religion, mass media, medicine, and employment. The series provides a broad public venue for nurturing debate, cultivating talent, and expanding knowledge of human sexual expression, past and present.

Recent volumes in the series include:

Reconsidering Radical Feminism: Affect and the Politics of Heterosexuality,
 by Jessica Joy Cameron
A Queer Love Story: The Letters of Jane Rule and Rick Bébout, edited by
 Marilyn R. Schuster
We Still Demand! Redefining Resistance in Sex and Gender Struggles, edited
 by Patrizia Gentile, Gary Kinsman, and L. Pauline Rankin
*The Nature of Masculinity: Critical Theory, New Materialisms, and
 Technologies of Embodiment*, by Steve Garlick
Making a Scene: Lesbians and Community across Canada, 1964–84,
 by Liz Millward
*Disrupting Queer Inclusion: Canadian Homonationalisms and the Politics
 of Belonging*, edited by OmiSoore H. Dryden and Suzanne Lenon
Fraught Intimacies: Non/Monogamy in the Public Sphere,
 by Nathan Rambukkana
Religion and Sexuality: Diversity and the Limits of Tolerance, edited by
 Pamela Dickey Young, Heather Shipley, and Tracy J. Trothen
The Man Who Invented Gender: Engaging the Ideas of John Money,
 by Terry Goldie

For a complete list of the titles in the series, see the UBC Press website, www.ubcpress.ca/sexuality-studies.

QUEEN OF THE MAPLE LEAF

BEAUTY CONTESTS AND SETTLER FEMININITY

Patrizia Gentile

UBCPress · Vancouver · Toronto

29 28 27 26 25 24 23 22 21 20   5 4 3 2 1

Printed in Canada on FSC-certified ancient-forest-free paper (100% post-consumer recycled) that is processed chlorine- and acid-free.

Library and Archives Canada Cataloguing in Publication

Title: Queen of the maple leaf : beauty contests and settler femininity / Patrizia Gentile.
Names: Gentile, Patrizia, author.
Series: Sexuality studies series.
Description: Series statement: Sexuality studies | Includes bibliographical references and index.
Identifiers: Canadiana (print) 20200287818 | Canadiana (ebook) 20200287869 | ISBN 9780774864121 (hardcover) | ISBN 9780774864138 (softcover) | ISBN 9780774864145 (PDF) | ISBN 9780774864152 (EPUB) | ISBN 9780774864169 (Kindle)
Subjects: LCSH: Beauty contests – Social aspects – Canada. | LCSH: Feminine beauty (Aesthetics) – Social aspects – Canada. | LCSH: Beauty contests – Canada – History.
Classification: LCC HQ1220.C2 G46 2021 | DDC 791.6/60971—dc23

Canadä

UBC Press gratefully acknowledges the financial support for our publishing program of the Government of Canada (through the Canada Book Fund), the Canada Council for the Arts, and the British Columbia Arts Council.

This book has been published with the help of a grant from the Canadian Federation for the Humanities and Social Sciences, through the Awards to Scholarly Publications Program, using funds provided by the Social Sciences and Humanities Research Council of Canada.

Printed and bound in Canada by Friesens
Set in Segoe and Warnock by Apex CoVantage, LLC
Copy editor: Robert Lewis
Proofreader: Helen Godolphin
Indexer: Christine Jacobs
Cover designer: Martyn Schmoll

UBC Press
The University of British Columbia
2029 West Mall
Vancouver, BC V6T 1Z2
www.ubcpress.ca

For Pauline

Contents

Illustrations

Acknowledgments

Writing this book has been a long, long journey. I won't be able to thank everyone by name here – all the archivists, librarians, and people who have told me stories about beauty pageants – but this book would only be an idea if not for them.

I am truly grateful to have an aquistions editor like Darcy Cullen. Her unwavering faith in this project and her encouragement have been a lifeline for me. Darcy and the staff at UBC Press, especially Carmen Tiampo, Ann Macklem, and Robert Lewis are a dream team. Cameron Duder edited a version of this manuscript and made it better. All errors remain my own, of course. Mike Dawson photocopied beauty contest souvenir programs from the Vancouver Public Library and sent them to me. Susan Prentice sent me the archival material on the protest of the Miss Canadian University Pageant. Dionne Brand gave me information that helped me locate material on Miss Black Ontario and other Black beauty contests. Thank you, Mike, Susan, and Dionne for your generosity and collegiality.

Parts of this book were written in different cities, including Paris. I want to thank my guardian angel, Nancy Marioles, who plucked me from a bad situation while I was in Paris and helped me to get back on my feet. Ron Shaw, a man I have never met, is Nancy's friend and the owner of the apartment I rent while in Paris. His place has played a central part in the writing process, and I am thankful to him for always making his apartment available to me. I also wrote the bulk of this book at a log house located in rural

Vermont built by my friend, Laurent Gaudin. I am so grateful to have access to this place; it's beautiful and peaceful.

There are several key people who have made my daily life happier, fuller, and better because they are in it – people like Emilia A. Fernández, Lou Gaudin and Téo Gaudin (my soul niece and nephew), Dan Irving, Kouky Fianu, Nick Hyrnyk (who conducted some research for this project), Jane Nicholas, Karen Dubinsky, and Gary Kinsman. I feel pretty lucky to have Josie, Rae, Nadia, and Charlie in my life. I have sisters and a brother who love me very much. I am blessed with eight nieces and nephews because of them: Amanda, Jonathan, Christopher, Nicholas, Alexander, Massimo, Matteo, and Olivia. My parents, Giuseppe and Giovanna, don't really understand what I do, but they believe in me anyway; I am always grateful to them. As I finish this book, my life is enriched by watching three spectacular little girls make their way in the world. Eleanor Ruth, Naomi Miriam, and Audrey Pearl give me hope.

Dino Zuccarini is my mentor, guide, and oldest friend. I can't imagine my life without him in it. Corinne Gaudin has listened to all my rants, made me dinner, wiped away my tears, distracted me with the latest news, taught me how to be a better researcher and teacher, and edited my work. The book you hold in your hands is possible because of her.

L. Pauline Rankin edited and read every version of this book. I write in this book that beauty is undefinable, but that's a lie. I know what beauty is, and I get to experience it through her every day.

Abbreviations

CBC   Canadian Broadcasting Corporation
GECO   General Engineering Company (Canada) Ltd.
ILGWU   International Ladies' Garment Workers' Union
IWY   International Women's Year
MCST   Maltese Canadian Society of Toronto
NCWC   National Council of Women of Canada
NFB   National Film Board
NIPC   National Indian Princess Committee
OPC   Ontario Provincial Council
RA   Recreation Association of the Public Service of Canada
RCMP   Royal Canadian Mounted Police
TLCW   Toronto Local Council of Women

QUEEN OF THE MAPLE LEAF

Introduction

Beauty pageants in North America flourished alongside the dime museums and freak shows of the 1870s. Like freak shows, beauty contests are institutions designed to entertain. They are spectacles where bodies are put on display: dangerous, extraordinary, fascinating bodies. Far from faddish, freak shows and beauty pageants endure, even if modified or seemingly anachronistic.[1] The reason for their longevity and popularity is their continued entrenchment of gender, class, and racial hierarchies – and in the case of beauty pageants, settler nation through bodies. Beauty pageants, like freak shows, are cultural institutions meant to anchor consistent images and ideals about beauty, bodies, and nation.

Most historians of the body concur that beauty itself is a complex phenomenon that is constantly contested, negotiated, and entangled with prescribed cultural practices.[2] A major theme of *Queen of the Maple Leaf* is how beauty contests[3] institutionalize and transform our private ritualized practices around beauty into public spectacles aimed at reinforcing white, middle-class, respectable femininity as a national discourse of white settler subjectivity. Beauty contests play a significant part in the making and sustaining of a modern version of *settler femininity* that codes white, heterosexual, female bodies as racially superior and exemplars of the healthy, prosperous, and strong settler nation. Settler femininity is a racialized and gendered signifier of the civilizing process not based solely on the dichotomy of the white, Victorian, respectable, chaste woman versus the "squaw," a derogatory and offensive term used to describe Indigenous women as promiscuous and sexually available (see Chapter 4). Although the term draws and feeds on this late-nineteenth-century dichotomy, it also adheres to a civilizing logic and is thus a tool directly linked to settler anxieties about the sexual and gendered character of colonial violence and nation building that characterized the twentieth century.

In her article "Taming Aboriginal Sexuality," Jean Barman reminds us that the construction of the sexually promiscuous Indigenous woman was possible only against the foil of Victorian women's chasteness in relation to the making of colonial masculinities.[4] Although they do not focus directly on settler femininity, scholars such as Barman, Sylvia Van Kirk, and Jennifer Henderson all offer a mapping of how settler femininity came to be a critical part of settler nation building.[5] One of the most important contributions to the scholarship on bodies, colonialism, and settler femininities is historians Katie Pickles and Myra Rutherdale's edited volume *Contact Zones,*[6] which examines the body as a site of colonial encounter revealing the body's centrality in settler world making and logics in Canada's "colonial past." In *Queen of the Maple Leaf,* I centre the bodies of beauty contestants and queens – white, immigrant, Black, or Indigenous – as a site of white settler logic and fantasy and suggest that these elements are in play in the historical past and present. In the 1920s, political and cultural regulatory practices that sustained Victorian codes of femininity and sexuality for settler and Indigenous women and for women of colour gradually began to be replaced by other social forces designed to transmit proper gender and sexual values. As a form of "banal nationalism," which refers to social psychologist Michael Billig's notion of how Western nations reproduce nationhood through continual and unconscious "flagging," beauty pageants in the twentieth century became an unthreatening, even seductive, tool in the replacement of Victorian gender and sexual codes as a means to communicate settler femininity as a civilizing logic in the face of anxieties about gender and sexuality.[7] That these settler anxieties continue to manifest on women's bodies is part of the long history linked to the racialization and feminizing of the nation discussed below.

Centring embodied allegories to represent the nation, especially the modern, white, progressive nation, is featured in literary scholar Daniel Coleman's work on nineteenth- and early-twentieth-century tropes of white civility in Canadian literature, which illustrates how claims of civility were part of a racial project that drew on a sense of Britishness.[8] In *White Civility,* Coleman shows how white settlers as the modern, progressive, and true inheritors of the Canadian nation are reified throughout key texts in Canadian literature from 1820 to 1950 to showcase and teach white superiority. All of Coleman's tropes – the Loyalist fratricide, the enterprising Scottish orphan, the muscular Christian, and the maturing colonial son – are male and thus centre the national allegory as masculine. Like Miss Canada, these tropes functioned in the same fashion as emblems of racial superiority and as conduits for quelling fears and anxiety about the continued presence of Indigenous and Black bodies.

Canadian beauty contests transmit this settler femininity over time and in a systemic and institutionalized way, thereby solidifying their value for white settler nationalism. Although the ideals of settler femininity underwent shifts throughout the decades from the 1920s to the late 1980s, these shifts cannot be measured neatly and in a linear fashion. Changes in social practices or political events such as the Second World War or the women's movement in the later part of the twentieth century obviously modified definitions and ideals, but the elimination and erasure of Indigenous and Black bodies continues to drive the vision of settler futurity, thus shaping femininity. In other words, tracing these shifts in a Eurocentric, linear, and progressive fashion to mark temporal change functions only to reinforce the settler logic that this book attempts to destabilize. This book traces how contested definitions of gender, race, modern consumer culture, community, citizenship, belonging, and nation were inscribed on the bodies of beauty queens through settler femininity over the twentieth century, but this tracing does not follow a linear narrative despite attempts to organize the chapters from the 1920s to the early 1990s. Beauty contests, in their multitude and variety, enable us to explore how the ideals and symbols of the white settler nation – in this case, Canada – were established within the framework of twentieth-century settler femininity and consumer culture. Canadian beauty contests took the rituals and spectacles of beauty and representations of the female body and created them as a "text" imbued with community values and white settler national identity. Although we can witness changes in this text over time, the choices about which bodies would be used to narrate this complex relationship between community values and white settler national identity were messy and do not fall neatly into a structured view of temporality often valued by historians.

There can be no doubt that beauty contests mattered in twentieth-century settler societies. Beauty pageants became ubiquitous because their structure and messages widely and effectively promoted the white settler values of competitiveness, individuality, respectability, and conformity as these social codes changed throughout the twentieth century. They strived not only to sell goods but also to spread ideals of community, racial homogeneity, moral character, and national symbols critical to upholding the myth of the modern white settler society. Beauty contests are culturally significant and highly adaptable because in their effort to create a universal depiction of beauty by blurring and sometimes erasing race, class, and nonhegemonic sexualities, they actually render the idea of beauty problematic and exclusionary. Beauty pageants can amplify a settler future defined by scholars Eve Tuck and Rubén A. Gaztambide-Fernández as ensuring "the absorption of any and all critiques that pose a challenge to white supremacy, and the replacement of anyone who dares to speak against ongoing colonization."[9] Beauty contests are one way that white settler societies can institutionalize this futurity, wrapped in entertainment and flash. By attempting to promote normative values designed to universalize white settler subjectivities, pageants create discourses about beauty and community that are unstable, tenuous, contested, and anxiety-ridden. Beauty pageants, therefore, give cultural historians a unique way to explain gender and bodies as signifiers of morality, sexuality, class, race, and womanhood within the context of consumer culture and the drive to commodify the body.

The beauty contestant's body as text, as representative of or exemplifying femininity, race, community, or nation, was and continues to be an ambitious endeavour. Since a straight line connecting race or nation to the beauty contestant's body is tenuous at best, this embodiment is in constant flux, easily manipulated, and always changing. Representations of whiteness and modernity in settler nations are contestable since they are signifiers of what historian Lorenzo Veracini labels the "imaginary spectacle" of settler fantasy, a foundational operating system of white settler societies.[10] By definition, the beauty contestant's body as an example of settler femininity had to be malleable to fit this fantasy. The numerous examples of a range of beauty contests attempting to represent feminized and racialized symbols of the white settler nation are not considered to be static or ahistorical. The politics of beauty pageants demand a fluid relationship with ideals of femininity, race, consumerism, and nation in historical context. Who is included or excluded from these categories punctuates the politics of beauty pageants and defines which bodies are contested in white settler societies.

This book explains why beauty contests, as spectacles designed to embody ideals about nation and citizenship through the bodies of respectable, middle-class women, are critical to maintaining white settler nationalism. Beauty contests may seem like frivolous entertainment, and in many ways, they are. However, unlike other forms of spectacle and entertainment, the beauty contest persists because it is more than just another example of readily consumed popular culture. *Queen of the Maple Leaf* demonstrates that the longevity of beauty contests lies squarely in their capacity to act as a tool for reasserting and re-entrenching, in seductive ways, the racial supremacy and heteropatriarchy at the heart of white settler societies.

Beauty contest scholars have offered a variety of analyses to account for the origins, objectives, and impact of these events. Some of this scholarship focuses on local and small queen pageants, similar to queen pageants that aim to shore up community values and civic pride, such as Stephen Fielding's "The Changing Face of Little Italy: The Miss Colombo Pageant and the Making of Ethnicity in Trail, British Columbia, 1970–1977," Tarah Brookfield's "Modelling the UN's Mission in Semi-Formal Wear: Edmonton's Miss United Nations Pageants of the 1960s," Karen Tice's *Queens of Academe: Beauty Pageants and Campus Life*, and Blain Roberts's *Pageants, Parlors, and Pretty Women*. These beauty contest scholars highlight the history of the local pageant in question and offer an analysis of the motives behind its inception, which often include an eagerness to boost community values or to offer young women a means to better themselves. This scholarship shows how ubiquitous and useful the beauty contest model was for community boosterism or for selling products, turning a profit, or attracting people to an event, but it also highlights another important aspect of beauty contest culture: women's use of the beauty contest platform to create opportunity or social advancement. Tice and Roberts, for example, offer evidence of Black women's support of beauty contests as a resource to enhance racial pride or acquire social standing as respectable in the southern United States. The focus of this work positions beauty pageants as part of the politics of beauty, emphasizing that they can be deployed to wield social or economic clout for otherwise marginalized individuals.

On the whole, beauty contest scholarship considers beauty pageants to be vehicles through which ideas of nation and citizenship are gendered and racialized, such as the work of Sarah Banet-Weiser and Rebecca Chiyoko King-O'Riain. In *The Most Beautiful Girl in the World*, Banet-Weiser uses a cultural analysis of four controversial beauty queens throughout the Miss America Pageant's history to explore how beauty contests are about "gender and nation as racialized categories" and offers a thorough account of how the pageant's significant currency is linked to American values about femininity, race, and culture.[11] King-O'Riain's *Pure Beauty: Judging Race in Japanese American Beauty Pageants* deploys the theory and practice of "race work" to explain the complex gendered and racialized notions of ethnicity, nation, and citizenship at the core of the Nisei Week Queen Pageant in California from the mid-1930s to 1990s. In this book, King-O'Riain traces how beauty contests used the queen as a way to demonstrate loyalty to the United States by showcasing her body as an outstanding example of

"Americanness." It was through this race work that a "white hegemonic gaze" was used to make the queen "American."[12] Banet-Weiser and King-O'Riain critically engage with the interplay among beauty pageants, nation, race, gender, and citizenship but fall short in examining how white femininity, respectability, and settler nationalism – which lies at the core of this "Americanness" – become inscribed on women's bodies to create the contested images that beauty contests propose. How did female bodies come to be understood as symbols of the settler nation in the United States and Canada? How has whiteness become understood as "beautiful," normal, and desirable in the United States and Canada due to their histories of colonialism and the denigration and erasure of racialized bodies?

Scholarship on beauty contests is gaining in popularity because beauty pageants such as Miss Atom Bomb, Miss Tobacco, and Indian Princess make for fascinating historical studies about popular culture, politics, bodies, and spectacle.[13] An analysis that traces the cultural impact of beauty contests to their gendered and racialized representations of nation and citizenship *and* how these representations are rooted in racial and patriarchal settler hierarchies shows why beauty pageants continue to proliferate despite feminist critiques. The purpose of this book is to demonstrate that the common thread connecting local queen pageants (including "ethnic" beauty pageants) and national beauty contests that function as profit-making ventures is their compulsion to uphold white, respectable, middle-class femininity, or settler femininity, as the marker of the desirable body in settler societies. This book does not debate whether beauty contestants are dupes or victims of false consciousness or agents successfully manipulating the system to their advantage. My position is that women, whatever their racial, socio-economic, or ethnic identities, have engaged with beauty contests as participants, organizers, and spectators for a variety of complex reasons, but an in-depth study of those reasons is beyond the scope of this book. Instead, I am interested in understanding the contested values at the core of the Canadian nation in order to contest nation itself, metaphorically grafted onto the female body. This analysis necessitates a discussion of Canada's settler colonialism and its politics of diversity through multicultural policies as anxiety-ridden attempts to manage race and nation.

Anti-violence scholar Andrea Smith demonstrates that because white supremacy and settler colonialism intersect, a theory of racialization or race formation that ignores the roots of settler colonialism continues to miss the mark.[14] For Smith, state formation in the United States is grounded in what she calls the "three pillars of white supremacy": the logics of slavery, genocide, and Orientalism as anchored by capitalism, colonialism, and war that maintain white settler societies.[15] Unlike colonialism, the project of settler colonialism is one of displacement – or elimination – and replacement through the logics of genocide, slavery, and Orientalism. Theorist and historian Patrick Wolfe uses the analogy of a double-sided coin to explain the displacement-replacement logic of settler colonialism: "The eliminatory project of replacing Native peoples on their land was one side of the coin of European property, the other being the enslavement of imported Africans and their descendants."[16]

The logic of white supremacy is not part of the historical *past;* it is a logic that is perpetuated in the historical *present* through a multitude of narratives. These narratives are embedded in a range of political, economic, legal, and cultural institutions that manipulate race, bodies, and nation, such as residential schools, multicultural policies, and even "frivolous" beauty pageants. At the moment of her victory, the beauty queen – the "winner" – stands as the personification of the white settler nation and community. Her "victory" signals that she successfully belongs to a narrative of citizenship steeped in a specific gendered, racialized, and sexualized definition of nation. Although beauty contests such as Miss Grey Cup and Miss Carleton University may not have been explicitly about nation or citizenship, the celebration of white, middle-class, respectable, and "wholesome" femininity through these pageants signalled the de facto racialization of white female bodies as sites of privilege, supremacy, and power.

In Canada, owners and organizers of beauty pageants past and present have lent credibility to their ventures by claiming to be searching for the "ideal Canadian girl." This phrase is not accidental or simply a gimmicky way of attracting participants and curious onlookers. Finding the "ideal Canadian girl" reinstated whiteness and class hierarchies at the centre of the making of national subjectivities when questions of nationalism were at their most heated, whether in the early 1920s with the rise of the modern girl or during the protests by feminists in the late 1980s. But what happens to those bodies that are not easily included within the boundaries of settler femininity? *The Queen of the Maple Leaf* is also concerned with revealing how some contestants are deemed unacceptable symbolic representations of settler femininity. The seductive character of beauty contests, bolstered by the idea that they are "harmless" or even "good clean fun," means that nonwhite women's bodies, which are often excluded from national discourses about femininity, also participate in these competitions and sometimes win. These beauty queens are victorious because they perform a version of settler femininity successfully, or at least exceptionally in the case of Indigenous and Black beauty contestants, but several examples exist of how their subsequent reigns have been fraught with problems and controversies. There are many instances of these "mistakes": Bess Myerson, Miss America 1945, the first and only Jewish woman to win the title, which resulted in sponsors withdrawing support because of her "race"; Vanessa Williams, Miss America 1984, the first Black woman to win the title, who was dethroned due to a controversy regarding photos appearing in *Penthouse* magazine; Danielle House, Miss Universe Canada 1996, who was dethroned after assaulting another woman over a former boyfriend; kahntinetha Horn, winner of the Indian Princess title, who used it as a platform for Red Power and was stripped of her crown because of her political beliefs; Alicia Machado, Miss Universe 1996, who was told she was "too fat" by pageant owner Donald Trump; Jenna Talackova, a Miss Universe Canada 2012 finalist, who was eliminated from the competition because she was discovered to be a transwoman; and Nina Davuluri, Miss America 2013, the first Indian American to win the title, who endured a rash of racist tweets questioning her "Americanness." When so-called controversial winners are chosen for national titles, the lines and boundaries of who belongs in the nation are made most visible.

Although this book focuses on queen pageants such as Miss Malta of Toronto (also Miss Malta) and Miss War Worker as well as on national beauty pageants in Canada, beauty pageants exist in relation to one another internationally, especially since many winners of national contests pursue global titles. But the relational character of beauty contests is also prevalent between local and community-based beauty contests and larger pageants such as Miss Canada or Miss Teenage Canada. The format of queen pageants is the same as or similar to the structure of national beauty pageants. Queen pageants are often used by the winners as stepping stones to provincial or national pageants. In this way, beauty pageants are part of a network whose tiers are not unlike the different levels of sports, such as Little League, Bantam, and so on. However, queen pageants are often organized as separate from national or provincial pageants – at times, deliberately so. In fact, some queen pageants, organized around a theme or a community event, are considered more relevant than national beauty pageants precisely because members of the audience and even the organizers themselves know the contestants intimately as daughters, nieces, or sisters. Queen pageants also differ in terms of the competitive component. Although no less demanding than provincial or national pageants, the "winner" often shares her victory so that no discernible winner is identifiable. However, the presence of judges does mean that someone has to win.

In *Queen of the Maple Leaf*, I argue that although queen pageants such as Miss War Worker, Miss Malta, and Miss Civil Service were local, the values and codes they exemplified shed light on how certain messages about femininity, class, sexuality, and race shaped narratives of the white settler nation. This book, therefore, focuses on the part that they played as building blocks for the national pageants and on how they functioned to solidify networks for the making of white settler nationalism in the context of the beauty pageant industry. Performing settler femininity was still the overriding aim even though the pageant title was not expressly "national." Although queen pageants are the poorer sisters of national beauty contests, they are still spectacles of racialization and gender. Whether the queen pageant in question is Miss Chinatown (a popular contest held in Vancouver in the late twentieth century) or Miss Restaurant, the goal of all beauty contests is to connect female bodies in some way to white, middle-class, respectable femininity and wholesomeness.

Beauty contests organized by unions were also very much involved in the entrenchment and reification of settler nationalism and white, middle-class, respectable femininity. It is no accident that immigrant women were not involved in the pageant of the International League of Ladies' Garment Workers' Union, called La Reine des Midinettes/Queen of the Dressmakers. This pageant was the enclave of francophone Quebecois women performing settler femininity. Queen of the Dressmakers was a way to uplift working-class francophone women as an example of acceptable bodies in the context of white settler society. However, viewing these queen pageants as less critical to our understanding of the connections between body, settler nationalism, and popular culture reifies a false dichotomy between the local and national. This book challenges this dichotomy, placing queen pageants on a continuum of beauty pageants and explicating their role in entrenching settler femininity. *Queen of the Maple Leaf* continues the dialogue between beauty pageant scholars and beauty pageants themselves and argues for the need to continue to understand beauty pageants in the context of settler nationalism and white supremacy.

Beauty, White Settler Femininity, and Canadian "Character"

Before the first beauty contest appeared in Montreal in the early 1920s, iconic representations of the Canadian nation and character were already a common feature of the political and cultural landscape, as was certainly the case in literature, as documented by Daniel Coleman.[17] By the late nineteenth century, the Mountie's red serge represented Canadian "honesty, justice and honour."[18] Johnny or Jack Canuck, a cartoon character that first appeared in 1869 in the Montreal journal *Grinchuckle*, symbolized young Canadians, like the country he represented.[19] The cartoon character sometimes morphed into a *habitant*, a farmer from seventeenth-century New France, who was a figure that romanticized and mythologized that chapter in Canadian settler history. Other historic symbols or icons of Canada included Niagara Falls, the beaver, the Canadian National Exhibition, Laura Secord, the Stanley Cup and hockey, and of course, the maple leaf.[20] To varying degrees, these geographic features, flora and fauna, sports, and people symbolized Canada's highlights, notably its natural attributes, its imagined colonial history, its international status in sports via hockey, its role in industrial progress, and its loyalty to the British Crown. Each one was framed, however, within a gender, race, and class discourse constructed for particular political, economic, and cultural uses. Veracini describes these settler society narratives as part of "a recurring narcissistic drive" based on the need to disavow the violence at the heart of all settler projects.[21] In settler societies, the fantasy of a peaceful nation reinforced through benign symbols and narratives of state formation functions to reconcile, even if tenuously, the violence of the settler colonial projects. The figure of a young, white female as a symbol of the nation is foundational to this settler fantasy.

Gender historian Carmen J. Nielson has revealed an important precursor to the twentieth-century beauty queen: a rendering of a young, white woman in "Indian" garb representing the image of British North America that appeared in popular nineteenth-century political magazines such as *Grip* and *Punch*. In this research, Nielson demonstrates the ways that the visual representation of this Miss Canada is rooted in the imperial gaze of the "indigenized, feminized body."[22] Political cartoonists used the image of Miss Canada when they wanted a symbol that conveyed "Canadian virtue."[23] According to journalist and author Ken Lefolii, Miss Canada arrived on the scene at the turn of the twentieth century because "some cartoonists found Johnny too crude a figure" and they needed another image to stand for "Canada's moral superiority in her quarrels with the U.S., the U.K., or the Métis of the Red River."[24] This rendering of Miss Canada is part of a long tradition in which nations have used the image of a young, white woman to represent them. Take, for example, the image of "Britannia" for England, "Marianne" for France, and "Lady Liberty" for the United States.[25] The problematic image of the female savage has also adorned maps, books, paintings, cigar boxes, and a multitude of products since the late eighteenth century to symbolize colonized lands. In the case of the pictorial representation of the early modern nation-state, the white, feminized (usually European) nation was sometimes in armour and wielding a sword and sometimes in a flowing tunic with at least one breast exposed. For Latin America or

Africa, the body of the Indigenous woman was almost always naked and some-times hairy, emphasizing the primitiveness of the land and people.[26] Nielson also argues that the "repetitive deployment of feminised and eroticised images of the nation summoned particular gender, sexual and political identities into being and entangled viewers' psychic investment in masculine, heterosexual and nationalist subjectivities," as evidenced in editorial cartoons and political campaign posters published in English Canada between 1867 and 1914, a par-ticularly critical period in nation building.[27] Settler nations such as Canada continue this legacy of the violent rendering of colonization, sexuality, and gender through the beauty pageant format in the historical present.

Like the beauty queen that would succeed her as the representative of Canadian womanhood, the Miss Canada figure used in political cartoons, on cigarette boxes, on magazine covers, and in propaganda posters during the Second World War represented the all-Canadian girl, and her looks and attire shifted accordingly.[28] The point was to create an image of Canada that would appeal to the middle-class settler gaze. In her work on cartoonist John Wilson Bengough, historian Christina Burr shows quite effectively how the image of Miss Canada used in political cartoons functioned to make Miss Canada "a symbolic [bearer] of the nation."[29] Bengough capital-ized on the shared view in nineteenth-century Canadian society that women were the guardians and protectors of the nation. Miss Canada as the whole-some fair maiden – Bengough's favourite depiction – signified "faith, hope, charity, justice, prudence, temperance, and fortitude" and could thus convey powerful messages about nation to both Canadians and politicians.[30]

Miss Canada sometimes appeared in a *ceinture fléchée*, or sash, another appropriated fantasy of Canada's settler historical narrative about whiteness, this time from the *coureurs du bois*, who were trappers in the fur trade. At other times, she was shown skating or as a sports girl, an image that would become synonymous with the Great White North, a label that was used to romanticize Canada both as a tourist ploy and as a reminder of its citizens' fortitude.[31] The female bodies representing Canada were exclusively white, with no reference made to the increasingly complex ethnic and racial differ-ences that accompanied the waves of immigrants entering the country in the nineteenth and twentieth centuries. Immigrant others complicate the racial and class hierarchies of white settler societies since their ability to legitim-ately belong to the white settler nation is called into question by the fact that their status as legitimate citizens is in a state of flux, even though they benefit from the dispossession of Indigenous people and the slave system. This lim-inal status is reinforced in the symbolic narrative: immigrant women's bodies are rarely featured as credible representations of Canada, and when they are used in this way, their selection is riddled with controversy.

The white settler gaze is crucial to understanding beauty contests. The act of consuming an image, symbol, or icon necessitates several "gazes" mediated by the categories of gender, race, ethnicity, sexuality, and class. After all, beauty contests are not about finding a "truth" about beauty; rather, they are unequivocally about performing settler femininity. Banet-Weiser suggests that what we experience additionally when we watch beauty pageants is a specific "gendered notion of citizenship" based on a "national field of shared symbols and practices."[32] The white settler gaze, then, is informed by the messages that it receives, and it reinvents meanings based on a common set of cultural values and practices embedded in a white settler consciousness. *Queen of the Maple Leaf* surveys the multiple voices involved in organizing, protesting, sponsoring, and participating in beauty contests in order to illustrate the links between beauty, state formation, and the making of white settler subjectivities.

Historian Véronique Nahoum-Grappe suggests that the erotic gaze allows for the consumption of femininity, ethnicity, and nation on a vast scale. This gaze uses female beauty "tactically, to persuade, as if it were a kind of rhetoric," with the result that the "effect of beauty is to divert attention from one object to another," making it socially efficient.[33] This conceptualization goes beyond Banet-Weiser's claim that "beauty contests produce the female body as a site of pleasure."[34] Indeed, the idea here is not just that "sex sells" but also that beauty and women's bodies were accepted as important tools in reifying abstract ideals like femininity, nation, community, or "whiteness," which, I argue, then became part of collective settler consciousness. Beauty is not definable because it is rhetorical. Instead, the beauty queen's body was exploited as an object of desire in contexts where white settler anxieties about categories of class, gender, race, ethnicity, and nationalism were debated and resolved.

Queen of the Maple Leaf does not offer an exhaustive history of beauty contests or beauty contestants in Canada. As a cultural history of beauty contests, it describes the history, structure, and format of several beauty contests to help situate the main narrative: beauty pageants are cultural institutions used to reinforce and entrench, however ambiguously, versions of settler femininity as an exemplar of the desirable body, past and future, in settler nationalism. This narrative does not discount the fact that Indigenous and Black beauty queens destabilized this settler futurity. As incongruent and always outside of settler normativity, these bodies are a reminder of colonial racial hierarchies that are at once forgotten and remobilized when needed. I focus on what was *said* about beauty contests and beauty queens in order to offer a better understanding of how the multiple ideals of settler femininity embedded in beauty contests became entangled with ideals of race, community, consumerism, and nation. I argue four main points throughout this study. First, beauty pageants are embedded in the beauty industrial complex, which includes representations of the white settler nation. We "consume" the beauty contestant's body as both a "product" and an embodiment of the values entrenched in nation, which gives us the notion of the consuming nation.

I employ the term "beauty industrial complex" to describe the dependency between business interests, the national or local imagination, and beauty contests, which is central to understanding how pageants were imbued with the gendered discourse of consumer culture. My use of this term refers to the connection between beauty contests, the media, and the corporate sector, namely the "beauty industry," which encompasses cosmetics, fashion, modelling, and advertising. The term adapts historian Kathy Peiss's "beauty industry" and scholar Varda Burstyn's development of the notion of a "sport-media complex."[35] In her book on beauty culture, Peiss describes the modern beauty industry as "large-scale production, national distribution, and advertising" accompanied by a "mass market of beauty consumers."[36] It was this beauty industry and its ability to make cosmetics "affordable and indispensable" and then to establish a dependency between fashion and cosmetics, or the "face as a style," that entrenched the buying and selling of cosmetics as an integral part of consumer culture.[37] The term "sport-media complex" refers to the forging of "deep links" between sport and commercial media in the twentieth century.[38] For Burstyn and her project on masculinity, sport spectacle, and business, the root of the sport-media complex is what she dubs the "sport nexus," or the existence of a "highly lucrative, multibranched transnational economy of enormous scope and influence."[39] It is this nexus that has established sport and its pervasive culture as "a spectacle of elite/professional performance."[40]

The idea of the beauty industrial complex helps to underscore the intersections among the corporate sector, the media, and beauty pageants. From the outset, beauty pageants played a pivotal role in the beauty industrial complex because they were easily manipulated to serve corporate interests attached to the fashion, cosmetics, modelling, entertainment, and advertising industries. Whether the contest was local or national, the integration of beauty pageants into corporate interests made sponsoring pageants an obvious business endeavour. It is no coincidence, for instance, that beauty pageants historically were organized by Chambers of Commerce and funded by businessmen. For corporations, beauty pageants were ideal venues through which to promote products because they appealed to the masses as vehicles of popular and consumer culture.

Second, I argue that beauty pageants are a product of the modern need to make oneself "special," which had arisen by the turn of the twentieth century as an embodied reinvention that dovetailed with the settler fantasy of racial and class hegemony.[41] I use Warren Susman's culture of personality because it allows me to link the concept of the erotic gaze with the beauty industrial complex; however, he did not question the racial character embedded in this modern subjectivity.[42] Susman identifies the culture of personality as an outcome of the emerging consumer culture of the early twentieth century, which focused on a person's ability to construct a pleasing and attractive shell. In other words, being liked and selling one's *self* became more important than what one thought or felt. By the turn of the twentieth century, North American society increasingly defined itself through the purchasing of goods, or consumerism, whereby individuals were valued for what they had, not for who they were.[43] As Susman explains, the culture of personality signalled the breakdown of the culture of character and the rise of anonymity in urban society.[44]

Within this emerging culture of abundance and anonymity, the culture of personality thrived as the emphasis shifted to projecting a personality based on charm, attractiveness, and distinctiveness but always within a white, middle-class respectability. This process allowed for a sense of "liberty and democracy" to flourish separate from the structures of class and race hierarchies.[45] Beauty contests in the context of twentieth-century consumer culture reinforced defining one's self in terms of external signifiers by providing fertile ground for the labour of "making yourself," a fundamental tenet of the culture of personality and the construction of the public self in the twentieth century. Coupled with this process, advances in technology and mass communication, such as radio and television, ensured that the normative discourses of femininity and whiteness were widely disseminated, thus rooting self-worth in external beauty defined by the hegemonic ideals of whiteness, class, and citizenship.

Third, I illustrate how beauty pageants are competitive enterprises entrenched in the idea that beauty practices, literally, are part of women's work. In other words, daily beauty rituals within a beauty culture are labour practices and an integral part of the beauty industrial complex. Looking beautiful is central to the daily ritual that women must undergo in order to engage *successfully* in society. Engaging in beauty practices – applying cosmetics, exercising, counting calories, removing unwanted hair, and keeping up with the latest trends in fashion – is unpaid work but labour-intensive nevertheless. These beauty regimens and cultural practices take time and sustained commitment. In the world of beauty contests, the beauty contestant, especially the winner, is held up as the exemplar of a woman who has done the job well and therefore succeeded in this work. The process of crowning this woman epitomizes the value accrued to these beauty practices, while reinforcing the competitive nature of beauty culture in white settler society. Performing settler femininity is hard work; sustaining it requires a certain level of engagement in the fantasy narratives of white settler society and in the politics of race and beauty on a daily basis. This beauty labour is different for women of colour since performing femininity, settler or not, is not just about ensuring legibility; rather, it is often seen as a duty to uphold racial pride in the face of a society that denies your existence. The format of the beauty pageant mimics the politics of competition at the core of ritualizing beauty practices and the winner-take-all character of settler projects, even when the terrain is anything but equal: just like on stage, women compete with each other on the streets, in office buildings, and in their homes.

The ideology of beauty is central to beauty contests and their competitive organization. The association of beauty and youth with goodness and truth often frames the use of beauty queens as props to promote and advertise an event or product. I use the term "ideology of beauty" to refer to the meanings that emerge when we think about the value placed on the concept of beauty. The ideology of beauty refers to the evolution of thought associated with the shifting definitions of beauty. The terms "beauty culture" and "cult of beauty" are employed in the book to describe the practices that men and women engage in so as to beautify themselves.[46] Beauty culture generally encompasses these elaborate rituals as well as our use of fashion magazines, commercials, newspapers, celebrities, and even the oral tradition of passing beauty secrets from mother to daughter as coaching material. The ideology of beauty and beauty culture are related in that the former informs the social value of beauty, whereas the latter organizes the cultural importance and prominence of beauty in the lives of men and women.

As this book documents, beauty contests transmit cultural messages because they belong to the cult of beauty, coded white, middle-class, and wholesome, past and present. Without the context of rules and rituals defined by beauty culture, beauty contests could not convey such powerful images, and beauty contestants would not be marked as the "success stories" of ritualized beauty practices. As an integral component of the beauty industrial complex, beauty pageants have always been seen as important purveyors of those very beauty practices. For example, beauty contests mirrored the cosmetic and clothing fashions that were in vogue at particular historical moments and, in turn, were used to introduce the latest fashions.[47] The ritualization of beauty practices in this way can be traced to practices institutionalized in beauty pageants as early as the nineteenth century.

Finally, this book critically examines how beauty pageants function as a seductive tool to reinforce gender, race, and class anxieties in white settler societies such as Canada. The bodies of beauty contestants and beauty queens have become a modern representation of legitimate white, respectable, middle-class femininity central to the fantasy of racial and social supremacy needed to support the narratives of settler societies. The winners of Miss Canada or Miss War Worker or Miss Malta appealed to the white settler gaze because they were all performing a version of settler femininity that was considered appealing. That beauty contests are annual events helps to sustain repeatedly the legitimacy of the white, middle-class body as the embodiment of the nation. The women who won beauty contest titles represented the national body – the desirable and desired body of settler nationalism. In the performativity of settler femininity, beauty queens and contestants reinforced and maintained gender, class, heteropatriarchal, and racial codes. The beauty contest format and structure, with its gendered division of labour – chaperones and coaches were female, whereas judges were male – its focus both on displaying bodies and on competitiveness and individuality, and its anxieties about legitimacy contributed to the predominance of white contestants, as revealed by the pictures in this book.

Settler femininity as a practice and ideal required a steady diet of advice. Advice about how to be beautiful, charming, and respectable was forthcoming from every corner. Beauty contests, manuals, modelling agencies, and finishing schools were institutionalized versions of what women and girls would have heard from earlier generations about how to stay youthful, beautiful, and pure. However, modernity and consumer culture changed how these messages were constructed and received, making beauty pageants all the more powerful. Attempting to avoid a trap that would label beauty pageants as exploitative and greedy, pageant organizers often claimed that their competition "was not a beauty contest!"[48] Chapter 1 explores this conundrum and what I call the *pageant paradox*, the delicate balance between selling desirable bodies and maintaining the illusion of Victorian white femininity and moral standards. The pageant paradox has a long history in the European context dating back to the sixteenth century with the arrival of the May Day queen, and it continues to make its mark in the contemporary period. Understanding this contextualization is critical to understanding how beauty pageants – local, national, and thematic – were not harmless "shows" but intricately tied to white settler nationalism.

Arguably, the most important beauty contest to illustrate the interplay between settler femininity, pageants as cultural institutions, and white settler nationalism is the Miss Canada Pageant. Not surprisingly, the Miss Canada Pageant enjoyed attention from the business community and government officials. The first national Miss Canada contest was organized as part of the Montreal Winter Sports Carnival in 1923. It was officially trademarked in 1946. Throughout its history, the pageant underwent major shifts based on economic and political changes and was always influenced by the context in which it thrived and failed. Chapters 2 and 5 examine the history of this specific pageant and its central role in shaping and entrenching ideals of settler femininity and nationalism through white bodies. Chapter 2 focuses on the pageant's history from 1923 to 1961, when it changed hands, passing from beauty salon owners in Hamilton, Ontario, to a public relations firm. The growing pains experienced through the first half of the pageant's history reveal the deliberate and methodical development of settler femininity as an exemplar of the only legitimate desirable body in the settler society.

The workplace was another arena where beauty pageants flourished. Grooming working-class women to emulate and perform settler femininity became a popular pastime. Employers and union officials alike used the beauty pageant format to boost morale while promoting their companies, products, and union principles. Chapter 3 highlights four examples of workplace pageants: Miss War Worker, Miss Civil Service, Miss Secretary of Canada, and Queen of the Dressmakers. I chose these beauty pageants to highlight both their intermittent existence on the public stage from the 1940s to the 1970s and how they largely used working women's bodies in similar ways despite being organized by different interests: the private sector in the case of Miss War Worker and Miss Secretary of Canada, the public sector in the case of Miss Civil Service, and a union in the case of Queen of the Dressmakers. These pageants drew large crowds from the workplace and the community because they functioned as queen pageants in what would be considered the most unlikely places: a munitions plant, a government office, and a union hall. But these pageants played a critical role in reinforcing and entrenching settler nationalism since they helped to sustain gender, class, and racial hierarchies in the guise of harmless fun. In fact, it was the very banality of the beauty contest format that made them so influential.

Although I organize Chapters 3 and 4 thematically, they continue the discussion about the use of the queen pageant format to celebrate community through the performance of settler femininity. The main difference, however, is that Chapter 4 focuses on ethnic and racialized communities. Pageant organizers for these competitions fashioned the beauty contest format as a venue through which to educate Canadians about their respective cultures as part of the centennial celebrations in the 1960s. I use Miss Malta of Toronto as an example of an ethnic/immigrant community's beauty contest and Miss Black Ontario, Miss Caribana, and Indian Princess as racialized community pageants to analyze the way that these competitions were used not only to educate white settlers about these communities through emulation but also to destabilize settler futurity. The complexities, negotiations, and challenges of performing settler femininity for the Miss Malta of Toronto contest, which exemplify the politics of diversity framed by settler discourses of multiculturalism launched in the early 1970s, differed in comparison to those evoked by the performances of the alterior bodies of Black and Indigenous contestants. Settler logic allows Black and Indigenous bodies to "improve" by performing the tolerated other, but the politics of beauty allow these bodies to use the settler logic of improvement to create opportunities otherwise inaccessible. Although this is a complicated relationship, it does present a way to destabilize settler femininity.

Chapter 5 returns to the Miss Canada Pageant but begins with the history of how television changed the way that settler femininity was literally broadcast to Canadians through this competition. By the late 1960s and throughout the 1970s and 1980s, the Miss Canada Pageant tried to negotiate critical national debates about identity, multiculturalism, bilingualism, and feminism while maintaining its hold as a credible expression of white settler nationalism. From the 1920s to late 1980s, settler femininity underwent several changes, but its function as a performance of white civility and respectability was still in play throughout the roughly seventy-year span that *Queen of the Maple Leaf* covers. The main reason for this continuity is that these versions of femininity responded to the changing nature of settler anxieties throughout this period and corresponded to the futurity imagined by settlers who foresaw a Canada free of bodies that refused to disappear. From the mid-1960s, a moment when Canadians were in the throes of debating the parameters of the settler nation beginning with the centennial celebrations, the pageants discussed in Chapters 4 and 5 played a part in anchoring a version of settler normativity that matched those internal debates about multiculturalism, language, regional differences, dispossession, feminism, and what it meant to be Canadian.

1

Beauty Queens and (White) Settler Nationalism

The rise of personality culture in the modern era, especially as a cornerstone of mass consumer culture, partially explains how "being beautiful and charming" shaped settler femininity in the early twentieth century regardless of socio-economic status. Although the notion that one is either born beautiful or not – that is, the idea of beauty as a genetic trait – persists in settler cultures, poise and charm were increasingly thought of as characteristics that one could acquire. The proliferation of charm schools, articulation classes, and finishing schools underscored a tenet of mass consumer culture: money can buy happiness. In other words, a woman who displayed charm and poise, a "classy" woman, could compensate for any "deficiencies" in terms of beauty, however that was defined. Beauty contests trumpeted the virtues of charm and poise specifically to distract audiences from what was ultimately an event that displayed a particular vision of the female body.

Pageants represent the culmination of beauty practices and rituals adapted for the consumer culture of the late nineteenth and twentieth centuries. Most historians of the body argue that concepts of beauty changed over time, as did the social values associated with beauty.[1] Below I offer, in broad strokes, the development of the modern meanings of beauty and how those meanings eventually were institutionalized in the form of the beauty contest. The focus is on how and why discourses associated with beauty and the body changed, in turn influencing the premise of those values upheld in competitions such as beauty contests. Finally, this chapter explores what I call the *pageant paradox*. The pageant paradox is the manifestation of the intricate and contradictory interplay between the beauty contestant's performance of sensuality and moral respectability, or the balance between the modern and the traditional.[2] In a section titled "This Is Not a Beauty Contest," I consider how and why pageant organizers attempted to reconcile the pageant paradox by denying the label of the beauty contest as a competition to decide which *body* was the most beautiful. This denial was used strategically to downplay the lure of sexuality and beauty and to promote moral respectability, wholesomeness, and charm in the hope that the beauty contest would appeal to white, middle-class women and the spectator's white settler gaze. Negotiating the complex balance among sensuality, beauty, and good character to perform an acceptable version of femininity and the making of the modern self was usually achievable only by white women. The pageant paradox has a third purpose. Beauty contests could survive only with the support of corporate sponsors, and they invested in beauty contests that could turn a profit. Without the active participation and buy-in of white, middle-class women, beauty contest organizers could not count on the vital support drawn from corporate sponsors. The success of the beauty contest as an institution depended on its ability to market an image of the "girl next door" as morally upright in a white settler society.

Making the Modern Beauty Pageant White

Settler ideals about physical beauty are by no means homogeneous. The roots of these ideals can be traced to Italian artists and humanists of the 1500s who, ironically, had inherited a basic mistrust of the body from the Middle Ages.[3] Framing women as temptresses meant that the practices and rituals for beautifying the body were placed under rigid moral and religious scrutiny. The result was that the pursuit of physical perfection and beauty was accompanied by a strict obligation to social and religious duty.[4] Beauty became synonymous with the female sex because of its denigrated status.[5] By the Renaissance, the narrow-hipped, small-breasted female body of the Middle Ages had given way to the plumper and full-breasted ideal of female beauty that reigned until the late 1700s.[6] "Plumpness" was considered a sign of health as well as beauty and was associated with women from the wealthier classes. Thinness was deemed ugly and considered a fate of the poor.[7] Such European ideals of beauty established in the sixteenth and seventeenth centuries were central to ritualizing beauty practices and canons. What became important was the ability for women to distinguish themselves from men in dress, appearance, and behaviour.[8] Behaving in a chaste, delicate, graceful, and unassuming manner was deemed an essential part of being beautiful.

Another enduring element from these periods was the discourse of beauty as a "visible sign of an inward and invisible goodness."[9] Beauty was considered an outward sign of a solid moral character. This discourse was codified in art, literature, and the use of cosmetics so that "beauty followed a formula, and women went to a great deal of trouble and expense to make their appearance conform to standards that remained virtually unaltered throughout the early modern period."[10]

Eighteenth-century Romanticism rejected a formulaic approach to beauty but retained the notion of ritual that continues to inform contemporary discourses of beauty. Books and manuals that concentrated on the use of cosmetics and the act of "painting" oneself to achieve and maintain a Eurocentric ideal of feminine beauty focused on the parts of the body that were visible to the public, namely the hair, face, neck, breasts, and hands.[11] Emphasis was placed on arousing the senses by creating an alluring public persona. It is noteworthy that, even as early as the eighteenth century, beauty was equated with whiteness, which was understood as the colour of purity, femininity, and civilized races.[12] In her study on beauty and ugliness, Véronique Nahoum-Grappe argues that beauty is a form of communication that carries messages and symbols about gender, class, race, and ethnicity, noting that it was employed as a tool in earlier eras when European women were prevented from using legal, economic, and political strategies to institute change or ideas.[13] Beauty, then, was a mask or a facade that produced meaning in the lives of women as they engaged with society.

By the late 1800s and early 1900s, the natural look heralded another change in the discourse of beauty practices. The natural look is a central tenet of modern beauty pageants since contestants must perform a "girl next door" ideal based on a clean, wholesome femininity. The rise of the bourgeoisie, who espoused simplicity and puritan virtuousness, supplanted the artifice that dominated the *toilettes* popular in the mid-1700s.[14] For the bourgeoisie, the emphasis was on building the inner self. Extravagant displays of wealth and beauty were deemed contrary to this process. Positive self-image was thought to reside in a pious, self-sacrificing character based on the ideals of utilitarianism and simplicity, with truth and goodness identified as the essence of beauty. The idea that the eyes offered mirrors to one's soul was commonplace by the beginning of the nineteenth century.[15] Beauty as an individual experience that was communicated to the world in an unadorned fashion informed the nineteenth-century "culture of character."[16] In the period after the First World War, the advent of consumer culture and the focus on one's public image saw the cult of character replaced with an approach and discourse of beauty that emphasized the self, especially the packaging and making of the self. This cultural shift, often associated with the rise of modernity, is explored in *Queen of the Maple Leaf*. Beauty pageants gained popularity on this fertile ground.

The history of beauty contests dates from seventeenth-century Europe. They are part of a tradition that began with the May Day queen, who represented at once both fertility and virginity.[17] What might seem like a contradictory dualism was but an exaggerated feature congruent with the manner in which modern beauty queens were later portrayed. Contestants were expected to be physically attractive and sexually appealing while exuding a virtuousness bordering on childlike innocence. The emphasis on attractiveness and sexual purity shifted with changing cultural influences. In France, as religious influences infiltrated the premodern festivities of the May Day celebrations, the May Day queen, usually a young woman, was replaced by a girl who received gifts from the townspeople while sitting on her throne.[18] This shift was meant to downplay the festive character of the celebrations by instilling a sense of piety through the body of a child.

Young virgins as symbols of beauty also functioned as a way to honour Catherine of Alexandria, the patron saint of virgins, nuns, spinsters, and dressmakers.[19] By the end of the nineteenth century, Miss Catherinette, a beauty contest for dressmakers in France, had been substituted for the religious Saint Catherine celebrations. In the Miss Catherinette beauty contest, contestants were either virgins or invoked the spirit of a saint who was a virgin, indicating the power that virgins held as symbols. In particular, the notion that virgins were pure of heart, chaste, and thus untainted by sin or evil established them as emblems of hope for the small villages and towns that wanted to be free of what were believed to be earthly manifestations of evil, such as drought, bad crops, or disease.

The tradition of selecting a May Day queen was eventually incorporated within and adapted to the main events at carnivals, tournaments, and community fairs. Competitors' bodies became sites upon which utopian views of community spirit, youth, beauty, and hope were sketched. By the eighteenth and early nineteenth centuries, "the beauty" was a regular feature of public festivals. In addition to celebrating civic pride and hopes for a better future, the selection of a queen "reinforced the centrality of physical beauty in women's lives and made beauty a matter of competition and elitism and not of democratic cooperation among women."[20]

American Phineas T. Barnum, famous for his sideshows and dime museums, was the enterprising mind behind the commercial success of beauty contests.[21] Barnum's first attempt to stage such a contest in 1854 was a failure, due mainly to Victorian distaste for the display of women's bodies in a public space. Traditionally, participants in Barnum's sideshows were working-class women whom he paid a fee for their time. In the Victorian era, what one wore in public defined class, level of affluence, and in the case of women, sexual status.[22] Prostitutes wore revealing clothing and rouge while putting themselves on public display. The commercialized beauty contest held no appeal for the middle and upper classes. Respectable young women of marriageable age were expected to sit demurely in parlour rooms entertaining suitors.

Photographic beauty contests offered a solution to Barnum's dilemma. In this format, young women were asked to send in daguerreotypes that would then be painted into portraits and hung in his museum. These portraits would be displayed in a gallery called the "Congress of Beauty" where visitors to the museum voted on which portrait they thought should win.[23] Barnum's idea did not come to fruition, but Adam Forepaugh, also a circus and sideshow owner, elaborated on Barnum's idea in 1888 by advertising in newspapers for photographs in order to find the nation's "most beautiful woman." The winner of this highly successful beauty contest was Louise Montague, who became famous as the "Ten Thousand Dollar Beauty."[24] By the early twentieth century, photographic beauty contests were a regular occurrence in the United States and to a lesser extent in France, but whether these women were considered refined or respectable was still open to debate. In her work on French beauty culture at the turn of the twentieth century, historian Holly Grout argues that photographic beauty contests were more prevalent in the US context but demonstrates their popularity in France by showcasing a 1920 contest organized by journalist Maurice de Waleffe called Concours de la plus belle femme. Participants in this contest heralded from the working class and were required to be amateur beauties – that is, not to be associated with the modelling or professional entertainment industries. De Waleffe insisted that his contest focus on an "ethnically French model of womanhood that would restore gender norms and racial order."[25] The Concours de la plus belle femme was de Waleffe's response to "urban degeneration, overcivilization, and national decline," which he believed threatened the racial hierarchy that defined France's superiority.[26]

The modern beauty contest is based on the principle that beauty and its maintenance are central to feminine charm and health. The beauty principle is coded white and is driven by presenting women's bodies as a platform for sustaining white supremacy. The ideals of beauty preached at the end of the nineteenth century focused on behaviour and practices that ranged from how to be cheerful and charming to maintaining a complexion free of, say, pimples. But these guidelines were meant for white, middle-class women. *The Ladies' Guide to Health, Etiquette and Beauty and General Household Knowledge*, a Canadian health and beauty manual published in 1891, was available to women who wanted to achieve "beauty" for the purposes of finding or keeping a husband. In the nineteenth century, for example, "cheerfulness" and an absence of "nerves" were two characteristics identified as helping a woman to achieve charm and beauty.[27] The reference to "cheerfulness" as a "beautifier" was based on the prevailing cult of character, which judged one's disposition or attitude to be more valuable than how one looked. *The Ladies' Guide* defined the cheerful woman as one who had the ability to accept her lot in life and to

> walk half a mile to see a beautiful view, or who, if the cook or chambermaid gives sudden warning, can make a bed or use a carpet sweeper or prepare a toothsome meal. There isn't a man living who would fail to appreciate such a wife, mother or daughter, especially if she were strong enough to do it well and cheerfully, and had nerve enough (or lack of nerves) to treat the matter as a joke rather than a misfortune. And she would be far more beautiful while so engaged, than if attired in the most becoming toilet, helplessly bewailing her fate.[28]

Adaptability, cooking and cleaning skills, and good humour were considered desirable traits in a pleasant Victorian woman of means, but so was the ability to walk a half-mile. The healthy and hygienic body was a mainstay topic in beauty manuals. In France healthcare professionals equated the pursuit of the beautiful body with health and hygiene as a "civic responsibility."[29] In a period when character was synonymous with good breeding and moral superiority, femininity and thus beauty were equated with cheerfulness and by extension racial superiority.

Vestiges of this cheerful character continued to be incorporated into beauty pageants, especially in the form of Miss Friendship and Miss Congeniality titles. These titles are the only part of the modern beauty contest that continues the cult of character prevalent in the Victorian era.

However, even *The Ladies' Guide* knew the "limitations" of a cheerful character and included a lengthy section on rituals and practices to enhance physical attractiveness because "a good complexion ... is essential to beauty in women, and most healthy women possess it."[30] *The Ladies' Guide* described the various methods and ingredients needed to maintain beauty, such as glycerine, carbolic acid, the juice of chickweed or onion, vinegar, magnesia, borax, olive oil, rum, almond oil, ammonia, rosewater, rosemary, and walnut juice. Special mixtures and concoctions could assist women to improve or eliminate features that enhanced or detracted from a person's physical attractiveness. Even in the late nineteenth century, body parts that were exposed to the public continued to garner attention, and so *The Ladies' Guide* shared advice for whitening hands, keeping hair clean, and removing wrinkles, pimples, spots, and blemishes from the skin. The advice offered in *The Ladies' Guide* ended with a reiteration of the value of cheerfulness as the most beautiful attribute a wife, mother, or young lady could possess.

It was only with the rise of professional modelling, the emergence of the modern girl, and the introduction of the swimsuit in North America that respectable women began to flock to beauty contests as contestants. Bathing suits, fashion models, the rise of cosmetic use, and the urban-based confident modern girl created acceptable conditions for the public display of women's bodies despite socio-economic status and produced possibilities for opportunities beyond the home. The commercialization of beauty culture created a fertile ground upon which to perform a self and "provided modern women with the tools and strategies necessary to make themselves visible, to shape how they viewed themselves and, to some extent, how they were seen by others."[31] Prizes for beauty contests at the turn of the century often included an opportunity to model or to act in the theatre. Beauty contests have long been perceived as stepping-stones to successful careers in the entertainment industry. The entertainment and cosmetic industries seized on the potential profits to be derived from encouraging the modelling and display of the feminine figure.[32] Utilizing a beauty queen who had already acquired public acceptance based on physical attractiveness eliminated some of the logistics and work needed to locate women who were willing to be put on display. The bathing suit was critical to the success of this venture. The bathing beauties of the 1920s and the swimsuit segment in beauty contests attest to the connection between the legitimate display of thighs and shoulders (and later, cleavage) and the public enthusiasm for beauty contests.[33]

Beauty Pageants, Healthy Bodies, and White Settler Subjectivities

Theories abound that posit the body as performative and/or as a cultural space mediated by social forces.[34] In the twentieth century, beauty contests were part of a political and social context in which the body was used as a site for promoting the agendas of various sectors of society such as the health movement (in terms of dieting, exercise, and physical culture), the social purity movement, and the eugenics movement. The social purity movement originated in late-nineteenth-century England but quickly took hold in Canada and the United States until the First World War. Social purity reformers (mostly women) advocated for sexual chastity and for social and political control of what were increasingly understood as urban vices, notably drinking, prostitution, and entertainment. The focus on sexual conduct enabled reformers to tie the social purity movement to the protection of the Anglo-Saxon race, linking its mandate to fighting against "the degeneration of the races."[35] Closely related, the eugenics movement, spanning the period of the 1920s to the 1980s, was based on theories of selective reproduction and on weeding out undesirable traits to ensure the health of the nation. Medical scientists and politicians who supported theories of racial hierarchies at the core of eugenics believed that the survival of the white race depended on the systemic sterilization of immigrants, people living in poverty, people living with disabilities, and Indigenous women.[36]

These movements constructed white women as the legitimate producers and nurturers of the next generation of citizens. Coinciding with the social purity movement and with the early years of the eugenics movement was another movement committed to educating society on the benefits of a healthy lifestyle based on diet and exercise. The health movement built momentum in the late nineteenth century and was in full force by the 1920s as a result of information compiled on the health of men drafted for combat during the First World War. Activities such as dieting and exercising quickly became a major aspect of beautifying and personal improvement rituals in settler societies such as Canada and the United States.[37] Like most social phenomena concerning the body, the health movement was enveloped in discourses of race, class, beauty, moral superiority, and strength (weakness and flabbiness being emblematic of larger social and national problems), issues also pertinent to beauty contests. For example, the swimsuit portion of beauty contests replicated these discourses, with the contestants expected to demonstrate that they were lean and healthy but still feminine. The swimsuit segment allowed unprecedented visual access to what were considered exemplars of feminine health, placing beauty pageants within the larger discussion about well-being in this period.

The emergence of beauty contests alongside the health and eugenics movements was no coincidence. Pageants were another platform from which to spread eugenic values regarding the healthy, white, and strong nation. A characteristic practice of the eugenics movement was the so-called scientific measuring of bodies in an effort to determine a normative discourse on health, physical perfection, and racialization. At the height of Japan's eugenics period in the 1930s, for instance, beauty pageants required contestants to undergo "physical examinations, including gynaecological examinations to establish their health, fertility, and virginity."[38] That legacy continued to surface in beauty contests, where contestants were measured to record their vital statistics. A vestige of earlier eugenic practices, this system of ranking, rating, recording, and evaluating the "best attributes" was used by judges of beauty contests to reach what they believed to be an objective decision. The bodies of beauty contestants, therefore, were to reinforce the racial (in)securities of the settler nation by repeatedly displaying on a stage white, youthful, feminine, and potentially reproductive women. "Rewarding" these bodies through a crowning ceremony served to ease these racial anxieties, even if only temporarily.

By mid-century the obsession with measuring and accounting for physical attributes had faded, and this approach was replaced by reproductive policies such as pro-natalist legislation, another important tool used to establish hierarchies of white supremacy in settler societies.[39] As the reproducers of the nation's citizens, white women were situated at the centre of the legal, state, medical, and religious discourses on state formation and were expected to fulfill a moral obligation to maintain their health and fortitude in order to sustain the health of the nation. The pro-natalist policies of the mid-twentieth century in Canada rested on racialized discourses that claimed it was the duty of white, healthy, and middle-class women to produce children in the name of nation building.

These same social and legal discourses were manifested in other forms of beauty pageants. From the 1920s to the 1960s, child beauty pageants were often part of community and national festivals. In 1923 the *Toronto Star* sponsored and organized a pageant called Canada's Loveliest Child, which nearly 8,000 children entered to compete for "the most representative of the loveliest of Canadian childhood."[40] In 1949 the Rotary Club in Niagara Falls conducted a "bathing beauty" pageant for the members' daughters in which all the participants were named "queens."[41] In 1962 the Canadian National Exhibition, held in Toronto, included a beauty contest for infants. About 1,000 babies, all dressed in white, were weighed, measured, and then judged. The "best in show" was a boy labelled a "little charmer."[42] The visual representations of these pageants show that all of these children were white. Clearly, vestiges of eugenic discourse circulated throughout Canadian society, even infiltrating beauty pageants.

It was, however, the Miss America Pageant that marked a milestone in the history of beauty contests and children's bodies as exemplars of the settler nation. The 1921 beauty contest was only one aspect of the festivities used by Atlantic City businessmen to lure tourists back to the boardwalk. Parades, concerts, sporting events, and fancy-dress balls were also designed for children and involved their active participation.[43] The presence of children at these events, including the beauty contest (whose winner was a fifteen-year-old girl), provided implicit support for pageants by the very audience that in an earlier period had rejected beauty contests as lewd. Ensuring that children could participate in the events enabled the beauty pageant promoters to harness the elusive and all-important respectability that had escaped Barnum's dime museums.[44]

The Modern Beauty Contest and Consumer Culture

The cultural shifts associated with modernism and mass culture proved especially fertile for an explosion of beauty contests across North America, and beauty queens came to represent virtually every ethnic community, sporting event, festival, parade, association, union, product, government institution, and ultimately, nation.[45] Beauty contests were part of a modernist period beginning in the nineteenth century and ending in the 1930s that was characterized by a cultural and philosophical movement that rejected tradition. To be "modern" meant to embrace the practices of modernism, which entailed making meaning in the context of mass culture, commodification, and performativity of the self based on a heightened sense of individualism. Modern forms of settler femininity are linked to colonialism conceptualized as a structure, not an event, and are a product of modernity.[46] The beginning of the period known as modernity started in roughly the late seventeenth and early eighteenth centuries, otherwise associated with the period of the Enlightenment, the rise of rational thought as defined by European thinkers, and the French Revolution. To suggest the existence of a modern femininity or femininities without linking these performances with settler colonialism in the case of Canada and the United States is to accept the periodization of modernity as the end of colonialism and the beginning of "world history," a precept rejected by decolonial theorists such as María Lugones, Aníbal Quijano, and Walter Mignolo. This epistemological construct of history and knowledge production enables a set of violent processes that imply, sustain, and reproduce racial hierarchies over time through the female body. Lugones's "colonial/modern gender system," based on Quijano's and Mignolo's theories about the coloniality of power, posits that so-called modern femininities play an important part in the colonial violence of heteropatriarchy and the way that it structures gender and sexuality.[47] In this colonial/modern gender system, white European men are the source of physical, intellectual, and moral power and white women are superior to all other women because of their sexual purity. The formation of nation in settler societies such as Canada depended on this gender system and the heterosexuality that framed it.[48] Throughout the twentieth century, performing settler femininities was directly connected to this "colonial/modern gender system."

The modern beauty contest – that is, the development of an institutional and commercial entity beginning in the mid-nineteenth century – consisted of women parading before a panel of judges who were responsible for ranking them according to a set of pre-established criteria. The social acceptance behind this explicit form of displaying mostly white women's bodies was based on several factors related to the rise of consumer culture, mass marketing such as advertising, rapid changes in technology, urbanization, and commercialization. Whereas this unabashed display of young women's bodies would have been considered scandalous in the Victorian era, parading in front of men clad in a bathing suit became permissible because the commodification and public display of bodies became a significant part of cultural and commercial exchange. The modern beauty contest's popularity as spectacle and commercial exchange coincided with the rise of the fashion show with live *mannequins* around 1910 in Paris, the appearance of the freedom-loving flapper and/or modern girl around the world, and the emergence of the working woman after the First World War.[49] Like fashion shows and, for example, the flapper version of the modern girl, beauty contests were a product of the turn toward the modern and had their own mechanisms to convey modalities of class, gender, race, and sexuality. Beauty contestants and the beauty pageants in which they competed embodied the pace, power relations, and rationalization that characterized what was understood as modern and thus became important transmitters of daily beauty rituals to a mass audience.

The cultural significance of beauty contests is not dwindling despite the fact that they are considered part of a bygone era. For instance, as recently as 2005, long after the mid-century heyday of beauty pageants, the venerable *New York Times* saw fit to report on the morale-boosting visits by beauty queens to American troops in Iraq.[50] The beauty queen holds a cachet that is as valuable as that of models or celebrities, especially in connection with military or paramilitary events. As symbolic representations of settler nationalism, beauty queens evoke what Michael Billig calls the "special feelings" associated with banal displays of nation and citizenship.[51]

Beauty pageants as we know and understand them today emerged with the advent of the Miss America Pageant in 1921. From 1921 onward, the history of beauty contests is a story of controversy, adaptation, and growing popularity.[52] The question is not how many there were but rather what made them such a convenient vehicle through which to represent gendered and racialized ideals of citizenship and to sell white settler nationalism. The answer lies in the connections between the practice of beauty, racial hierarchies, and the institutionalization of beauty contests. On their own, beauty contests had little value, but since they were an institutionalized form of daily beauty rituals and labour, their utility was legitimized. As institutions – a consistent, recognizable way to order social or political codes – beauty contests communicate beauty practices and racial ideologies that are repeated and taken for granted in everyday lives. For instance, beauty practices such as staying thin, buying and applying cosmetics, bleaching skin, straightening hair, or making the "right" fashion decisions are performed completely or successfully through the beauty contestant's body in the beauty pageant format and are accordingly rewarded. Based on specific settler values manifested in each decade from the 1920s to 1980s, such as individualism, competitiveness, performativity, and uniformity, beauty contests and beauty queens became powerful tools with which to promote products, communities, and settler nationalism. Simultaneously, they also served a range of entirely utilitarian purposes. Most simply, they fulfilled the task of promoting a company, an event, or a nonprofit organization. Aspiring to extend the vacation period beyond the Labour Day weekend, for example, the Atlantic City business community believed that a beauty contest featuring girls and young women wearing bathing suits, a practice that was just beginning to gain societal acceptance, would attract people's attention.[53] When Margaret Gorman won the first Miss America title, tourists and their money stayed in Atlantic City out of curiosity about the event, not necessarily due to patriotic pride.

The link between respectability and beauty contests, however, is rooted in a particular understanding of beauty as a signifier of character. Equating beauty with goodness and vice versa is a critical aspect of beauty rooted in a tradition extending back to Plato, who believed that to acquire true beauty, one must reject sexual or physical beauty and work toward love.[54] Sociologist Anthony Synnott refers to the symbiotic relationship between beauty and goodness as the "beauty mystique," which also includes the reverse idea that all that is ugly is evil. He argues that the beauty mystique permeated Western thought on beauty and the face. Beauty and ugliness have been posited not only as physical opposites but also as moral opposites.[55] The ugly person embodies the moral qualities attributed to the other. Without the ugly, the normative discourses of beauty are empty of cultural meaning. The beautiful body is always contrasted with bodies considered gross, freakish, wrong, fat, old, nonwhite, lesbian or gay, or disabled. It is in the process of establishing this contrast that ugliness becomes linked to being bad or morally corrupt.

The association between ugliness and evil in European-based myths and folklore is well established. Scholars have also discussed at length the significant cultural consequences of the idea of "abnormal bodies."[56] Bodies that are described as ugly exist outside societal ideals of acceptability. Women's bodies that do not conform to (literally, "don't *fit*") ideals of beauty and femininity are usually posited as out of control, lazy, deviant, dirty, comical, diseased, and/or unfeminine. Ugly bodies have also been put on display. In contrast to beautiful and feminine bodies displayed in organized pageants, ugly bodies were used as objects of fascination and spectacle in freak shows.[57] Freak shows and later circuses regularly featured tattooed, hairy, skinny, fat, tall, and short bodies as well as people with intellectual disabilities and bodybuilders as examples of people living outside the discursive bounds of normality. The same Phineas T. Barnum who assumed such a key role in transforming the exposition of beauty into its modern, commercial form was much better known for his three-legged boy, his smallest man on earth, and his fat and bearded ladies. That both extremes of the beauty-ugliness continuum were staged by the same organization is no coincidence.

The connections between ugliness, being unfeminine, and immorality inform beauty practices as intensely as do gyms, cosmetics, and fashion magazines in the beauty industrial complex. The strong cultural messages that ugliness and the unfeminine communicate create a rupture in established gender codes and behaviour and have been used as a potential form of resistance. For example, since the nineteenth century, the practice of tattooing and the "monster beauty" of tattooed women have caused an aesthetic revolution in what is understood as feminine.[58] Fat bodies are also being theorized and historicized as radical because these bodies challenge normal conceptualizations of beauty, especially in the twentieth century.[59] Feminists who protested the Miss America Pageant in 1968, for instance, were referred to as "fat," "man-haters," or "lesbians" because many of them resisted societal norms of beauty.[60] The bodies of bodybuilders, homosexuals, and racialized others have also fallen within the discursive rupture of ugliness. However, all of these radical sites of so-called anti-beauty have spawned competitions modelled on the beauty contest both to exploit the potential for spectacle and to establish legitimacy.[61] In a society where the essence of the person is *worn* on the body, finding a social space in which to exist becomes a consuming endeavour.

Indeed, throughout the nineteenth and twentieth centuries, beauty manuals and ads for cosmetics insisted that "if you look good, you will feel good," emphasizing the alleged connection between manipulating the external surface of the body and the inner self. The influx of rural populations into urban centres and the daily proximity of people on streets, in the workplace, and in social spaces accelerated the development of the public face. Once the face was transformed into a deceptive mask that identified the social self as opposed to the so-called true character within, it lost its meaning as the mirror to the soul. In effect, the social self was the manifestation of individuals' performance of that self as they wanted it to be perceived. By the twentieth century, the social self had superseded the cultural value formerly placed on the inner self, and one's personality had become synonymous with the intricacies of one's soul. The social self, then, became an indicator of moral goodness or beauty.

For most beauty pageants, contestants had to display not only their physical attractiveness according to dominant norms but also their charm, poise, and personality. The notion that outer beauty, or a component of the social self, corresponded to inner beauty was a prerequisite for consideration of whether one was a viable beauty contestant. This emphasis hearkens to the notion that beauty is good and, more importantly, that beauty equals moral goodness, whiteness, and a wholesome character. Consequently, pageant officials were diligent about monitoring contestants' sexual status and moral habits and behaviours. The modern beauty queen had to be a morally upstanding individual in order to be defined as beautiful or, more accurately, had to perform the signifiers of what was constructed as morally upright. In the Miss America and Miss Canada Pageants, where ideals of white womanhood were linked to ideals of the white nation, the beauty queen had to emulate a wholesome goodness as well as to be physically attractive. Ultimately, a beauty queen had to demonstrate that inner goodness informed her public self; in other words, the onus was on her to prove that she could conduct herself appropriately in public. The questions asked of contestants during the interview segment were geared toward establishing their public credentials.

Additionally, beauty contests figured into the societal demands placed on women in settler society to compete for attention or respect – that is, to create a public face that stood apart from and eclipsed that of other women. Beauty practices were emblematic of competitiveness and individualism, two tenets of consumer culture and the beauty industrial complex. Beauty contests exploited and exaggerated these tenets to inject an element of excitement into the pageant proceedings but also, ultimately, to re-create cultural behaviours at a more intense level. Competitiveness and individualism underpinned the success of the market-driven cosmetic and diet industries that structured many of the beauty rituals in which men and women engaged. Feminist journalist Susan Brownmiller has demonstrated that the way we compete for sexual partners, jobs, and approval in settler society is linked to our obsession with beauty. Women who participate in this process open themselves up to reproach as they attempt to "match the femininity of other women, and especially to outdo them, [which] is the chief competitive arena ... in which the American woman is wholeheartedly encouraged to contend."[62] Although Brownmiller does not explain to whom she refers as the "American woman," women of colour were not even considered in the game; they were defined as the other. The competitiveness that she refers to can be assumed to be between white women. The competitive discourse embedded in the pursuit of beauty exposes another dichotomy that further complicates social relations. White women's primary role has been to act feminine, a concept that is culturally defined, although the labour involved in acting feminine, including an array of beauty practices and behaviours, must look effortless. Beauty pageants reinforce and legitimize the competition embedded in beauty practices and feminine ideals in a context that exemplifies capitalist values such as discipline, individualism, and liberalism.

Perhaps the elusive character of beauty is precisely the reason why women and men pursue it so relentlessly. Beauty has been posited as unattainable because beauty is trumpeted as a gift that is bestowed on the luckiest among women through birth. Nevertheless, the beauty industrial complex assures women that natural beauty is a state that is attainable, such as by applying the appropriate shade of foundation, but only for white settlers. The wide use of skin whiteners, bleaching, and hair straighteners demonstrates the deep entrenchment of beauty's association with whiteness and white supremacy.[63] For those women supposedly not born beautiful, beauty is possible only through hard work, discipline, and money. Cosmetic surgery, buying the right products, exercising, diets, and taking the advice of experts (usually found in fashion and beauty magazines) are all beauty practices that can help us in our pursuit of the cultural ideals of physical attractiveness. The (il)logical extension of this conceptualization is that there is no excuse for being "ugly." The beauty queen, therefore, is judged on her success at her *job*, which is to strike the right combination of physical attributes that make legible settler discourses of beauty, race, and class. If she has successfully exercised, dieted, and trained herself into beauty, she *belongs*. However, it is also the case that Black and Indigenous women's bodies, like the bodies of the contestants who participated in Miss Black Ontario or the Indian Princess Pageant, can improve only to a certain point. This limited improvability works as a key component in sustaining the logic of settler futurity as squarely placed on the shoulders of white female settlers.

Beauty, Personality, and the Pursuit of Charm

Over time, the Miss Friendship title became an integral part of the Miss Canada Pageant's content. Contestants had to exemplify a trio of attributes in order to be victorious: beauty, poise/charm, and intelligence.[64] Roughly equal points were assigned to each attribute. The interview segment, in which contestants had the opportunity to speak, measured intelligence but, in truth, was yet another way to judge charm or personality, traits associated with the contestant's public face. The Miss Friendship title was bestowed on the lucky contestant whose charm and personality suggested so-called sincerity and amenability rather than a calculated performance of the social self. In the world of beauty pageants, however, calculated performances of the social self were deemed more believable. What is perhaps most revealing about what it takes to be a beauty queen is that no winner of the Miss Canada or Miss America titles has ever held the national crown and Miss Friendship title concurrently.

There are two reasons for this fact. First, the Miss Friendship title was not part of the formal judging process. Because the judging process was based on norms of expertise and objectivity (with a chartered accountancy firm doing the calculations), organizers considered any title that fell outside the process to be subjective or "emotional."[65] Contestants themselves chose the winner of the Miss Friendship title to celebrate or reward a fellow contestant whom they felt exemplified kindness and sportsmanship. It was, of course, the only opportunity for the contestants to judge the qualities of the other competitors without the high stakes associated with formal judging. Second, winning the Miss Friendship title somehow meant that the winner was never really in the running for the *real* title. The issue was not that she was considered ugly or unfeminine but that she was simply too wholesome. Miss Friendship could never convincingly perform the pageant paradox, the intricate balance of sensuality and respectability, to be a successful Miss Canada.

Personality culture is central to the cultural significance of beauty contests. The discourse of beauty was only one aspect, albeit a crucial one, of what was meant by Miss Canada. Personality or charm – the ability to portray a public self – was the other critical attribute. As Warren Susman argues, the shift from a "producer to a consumer society" brought about a new social order where "the vision of self-sacrifice began to yield to that of self-realization."[66] Self-realization was a project integral to the ritual of beautification. For individuals in this new, largely secular social order, the emphasis was on the development of the self, a process that involved "less interest in moral imperatives."[67]

The shift from the cult of character to the culture of personality captures the manner in which settler societies adapted and coped with the change from a culture of scarcity to one of abundance and the emergence of the modern. At the beginning of the nineteenth century, a "person of character" was held in high esteem because he or she had achieved mastery and self-control over emotions and surroundings, characteristics considered essential for the making of a settler nation. The words most often associated with character were "*citizenship, duty, democracy, work, building, golden deeds, outdoor life, conquest, honor, reputation, morals, manners, integrity, and above all, manhood.*"[68] These buzzwords were meant to separate white settlers from Indigenous peoples, who too frequently were labelled as boorish, savage, unclean, amoral, pagan, and effeminate.

Although the cult of character was linked significantly to settler values anchored in gender, racial, and sexual hierarchies, religious beliefs, and liberal ideologies, it is important to note that women were also expected to "master" themselves. The cult of womanhood was part of this context of "building character."[69] In an 1888 article titled "Personal Beauty and Some of

Its Canadian Characteristics," reporter Cermer Mada delved into what constituted Canadian womanhood.[70] Written in the period when the cult of character was making its initial shift toward the culture of personality, the article focused on the importance of beauty of form and face but still emphasized the inner qualities needed for feminine character. This article also provides a glimpse into how a woman's body functioned as an allegory to bolster ideals of the white settler nation. Mada compared the Canadian woman's beauty to that of her English "sister" and American "cousin," arguing that the Canadian climate and lifestyle made them robust and healthier and thus somehow better and more beautiful than their English and American counterparts. Mada regarded Canadian women as superior to American women because they retained more of their English heritage, such as "charming plumpness which gives body as well as form to beauty, and, bespeaking their truly English origin, allies them to the Norman types of the Motherland more than those which prevail in the neighbouring States." Mada suggested that in the use of women's bodies as symbols of racial superiority and order, the "healthy beauty" of Canadian womanhood indicated the promise and potential of the settler nation.[71]

When Mada discussed character within the context of beauty, he referred to the nuances of the female character. He identified the "chief ingredients" of beauty as "health, love, and intellect" but added that, in fact, there were as many definitions of beauty as there were people. This characterization of beauty as elusive and unstable was one of the reasons why beauty was downplayed as a worthy pursuit for women of character within the cult of character. What was deemed worthy was "inherent goodness," a virtue surpassing "mere loveliness of the face."[72] Goodness was believed to be the true indication of a woman of character because it could be found in, presumably, both beautiful and ugly women. In the cult of character, therefore, a "good" woman possessed grace and charm that no amount of cosmetics could emulate, a notion that would diminish with the rise of the culture of personality.

But how could one know that a woman had character when she did not strike one as being as "sweet as the honey of Hybia?"[73] According to Mada, the one trait that had "no rival superior to it in charm" was the speaking voice. Like the eyes, the voice functioned as the "true index to the character within"; its charm was powerful because it became a distinguishing racializing marker of respectability, of being cultured, and of "good breeding."[74] Women of character spoke in soft, deliberate tones underscoring their submissiveness and goodness, racial superiority, and economic station. The class dimension of beauty was another central character element in the nineteenth century that spilled over to the culture of personality. The abilities to modulate one's voice and to speak in an articulate manner were an indication of class, just as fashion and manners similarly marked one's wealth. These abilities also solidified one's place in the racial hierarchy, as speaking "properly" signified a cultivated sense of self in settler societies.

The culture of personality emerged with mass production and consumption, playing a critical cultural part in early-twentieth-century settler society. By the 1920s the notion of "self-realization" as opposed to "self-mastery" premised a belief in the ability of people to improve themselves so as to be distinguishable in mass society.[75] This aim was attainable through habits and practices developed as part of consumer culture. Manuals on how to develop personality flourished at the turn of the twentieth century. The key words that Susman found most often describing someone with personality were *"fascinating, stunning, attractive, magnetic, glowing, masterful, creative, dominant, forceful."*[76] What became paramount, however, was the ability to be different and unique, especially in the modern era. The often isolating and secularized culture that surfaced with industrialization and urbanization necessarily meant that being "somebody" in a crowd required more than strong moral values. Beyond the era of the cult of character, those who now called attention to themselves without disrupting normative ideals were deemed "magnetic."

Beauty contests thrived in the culture of personality. Indeed, without the culture of abundance and personality, beauty contests could not have developed into the cultural institutions that they became. In the late nineteenth century, Victorian restraints on women's public movement and sexuality made it virtually impossible for women to develop a dominant or forceful personality translatable in a public forum. As we have seen, Victorian middle-class women could not participate in beauty pageants organized by newspapers for fear of compromising their social status. Participation in these contests would have meant that such women had questionable moral values or were not respectable. By the 1920s personality culture had created opportunities for men and women previously constrained by prescriptions of respectability. In an environment that increasingly placed worth on celebrity, beauty contests offered a normative arena for women to showcase their "magnetic, creative and fascinating" personalities.[77]

The proliferation of how-to manuals for both men and women from the 1920s to 1950s enabled "ordinary" people to acquire knowledge, such as to how to attain a "fascinating" personality and develop poise and charm (or personal charm, as it was sometimes called). Visions of the self in personality culture "are assumed from the start not to be natural but to be things that can be learned and practiced, through exercise and by study of guidebooks to success."[78] The message that women received, therefore, was to rely on physical beauty, poise, and charm to build a sense of self that distinguished them from others.

Women learned that poise and charm, like physical attractiveness, were traits that could be attained through hard work and discipline. Although physical beauty was sometimes out of reach, any woman, whether working-class, a person of colour, or the wife of a billionaire, could learn how to be charming. Poise and charm combined manners, posture, and grooming and were almost always regarded as attributes of settler femininity. Women could learn how to dress correctly, to apply makeup based on accepted practices, and to sit, eat, and walk in ways that accentuated femininity and exemplified poise and charm. The daily beauty rituals practised by Black women across Black college campuses are an example of how critical this politics of respectability was to securing public acceptance. Scholar Karen Tice argues that in the 1940s and 1950s, the ability of women at Black colleges to gain "distinction and acceptance" rested not only on intellectual achievement but also on "how they performed a constellation of middle-class norms for poise and charm, and how these efforts were judged by men."[79] In the case of Black women, this expectation of discipline and self-representation was based on "class-coded norms" that helped to refute structural racism.[80]

Charm schools were at the ready to help women. In general, former models or dancers operated charm schools that catered to a variety of clients, including models, public relations professionals, and women interested in self-improvement. Some charm schools in the 1940s and 1950s supplied models for local fashion shows and thus were drawn into the beauty contest industry. Beauty contestants used charm and beauty coaches, often hired from charm schools, to help them refine their personality. These charm coaches taught them how to walk, talk (or articulate), sit, and apply makeup, furnished them with fashion tips, and, most importantly, advised them on exercise and diet. Charm schools and coaches therefore became indispensable actors in the beauty pageant industry and the broader beauty industrial complex.[81] Such schools were pivotal to success in the beauty contest world because charm and poise were the basis of the settler feminine ideal, and this same feminine ideal equated charm and poise with goodness, whiteness, wholesomeness, and beauty. Beauty contestants who looked and acted like professional models did not fit the feminine ideal of wholesomeness.

Ironically, it fell to the former models operating charm schools to coach contestants on how best to act "naturally" like the girl next door. As experts on charm, poise, and trade secrets, charm coaches and schools could enhance a contestant's chances of beauty contest glory.

In the new consumer culture, these charm schools flourished. Beauty, although critical, was only one component of the personality package. Although personality culture affected men and women alike, in the twentieth century it was still incumbent on women who strove for social and economic success to behave "like women." In other words, being respectable, demure, feminine, and physically attractive were hallmarks of a good and marriageable woman. The advice contained in manuals written for women in the latter half of the nineteenth century continued to dictate rituals of beauty and femininity in the twentieth century, with the important distinction that the emphasis shifted away from cultivating inner beauty.

In 1950 the National Film Board's *On the Spot* television show visited the Barton Taylor School of Charm in Montreal. The footage followed the metamorphosis of a young woman named Pat Wilson from a gum-chewing, inarticulate slouch to a "lady."[82] Using Wilson as an "experiment," *On the Spot* wanted to find out if charm schools could do the "impossible" by transforming a woman racialized by the producers as "white trash" into a respectable, groomed white woman. In a thirty-minute episode, viewers were invited to follow Wilson as she took the charm course coached by Jay Barton, co-director of the school. The lesson for Wilson and the viewer was quite clear: anyone could change into a charming, feminine, and attractive young woman with hard work and expert guidance. With enough acquired charm, poise, and the right clothes, white women could find dates whether or not they were born beautiful. More importantly, the program insisted that women who wished to make themselves attractive and marriageable had to learn the secrets and traits of being feminine.

In his explanation of how they chose the woman who participated in their experiment, host Fred Davis acknowledged the potential problem of stopping a stranger on the street and asking, "Well, you're not very attractive. How would you like to take a charm course?"[83] From the beginning, in order for the segment to "deal with an intriguing intangible known as charm," the producers of the show constructed charm as something that attractive women possessed. Their solution was to phone the father of a family that they had worked with for a previous story and ask him whether they could contact his daughter (whom they presumably believed lacked "charm and poise") to participate in their experiment. The audience's consensus was that Wilson did indeed need Barton's help, and Wilson eventually confirmed her consent in an ensuing interview. The producers established this need by cleverly juxtaposing key questions about what Wilson thought was feminine with the visuals of other women at the beginning of the program. These women, who represented the supposedly elegant, graceful, immaculately dressed, and attractive "finished product," were depicted in various stages of applying lipstick, putting on jewellery, combing their hair, and pulling a lace veil over their face.[84] The contrast sent a powerful message about normative ideals regarding femininity and beauty while setting the stage for Wilson's metamorphosis.

The program further underlined the contrast between the two depictions of womanhood by featuring Lina Roth, a professional model exemplifying grace, femininity, charm, and thus beauty. To emphasize the message that being beautiful was hard work, Davis used Roth to demonstrate for him the proper technique for walking and sitting:

> DAVIS: Would you mind walking across the room? Like start from here and just walk across there.
> [Roth does as she is told as the camera focuses on her legs and feet.]
> DAVIS: No effort, at all. Now, how about sitting down? Would you show me how you sit down?
> ROTH: Of course, anything special you want?
> DAVIS: No, not as a model, particularly. How would you do it, naturally?
> [Roth sits down, crosses her feet, and places her crossed hands on her thighs.]
> DAVIS: And the feet and legs just automatically take, do they?
> ROTH: That's right.
> DAVIS: You certainly made it look easy.
> ROTH: Thank you.
> DAVIS: That's wonderful. Well, that's what technique will do when added with feminine grace.[85]

This brief exchange solidified two aspects of charm. First, Roth established for the audience that because of her hard work and discipline, she had acquired expertise pertaining to walking and sitting. This expertise extended to her ability to meet special requests regarding technique. In other words, there were different, specialized ways of walking and sitting depending on the context. Second, Davis used Roth's body to show that the expert could demonstrate graceful walking and sitting and make it seem easy and natural. In this exchange, there was no recognition that having good technique and being natural were contradictory; rather, this discourse was invoked to downplay the labour involved in performing respectable femininity through charm and poise.

The segment of the show that listed and examined Wilson's "issues" was perhaps the most revealing. When Wilson's progress was then discussed with Davis, Barton pointed out that Wilson's attitude had "shifted" once she "admitted" that she had "bad habits."[86] Wilson's areas of improvement included hair, complexion, gum chewing (not done in public), eyebrows, clothes, voice, nervous twitches, walking, and facial expressions. She was filmed exercising, trying on new clothes under Barton's supervision, and doing articulation exercises. When Roth and Wilson were first shown together, the latter was shunned and even regarded in a disdainful manner. Roth's attitude toward Wilson appeared to have changed when the camera "listened in" on Roth offering Wilson a ticket to a show. By this point, viewers were to believe that Wilson had achieved a significant transformation. Apparently, her bad habits were now under control, and her reward was an invitation to a social event. Her ability to perform respectable femininity and, through hard work, to learn the skills involved in being charming, pretty, and graceful meant that she now belonged.

An aim of the charm course was to build Wilson's allegedly nonexistent self-confidence, but the underlying message was to demonstrate that proper training, especially for women, could subvert the material reality of class. The show conveyed the message that any shy, unsophisticated person could exude confidence simply by bolstering her appearance and sculpting her mannerisms. By the time of her final interview with host Davis, Wilson had been transformed into a lady and was grateful for the opportunity given to her by her benefactors:

> DAVIS: Well, Pat, I'm really proud of you, and you haven't even finished the course. [He guides her to the door.] You know, I probably won't even know you next time you're in Montreal. Remember how you felt and looked the first time you came in here?
>
> WILSON: I certainly do, Fred. But you know I feel so different now. Well, I have a different attitude about things. I mean, I don't envy people foolishly like I used to.
>
> DAVIS: How do you feel now?
>
> WILSON: Well, I feel like I'm somebody.

DAVIS: Well, that's wonderful! That's the way you should feel.

WILSON: You know, Fred, this is kind of hard for me to say, well, thanks.

DAVIS: Oh, don't thank me. You did all the work! Now, you run along and lots of luck to you, Pat.[87]

Now that Wilson was a "somebody," the audience was asked to believe that she was equipped to face the world. The notion of being a "somebody" echoed the main principle of the culture of personality. It was also a pivotal element of the beauty contest, where the contestants' project was to mark themselves as special or different from their competitors. Wilson's transformation, considered a positive result, stood as evidence that charm schools were benign entities. It was the same argument used to justify the existence of beauty contests at the height of the feminist protests in the late 1960s and early 1970s.

Bob Anderson, the executive producer of *On the Spot*, offered a critical commentary on the show's agenda. Anderson did not question the necessity or the popularity of charm schools. In fact, he agreed that a "certain amount of instruction" on how to present oneself was "desirable" and that a "good appearance gives you confidence." However, Anderson was uncomfortable with the danger that these new schools of charm could foster conformity. In a reversal, Anderson pinpointed the very problem that had inspired the emergence of the culture of personality as described by Susman. What was "disturbing" for Anderson was that "when you put on charm, like a uniform, the individuality seems to disappear."[88] His anxieties stemmed from the idea that charm and beauty could be achieved through work and that they were contrived discourses constructed for public consumption that negated any need to examine one's *character* or to believe that character could be substantive. Of course, Anderson missed the point. A hallmark of the rise of mass consumer culture was that individuality became the norm, but it also presented a space for some to carve out new possibilities and opportunities as they adopted class and gender codes that helped to subvert socio-economic or racial discrimination. Acting the part – performing charm, poise, and middle-class habits – reified settler femininity, but it also helped people of colour or from the lower classes, for example, to challenge and destabilize.

"This Is Not a Beauty Contest": The Pageant Paradox

The historical evolution of the beauty contest from the May Day queen to the bathing suit competitions on the Atlantic City resort strip suggests that, as institutions of popular culture, these contests reflected entrenched social values about women's bodies, race, and beauty practices, but it also shows how these social values changed. The shift toward acceptance of the public display of the feminine figure necessarily divested women of the restraints placed on them by the Victorian value system. An important indication of this phenomenon was the insistence on the part of pageant officials that their beauty contest "is not a beauty contest." This often repeated phrase sought to recast beauty contests as respectable and viable enterprises for white women while maintaining the entrepreneurial objectives underlying them, which I call the pageant paradox. Insisting that beauty contests were not really *beauty* contests became a crucial strategy in maintaining a hold on the values of chastity and virtue even as the last vestiges of the Victorian era disappeared.

However, some pageant officials were not interested in upholding Victorian ideals of feminine decorum and moral virtue while putting women on display, a shift increasingly present in the modern era with the development of the beauty industrial complex. For example, when Yolande Betbeze, Miss America 1951, refused to model in a bathing suit provided by the Catalina swimwear corporation because she felt that it was demeaning, the executives at Catalina ensured that no future Miss America would impede their ability to promote the product line by establishing and funding the Miss USA and Miss Universe Pageants for the sole purpose of selling bathing suits.[89] Obviously, the executives at Catalina were not concerned with safeguarding Betbeze's personal sense of dignity.

Another exception was the Miss Dominion of Canada Pageant (1960–79), founded and directed by John C. Bruno and his company, Canadian Beauty Spectaculars Limited. The Miss Dominion of Canada Pageant was established in Niagara Falls, Ontario, as "a promotion of international friendship."[90] Unlike her rival, Miss Canada, Miss Dominion of Canada had the rights to compete and represent Canada in the Miss World, Miss Universe, and Miss International Pageants.[91] The pageant itself operated only sporadically, but it did manage to sustain itself until 1979, when it finally folded. The Miss Canada Pageant took over in 1980, and the winner became the official representative of Canada at the Miss Universe Pageant until 1992.[92] Unlike Miss Canada, Miss Dominion of Canada was not televised. It did not enjoy the same popularity and cultural legitimacy as its cousin. As owner of the Miss USA counterpart in Canada, Bruno also believed in making transparent his real intentions behind the Miss Dominion of Canada Pageant. For example, in her manual *How to Be a Beauty Pageant Winner,*

Marie Fenton Griffing, a pageant consultant, readily identified the financial interests behind the pageant:

> One reason for stacking the odds in a contest is cold hard cash. In some pageants it is imperative to the sponsor that the right girl wins and goes on to represent him in other larger pageants. Each time she does well in those pageants, her financial value to him increases. For instance, one of the primary sources of income for the Miss Dominion of Canada pageant sponsor, John C. Bruno of Hamilton, Ont., stems from the contract his girls must sign with his firm, Canadian Beauty Spectaculars Ltd.[93]

Not surprisingly, Catalina provided the Miss Dominion of Canada pageant with its official swimwear.

Although the officials of the Miss America and Miss Canada Pageants insisted that their events were "not a beauty contest," some pageant officials, such as Bruno, had little interest in promoting respectability. Bruno expressed concern only that the women who entered his contest "look good in a Mountie costume."[94] According to reporter Alexander Ross, Bruno's company made "$45,000 dollars in product endorsement, franchises for a string of charm schools and sales of Miss Dominion of Canada cosmetics to charm-school students" in 1964.[95] This Canadian example underlines the connection between beauty, big business, and national identity since the Miss Dominion of Canada Pageant was an important player in the national arena of Canadian beauty contests. Miss America and Miss Canada officials might have insisted that their pageants were not beauty competitions, but the owners of Miss USA and Miss Dominion of Canada were clear about the commercial intentions of their business ventures.

Part of the reason for the phrase "this is not a beauty contest" was to avoid conflicts over ideas about beauty, sex, and respectability posed by the Miss USA, Miss Universe, and Miss Dominion of Canada Pageants. If a contest was interested solely in selling products using the *image* of beautiful, white, sexy women, then a beauty queen could not fulfill the role of community ambassador or represent unions, associations, or a government department. For these roles, the beauty queen required other traits that would make her an acceptable representative, such as the perception of sexual innocence, musical skill or public speaking skills, charm, poise, a sense of civic responsibility, and a respectable demeanour, all of which could be easily attributed to a wholesome young woman. The key to a successful beauty contest and beauty queen, then, was the ability to sell sensuality while denying that sensuality and sex were central to beauty and physical attractiveness. This balancing act is a core aspect of performing settler femininity since it continues to differentiate beauty queens as respectable and legitimate signifiers of the settler nation. This conundrum presented pageant organizers and beauty contestants alike with a paradox. National and small-town pageants were held hostage to this paradox since the purpose of these pageants, the rules the contestants had to follow, and whether or not swimsuits and even formal evening gowns were worn determined whether a pageant was something more than a *beauty* contest.

In his research on late-twentieth-century, small-town community pageants in Minnesota, anthropologist Robert H. Lavenda suggests that the phrase "this is not a beauty pageant" stemmed from the need to reconcile "two different and perhaps contradictory prototypes of [the] event: the debutante presentation and the beauty pageant."[96] For Lavenda, the differences between the "queen pageants" in small towns and the larger, national beauty contests like Miss America was that locally the contestants were the "community's daughters," not sexual objects on display. The swimsuit competition, so popular in the national competitions, was often eliminated in queen pageants to highlight the message that the queen pageant was mainly about finding a suitable representative for the community and was not an exploitative commercial venture. The most important difference, however, was that unlike the national pageants, where contestants were strangers coming together to compete (with some contestants competing in contests as part of a circuit of professional competitors), in the queen pageants the contestants were literally "the girl next door."[97] The contestants themselves would have gone to the same schools, parks, and churches. They were well known in the community through their volunteer work or outstanding academic and extracurricular activities.

According to Lavenda, the organizers of the queen pageant were not looking necessarily for the most physically attractive young woman based on a standard of beauty; rather, they were "looking to recognize and train an elite cadre of young women within the town [and] for someone to represent the town at a series of similar events held in other small towns around the region."[98] He describes this process as similar to a debutante cotillion, where upper-class, white women gain introduction into elite society. In the queen pageant, the "community's daughters" were introduced to the community via the pageant. The community was well aware of the process that queen pageant participants had undergone in the same way that the debutante's audience at the cotillion were well versed in her year-long networking activities.[99] In the Minnesota queen pageants, participants were sometimes sent to beauty colleges for training in makeup, grooming, and walking and standing on stage.[100] This training usually took two months and required enormous dedication on the part of the contestants and their parents in a fashion similar to the process experienced by the debutante and her mother.

Yet Lavenda's analysis requires qualification, specifically his view of the differences between queen pageants and their "lewder" sisters, beauty contests. Without the beauty contest, the queen pageant would not exist. The latter exists in the cultural meaning created by the former, and both use racial and class codes reflected by white settler nationalism. In fact, once the contestant is "introduced" as part of the formal pageant, the beauty contest element is in play. The young women are asked to parade in front of a panel of judges who award points based on physical attractiveness, among other things. The Minnesota queen pageants, therefore, were "hybrids" of national beauty contests only insofar as the contestants knew most of the audience members.

Officials of national pageants faced the same problem as the organizers of the queen pageants – that is, the need to legitimize a ritual that was imbued with references to qualities perceived as virtuous in the context of white settler society. It comes as no surprise that the officials of national contests *and* queen pageants insisted that their pageants were "not beauty contests." All of these pageants appropriated the beauty contest model to project a symbol that encapsulated ideals proudly held by settlers as they formed particular fantasies about community and nation. Arguably, the performance of settler femininity was forged in the more intimate and local setting of the queen pageant, where the social and cultural discourses and practices of racialization were taught and learned or passed on. The national stage (literally and figuratively) became the place where the cumulative results of the racialized performance of settler femininity, consolidated at the local level, were consumed by a larger audience.

Certainly, queen pageants had their critics. Canadian journalist Gordon Sinclair wrote an article in 1949 condemning beauty pageants as "parades of girl meat on the hoof."[101] In his exposé, written after twenty years of "judging" beauty contests, Sinclair revealed that most of these events were charades where the winner was selected before the actual contest took place. He described a circuit of beauty contests where "professional" contestants were paid a sum of money, transportation, and food to participate in a small-town festival.[102] Sinclair had a cynical – almost bitter – perspective on beauty contests, ending his attack on beauty queens and beauty contests with the following: "While skilled experts judge hens, sheep or even white mice, camera-conscious politicians and cynical reporters sit in judgement on the girls [sic]. In an atmosphere of confused expectations and selfish vanity the judges know, as you know, that better-looking girls can be found in any factory office or packing plant."[103] In contrast to the community affairs that Lavenda described, Sinclair characterized beauty contests as fabricated events meant to serve local business interests.

This indictment of local beauty contests as staged business transactions was quite incriminating for the queen pageants. Sinclair emphasized practices that he felt were questionable, such as the use of "professional" contestants who were paid to compete but never won. His comment may have been a reference to the impresarios or "promoters" who received money from the local chambers of commerce to organize the pageants. According to Sinclair, far from being community-based pride boosters, the pageants over which he presided were advertising gimmicks for everything from tobacco and cheese to the West End Business Man community. Certainly, the variety of products and business interests that inspired the titles and pageants confirmed the business function of the local pageants. For Sinclair, the exchange of money made these local pageants reprehensible and "phony," but in his diatribe Sinclair confused the purpose of these local pageants with the discourse of beauty contests as exemplars of beauty.[104] Sinclair failed to realize that the primary purpose of queen pageants was to satisfy local interests, raise funds, solidify social values, boost community pride, and entrench racial superiority.

Sinclair was careful to distinguish the Miss Canada Pageant from the other ten contests over which he presided each year during his judging career.[105] It is clear in his article that he viewed the national pageant as "not a beauty contest" because it did not resemble the bathing beauty shows of his judging circuit. Instead, the *beauty contests* he referred to were "30% ballyhoo, 30% buttocks, 30% baloney and 10% associated ingredients" and thus not in the same class as the Miss Canada Pageant.[106] Presumably, Sinclair considered the Miss Canada Pageant to be closer to what he understood as a *beauty pageant*, an event that contained contestants who exhibited poise, charm, and beauty. The Miss Canada Pageant was "culturally on the level" even if it failed to fill Maple Leaf Gardens to the rafters.[107] Yet the Miss Canada Pageant was as much a business venture as the local beauty contests that Sinclair mentioned. Like Bruno, S. Radcliffe Weaver and his wife, Edna, co-organizers of the Miss Canada Pageant, were impresarios interested in selling beauty products and using the contest as a venue for their business activities. The Miss Canada Pageant, however, did an effective job of packaging itself to the satisfaction of even a perennial gadfly like Sinclair.

Miss Canada was "culturally on the level" by 1949 because it had fulfilled its image as more than a beauty pageant and not *really* a bathing beauty contest. It had all the accoutrements of a beauty contest – women in bathing suits, judges, and prizes – and Miss Canada represented Canada's version of the white settler nationalism seen in the Miss America Pageant. Although it was a corporate entity, the pageant developed into an institution that used women's bodies to simultaneously promote wholesomeness and white settler national pride. Local pageants also had the capacity to promote community pride, and many of them could boast that they were not beauty contests, but these pageants did not have the clout and exposure of their national counterparts.

The interplay between beauty and personality enabled beauty contests like Miss Canada to claim that they were not beauty pageants. In the Miss Canada and Miss America Pageants, the bathing suit segment of the competition was framed not merely as a way to show flesh; rather, organizers argued that it was the only way for the contestants to demonstrate poise and for the judges to ascertain a contestant's personality. Although this reasoning may seem disingenuous to some, the ideas being proposed are congruent with the logic of beauty pageants as literally *contests* of white bodies and performativity. Personality, therefore, was the cultural framework within which beauty contests became popular and acceptable forums for middle-class women in the twentieth century and for embodied representations of the white settler nation.

National beauty contests in Canada aspired to have their titles represent the all-Canadian girl or Canadian white womanhood. The social meaning attached to these symbols was centred on the traits of charm and personality. Given the significant cultural influence that a version of Canadian settler femininity presented, beauty contests were excellent venues through which to magnify these ideals on a national scale. The culture of personality enhanced women's abilities to sell themselves as iconographic figures of settler femininity and charm, which were considered useful to various areas of the business community. Consumer culture made these institutions and the beauty queens that they produced an integral part of selling ideas and products. It is no wonder, therefore, that manuals on how to be a beauty queen had proliferated by the late twentieth century.[108] As beauty contests became serious business, books and manuals appeared in order to reassure potential contestants that with enough knowledge and hard work, they could participate successfully in a beauty contest.

Cultural discourses of beauty took several forms throughout the nineteenth and twentieth centuries. Ideals of femininity, beauty, white supremacy, and morality dictated beauty practices and beauty contests. The connections between femininity, beauty, white supremacy, and morality were difficult to grasp, making institutions like charm schools, beauty manuals, and beauty pageants into vehicles through which the signifiers of womanhood could be articulated more easily and consumed more effectively. The culture of personality was central to this articulation, as it explained the shift away from the cult of character and toward the social self that made one special, unique, and magnetic. It was possible only in the context of consumer culture, which in turn was fertile ground for performing the social self. In women, this social self turned on beauty practices such as dieting and exercising and on traits such as cheerfulness and submissiveness. Charm schools and beauty manuals helped women to learn about these practices and behaviours, and beauty contests reassured aspiring beauty queens that beauty was attainable.

Beauty contests were mounted by so many organizations because morality, beauty, whiteness, and femininity became intertwined with notions of goodness and youth. By framing beauty contestants as wholesome and good, pageants inspired feelings of truth, pride, and white nationalism. The use of beauty contests to represent an organization, such as a business or union, was seen as a way to bolster workplace morale, consumer attention, and even patriotic sentiments; however, they also played a role in entrenching racial hierarchies and heteropatriarchy. A central component of the bolstering of white settler nationalism is the representation of racialized bodies that adhere to its ideals of citizenship and nation. Beauty pageants were used to define and to differentiate between those who were included in the national body and those who were excluded from it.

2

Miss Canada and Gendering Whiteness

As an ideal of Canadian, white, feminine beauty and youth, Miss Canada embodied cultural and political discourses of a racialized and gendered nation. Promoting the nation through female bodies has a long history, and in turn nation is frequently allegorized as female. The first Miss Canada contests were enveloped by this discourse of citizenship and national identity framed by a violent history of white settler colonialism. By the early twentieth century, the Canadian settler nation had begun to forge its identity within a cultural discourse increasingly influenced by notions of independence and commercialization.[1] Canadians, coded as the "two founding nations" – English and French – had engaged in national and constitutional debates about conscription during the First World War, the granting of a limited franchise to women whose children or husbands were fighting on the front lines, and what was seen as an attack on the validity of Confederation by Quebec intellectuals.[2]

In 1923, the same year of the first Miss Canada contest in Montreal, Canada signed the Halibut Treaty with the United States, marking the Dominion's first negotiated international contract without the British government present. Canada also argued for greater forms of independence around decision making on the global stage at that year's Imperial Conference.[3] In addition to these political strategies for national independence in the global arena, Canadian governments from the 1900s to the 1920s initiated a major treaty-making campaign designed to secure the settlement of southern

Canada and to gain access to national resources in the North. In the treaty-making period between 1871 and 1921, sitting Canadian governments stole nearly half of Indigenous peoples' land mass.[4] Dubbed the "roaring twenties" by historians due to the shift to modernism, economic expansion, and the emergence of technological advancements, the 1920s were characterized by prosperity made possible because of a series of political decisions driven by the settler logic of elimination, dispossession, and expansion. It is within this context that the Miss Canada contests were formed.

In the 1920s beauty contests were still in the early stages of garnering public acceptance. Questions of appropriate public display of women continued to be debated by religious, political, and social groups. The emergence of the new woman and modern girl, the suffrage movement, and the increased presence of women in public spaces, however, meant that the Victorian values of the late nineteenth and early twentieth centuries gradually but assuredly were losing their grasp.[5] Women reformers of all stripes contested these pageants. They commented and took action on every issue that concerned women, from temperance to maternity to economic matters. Beauty contests were understood as a social problem and often came under their scrutiny.

Plagued with controversies since the 1920s, Miss Canada's growing pains took almost fifteen years to resolve. There are three reasons for this lengthy maturation period. The Miss Canada Pageant and title were officially incorporated only in 1946 due to the absence of a consistent corporate infrastructure. Second, when it was finally incorporated by a small business located in Hamilton, Ontario, the Miss Canada Pageant was mismanaged, did not have the necessary capital to function on a national level, and was mainly concerned with sending a representative to the Miss America Pageant instead of mounting a pageant for a homegrown audience. Finally, the gap between the first nationally recognized winner in 1923 and Miss Canada 1946 meant that the organizers of the pageant could not claim the longevity that held US audiences captive in the case of the Miss America Pageant.[6] This chapter's discussion of Miss Canada covers the period between 1923 and 1961, whereas Chapter 5 focuses on the period between 1962 and 1992. Although both of these chapters trace the history of the pageant, I have decided to separate them for two reasons: first, doing so serves to emphasize how the pageant shifted its meaning making in the face of contestation about nation throughout the twentieth century; and second, it serves to demonstrate the connections between national beauty pageants, such as Miss Canada, and queen pageants as either reifying, negotiating, emulating, or destabilizing settler femininity at the local, national, and international levels. All the contests discussed in this book, regardless of their mandate or sponsorship, functioned within a settler colonial context that shaped how they defined beauty, bodies, femininity, and race.

What made the beauty queen's body seductive as a national metaphor in 1920s white settler society? How did the shift to the culture of personality and the changing ideals of femininity after the First World War enable mostly white women to participate in an event previously defined as lewd and improper? I argue that the shared values that came to define ideals of what it meant to be Canadian were entwined with settler conceptualizations of gender, class, and race transcribed on the bodies of young Canadian women. Although the Miss Canada title did not become incorporated as an annual event until the mid-1940s, beauty contests appeared throughout the interwar period in order to soothe social and cultural anxieties regarding changes in public space, consumer culture, and women's roles. From 1923 to early 1963, before the Miss Canada Pageant was televised, the contestants and organizers of the event contended with the challenge of establishing the beauty contest as a legitimate arena of participation for white women and used this venue as a way to translate a particular version of whiteness, class, and femininity. This version of the national fantasy had to be customized to Canadian ideals of nation and citizenship at a critical moment in its formation.

Pageantry and Protest: The "Sports Girl," Feminism, and the White Settler Nation

In February 1923 the Winter Sports Committee in Montreal decided to organize a national Miss Canada contest as part of the Winter Sports Carnival festivities. To the organizers' surprise, the response from young women and the general public across Canada was overwhelming. Miss Canada 1923 would visit various cities in Canada and the United States while acting – in the words of a *Montreal Gazette* reporter – as "a sort of social [hostess]."[7]

At the local level, Montreal women responded enthusiastically to the search for the "ideal Canadian girl." Twenty-six contestants representing various organizations entered their names for the Miss Montreal title in the hope of competing at the national level. The sport and labour organizations that submitted entries included Almy's Employees Athletic Association, Lodge No. 56 of the Benevolent and Protective Order of Elks, the Montreal

Baseball Club, the Ancient and Honourable Order of the Blue Goose, the Canadian Brotherhood Railroad Employees, the Loyal Order of Moose, the British Canadian Bowling Club, Bramson's Auto Service, and the Club de Hockey Dimanche Matin.[8] Local newspapers such as *Pathé News* and *La Presse* and hotels also submitted entries. The Miss Montreal contest, in fact, became an outlet for these organizations and businesses to support community spirit and sell products. Like other social and recreational events, the beauty contest offered another forum through which Montrealers engaged in so-called friendly competition. The contest also shored up support for the Winter Sports Carnival, an event created to boost the local economy.

The title meant more than just finding another pretty face. John J. Fitzgerald, the manager of the Winter Sports Committee, believed that "beauty of face and form alone would not govern in the choosing of the winner but only as such beauty contributed in the owner's charm, character and personality."[9] The judging for the Miss Montreal contest involved both a formal panel of men and a larger community-based system of selecting a winner, reminiscent of the photo contests organized by newspapers in the late nineteenth century. A *Montreal Gazette* article encouraged Montrealers to send in voting coupons marked with their preference, which they could cut out and submit to all local newspapers.[10] The fifteen candidates with the highest number of votes constituted the line-up from which the official panel of judges would select Miss Montreal.

The Miss Canada 1923 contest was billed as a national event. Cities and communities from across the country selected beauty queens with commercial and community fanfare equivalent to the Miss Montreal contest, attesting to the popularity and spreading cultural acceptance of beauty contests.[11] In Halifax, Mrs. Ora Doherty, one of two married women who participated in the Miss Canada contest, competed against over 300 contestants at a pageant organized and sponsored by the *Halifax Herald* while 5,000 spectators looked on.[12] The only judge for that contest was Laura MacCallum Grant, wife of Nova Scotia's lieutenant governor. In Winnipeg about seventy women competed for the Miss Winnipeg title at the Royal Alexandra Hotel, where the *Winnipeg Free Press* put on a cabaret and dance for the occasion.[13] In this pageant, the sixteen judges were chosen from the community's female social and political elite in the community. The involvement of members of Winnipeg and Halifax high society lent legitimacy to the pageant. Without them, the beauty contest would have continued to be considered morally suspect. Instead, their participation reinvented the beauty contest as an acceptable cultural event for white, middle-class women.

The business community also played a role in reinforcing the beauty contest as a legitimate cultural practice and discourse. In an effort to show support for Anna L. Walsh (Miss Quebec) and to boost her chances in Montreal in the main event, Quebec City's department stores cooperated to supply Walsh with an "abundant wardrobe."[14] Department stores saw new advertising possibilities in the contest, which gave them access to a free or cheap spokesperson and to a range of potential consumers. Although a free wardrobe was a welcome prize for Walsh's efforts and victory as Miss Quebec, it also afforded the department store owners maximum attention at a small price.

From the outset, the Miss Canada 1923 contest exemplified the highly gendered and racial character of pageants, where the white settler male gaze was used to bolster certain ideals of modern settler femininity. While in Montreal, the contestants received the "royal treatment" from Montreal's labour and fraternal associations, civic officials, and local hotels, namely the Windsor and the Mount Royal. The Westerners Club, an association of western Canadian residents in Montreal, sponsored a reception in the Rose Room at the Windsor Hotel in honour of Miss Winnipeg, Miss Regina, and Miss Edmonton.[15] Approximately 300 people attended the affair. Club officials introduced Miss Montreal, Miss Halifax, and Miss Saint John to the assembled crowd.[16] Later the same afternoon, the mayor of Montreal formally welcomed the contestants at a civic reception in the hall of the *La Presse* building.[17] At this reception, the Miss Canada contestants were presented with the keys to the city, a gesture meant to welcome acceptable citizens into the city's social boundaries.[18] That evening, another reception was held at the Mount Royal Hotel. Presided over by Miss Montreal, it was organized specifically to give the general public an opportunity to meet the contestants.[19] McGill University and the University of Montreal also contributed to honouring the beauty queens by hosting receptions and by extending special invitations to watch their hockey games.

As enthusiasm for the event gathered momentum, so did the problem with issues linked to the judges' identities and the criteria for choosing Miss Canada 1923. These controversies added excitement during the selection of Miss Canada but put pressure on officials of the Winter Sports Committee and may have contributed to the general belief that the pageant was having organizational problems. The *Montreal Gazette* first reported on the issues by noting that although the many receptions and teas organized to introduce the contestants would have given the judges ample opportunity to do their job, there seemed to be no judges to be found.[20] That evening, the Winter Sports Committee announced that the names of the judges would not be released until Saturday night at the Windsor Hotel during the Winter Sports Ball. The committee believed that keeping the judges' identities secret put them in a "better position to observe the claims of each contender."[21] The issue of favouritism also surfaced when it was announced that all the judges were Montrealers. Concern was voiced over the possibility that they would select Miss Montreal by default.[22]

The question of the exact qualities that Miss Canada was to embody became a debate between the organizers and the contestants about legitimate forms of femininity as representational of the nation while obscuring the underlying racial character of that performativity. When the names of the judges were finally announced, the five men were left to their own devices to select Miss Canada. The only guidance they were given was the original letter from the Winter Sports Committee to the several newspapers across Canada that sponsored contestants.[23] Based on that letter, candidates were to be judged on "attractiveness, personality, style and general appearance," and they had to appear at least once in a winter sports costume.[24] Much importance was placed on the latter because it represented the "official" reason for the beauty contest. The detail and attention given to the winter sports costume worn by the winner, Miss Saint John, indicates that fashion, or at least appearing fashionable, was an essential ingredient:

> Miss St. John who appeared at home on skates and sped gracefully over the ice, was dressed in a sport costume of jade green broadcloth, with white fur trimmings. Her coat was of the close waisted, rippled style, with cuffs of white fur. She too wore knickerbockers and golf stockings. Her boots were of silver color. A white fur hat to match, with jade trimmings and a rhinestone ornament, sat jauntily on her raven black hair.[25]

Discussion of clothing and behaviour also led to the issue of who looked the most "athletic" or personified the "athletic type." The debate over whether Miss Canada should be selected on the basis of beauty or athletic ability was extremely controversial since lurking behind this debate were questions of what constituted codes of settler femininity in the context of the pageant. The candidates themselves contended that the winner should be selected based on "abilities in Canadian sports," but Fitzgerald insisted that "proficiency in sports is not necessary."[26] The contestants saw themselves as "sports girls," not as "beauty candidate[s]." For them, Miss Canada 1923 was a "sports title," and the expensive hotels, teas, and luncheons were simply part of the fanfare that accompanied their participation in the contests.[27]

Historian M. Ann Hall argues that much of women's sport history in Canada has been influenced by the ability of female athletes to sustain their femininity and to establish their heterosexuality while participating in sports often seen as masculinizing women's bodies.[28] Female athletes of the time were expected to behave with "appropriate female decorum" on and off the field or ice rink.[29] Notwithstanding the contradictory messages behind Victorian sensibilities and debates over female athleticism, being an all-around Canadian girl *meant* being athletic, active, sport-oriented, and a year-round lover of the outdoors. The settler fantasy that Canadian girls are "hardy" and can withstand the Great White North played a part in this discourse.

The definition of the "sports girl" merged with contemporary cultural trends in which "a distinct youth culture [and] transformations in the fashion and consumer industries" gradually replaced Victorian ideals of submissiveness and femininity.[30] The modern girl of the 1920s was often personified by the image of the flapper with her short shirt, slender body, and bobbed hair. Fashion styles rapidly changed in the context of "flapper-ism."[31] The flapper image introduced a new ideal of femininity based on independence, mixed-sex socializing, and sexual and youthful energy. Possessing a version of this modern settler femininity, the "sports girl" placed a stronger emphasis on athleticism and a healthy body, coinciding with a myth central to the Canadian settler imagination about resilience and the idea of the North. The contestants were echoing a gendered and racialized discourse that historians suggest had been largely integrated into settler society by the 1920s.[32]

What constituted the elements of this discourse, however, varied even among the Miss Canada 1923 contestants. Miss Regina, Miss Halifax, Miss Edmonton, Miss Sainte-Anne-de-Bellevue, Miss Sherbrooke, and Miss Winnipeg went public with their claim that they had been chosen in their local competitions based on their competency as "sports girls." Miss Sherbrooke, for instance, said that she "would never have come if I had felt that it was to be a beauty contest."[33] Miss Montreal, in contrast, who disagreed with her fellow competitors, said that "talents to appear well in the social life will play a more important part than ability in sporting circles."[34] Winter Sports Committee officials insisted that they had never implied that sports ability was a top consideration for winning the title. However, a candidate's chances of winning seemed to be influenced by her capacity to emulate the "sports girl" or a particular kind of athletic femininity that did not destabil-ize the association between healthy white bodies and respectable feminin-ity. In response to a question about whether a candidate would still be a contender if she did not perform in the various sports events, Fitzgerald said that she could, in fact, be victorious but that she would have to be "excep-tionally charming" to do so.[35] The contestants were concerned about their ability to maintain their respectability while participating in a forum that was a relatively new phenomenon with a questionable history, especially for white, respectable women. In the context of the health movement, the "sports girl" trope, with its focus on a healthy, youthful nation, was used to guard against any potential backlash that the contestants might experience for participating in what was essentially a beauty contest.

This debate over the meaning and characteristics of the "sports girl" and her association with the Miss Canada title demonstrates the complexities of using the beauty contest format to institutionalize the white settler nation in the 1920s. The members of the business community behind the Montreal Winter Sports Carnival and the Miss Canada contest were motivated by drops in sales in the post-holiday season and wanted to find a gimmick that would entice people out of the home and into Montreal's downtown core to spend money. One way to accomplish this goal was to help consumers make a connection between a "pretty face" and a product. But what made the Miss Canada title instrumental in this branding exercise were the winner's embodiment of charm and her representation of white settler values that could increase sales *and* brand loyalty. The seductive co-optation at play made beauty contests a powerful advertising tool.

Debates and discomfort over the ideal image of a national titleholder were not unique to Canada. In her study on the Miss America Pageant in the 1920s, historian Kimberley A. Hamlin suggests that the pageant was a "revolt, conscious or otherwise, against women's increased independence and presence in the public sphere."[36] Hamlin shows that the winners of the Miss America title "popularized the image of the traditional Victorian woman who wore her hair long and espoused no personal ambitions or aspirations other than to be a good wife and mother" while rejecting the ideals of womanhood heralded by suffragettes and women who espoused flapper styles.[37] It was this contested terrain between Victorian woman-hood, on the one hand, and the emerging femininity of the modern girl and personality culture, on the other hand, that rendered national beauty contests a delicate balancing act. Protests against the contest from various groups resulted in a brief cancellation of the Miss America Pageant between 1928 and 1933. Members of the Atlantic City business community worried that the national debate over which discourse of femininity would prevail at the Miss America Pageant was detrimental to their business interests and to fulfilling the initial objective of the pageant, which was to attract tourists, namely middle-class consumers ready to spend money.[38]

Women reformers emphasized both the moral component of beauty contests and the economic exploitation of young women. In fact, the practice of protesting beauty contests is as old as the modern beauty contest.[39] Although I elaborate below on the motives and protest strategies used by two prominent feminist groups, the National Council of Women of Canada (NCWC), including its provincial and municipal chapters, and the Canadian Federation of Women's Labour Leagues, which published a labour newspaper called *The Woman Worker*, these women reformers did very little to mount attacks against the way beauty contests were used to reinforce white settler nationalism.[40] In addition, these women's groups rarely worked as a common front on women's issues, mainly because they positioned themselves at opposite ends of the feminist continuum.

By 1921 white, middle-class women in Canada had already transcended many of the former barriers to their presence in public spaces. Working- and middle-class women exploited newfound opportunities in the labour market due to the shortage of workers brought on by the First World War. Although this trend had reversed by the war's end, the social changes that ensued could not be ignored. The modern girl, like the new woman before her, embodied a mixture of this possibility for economic independence accompanied by the ability to move more freely in what was understood as a male preserve. Still, the home remained widely accepted as the only viable and acceptable place for women to live out their lives as mothers and wives, upholding the moral values of the family. This artificial separation of spheres functioned to maintain the gender hierarchies sustained by heteropatriarchy. Despite the new "freedoms" experienced by white, middle-class women, especially through the discourse of the new woman and modern girl, the heterosexual family continued to reproduce gender and racial ideologies that upheld white settler nationalism.

Majoritarian women gained the vote during the Great War, altering women's political consciousness and demands. The right to vote in a federal election was first given to female relatives of men serving in the war. This right to vote, even if extraordinarily limited, meant that women's former status as noncitizens was eroding.[41] A clear result of this wartime political gain was the suffrage movement, which entailed the establishment of several women's groups dedicated to winning the franchise for white, middle-class Canadian women. Racial ideas about who could vote were gendered; Indigenous women did not gain the right to vote until 1960, and white women reformers were outraged at the fact that immigrant and Black men were granted the franchise before them. The Woman's Christian Temperance Union and the National Council of Women of Canada were two examples of women's political organizing, but women who participated in the labour movement also joined in this fight.[42]

Women's increased participation in the labour force and the temporary gain of the franchise in 1918 created confusion stemming from the clash between this new extension of rights and the cult of domesticity that continued to be enforced. As women began to imagine a life beyond economic dependency and moral regulation, legal, political, and religious forces began a campaign to reimpose women's traditional roles as a way to safeguard the "health" of the nation through the reproductive labour of white bodies. It was precisely the anxiety produced by wartime activities and the suffrage movement that created the need for a ritual and symbol of Canadian settler femininity that would re-establish prewar gender, class, and racial roles.

Beauty contests are an ideal venue through which to showcase these rituals and symbols on a stage and in a public manner. However, the reputation of beauty contests in the 1920s created a dilemma for women reformers. Although using beauty contests to promote their vision of the settler nation through white female bodies may have proven fruitful, it conflicted with the code of respectability dictating that the moral superiority of white women lies in their character. The reproductive health of Indigenous, immigrant, and Black women in Canada was excluded from the discourses of moral character, which was understood to be within the reach only of white women. Consistent with the fact that women of colour were considered a threat to the healthy, white nation and were often the targets of eugenics programs, the bolstering of settler femininity and respectability was an important mission of white women reformers.

Faced with the need to advocate for the moral superiority of white female bodies, women reformers stressed that women's potential as the moral educators of future citizens, not as objects in bathing suits (even if they were bloomers!), uniquely positioned them to influence politics and the law. Launching protests against beauty contests further entrenched reformers' reputation as moral citizens. At the core of their criticism was that beauty contests focused on beauty, not on the values or character found in white settler femininity. Beauty contests were construed as destructive forces. Women reformers feared that too much attention to physical concerns would distract white women from their vocations as mothers and wives, leading to moral corruption because these concerns were so seductive. But these protests and criticisms were unsuccessful in eliminating beauty pageants. As big business, pageants held too much economic clout. After all, these early reformers were competing against the male organizers of the contests in the 1920s in Canada and the United States, who were also interested in female representatives of "morality," albeit for different reasons.

The editors of *The Woman Worker*, for example, were well aware of the powerful influence of the business community and chose to circumvent the morality issue in favour of focusing on the exploitation of women as commodities. *The Woman Worker* was first published in July 1926 under the editorship of Florence Custance, a schoolteacher from Britain and a staunch labour activist. The newspaper – or "magazine," as she called it – was the first separate English-language socialist paper with the goal "to champion Protection of Womanhood, and the Cause of Workers generally."[43] In a brief September 1926 article, *The Woman Worker* commented on a beauty contest that had taken place in Toronto at Sunnyside, a popular beachfront tourist attraction in the east end of the city: "The recent beauty contest in Toronto has brought forth condemnation from ministers of the church and artists. Both object to the display of feminine beauty in such a vulgar fashion. The onus of the responsibility for thus exposing themselves is placed upon the girls who take part."[44] It was not, however, the beauty contest as a display of women's bodies to which *The Woman Worker* objected but the use of working-class women as advertising gimmicks.[45]

In fact, the notion that the "daughters of the working class" were maintaining their "beauty and physical fitness" did not seem problematic to the newspaper's editors.[46] On the surface, the mere acts of exercising, grooming, and making oneself attractive were not considered abhorrent, but making a profit from the display of the working-class female body was a different matter. For *The Woman Worker*, the criticism emanating from the religious quarter, which fell squarely on the shoulders of the young women participating in the beauty contests, was misplaced. Rather, they insisted that disapproval should be heaped on the City of Toronto. They argued that the city used the contest to advertise Sunnyside and increase revenue for the transportation system while facilitating the sale of merchandise as part of the festivities.

Arguments that women on the left were against beauty rituals or pageants because of their potential distraction ignore these women's real concerns.[47] The editors of *The Woman Worker* were careful to deflect the idea that women participating in beauty pageants were morally questionable and instead focused on the fetishization of women's bodies and on suspect business practices in the context of the emerging consumer culture. Ultimately, like their conservative sisters, women on the left entertained the notion that white, working-class women could be folded into the civilizing narrative of the settler nation through femininity and beauty contests in the same way that working-class women would be co-opted into this narrative through their participation in the Miss War Worker, Miss Civil Service, and La Reine des Midinettes/Queen of the Dressmakers pageants later in the century. In February 1927, *The Woman Worker* applauded the Toronto Local Council of Women (TLCW) for "protesting against commercializing the beauty of young women," suggesting that the newcomers to the council's original protest were most welcome.[48]

Nevertheless, women reformers continued to have their say in the battle against beauty contests. On February 26, 1927, Agnes Lind Smythe, president of the Ontario Provincial Council (OPC) of the NCWC, wrote a letter to William Herbert Price, the province's attorney general, regarding the issue of beauty contests:

> The consensus of opinion seems to be entirely against these contests. I have been asked to write you regarding this matter and to find out if anything can be done to ban these from Ontario. Is this a municipal or a provincial or perhaps a federal issue? The women, I feel sure, are anxious to attack this problem in the proper way and will be glad of your advice.[49]

The OPC viewed beauty contests as a "problem" because its members considered them to be a moral issue. According to women reformers, beauty contests created opportunities for male and female audiences to gaze at women while they displayed themselves in bathing suits. They disrupted the moral constraints popular in this era by creating social space deliberately constructed to look at women's necks, hands, arms, and thighs. It gave young women the opportunity to apply makeup, a practice considered antithetical to the morally upright and respectable white woman. Their use of the legal arguments for the interdiction against beauty contests illustrates that these women reformers regarded beauty pageants as dangerous institutions.

It was the deputy attorney general, Edward Bayly, who was charged with the task of responding to Smythe. In his first letter to Smythe, Bayly cited Section 208 of the Criminal Code of Canada as a possible legal stance against beauty contests, noting that it is a criminal offence to present or participate in theatrical performances where a "play, opera, concert, acrobatic, variety, or vaudeville performance, or other entertainment or representation" is deemed "immoral, indecent or obscene."[50] He continued by suggesting that even if there was no conflict with the above law, the Municipal Act of 1922 could also apply, as it allowed municipalities to pass bylaws in order to regulate "the morality of the inhabitants as may be deemed expedient."[51]

The regulation of morality was precisely the core of the issue, and in his initial letter to the OPC, Bayly understood quite accurately the nature of Smythe's inquiry. However, it was in his draft response, prepared on March 9, 1927, that he revealed the political complexities associated with such laws, urging Smythe and her colleagues to abandon their legal strategies against beauty pageants. Regardless of his reaction, Bayly's legal opinion was vital in legitimizing the notion that beauty contests were immoral and obscene.

In a memo to Price on March 9, 1927, Bayly suggested that the Ontario government had the "power, no doubt, to stop beauty contests (the same as it would have power to stop or regulate athletic contests or any other contests which took place in the Province) under the British North America Act, Section 92, sub-head 16 which gives the Legislature jurisdiction to make laws respecting matters within the Province."[52] Indeed, if Attorney General Price had felt compelled to move forward on the issue, Ontario, like any other province, could have passed laws either regulating or eliminating beauty contests. Price and Bayly, however, were seasoned politicians. They recognized that unlike the vaudeville or burlesque shows of the 1920s, where the issue of obscenity seemed more obvious, implementing laws against beauty contests would create an uproar. Bayly ended his letter with the caveat that although he had not been asked to voice an opinion, he felt that such legislation would be "inexpedient and ineffective."[53]

Explaining the legalities of regulating morality in the city, province, and country was not the difficult part; demonstrating to the OPC that such regulation was politically unacceptable was the true challenge. Here, Price and Bayly had to show that they supported, in principle, the concerns voiced by the OPC and its membership without encouraging them to take further action. They did that first by appealing to the OPC's reputation for wanting to protect women from going astray and then by focusing attention on the organization's skill at influencing the social climate of the day:

> It would, as you will appreciate, be an impossible matter to pass an Act prohibiting beauty shows or even regulating them (apart from any immoral feature) without punishing those who violate the Statute. This might mean prosecutions in the Police Court which would probably bring about a greater evil than the Act might be designed to prevent. I think on consideration you will appreciate that in so far as beauty shows are objectionable from a Social or individual standpoint, they can be prevented more effectively by that social pressure which women when they are in earnest, know so well how to exercise.[54]

Deflecting the issue away from the legal Pandora's box that the OPC was asking them to open, Bayly and Price needed to steer the beauty contest issue back to the realm of morality. By putting forward the possibility that the participants might be the ones to suffer most, Bayly and Price probably believed that they were appealing to women's "nature" to protect the least fortunate, presumably the women naive enough to participate in beauty contests.

The OPC refused to be shaken by the bad news and patronizing tone of the letter and instead continued to protest beauty contests well into the 1930s. The Toronto Local Council of Women moved a resolution to "strongly oppose" beauty contests and pushed that petitions be established to persuade Toronto City Council to cooperate in "not allowing the same to be held" because "beauty shows place a premium on external appearance rather than beauty of character, resulting in a lowering of the true ideal of womanhood."[55] This resolution introduces the complexities involved in protesting beauty contests in the context of the interwar decades. For the TLCW, at least, the question went beyond the idea of obscenity or the indecent display of white women's bodies and centred more on late-nineteenth-century ideals about "beauty of character." The members of the TLCW believed that beauty of character consisted of the Victorian values of simplicity, submissiveness, duty, virtue, and self-sacrifice. The TLCW's efforts against beauty contests were announced in the "Moral Standards" section of the proceedings of the National Council of Women of Canada's annual meeting in 1927.[56] Recognizing that there were "strong forces behind these shows," the NCWC conceded that beauty contests were "a difficult subject to attack."[57] Presumably, the forces referred to were the business community and City Council.

The TLCW and the OPC refused to be intimidated by these "strong forces" and continued their tireless campaign against beauty contests. Throughout 1928 the provincial and local councils in Ontario undertook a more systematic approach, formulating a petition to Toronto City Council. The petition advanced three arguments: (1) that beauty contests "lower the true ideal of womanhood by creating a false standard"; (2) that beauty contests were different from athletic contests because, unlike the latter, they "possess nothing of the appeal of skill and courage and perseverance"; and (3) that the winners of beauty contests "obtain a dangerous popularity" and were subject to "unwholesome" commercial exploitation.[58]

The petition was a clear, decisive statement. The OPC and TLCW were careful to show that beauty contests were repugnant to them not only because they considered them morally corrupting but also because they were essentially commercial ventures. Beauty contests were problematic for promoting fame as a way to gain social favour, making them dangerous and "unwholesome." Using language such as "dangerous popularity" was an attempt to connect beauty contests with public encouragement of sexual permissiveness, even suggesting sexual danger.[59] The TLCW implied that young women who participated in beauty contests were expressing themselves in ways that were disrespectful and that clearly threatened "civilized morality."[60] The petition explicitly recognized the commercial issues at the core of the beauty pageant as well as the contest's ability to disrupt social and sexual mores.

From 1929 to 1934 protests against beauty pageants all but vanished from the NCWC's agenda. The economic turmoil of the Depression demanded other uses of its time. In fact, the next time that beauty pageants surfaced as a contested issue was in 1935 when the Border Cities Local Council of Women unsuccessfully petitioned the OPC to urge the Ontario government to pass a bylaw prohibiting beauty contests.[61] Once beauty pageants were incorporated into the festivities associated with the Toronto Police Department Amateur Athletic Association in the later 1930s, the drive to demonstrate that they were outside the realm of respectable white womanhood fell by the wayside. The popularity and legitimacy now associated with the beauty pageant left women's groups such as the OPC and TLCW scrambling to prove that these contests were morally corrupt or exploitative. Who would accuse the Toronto Police Department of paving a path of debauchery and indecency by holding these shows? By the late 1930s, therefore, the arguments against beauty pageants found few supporters. For women reformers, the pageants challenged the cult of white womanhood and increased social anxieties regarding moral and sexual purity, thereby threatening heteropatriarchy anchored in white settler nationalism. Nonetheless, they also helped to situate white Canadian women as the mothers of future citizens, thus bolstering arguments forwarded by the social purists. The tug-of-war within feminism regarding how best to respond to the beauty contest phenomenon continued in the mid-twentieth century but was tempered by a grudging acceptance of beauty contests as cultural institutions with popular appeal.

"She Knows Canadian History": Winnifred Blair and the Miss Canada Pageant 1923

It is impossible to say whether the winner of the Miss Canada 1923 contest put to rest the debate in Montreal about "sports girls" or the morality of beauty contests, but the discourse created around her did reinforce the connections among the beauty queen's body, femininity, and the racial fantasy of the white settler nation. It seems that the lapse between Miss Canada 1923 and the contest's re-emergence in 1946 as the Miss Canada Pageant was based not necessarily on this debate but on a lack of willing organizers and a sustained corporate infrastructure to supply much-needed capital.[62] Indeed, a compromise was reached when Winnifred Blair was selected as Miss Canada 1923, for she represented the independent-minded new woman and modern girl mixed with the traditional Victorian woman, thus embodying an ideal that did not disrupt the white settler discourse of nation.[63]

When Blair won the title, her life as an unknown "business girl" ended.[64] As a laurel wreath was placed on her head, the orchestra played "O Canada." Miss Saint John was, apparently, the choice for most of the people who attended the ball because she represented a "type of wholesome Canadian womanhood," the defining characteristics of which included someone who was "simple and unstudied in demeanor, clear of eye and complexion ... mildly animated rather than vivacious – a girl of the people of the country, whose head seemed in small danger of being 'turned' by the ephemeral honor."[65] Blair was a consensus choice. She appealed to the cult of character and white womanhood valued by an older generation since she was "simple and unstudied in demeanor" and encompassed some of the transitional qualities entrenched by the culture of personality within the bounds of whiteness as "a girl of the people of the country." One of the judges, George Driscoll, explained why Blair won:

> Ideal Canadian Beauty was in my opinion pretty nearly represented and demonstrated in the little girl, Miss St. John in the Montreal carnival contest. She had natural color, fine rosy cheeks, she was well formed, not too slight, and yet not too stout. She is wonderfully athletic, vivacious, modest, and a real outdoor girl, while, on the other hand, she conducted herself in the drawing room with perfect grace and ease. In her conversation there was no attempt at colloquial slang, yet at the same time she was not "upstage" or affected. Of course the contest was not a beauty contest, though that entered into it.[66]

Blair's victory signalled a successful representation of whiteness, the innocence of a "little girl," and the demeanour appropriate to perform middle-class respectability. Blair was an acceptable choice as long as she was "athletic" in the right context, such as skiing down Mount Royal, where many of the carnival activities took place. Apart from confirming whiteness, the mention of "natural color" usually meant that a woman barely used makeup, the application of which was still not considered entirely acceptable, at least not for women who were chaste. Blair, therefore, appealed to heteropatriarchal ideas of sexuality and femininity. It was precisely her ability to behave according to what Driscoll considered appropriate for a "lady," whether she was sliding down a hill in a toboggan or sipping tea in the drawing room, that secured her success as an emblem of settler futurity.

In keeping with his understanding of appropriate feminine behaviour, Driscoll felt that Blair's modesty meant that she was more than "just another pretty face." He explained, "It was not an athletic contest either: you can get a lot of beauty without much mentality. Miss Blair could sit down and carry on a conversation modestly, gracefully and intelligently. She knows Canadian History and is indeed an ideal wholesome type of Canadian young womanhood."[67] Graceful behaviour was another way of suggesting that Blair had the social skills needed to speak in public, a trait that the businessmen behind the Winter Sports Carnival needed if she was to help with boosting sales. But Driscoll was also keen to show that Miss Canada 1923 was a good choice because she upheld a characteristic that he believed was necessary for the bearer of the title: a knowledge of Canadian history. What this knowledge consisted of is not revealed, but it was important enough for this journalist to imply that Blair's knowledge of Canadian history carried some sort of patriotic value and was emblematic of Blair's *Canadianness*. In this instance, Driscoll wanted his readers to embrace the possibility that intelligence in women did not contradict Victorian sensibilities, but these statements also reinforced the idea that part of white settler nationalism included "knowing" the myth-making narratives that sustained the fantasy that upheld it. As an embodiment of the Canadian nation, Miss Canada had to show the ability to communicate this fantasy.

The reference to Blair as "wholesome" referred to her perceived sexual innocence. It was Blair's performance as modest, gracious, and virtuous that made her different from the images of the modern girl prevalent in the early 1920s. This was an image of which Driscoll (and many others) did not approve: "I was struck by the complete absence of flapperism in Miss Blair. She is certainly no flapper, but a nineteen-year-old woman, who would make a favorable impression in any society, and would hold her own in fashionable circles, while quite as easily she would make friends among the masses."[68] According to Driscoll, her lack of "flapperism" made her the right choice to exchange niceties with both the upper and the working classes. Blair's success entrenched the image that was most valued in white settler heteropatriarchy: a Canadian *girl* who used her racial and gender status to stabilize a version of settler femininity entrenched in sexual innocence and modesty. This settler femininity upheld the fantasy of settler heteropatriarchy as a contrast to the sexual unruliness of immigrant women, the whore status of the "squaw," Black women's unbridled sexuality, and to a lesser extent, the promiscuous flapper.

As Miss Canada, Blair quickly acquired status as a national icon, but before her victory she had worked in the office of a custom broker as a stenographer. Her father died three months prior to her victory from an illness contracted while on active service overseas in the First World War.[69] She lived with her mother in Saint John. When she was asked what it felt like to be Miss Canada, Blair said that she had "no feelings left" and that she was "stunned" that the judges had chosen her.[70] When asked whether she had any aspirations for a career in the entertainment industry, Blair responded that she was not interested in the movies and that "when this is over I am going back to my typewriter."[71] Blair might have been a private citizen, but her life as an ordinary person was over once she was crowned. In anticipation of her arrival, the City of Saint John put up archways over the streets, organized receptions, and set aside a suite of rooms at the Royal Hotel as Miss Canada's headquarters.[72] After she disembarked from her train, Winnifred Blair was led into a "royal coach" especially designed for her that had "been gilded all over with a huge crown set over the top and with the driver's seat raised quite high. Old-fashioned doors have been placed on it and painted on them are royal crowns with the initials 'W.C.I.B.' and underneath 'Miss Canada.'"[73] She then made her triumphant march along the route to the headquarters of the Saint John Winter Carnival Committee. After an official welcome by Mayor G.F. Fisher, Blair was whisked off to the Royal Hotel, where a reception organized by the carnival's ladies committee awaited her.

The reception that Blair received was tremendous. As the St. Mary's Band played "O Canada," thousands of people gathered to cheer and greet the new Miss Canada at the train station and along the processional route.[74] The sudden upsurge in enthusiasm and spirit for the carnival activities in the city was directly linked to Blair's victory, allowing carnival organizers to breath a sigh of relief. Blair received telegrams from the mayors of Moncton, Halifax, and Edmonton, the premier of New Brunswick, the editors of major newspapers, and organizations such as the Knights of Columbus.[75] She became the unofficial ambassador for the towns where she was born, lived, and went to high school. The Women's Canadian Club made Blair a life member during an elaborate luncheon.[76] In an editorial on the new Miss Canada, Blair's popularity was placed squarely on her "charming modesty." This editorial was proud to mention that the sudden fame had not "turn[ed] her head" toward notions of grandeur.[77]

A *Toronto Star* journalist captured the reason for Blair's popularity. In an ironic twist, Blair's "aloofness" about gaining commercial benefit from the notoriety fed the perception that she was indeed just another "ordinary girl."[78] On a quest to define this elusive persona, the journalist decided that it was neither Blair's beauty nor her athleticism that made her a national icon. According to the reporter, one could find a dozen more beautiful women at the corner of King and Yonge Streets and athletes with more talent than Blair.[79] Blair's success was attributed to her "unaffected and seemingly unspoilable naturalness" and to her "enthusiastic spirit of a sports-loving Canadian youth."[80] It was Blair's ability to maintain her image as an ordinary person with the "invulnerable armor of a perfect wardrobe" that held the attention of newspapers across the nation and warranted so much appeal for Canadians. Her refusal to entertain the possibility that she escape to Hollywood and try her hand as a movie star endeared her to Canadian audiences. Blair was held up as an exemplar because she performed the role of a charming and wholesome person while maintaining the Victorian ideals of youth and settler femininity. More importantly, Blair demonstrated that this ideal was not entirely overshadowed by the spectre of the modern girl. On the contrary, some elements of the "sports girl," a mollified and modified version of the flapper, could be incorporated into the ideal of wholesome settler femininity, in effect taming what were considered the dangers of this shift. In other words, Blair was constructed as embodying the best of both worlds: the energy of youthful womanhood and the settler moral and sexual codes of an undisrupted heteropatriarchy.

Although the Miss Canada title lay dormant until the mid-1940s, its absence did not sound the death knell for other beauty contests in the 1920s and 1930s. Throughout the interwar period, women continued to represent cities, towns, or festivals as beauty queens. The Miss Toronto Pageant, first organized by the attraction manager of Sunnyside's amusement park in 1926, arose as one of the more prominent contests.[81] It continued to be associated with the park until adopted by the Toronto Police Department Amateur Athletic Association in 1937 as an annual event. The winner of the 1937 Miss Toronto Pageant was May "Billie" Hallam.

In 1975 Ed Reid, host of the CBC television series *Take 30*, interviewed Hallam for an episode devoted to the Depression years. At the time of her victory, seventeen-year-old Hallam was a softball pitcher from a working-class Toronto family. Hallam recalls how her grandmother entered her in the contest based on her "healthy" appearance.[82] As a beauty queen of the Depression era, Hallam's working-class roots made her all the more appealing in the context of white settler society and posed little contradiction to middle-class respectability. Her "success" was imbued with cultural meaning about perseverance, uplift, and good character – traits valued in narratives extolling the ability of a country to survive economic, social, and political turbulence.[83]

Being "healthy looking" in the context of the late 1930s was as important as "being beautiful." According to historian Charlotte Macdonald, the rise of a healthy body culture in this period was new and linked to modernization across the settler colonial societies.[84] The idea that bodies can be reconstructed, or malleable, matched the advancements in industries and technologies as well as the shift from production to consumerism that called for a constant drive toward "novelty."[85] In her book, Macdonald refers to a "sporting citizenship" among "white Dominions" that encompassed the values of freedom and a restraint against violence, thus signalling the civilizing project of progress and modernity. The strong body, not just a healthy one, became a metaphor for the nation; engaging in the physical activity of sports, especially for women, was considered a duty of citizenship.[86]

Hallam's participation in the event after receiving her grandmother's blessing and encouragement shows acceptance of the public display of women by the late 1930s. Hallam's grandmother would have come of age when proper young women did not venture into the streets without chaperones and when those who participated in beauty contests were considered morally corrupt. Use of the word "healthy" by Hallam's grandmother signals the times since at the turn of the twentieth century, it was often used as a synonym for beauty. To be sure, Hallam did not fit the image of a glamorous beauty queen. When asked by Reid how she was handling her new life in the spotlight and the material wealth that she acquired as Miss Toronto 1937, Hallam's understanding of class prompted her to characterize the rich as different from her. Yet it was precisely the ability to mimic ideals of settler femininity, charm, beauty, and glamour that made beauty queens amiable to middle- and upper-class people. Once she won, her socio-economic background was lost behind the royal title of a beauty queen.

The ideals and qualities of Miss Canada continued to create debate and controversy in the 1940s and 1950s. These controversies, such as the one reported in *Le Devoir* in 1947 involving allegations that the Miss Montreal and Miss Quebec titleholders were "prostitutes," reveal the challenges that pageants had to face in order to claim legitimacy.[87] As the pageant became a Canadian institution embedded within the beauty and entertainment industries, the urgency to establish the shared values that defined the symbol of Canadian settler femininity increased. Not to be deterred by the Second World War, Canadians were able to continue their affair with beauty contests and their ability to solidify nationalistic feelings during the war years with pageants such as Miss War Worker, one of the contests discussed in Chapter 3. Under S. Radcliffe Weaver and his wife, Edith, the new owners of the title, the Miss Canada Pageant became a business venture, albeit a small one. The dilemma for the next twenty years would be how to strike a balance between the shared values of the white settler nation and those of corporate Canada without overtly exploiting the bodies of white, middle-class women. What may seem like a daunting task was essential to the pageant's success.

Gendering the White Nation, 1946–62

The Miss Canada title was resurrected in Ontario in 1946 as part of the City of Hamilton's centennial and received an official patent in 1947.[88] Marion Sayer from Newtonbrook, Ontario, a veteran of another beauty contest in 1943 when she clinched the Miss Toronto title at the Toronto Police Games, was the first Miss Canada Pageant winner. A secretary by profession, Sayer worked for the cosmetics department of the Robert Simpson Company at the time of the crowning.[89] She was twenty-one years of age. Sayer won a free trip to Hollywood, New York, and Washington, DC, where she was to invite President Harry S. Truman to attend an airplane show scheduled to take place in Toronto.[90] Under the hot lights at Scott Park in Hamilton, fifty-nine women in bathing suits competed for the title with 7,000 spectators present. Sayer received her honour from Mayor Samuel Lawrence while her mother, Melba Sayer, stood proudly beside her. When asked how she felt when she heard her name announced as the new Miss Canada, Marion Sayer said that she was "so thrilled" that she was "at a complete loss for words."[91] Sayer attributed her victory to a rabbit's foot that she had received from her brother for luck.

The Weavers owned the rights to the pageant, but they also owned a beauty salon, a steam bath, and a palomino stable.[92] Originally, the Miss Canada Pageant was a franchise of the Miss America organization. From 1946 to 1962, before the pageant changed hands from the Weavers to Walter Pasko and Tom Reynolds (and their associates), pageant officials concerned themselves with sending a Miss Canada to the Miss America Pageant in Atlantic City. Consequently, whether the contest represented each region of Canada was not the pageant's main focus. In those sixteen years, nine Miss Canadas were from Ontario, three from British Columbia, two from the Atlantic provinces, one from Quebec, and one from the Yukon. Despite the organizers' preoccupation with their American counterpart, and not surprisingly, a Miss Canada titleholder never won a Miss America title.

While in the hands of the Weavers, the pageant found various venues in southern Ontario: Hamilton, London, Toronto, Burlington, and Niagara Falls. The chambers of commerce, Lions Clubs, and Kiwanis Clubs of these cities took turns sponsoring the event. Throughout its history, the administrative structure of the Miss Canada Pageant was based on a strict gendered division of labour. The men dealt with the business and production aspects, whereas the women (often referred to as hostesses) focused on the contestants, whom they chaperoned, managed, trained, and helped with clothing, hair, and makeup.

For the Weavers, the main adjustment needed was with public perceptions of the contest. As a national title, Miss Canada struggled to attain respectability and public acceptance, and it looked to the Miss America Pageant for answers. Although still controversial, by the late 1940s the Miss America title was already well on its way to establishing itself as an

Miss Canada 1946 basking in her victory. | Archives of Ontario, C109-4-2-35.2, 5104.

American institution. However, the reason for this success was the establishment of a new scholarship program, which attracted "legitimate" contestants. By establishing a scholarship program, headed by a committee
of several Quaker women from Atlantic City, Lenora Slaughter, the Miss
America Pageant's first female national director, was able to change
people's assessment of the pageant.[93] The scholarship program allowed
them to effectively argue that Miss America was more than just a swimsuit competition aimed at titillating audiences with exposed flesh. In an
effort to further convince the public of the pageant's legitimate status as a
respectable organization, "talent" and "personality" were added to the list
of qualifications for future Miss Americas. Nevertheless, in the 1950s the
bathing suit segment drew crowds more than any other part of the
pageant.

In Canada, S. Radcliffe Weaver was never far behind in implementing
the same requirements and qualifications. In an attempt to enhance the
prestige and respectability of the scholarship program, he appointed Ellen

Fairclough, Canada's first female Cabinet member and the minister of immigration who presided over official nondiscrimination in Canada's immigration policy, to chair the program's board of directors.[94] Commentators such as journalist James McHardy saw the addition of a scholarship program to the Miss Canada Pageant as central to ensuring a positive reputation for the contest and its contestants:

> The offer of a handsome scholarship for the winner of a "Miss Canada" contest will attract girls who have background and are ambitious, and the assurance of a properly-chaperoned, well-conducted contest will overcome the objections of many parents to their daughters parading before the public. Then the girl who emerges with the "Miss Canada" banner should be able to represent her country at Atlantic City or anywhere else and be armed with beauty, talent, personality and intelligence.[95]

In the late 1940s beauty contest officials had to recalibrate the relationship between the display of white feminine sexuality and moral innocence. McHardy's arguments for a "properly-chaperoned, well-conducted contest" forced the issue for beauty contest officials who wanted the contestants to represent "wholesomeness" while entertaining crowds in bathing suits and high-heeled shoes. A scholarship program catered to the idea that only women interested in so-called serious careers would become eligible for participation. Organizers banked on the fact that this focus would appease parents' concerns about their daughters "parading before the public."

Notwithstanding the drive to establish the contest as respectable, no pageant wishing to attract big audiences could survive without a swimsuit competition. Justifying the swimsuit segment was an annual challenge for the Miss Canada Pageant, one that could never be put to rest. Sarah Banet-Weiser suggests that, unlike the bathing beauty contests of an earlier era, the swimsuit competition helped to maintain a tradition that "recoups the crucial materiality of femininity: the seemingly changeless female body, fixed in age and the embodiment of heterosexual desire."[96] According to the Miss Canada organizers, bathing suits enabled the judges to "adequately and unquestionably" assess the "Beauty of Face and Form" segment of the criteria. By the mid-1950s, standardizing the style and colour of bathing suits to create the illusion that contestants were judged on an equal footing was part of this discourse of objectivity and respectability.[97] By making "regulation swimsuits" mandatory, pageant officials could argue that the swimsuit competition maintained the integrity of the event while ensuring that white female sexuality remained on display.

The gender and race of judging, Miss Canada 1946 Pageant. | Archives of Ontario, C109-4-2-35.1, 5100.

The swimsuit segment was also a crucial element in securing sponsor-ship from the business community since this was the component of the pageant that ensured large numbers of viewers. The practice of having bath-ing suit manufacturers supply the swimsuits for the contestants helped to boost sales for the companies involved and instituted the image of uniform-ity and fairness. As we have seen, Catalina used this tactic in its newly cre-ated Miss Universe Pageant and in supplying the official swimwear for the Miss Dominion of Canada pageant. Companies like Jantzen and Sea Queen were mainstays of the Miss Canada Pageant's swimsuit segment, which included a Miss Swimsuit title by the mid-1970s. This annual feature of the Miss Canada Pageant meant that corporate interests permeated every aspect of the contest, not just in the commercial breaks.

From 1946 to 1962 the Miss Canada Pageant's main objective was to enter the beauty pageant industry as a formidable player by associating itself with the Miss America Pageant. To accomplish this goal, the pageant had to establish itself as a viable representation of white, respectable femininity and do so in a dignified manner. However, where it occasionally wavered in deploying a stable version of settler nationalism and citizenship with the eruption of a scandal or claims of illegitimacy, it gained in instituting a fantasy of white settler ideals of gender and race. All the winners of the Miss Canada title in this period were white, reinforcing the notion that *Canadian beauty* was white, youthful, and tinged with the allure of innocence. The Weavers were attempting to win the hearts and minds of a white settler public since such acceptance would eventually translate into a pageant title that could become an iconic symbol of the settler nation and its citizenship.

Issues of public image were a constant problem at the beginning. In September 1954, *Maclean's* magazine published an article featuring a former and disenchanted titleholder. Marilyn Reddick, Miss Canada 1952, exposed some of the problems and controversies behind the scenes at the pageant. In a scathing account, Reddick described the beauty queen as a "musical-comedy actress" with the ethics of a "Girl Guide" and the constitution of a "Clydesdale mare."[98] Reddick was a regular on the beauty contest circuit by the age of sixteen. She entered the Toronto Police Department Amateur Athletic Association's annual Miss Toronto Pageant and placed third. She then tried her luck with the Miss Bloor contest organized by the Bloor Street Business Men's Association of Toronto and won. In the *Maclean's* article, Reddick admitted that she participated in beauty contests because she believed that they would enable her to enter the "showbiz" world, which she and her parents desperately wanted her to penetrate.[99] When Reddick's plans failed, she went public with her disappointment. Drawing on a discourse of sexual danger, *Maclean's* spotlighted the "wolves" that surrounded the contestants throughout pageant week:

> The male attack was tremendous. We were all billeted in hotels [in Atlantic City] and every time we left or arrived there were packs of wolves trying to cut girls out from the flock ... These total strangers telephoned our hotel rooms asking for dates. But the chaperones were always there, dashing in and breaking it up if ever the girls and the wolves looked like getting together, and snatching up the phone every time it rang. Mrs. Weaver didn't say much but I could tell she thought the affair lacked the tone of the Miss Canada contest.[100]

Reddick's account of her experiences as Miss Canada at the Miss America Pageant highlighted the competitiveness of beauty contests and the emotional damage that contestants risked even as the pageants presented women with financial and employment opportunities. Reddick found the American contestants to be more sophisticated and professional than anything she had experienced. She recounted incidents when fellow contestants were openly hostile toward her and made derogatory remarks about her body.[101] As Miss Canada 1952, Reddick was eliminated in the first round at the Miss America Pageant. The disappointment proved too much for her to handle. Shortly after her return from Atlantic City, doctors ordered her to take a two-month rest, but S. Radcliffe Weaver had other plans. He decided that the best way to get Miss Canada back on track was to send her to the 1953 coronation of Queen Elizabeth II in England in the hope that she would get an audience with the queen. When Reddick recounted this story to the press, Weaver appeared insensitive to Reddick's emotional state and emerged as the classic villain, interested only in turning a profit.

The *Maclean's* article was more than just bad publicity for the Weavers. The pageant was riddled with problems, but for the first time someone directly involved had revealed the commercial and exploitative side of the beauty pageant industry.[102] By painting herself as just a pawn of a pageant hungry for profit and publicity, Reddick created a controversy that went beyond financial insecurity or contestants who broke the rules. A response to these claims had to be formulated, but one from the Weavers would seem inappropriate and defensive. A response from Reddick's successor, Miss Canada 1953, was more credible. Kathy Archibald's article appeared in *B.C. Magazine*, a Saturday insert of the *Vancouver Province*. At the time the article was written, Archibald was studying to be a veterinarian at the University of Guelph.[103] The *B.C. Magazine* article disputed Reddick's account while offering Archibald's own personal opinions and constructive criticisms of the pageant.

Archibald recalled how she had entered the Miss Canada Pageant as the Kelowna Regatta's Lady of the Lake. When Archibald was told that she would travel to Burlington to represent Kelowna, she was first "thrilled" and then scared because she realized that she did not have a "talent." But she said that her bigger worry was her age. At nineteen, she felt she was too young and that the other contestants would be far more "sophisticated" because the beauty queen reign "gives you a year which is on the most part rather strange and decidedly unnatural."[104] She saw the age issue, rather than petty tensions, demands, and commercial exploitation, as the reason for Reddick's nervous breakdown. The culprit was not the profit-making interests of the pageant officials and sponsors but Reddick's lack of maturity and the "unnatural" strain of the one-year tenure as queen. By placing the blame on Reddick's inability to deal with the stress associated with the Miss Canada title, Archibald effectively exonerated the Weavers and the sponsors of responsibility.

The Reddick-Archibald debate ended there, but the Miss Canada Pageant continued to grapple with issues of public image. In 1953 debate emerged about how much emphasis was placed on "beauty of form and figure," as opposed to "personality, charm, and intelligence," as highlighted in an editorial written some days after the crowning of Miss Canada 1953 that cited "the inevitable vagueness as to just what qualities are required and in what proportions" as the problem.[105] Although the editorial noted the "difficulties," the reader was left with an overall positive impression of the contest. The editorial also pointed out that the Miss Canada Pageant "is not a beauty contest" because there was no bathing suit parade on the final night of judging. Instead, emphasis was placed on how "lovely" the contestants looked in their evening dresses and on Miss Canada 1953's speech about her hometown. Editorials or commentaries that questioned the reputation or criteria of the title were detrimental to the pageant's public image, especially when it was still being forged in the early 1950s. In this period, the contest struggled to establish itself as something beyond a bathing beauty event and to secure its place as a cultural institution designed to maintain racial and gender hierarchies.

Archibald's victory in 1953 marked the beginning of a period in which Miss Canada began to be perceived as a nationwide institution. For the first time since its inception, a British Columbian had won the title. By the time she reached Newfoundland in early October 1953, she had visited thirty cities across Canada and the United States. While in Newfoundland, she was interviewed by disc jockeys Bob Lewis and Art Harnett of CJON Radio. She met Premier Joey Smallwood, visited the tuberculosis sanatorium, and promoted one of her sponsors – Monarch Knitting Mills – at a mall.[106] Publicizing her appearance was an essential step in the process of representing the Miss Canada Pageant and her sponsors. The interview by CJON included Archibald's chaperone, Evelyn Webster, a southerner from Alabama who

called Hamilton her new home. She was prepared to put the issue of qualifications to rest:

> HARNETT: Can you tell us what qualifications are necessary for entry into
> the Miss Canada Pageant and also for winning same?
> WEBSTER: Yes, I'll be glad to. This thing of calling it a beauty competition –
> it isn't that. Of course, I think most are lovely, healthy. Canadian girls
> are beautiful, but we want intelligence, and we want character, and we
> want education and definitely fine personality and all the charms that
> go into making a real fine Canadian character and Canadian represent-
> ative or ambassador as she goes around the country and goes over to
> the United States.
> HARNETT: And Miss Archibald has all these attributes you're talking
> about?
> WEBSTER: I think she has a lot of lovely things – so many of them![107]

The shift toward an emphasis on "intelligence," "character," and "a real
fine Canadian personality" was based in part on the need to demonstrate
that the pageant was a serious venture and an emblem of settler femininity.
Beauty contestants who possessed these qualities could hold their own in a
public situation, like promoting knitted sweaters. Dispelling the notion that
the Miss Canada Pageant was a "beauty competition" coincided with promoting the scholarship program, enabling pageant officials to argue that the
beauty contest industry was more than just about pretty faces. Capturing
the white settler gaze meant ensuring that the winner of the Miss Canada
title *actively projected* white, respectable femininity. In other words, the
racial, class, sexual, and gender hierarchies represented by the titleholders
were not passive. Invoking the idea of Miss Canada as an "ambassador,"
someone tasked with *defending* and *advocating,* was imperative to creating
the fantasy that the pageant had the potential to institutionalize the white
supremacist ideologies at the core of Canadian political, legal, and cultural
systems.[108]

By the mid-1950s, the Miss Canada Pageant had achieved its goal of
establishing itself as both a Canadian institution and a viable business venture. Major companies such as Pepsi-Cola Canada, Samsonite of Canada,
the Philco Corporation, Trans-Canada Airlines, and the clothing manufacturer Miss Sun Valley contributed to the Miss Canada Scholarship
Foundation. In 1956 the CBC finally gave the pageant the venue that it
needed for promotion on the national stage. It produced a lengthy,

"inquisitive and light-hearted look behind the scenes of the Miss Canada competition." The feature consisted of impromptu interviews with several (white) contestants, beginning with footage of the pageant participants on a tour boat circling Hamilton Bay. The rules of the pageant were the focus of the first set of questions:

> REPORTER: Girls, what are the rules and regulations of this contest?
> CONTESTANT #1: Well, Frank, one of the rules is the girls ... in the contest must have won a beauty contest held in their own territory.
> CONTESTANT #2: The girls must be single and between the ages of eighteen and twenty-six and have to have a good character and personality.[109]

This segment's effort to promote awareness of the pageant was not intended to educate Canadians about the "rules" but to elicit excitement that would eventually translate into viewers. In this orchestrated question and answer format, both the Miss Canada Pageant and the CBC tried to reassure the public that the contest was legitimate by emphasizing that all the "girls" were young adults (as no children were being exploited) and of "good character and personality" (insofar as the delegates, if not virgins, could at least pass as innocent).

In an attempt to enhance the pageant's image as an upstanding organization by de-emphasizing looks and placing value on the perception of sexual innocence, the show tried to tease out the differences between "beauty queens" and "pretty girls":

> REPORTER: What's the difference between a beauty queen and a pretty girl?
> CONTESTANT: Well, a pretty girl, you could say, more or less lives her own life and goes her own way, whereas a beauty queen has to watch her step.[110]

Having "to watch her step" meant that a beauty queen shared a responsibility to behave in accordance with the dominant discourse on Canadian settler femininity and heterosexuality as defined in the postwar period. As the beauty queen became aligned with the shared values and hopes of the nation, her body and sexuality also became a focus of the beauty pageant itself. In her book on youth culture in mid-century Canada, sociologist Mary-Louise Adams argues that white, middle-class youth were considered "symbols of the prosperity and potential of their families and their society."[111]

Joan Fitzpatrick, Miss Canada 1958, and Prime Minister John Diefenbaker at Parliament Hill. | Library and Archives Canada, Duncan Cameron Collection, PA206933.

Beauty queens, like white, middle-class youth, were considered to be part of a counternarrative against the troublesome messages magnified by rebellious, unruly, and promiscuous "teen culture" and the sexual perils that it presented.

Regulating morality (coded as sexual regulation) became the singular element needed to ensure the cultural acceptability of the Miss Canada pageant to white settler audiences. The main focus of this project involved regulating the beauty contestants' sexual and social behaviour:

> *CHAPERONE:* Girls, I have a few suggestions to make to you while you're
> here at the pageant. First, this is to be a week with a manless menu.
> No speaking to men in the hotel or in the streets or in the forum.

No cocktails, please. And remember girls, you are being judged on form – beauty of form – and figure. And your figure must be your very own. And remember girls, if you have any questions, or any problems, see your chaperone. All right, keep happy, and now let's get back to the rehearsal.[112]

By reminding the contestants that pageant week meant having a "manless menu" and absolutely "no cocktails," this pageant official was attempting to set a moral standard adapted to white feminine sexuality in the 1950s. In the context of the Miss Canada Pageant, "good character and personality" meant that beauty contestants refrained from sexual activity and drinking while demonstrating an ability to fascinate and charm, a pageant paradox considered key to performing femininity, sexuality, and selling products in a consumer culture.

For the pageant judges, Dorothée Moreau, Miss Canada 1956, personified "good character and personality."[113] During her tenure, she met Prime Minister Louis St. Laurent and embarked on several commercial ventures. Moreau's itinerary during her reign included flying to England and having a screen test with the Arthur Rank organization, visiting France, serving as a semi-finalist in the Miss America Pageant, and appearing in the Raphael-Mack Fashion Show.[114] A pageant official described her as possessing "unspoiled sophistication." This attribute aside, it was her ability to entertain and to assume the role of "ambassadress" that brought her so much acclaim. In a promotional booklet, Moreau was congratulated for being "one of the finest Misses Canada the Pageant has been fortunate enough to seek out and present to an entertainment hungry Canadian audience."[115] Her ability to appeal to this audience while successfully promoting the Philco Corporation's newest product helped pageant officials to frame the contest as a safe and reliable form of advertising. Moreau possessed the right balance of good character and personality and thus perpetuated the idealized version of Canadian settler femininity and sexuality.

The personalities behind the pageant were as crucial to the discourses of white settler society and femininity as were the contestants themselves. As managing director, Frances Hollinrake supervised the contestants while in Hamilton. She owned Raphael-Mack Salon and Specialty Shops, sat as provincial treasurer of the Imperial Order Daughters of the Empire, and was a judge for the Miss Canada 1956 Pageant.[116] The brief biography in the pageant's souvenir program heralded her as an important Hamiltonian who always had the best interests of the city and youth at heart. Her candid views on Canadian youth, nation building, and the Miss Canada Pageant reveal the importance that she attached to beauty contests:

> I have a definite belief in the inherent good in Canadian youth. Those who will graduate this year are the future leaders in industry, business, society and politics. They are our nation's bulwarks against all that is bad in Communism. They give us more cause for joy than for complaint ... It is a pleasure to help provide an opportunity medium for suitable young Canadian ladies. The Miss Canada Pageant achieves that end.[117]

For Hollinrake, the Miss Canada Pageant was far more than a parade of beauty queens; it fulfilled a critical role in the fight to keep the nation stable, moral, and free. Historian Katie Pickles's study on the Imperial Order Daughters of the Empire explains the serious attention that the organization gave to the civil defence against communism, arguing that members approached national security through a community-based front.[118] It is possible that Hollinrake interpreted this approach as including the recruitment of young women as part of this project to win the fight against communism. The Miss Canada Pageant presented an opportunity to train the elite – "future leaders in industry, business, society and politics" – in entrenching settler nationalism as heterosexual, white, individualistic, and capitalist.

Accompanying these anti-communist sentiments was a heteropaternalist image of the pageant as a protector of white feminine virtue rather than an exploiter or "spoiler" of that innocence. The embodiment of this paternalism was Weaver himself. In his biography, Weaver is described as "a father among fathers" who "assisted some of the finest Canadian families to make it possible for their young daughters to pursue their special field of talent."[119] Not surprisingly, Weaver's business interests in the pageant were consistently downplayed. Instead, he appeared as an "eminent authority of beauty and poise." Weaver carefully established himself as an expert, someone to be trusted, a reliable man, and an honourable citizen working tirelessly and altruistically for the good of Canadian women. The promotion of this persona was accomplished with the help of the Hamilton Homemakers Club, whose members probably provided the many hours of unpaid labour essential to running the organization, as well as playing the part of chaperones.[120]

The 1957 souvenir program included an entire page dedicated to "How We Choose Miss Canada." The piece provided information on what it meant to be Miss Canada and an explanation of the entrance process, judging, and the issue of bathing suits. Its inclusion in the souvenir program functioned to define, defend, and dispel myths about the various aspects of the pageant. Ideals of Canadian settler nationalism and the fairy-tale element resonated throughout. The following passage portrayed the title as a portal to an exciting world:

> "Miss Canada" comes from every province in Canada. She becomes her nation's Ambassadress of Beauty, its Prime Minister of Talent. She lives in a dream world – become reality. The Pageant opens a whole new world for her. To the world outside her home, her native land, she does not come from easterly Newfoundland or westerly British Columbia. Nor does she hail from the colder Yukon or sunny Southern Ontario. She comes from Canada and stands resplendent in an association of Canadian beauty, talent and intelligence.[121]

Once crowned, Miss Canada encapsulated a moral, racial, cultural, linguistic, and regional homogeneity that dovetailed with settler nationalism. The illusion of homogeneity was central to selling Miss Canada on the international scene. The dream world referred to entailed new access to the international stage and the titleholder's iconographic status as the symbolic representative of Canadian femininity and beauty. Labels such as the "Ambassadress of Beauty" and the "Prime Minister of Talent" added a discourse of officialdom to the title but also underscored that the performativity of embodied racial and gender hierarchies in white settler society was active and purposeful. In other words, the promoters and organizers of the Miss Canada Pageant used the bodies of beauty queens representing this title as the anchors of a white settler nation precisely because the material body and its symbolism entrenched white subjectivity as a tool of the civilizing project on the global stage.

From 1923 to 1962, Miss Canada embarked on a bumpy road toward establishing itself as a cultural institution and spectacle featuring white female bodies. Despite the perennial controversies, sometimes highly publicized, Miss Canada became associated with white, middle-class femininity, making the title a potentially profitable advertising tool for scores of businesses that sold everything from pantyhose to cars. As a cultural institution, the Miss Canada Pageant had much the same success as the Miss

America franchise. Settlers did see their values reflected in the bodies of the contestants even if they continued to suspect that the investment of the beauty industry complex in the pageant meant that young women were open to exploitation and fetishization. By the time the Miss Canada Pageant reached solid ground in the mid-1950s as a national institution, much of Canadian society had accepted that women's bodies were a mainstay of advertising and that displaying their bodies for public consumption was a consequence of modernity. The participation of members of the middle and upper classes as organizers, national directors, and chaperones contributed to making Miss Canada an arbiter of white settler nationalism. People like the Weavers and Evelyn Webster became gatekeepers regarding white, middle-class, wholesome Canadian girls.

However, eschewing the flapper's open sexuality, shunning the feminist tendencies of the new woman and modern girl, and controlling adolescent sexuality are not preconditions for legitimizing a pageant. Pageants that get to claim national status must survive the test of time and the cultural changes that come with it. Miss Canada was no exception. By the early 1960s, the Miss Canada title was an established beacon of white settler pride, but it needed to pivot in response to the onslaught of new technologies and mediums such as television. Unlike the Miss America Pageant, Miss Canada in the period discussed above did not enjoy international standing for two reasons. First, the Weavers lacked the funds and know-how to take the pageant to the next level. They were small-business owners with connections to the social elite in Hamilton, not globetrotters with links to multinationals. By 1963 their hold on the Miss Canada Pageant was weakening. Second, through the sponsorship that they provided, big businesses were increasingly interested in marketing their products on the national and international stage. Miss Canada had to comply or vanish into oblivion. Televising the event was pivotal to its survival, not only because it appeased sponsor interest but also because it secured a stronghold in the national imagination in the same way as, but separate from, the Miss America Pageant. I discuss this evolution in detail in Chapter 5, where I return to the last twenty years of the Miss Canada Pageant's duration.

National beauty pageants from the 1920s to the beginning of the 1960s played a central role as exemplars of settler femininity, but local and queen pageants were instrumental in conveying *and* destabilizing settler nationalism. In Chapters 3 and 4, I introduce several of these local and queen pageants, focused on the bodies of working women from various sectors of the labour force and on the bodies of immigrant, Black, and Indigenous women. I organize these chapters chronologically and thematically to show the commonalities between contests and to demonstrate how they borrowed, modified, subverted, and performed distinct versions of settler femininity. In these examples, the performance of settler femininity was a response to the version embodied by Miss Canada but in a complicated, nuanced, and tenuous manner.

3

Labour of Beauty

In 1956 Dick McDougall of *Tabloid*, a CBC public affairs television program, interviewed Miss Advertising Specialty, Mary Ann Lenchuk, at the annual convention of the Ads and Sales Club, a mostly male enclave. The interview introduced a story on advertising. The program presented various advertising tools used by industries to sell their products and grab consumers' attention, such as a pencil equipped with a yo-yo, a calendar, or a gigantic set of matches ("for the chain smoker").[1] Lenchuk demonstrated the advantages of using a beauty queen to represent a product; she herself effectively became a specialty advertising item. Lenchuk wore the classic French maid's outfit, along with a coronet of roses and a sash. Although there was no actual contest for the title of Miss Advertising Specialty, Lenchuk was crowned by Judy Welsh, Miss Toronto 1956, before a crowd of over 500 businessmen.[2]

Miss Advertising Specialty was but one of many titles organized and sponsored by the business sector. Beauty contests linked to specific products and employment areas were popular because they captured people's attention. The rise in consumer culture was buttressed increasingly by advertising that promised sexual fulfillment with product identification.[3] In what is arguably the best-known example, airline companies sexualized flight attendants to sell seats, obligating their flight attendants to take charm classes and to learn how to apply makeup and maintain a certain weight, providing yet another example of the beauty industrial complex's reach. By the 1970s the "fresh-faced girl next door" flight attendants popular in the 1950s had been replaced by attendants who had to wear hot pants and "Fly Me" buttons if they wanted to keep their jobs.[4] The beauty, sexuality, and personality of flight attendants became a central promotional tool of the airline industry.

The growing presence of women in the paid labour force at the beginning of the twentieth century emerged as an increasingly contentious issue as women assumed pivotal roles in the manufacturing and clerical industries even before the onset of the Second World War dramatically increased their numbers and visibility. Women actively participated in the social organization of the workplace, and their presence heightened anxieties about sexual and gender relations. One of the main reasons for these anxieties stemmed from women's participation in nontraditional work and from their increased presence in a wide range of industries.[5] The focus on workplace beauty pageants in this chapter is meant to position these queen pageants as significant players in sustaining versions of settler femininity even as the values and codes underlying this performance of femininity shifted slightly in the postwar period. Although white supremacy and the racial hierarchies that it maintains still actively frame how settler women negotiate their *place* in the Canadian landscape, the postwar period covered in this chapter leaves behind discourses of the modern and introduces a version of settler femininity concerned with a more conservative vein regarding what it means to be wholesome, respectable, and white. To illustrate that this conservatism was not unique to national beauty contests in the same period but, in fact, was ubiquitous throughout pageant discourses, I showcase beauty contests organized by the blue- and white-collar sectors.

Established and funded by both employers and unions, beauty contests were used by the business community for a variety of purposes. On the surface, the contests advertised consumer products, promoted businesses to the mass public, or recruited new workers. However, beauty contests did much more. During the war years, for instance, the Miss War Worker contest had the added function of boosting patriotic sentiment and settler nationalism even if it was promoted as a "fun" event. One of the best examples of union-organized beauty contests is La Reine des Midinettes/Queen of the Dressmakers, a beauty pageant organized by the International Ladies' Garment Workers' Union (ILGWU). The ILGWU pageant shows how beauty contests and union-sponsored social activities "educated" garment workers. Queen of the Dressmakers was staged to "uplift" garment workers by encouraging them to emulate the ideals of femininity, whiteness, and class. Like employer-initiated pageants, they added glamour to work considered tedious and underpaid.

Underlying all these workplace beauty contests was the need to subdue settler anxieties created by the influx of white women into the labour force, which at times included their participation in nontraditional sectors. The increased numbers of women in the workplace created a social disruption that required a new calibration of settler femininity to re-entrench gender, race, and sexual codes in line with the white settler heteropatriarchal nation. By the Second World War, beauty contests helped to allay fears about eroding gender and sexual roles. Workplace beauty contests provided a space in which societal expectations about sexual conduct and ideals of beauty as well as a modern version of settler femininity could be reinforced, serving the same broader mandate of national beauty contests like Miss Canada. Pageants sustained the discourse that women's primary goal in the world of work, or another aspect of her job as a woman, was to adhere to proper notions of femininity, morality, and beauty.

Employers initiated and organized beauty contests in workplaces traditionally understood as the domains of female work. These numerous examples of workplace beauty pageants became part of the cultural landscape of work for women from the late 1920s to 1960s. Beauty pageants such as Miss War Worker, Miss Civil Service, and Miss Secretary of Canada eroticized and challenged mostly white women's presence in the workplace. Indeed, with the exception of one winner of the Miss Civil Service contest, all the winners of the pageants discussed in this chapter were white. It would be overly simplistic, however, to say that workplace beauty pageants merely reinforced and reflected dominant gender roles. They were also at the centre of the contestation over the meaning of women's work by both men and women and over how women's work could be reconciled with settler femininity. With the exception of Miss War Worker, the beauty queens associated with Queen of the Dressmakers, Miss Civil Service, and Miss Secretary did not make explicit mention of the nation as part of their mandate, but this fact does not mean that these beauty queens did not embody gender, race, class, and heterosexual signals underscoring white settler nationalism. The "success" of the settler nation depended on working women's adherence to these hegemonic values literally on stage and under bright lights.

"Beauty as Duty": Miss War Worker

As recreational and entertainment events, beauty contests were particularly important in workplaces and professions traditionally dominated by men but especially where women were an increasing presence, as was the case during the labour shortage of the Second World War. In such settings, women's presence in nontraditional employment was accompanied by a focus on beauty culture practices. A lipstick ad in *Chatelaine* magazine, for example, congratulated female munitions workers for "succeeding in keeping your femininity – even though you are doing man's work!"[6] During the war, women worked in factories, drove buses and streetcars, delivered mail, and worked on farms. Such places of employment furnished venues for other beauty pageants such as Miss Farmerette. The Miss Farmerette contest represented the "typical Ontario Farm Service Force Girl." The contest was organized to "honour the 1,300 girls who serve in Government labour camps and on private farms throughout Ontario." For example, the winner in 1942 was chosen based on her "service, personality and camp spirit."[7]

War plants, or munitions factories, used pin-ups, cartoons, the woman's page of their newspapers, and beauty contests to sustain ideals of white femininity and beauty culture. Historian Helen Smith and sociologist Pamela Wakewich explore the various ways that the Canadian Car and Foundry Company Limited (Can Car) used these tactics in its *Aircrafter* newspaper to both praise women and contain them.[8] The two central goals of the newspaper were to maintain high productivity and to prepare the workforce for the postwar economy. Can Car met these objectives by emphasizing teamwork and family, thereby linking war with homes, families, and nation.[9] Although Can Car did not organize a beauty contest, *Aircrafter* featured pin-ups and a woman's page that together emphasized Can Car workers' "decorative role" to ensure that the "masculine labour" performed by these women did not diminish their femininity.[10]

Pin-ups and beauty contests also permeated the work culture at Alberni Plywoods Limited, a factory that opened in Port Alberni, British Columbia, in 1942.[11] In her case study of how wartime employment impacted women at Alberni Plywoods, historian Susanne Klausen found that "sex-typing" tasks as suitable for women "feminized and devalued women's labour while justifying the sexual segregation of workers."[12] Sex segregation at the plywood plant was exacerbated by the company newspaper, *Harmac News*, which sanctioned the image of single female factory workers as "feminine or sexual beings ripe for romance or marriage." A Lumber Queen title was organized in the postwar period, in addition to the pin-ups featuring "Plywood Girls" and their leisure activities. This pageant was an event at the annual Labour Day celebrations, where the winner was chosen by a popularity poll.[13]

In her classic study of Canadian women's participation in the Second World War, historian Ruth Roach Pierson documents how government and military officials tirelessly employed aggressive propaganda techniques to reassure Canadians that white women could participate in the military without losing their femininity.[14] An important part of this propaganda included profiting from the "promotional value of 'sex appeal.'" Pierson notes that the first woman welder to be approved by the Canadian government for national defence work was selected by *National Home Monthly* magazine as its "Glamour Girl" in the September 1942 issue.[15] Women war workers and servicewomen were inundated with messages that their primary duty was to maintain their beauty and femininity even as they performed work traditionally viewed as masculine.

It was this "sex appeal" that made the Miss War Worker beauty contest so popular among blue-collar workers and Torontonians in general. The Miss War Worker beauty contest was held at Exhibition Park as part of the Toronto Police Department Amateur Athletic Association's annual festivities. From 1942 to 1944 the contest was held in conjunction with the Miss Toronto Pageant, sponsored and organized by the Toronto Police Department. The association's event attracted hundreds of people annually, and the beauty pageant was a big draw. The Toronto Police Department has a long history of organizing beauty contests. It held the Miss Toronto Pageant almost annually even during the years that the Miss Canada Pageant was on hiatus. Miss War Worker focused on the war effort in Toronto and surrounding towns, such as Ajax, where many of the munitions factories were located. As the ultimate example of "beauty as duty" – the idea that women were morally obligated to beautify themselves as part of the war effort – the Miss War Worker contest continued the tradition of inserting beauty culture into work culture.[16] The pageant was one of many social and recreational events organized by munitions plants. What made it unique was that it drew on the "Rosie the Riveter" stereotype popularized by Norman Rockwell, an image that exemplified settler femininity by using a white female body as a symbol and defender of home-front patriotism. Contestants competed in coveralls and bandanas, not as a way to downplay the ideals of beauty and femininity but as a way to use women's bodies to convey the connections between munitions workers, patriotic duty, and the needs of the wartime nation. In the case of the Miss War Worker contest, parading in bathing suits and evening gowns would have detracted from the war effort.

The Miss War Worker contest morphed into a corporate issue as the labour shortage increased. In a memorandum sent to the top executives at

"Beauty No Artist Could Paint!" Miss GECO 1943 contestants. | Archives of Ontario, F2082-1-2-1.

Miss War Worker 1943 and two finalists. | Archives of Ontario, F2082-1-2-1, 3455.

the John Inglis Company[17] on July 2, 1943, Archer Lee Ainsworth, vice-president of the company, urged them to take the Miss War Worker beauty contest seriously:

> We have, from time to time, engaged in certain Beauty Contest competitions without properly organizing to be sure that we had a reasonable chance of winning, and in the case of the selection of Miss Warworker [sic] last year which was won by Research Enterprises I am told by Colonel Philips that the publicity at the time and which continued has been responsible for certain types of girls who normally would not consider working in a factory applying to Research.[18]

Ainsworth wanted his company to win the title of Miss War Worker because it was a hugely successful event during its three-year run. He needed more employees and could not afford to have Research Enterprises, a rival company, take those resources away from him. If a "frivolous contest during wartime" proved to be a successful recruitment strategy to fill the assembly lines at his munitions plant, then Ainsworth was willing to do whatever promotion was needed.[19] More importantly, he could not be outmanoeuvred by the CEOs of other munitions factories in town.

Ainsworth wanted the Miss John Inglis contest to create such a stir around the country and among other working women that they would leave their current jobs to make bombs and guns at Inglis:

> The last, and most important point by a long way, is that we organize very thoroughly for nation-wide publicity and make a feature of the fact that this has been done on the employees' own time, and worded in such a way that it has in no way affected production. Every step should be taken to get the various reporters and photographers present and to see that we have first class photographers of our own so that the copy can be sent out to all publications across Canada, and the basic theme behind the whole thing should be that from a wide variety of types of employment entered into the contest, such as sales girls, stenographers, clerks, etc., the idea being to have the impression that it might be good business for some of these girls to quit their present jobs and come here.[20]

Top management took Ainsworth's instructions seriously and organized a full-fledged pageant with the help of the Labour-Management Committee. Although the Miss War Worker contest served as entertainment and boosted the local economy in Toronto, the John Inglis Company's principal goal was to recruit more women, especially office workers and housewives, by publicizing the plant itself.

On July 15, 1943, the John Inglis Company staged its beauty contest. On this night, over 800 employees and friends stretched the seating capacity of the auditorium of the Girls' Recreation Club on Cowen Avenue.[21] In keeping with the notion that this was a contest to select a glamourized version of a war worker on the home front, the judges themselves were chosen not only from the fashion and entertainment industries but also from senior ranks of the military.[22] Each contestant for the Miss John Inglis beauty pageant represented the department for which she worked. A 1943 article in *The Shotgun*, the company newsletter, described how the sheer volume of participants complicated the judging process.[23] From forty contestants, the judges chose six finalists dubbed the "Missus [sic] John Inglis," but June Pattison was nominated as the "Queen."[24] In keeping with the spirit of support for the war effort, each of the six finalists received Victory Bonds.

Other munitions companies that participated in the Miss War Worker contest included the National Steel Company, the de Havilland Aircraft Company, General Engineering Company (Canada) (GECO), Research Enterprises, and Ajax-Dominion. Munition workers from Quebec did not participate in the Miss War Worker contest, and no research has been conducted on similar pageants for that province despite the fact that munition factories such as L'Arsenal Saint-Malo, located near Saint-Sauveur, employed thousands of female workers.[25] As early as 1942, GECO was entering its very own Miss Scarboro to represent the company at the Miss War Worker contest. GECO's Miss Scarboro contest was considered an important part of the factory's social events culture.[26] The Munitions Workers' Association at GECO sponsored the beauty contests, dances, and Christmas parties. Like the Miss John Inglis contest, the Miss Scarboro contest was a popular venture. GECO workers came out in large numbers to lend support to the contestants, and the female war workers themselves participated with enthusiasm.

Posing in front of the Union Jack and the Ontario provincial flag, the contestants of the Miss GECO 1943 contest showcased the racial exclusivity of this competition. Although the number of Black women working for GECO is unknown, Black women worked in munitions plants all over the country. In response to the dearth of scholarship on the experience of Black women in Canadian war plants, author and activist Dionne Brand interviewed several women and revealed some of the working conditions that they endured, including working in the more dangerous areas (handling high explosives) and having to take the night shift.[27] In her book on the National Film Board of Canada's still-picture division, art historian Carol Payne includes a photograph of one of the few Black munitions workers I have encountered published in an academic book. Payne quotes from the full caption that accompanied a 1943 picture of Cecilia Butler, a former nightclub singer and dancer employed as a reamer at the John Inglis Company: "Negro girl workers are highly regarded in majority of munitions plants, display exceptional attitude for work of precision nature."[28] Yet Black women did not participate in the Miss War Worker contest, nor were they included in the various discourses on beauty culture swirling around factories traditionally designated as male enclaves.

One of the underlying functions of the Miss War Worker contest was to facilitate a "friendly" competition among the munitions plants in Toronto. This beauty contest stressed patriotic duty and drew attention away from war production and profits. *The Fusilier,* GECO's bimonthly newsletter, echoed Ainsworth's concerns about the recruitment of workers and about improving its public image across the nation: "It is understood that most if

Miss GECO 1943 contestants with the Union Jack. | Archives of Ontario, F2082-1-2-1, 1590.

not all of the other war plants in the Toronto area will be represented, and it was felt by both management and the M.W.A. [Munitions Workers' Association] Executive that 'Scarboro' has no reason to take backwater from anybody in the matter of feminine pulchritude."[29] All contestants had to be at least sixteen years of age and had to "be clad in their factory costume." Prizes for the winners included $400 for the titleholder, $100 for the first runner-up, and $25 for the second runner-up. The eight finalists who were selected to represent GECO at the Miss War Worker contest on July 18, 1942, were lauded as upholding the "honour and glory" of the plant. In the end, GECO did not "do well" at the Miss War Worker contest; Research Enterprises took the first and second prizes in 1942, with Ajax-Dominion placing third.[30] But as long as the war persisted, the articles in *The Fusilier* continued to encourage its readers to participate in the Miss War Worker contest as a way to promote the company and enforce ideals of duty to (militaristic) work, nation, and a version of settler femininity.

Managing Bodies and Bureaucracies: Miss Civil Service and Miss Secretary of Canada

The practice of integrating beauty culture practices into the fabric of the workplace also involved clerical workers. Like waitresses, clerical workers were a constant feature of the modern city. By the 1920s their presence in office buildings, banks, and malls had redefined public space significantly. Female clerical workers were often described as "business girls," conjuring up an image of single women in pumps, stockings, and trench coats who exerted a public presence – another version of urban and modern settler femininity. In her study on gender, space, and information technology, human geographer Kate Boyer suggests that most companies were class-conscious, insisting on a public image that emulated middle-class values.[31] The armies of female office workers were targeted as the exemplars of this value system. Clothing, behaviour, and even speech were expected to reflect the image of well-educated workers in a professional environment. The large numbers of clerical workers needed to support day-to-day business also introduced a heterosocial space that had been virtually nonexistent at the turn of the twentieth century.[32]

In 1954 Miss Civil Service, Betty Burton, met Miss Canada 1954, Barbara Markham, at Cornwall Night, an event hosted by the manager of the Connaught Park Raceway, T.P. Gorman. The guest list was impressive and included Ray Kinsella, president of the Recreation Association of the Public

Service of Canada in Ottawa, and association directors Len Hill of the House of Commons staff, Jack Vinokur of the Civil Service Commission, and Charlie Anderson of the Dominion Bureau of Statistics.[33] It was a big night for Cornwall but especially for Miss Civil Service. A photograph of Miss Canada shaking hands with Miss Civil Service, which served as an advertising gimmick, allows a rare glimpse into the different uses that were made of the image of settler femininity exemplified by the Miss Civil Service contest and the Miss Canada Pageant.

The crowning of the first queen of the civil service was an event linked to the Recreation Association (RA) Snow Carnival in 1950. Theresa Nugent won the RA Queen title that year and was crowned the first official Miss Civil Service in 1951. The civil service beauty contests allow for a more nuanced understanding of the existing climate in the federal government and Ottawa communities surrounding issues of proper gender and sexual behaviour. The Miss Civil Service/RA Queen contest served two purposes: first, to create possibilities for social class mobility for some members of the federal government; and second, to maintain workplace discipline in a heteropatriarchal context. The civil service beauty pageant was critical to educating an army of young women (some aged sixteen) on how to behave appropriately within a bureaucratic culture and city. They embraced the pageant because it made learning the interplay of white femininity and professionalism accessible, allowing them to increase their chances of keeping their positions as clerical workers. The investment in demonstrating interest in this pageant seems to have been high given that the women who participated in the Miss Civil Service/RA Queen contest were federal government workers toiling in Canada's capital, Ottawa, where their white-collar work was considered important and even coveted by some.

In a 1965 edition of the *RA News*,[34] the editor made specific references to the important role that the RA Queen played as the representative of the "Ideal Government Girl":

> The RA Queen of the Year contest differs from the ordinary beauty contest in that the girl who is selected reflects credit not only on herself but also on all of the thousands of girls who work for the Federal Government. The honour and esteem which the RA Queen receives are meant both for herself and for all of her colleagues without whose dedicated efforts the machinery of government would quickly grind to a halt ... Having chosen its Queen for the year, the RA proudly requests that she represents them at

many public appearances so that as many as possible can see the person whom you might meet any day in any office – the Ideal Government Girl.[35]

As the official ambassador of the ideal government girl, the civil service beauty queen was a symbol of pride for the Recreation Association and for the federal government. Winning the title of Miss Civil Service or, after 1960, the RA Queen of the Year was presented as an honour. For the beauty contest winners, many of whom came from rural areas or the working class, serving as Miss Civil Service meant instant fame, popularity, and upward mobility. The winner gained access to power brokers in the nation's capital, such as wealthy businessmen and high-ranking government officials. Photographs and stories of the latest winners made headline news in the *Ottawa Journal*, the *Ottawa Citizen*, and *Le Droit*, also an Ottawa newspaper. RA Queen 1966, Carole Fox, posed with Prime Minister John Diefenbaker for the opening of the RA Stamp Exhibition.[36] Fox was described as one of the "busiest" of the civil service beauty queens because she travelled to seven Canadian cities in five days prior to Ottawa's Tulip Festival as part of publicity for the event.[37] RA Queen 1963, Suzanne Perry, shared the limelight with Premier Ernest Manning of Alberta at the opening of the 1963 Tulip Festival.[38] Most importantly, being selected as Miss Civil Service/ RA Queen signalled the end of being an anonymous member of the female labour force necessary to running the "machinery of government."

After the Second World War, the expanding federal bureaucracy resulted in a labour shortage. Thousands of women were signed up to work as stenographers and typists. The shortage of office help was especially bleak in 1952, when, for the first time since the war, "untrained girls were taken fresh from high school and paid fifteen dollars a week to learn enough to pass civil service exams."[39] With the influx of women into the federal service by the mid-1950s, there seemed to be a need to define and create an image of the "typical government girl."[40] The process of selecting the winner of the Miss Civil Service/RA Queen contest played a central role in finding that typical government girl. Each division would send nominees to the internal competition to select the "girl" who would represent the department at the Night of Stars, the event where the judging for the Miss Civil Service/RA Queen contest took place. As shown in the profiles of the winners provided by the *RA News*, the typical government girl was a woman who worked in a position of administrative support. According to a 1953 memo outlining the prizes and providing the date of the contest, the deadline for entries, and a short paragraph on criteria by W.J. Bottomley, chairman of the Miss Civil

Service Committee for the Recreation Association, the candidates were to wear "conventional dress. This is not a beauty contest but we do want to choose a typical Miss Civil Service. Judging will be based on appearance, dress, hair, figure and poise."[41] Interestingly, this statement on the general criteria was changed slightly in a 1954 memo written by Len Law, Bottomley's successor, where the emphasis on physical appearance was replaced by "such things as posture, good grooming, neatness and personality," all middle-class attributes predominantly coded white.[42] Notwithstanding this modification, physical appearance continued to hold sway. Articles in the *RA News* announcing the winner for a particular year published the beauty queen's height, weight, and measurements along with her address, indicating that "appearance" was the predominant feature of the pageant. The statement "this is not a beauty contest" would have been sufficient information to help organizers and contestants understand the pageant's "official" mandate. In the case of the Miss Civil Service/RA Queen contest, this mantra was code for no bathing suits, no sexy evening wear, and no cleavage.

Local celebrities, high-ranking government officials, beauty industry proprietors, and media executives were among the people invited to sit as judges for both the departmental preliminaries and the Miss Civil Service/ RA Queen competition. For example, in 1955 the judges for the Miss Northern Affairs contest (sometimes referred to as Miss Resources) included Helen Turcotte of the *Ottawa Journal*, Austin Cross of the *Ottawa Citizen*, and M. Charles Daoust of *Le Droit*.[43] In 1962 the judges for the Miss Public Works competition were Peter Jennings, then a program host at CJOH-TV in Ottawa, and football personality Angelo Mosca of the Ottawa Rough Riders.[44] In 1961 the judges for the Miss Civil Service/RA Queen competition were Judy LaMarsh, a member of Parliament who eventually held the portfolios of the minister of national health and welfare, the minister of amateur sport, and the secretary of state; Senator Josie Dinan Quart, who was a member of the Imperial Order Daughters of the Empire; and Ernest L. Bushnell, director general of programs at the CBC.[45] In addition to using high-profile members of the Ottawa community to help boost audience attendance and ticket sales, the organizers of these beauty contests also employed the services of people such as Ellen Fairclough, the minister of citizenship and immigration, to crown Miss Civil Service in 1959. The objective of using high-profile people as judges or as part of the festivities was to lend legitimacy to the Miss Civil Service/RA Queen contest. Considered successful in their respective fields and "experts" on Canada, these judges were imbued with the ability to recognize and then *assess* what qualities were required for the "typical government girl." In other words, the label of "judge" made them *proficient* in profiling bodies as white, respectable, heterosexual, and typical.

To assist in their endeavours, the judges were given a document containing six items regarding the judging procedures, the ranking tabulations, and the criteria upon which to make their assessments. The third item explained that contestants would be "rated on 600 points" using a ranking of "poor, fair, average, very good, outstanding" as per the following "general guide":

A. DRESS – should be neat, well pressed and suitable for office wear.
B. FACE – should be attractive with regular features and suitably made-up.
C. FIGURE – should be well proportioned for contestant's height.
D. HAIR – should be well groomed and suitably styled for office wear.
E. GENERAL IMPRESSION – apparent personality and overall impression.
F. POISE – should have erect posture, and be outwardly at ease.[46]

As ambiguous as the above criteria may seem, they reveal the extent to which value was placed on how well a contestant could play the part of the government girl as another version of settler femininity. The objective was to reinforce and entrench ideals about whiteness, class, and heteropatriarchy that helped the federal government to uphold elements of white settler nationalism, such as having "regular" features.

Professional codes such as neatness, well-pressed clothing, "suitably styled" hair, a "suitably made-up" face, and an "erect posture" were supposed to signal a middle-class sensibility that had to be *learned*, especially among female government workers who were ostensibly from rural and working-class backgrounds. These codes were also barely veiled signals that the typical government girl was a white woman. Being read as professional required attention to minutiae regarding dress and the appearance of particular body parts, which effectively minimized or erased markers of class. The fifth item regarding judging procedures for the Miss Civil Service/RA Queen title included the scoring and measuring of class:

> The judges will receive additional score sheets for the final judging. This judging should be fairly exacting with particular attention being given to smile (contestant should have nice even teeth), hands (should be well manicured and shapely), stocking seams (should be straight), shoes (should be polished or well brushed). RA Queen of the Year should be a shining example of beauty, good grooming, and attractive personality.[47]

Dishevelled clothing such as a crooked stocking seam or the failure to have polished shoes, signs of an unkempt appearance such as uneven or defective teeth, and evidence of manual labour such as nonmanicured hands were discursively invoked as unprofessional and associated with working-class practices. This discourse was repeated in Queen of the Dressmakers, a beauty contest established for Montreal's garment workers. Attractiveness and "apparent personality" – another way to convey the tropes of the first impression, professionalism, and charm – underpinned the racial ideology connected to the Miss Civil Service/RA Queen contest. Like having "regular features," charm was a signifier of whiteness since it invoked a pleasant and friendly demeanour that was meant to establish a sense of social and racial neutrality.

Indigenous and Black women participated in civil service beauty contests. Their presence destabilized the settler logic of white femininity, but as beauty queens, they continued to embody feminine performances that were supposed to display an "apparent personality," or charming disposition. Two examples are Janet Morris, a member of the Eskasoni First Nation (Mi'kmaq), who was Miss Indian Affairs 1965, and Betty Gitten, a married Black woman, who captured the RA Queen title in 1962. The article in the *Indian News* announcing Morris as Miss Indian Affairs declared, "This time she really is!" demonstrating an understanding of some of the paradoxes at the heart of the department's preliminary contest.[48] However, this subversive tone was quickly supplanted by several statements geared at whitewashing Morris's heritage, including highlighting her membership in the Girl Guides and the 4-H Club in Nova Scotia. A reference to Morris's participation in the Girl Guide movement would have functioned to signal the limited improvability of this particular Indigenous body. As historian Kristine Alexander shows in her extensive study on the Girl Guides in England, Canada, and India in the interwar period, this movement was used as a "civilizing mission" to help promote and solidify white girlhood.[49] Making Morris "modern" included statements where she said that she "regretted" never having learned how to make the "excellent Micmac baskets" made by her mother since "it takes a very special feeling and although I worked hard I never made anything really good."[50] To establish Morris as a professional and respectable representation of femininity despite her alterity, she was described as "a quiet spoken young secretary" who was "admired almost (but not quite!) as much for her hard work and efficiency as for her charm and beauty."[51] In 1962, the year that the organizers "reinstated" married women as contestants, Betty Gitten won the title.[52]

According to D.O.T. Belle, RA Queen 1963, Gitten was "a very striking human being and a very professional, very charming woman ... I would imagine that she was probably one of the better ambassadors that they had."[53] Gitten's ability to perform charm and "professionalism" made her *exceptional* – Black bodies that passed as acceptable representations of femininity were supposed to be unique, a rare example, and infrequently repeatable, unlike the white bodies that were routinely marked as suitable.

In order to help women in the civil service to achieve this middle-class settler femininity, the *RA News* published numerous advice columns specifically addressing women in the government. Articles entitled "The Well Dressed Government Girl" or "Pretty Girls Are Nicer" advised women on how to dress and on why being "pretty" was equated with popularity. Fashion shows catering to the fashion needs of male and female federal employees (held in conjunction with beauty contests for two years in the 1960s), charm and modelling courses, diet classes, advice columns, and articles offering hints on how women should "hunt" for men or on how men could "play upon" their female "victim's sympathies" contributed to defining the typical government girl and by extension the new typical government man.[54]

The concern over establishing the ideal government girl was motivated by the need to create a specific and unique image of the government worker as a white, feminine, middle-class professional. Clothes were emblematic in producing and enacting that image. Proper office wear and fashion tips were by far the most discussed and written about topic in the Recreation Association's monthly newspaper. Miss Civil Service became the unofficial arbiter of proper and acceptable office wear for female government workers. Fran Jones, the main writer of the "Feminine Fancies" column, commented on the fashions that the Miss Civil Service winner, runners-up (crowned as the official "Princesses"), and contestants wore at the Night of Stars event. She pointed out the styles that were considered appropriate and those that were not, suggesting that "the contest could be used as a yard stick."[55] For Jones, "the well-dressed girl never over dresses ... She knows that there is plenty of sense in the well worn phrase 'plain but good.'"[56]

However, plain but good clothes were not the only things that the ideal government girl had to possess in order to win the Miss Civil Service title. There remained the question of exemplifying good personality, charm, and poise. To help female government workers who needed guidance in obtaining a charming personality, the Recreation Association established the RA Charm School for women only.[57] Charm was posited as a prerequisite or cornerstone of femininity and sophistication. Erasing any remnants of what were considered working-class or rural traits, such as by attempting to obtain a "properly modulated voice," was a critical feature of the "professional girl." It also became the last opportunity for the "not so pretty girls" to become "popular with the opposite sex": "Charm is being attractive but not necessarily beautiful. The emphasis is on mannerism, poise, conduct and speech ... To be popular with the opposite sex, it is far more important to have charm than anything else."[58] Learning how to be charming and graceful required effort and commitment, a lesson imparted to Pat Wilson of Montreal, discussed in Chapter 1. It required coaching, study, and a willingness to embrace the many beauty practices in order to attain charm and grace. For working-class white women and women of colour, learning the ropes regarding beauty also meant keeping a job or access to public space. Women who took this work seriously felt that they could *make* themselves attractive and reap the reward, such as acquiring a boyfriend or husband. In either or all of these cases, this work and the dedication to learn how to be charming and graceful were not to be underestimated.

The professional business girl was not solely within the purview of the Canadian federal bureaucracy. In 1960 the Remington Rand corporation announced that it was sponsoring the Miss Secretary of Canada contest in "recognition of the services rendered by secretaries in Government, Industry and Commerce."[59] The Miss Secretary of Canada contest took place across six regions centred on Vancouver, Edmonton, Winnipeg, London, Toronto, and Montreal. Six finalists were chosen at these regional contests. The national finals were scheduled for September 30, the birthday of Lillian Sholes, supposedly the first female typist and daughter of the inventor of the typewriter, Christopher Latham Sholes. It was a nationwide contest with prizes that included a two-week trip to New York with all expenses paid, a portable typewriter, and a cheque for $200. Clothes, an important appendage to any respectable beauty contest, were also one of the prizes. The national finals winner would receive a complete wardrobe from the Arnel Company that included "playsuits, cocktail frocks [and] afternoon dresses."[60] All regional winners would be flown to Toronto for the finals, courtesy of Remington Rand, and would receive a portable typewriter. Their bosses, for their trouble, would receive Remington Rand's "finest electric typewriter," the Statesman.[61]

Beauty contests such as Miss Secretary of Canada helped to bring some order to the rapidly changing urban landscape and to the competing levels of expertise in the workplace. The organizers of this contest, like so many organizers before them, announced that Miss Secretary was "not a beauty contest," even though "appearance is one of the several factors on which she will be judged."[62] The message of propriety was clear. Indeed, the ideal secretary required proficiency in "typing, shorthand, skills and poise."[63] As we have seen, the word "poise" signified being charming and demure, as well as possessing a certain form of "feminine politeness." Like in the Miss Civil Service/RA Queen beauty contests, contestants did not compete in bathing suits or extravagant evening gowns. Instead of presenting a talent, all participants had to submit an essay of 300 words "giving advice on what is required for a career as a successful secretary."[64]

Miss Civil Service, Miss Secretary of Canada, and the earlier Miss Sun Life, a beauty contest organized by the Sun Life Insurance Company in Montreal in 1927,[65] served educational goals aligned with the heteropatriarchal codes embedded in a white settler nation. These beauty pageants reminded clerical workers that their jobs required them to behave and dress conservatively and professionally. Beauty contests could also heighten what was seen as an eroticized environment. Boyer suggests that these workplace beauty queens "underscored women's distance from the ideal of rational (male) white-collar worker ... and re-asserted male (sexual) power and dominance in this space."[66] Like all recreational events organized by employers to boost workers' morale, beauty contests both contained and challenged gender, race, and class roles and heterosexual mores in mixed-gender workplaces.

"A Ray of Sunshine": Garment Workers and La Reine des Midinettes

In the 1940s the garment industry, like the secretarial pool, was predominantly viewed as a place of female work. Although men worked as clerks, waiters, and tailors, they consistently received better wages than women and usually occupied positions with more responsibilities attached to them. Employers and union officials did not organize beauty pageants featuring male workers because beauty contests were entrenched as feminized spectacles. The beauty contest organized by the International Ladies' Garment Workers' Union served a range of purposes and became an integral part of boosting workers' solidarity (among primarily female garment workers) through education and spectacle. How did La Reine des Midinettes/Queen of the Dressmakers act as the main promotional tool used by the Montreal ILGWU to communicate the strengths of the union to the business and political communities, in addition to the working-class community and the union's rank and file? Why did the pageant use exemplars of settler femininity to garner workers' solidarity and union loyalty?

The first Bal des Midinettes occurred in 1938. Yvette Charpentier, who would eventually become the director of the ILGWU's education department and creator of the Reine des Midinettes title, was a member of the committee that organized the ball. It was modelled after the Parisian annual ball, a tradition initiated by garment workers in France.[67] The program of activities for the evening included Parisian dances, skits, an array of folk and union songs, and a fashion show. The latter proved to be the highlight of the evening. Canadian Waist, one of the more successful clothing manufacturers in Montreal that hired only unionized workers, participated in the show by donating a dress decorated with maple leaves and a sash that read "Miss Quebec."[68] Although this particular dress may have sent mixed messages about English and French Canadian nationalism, symbols of a white settler nation were unmistakable. However, the official *midinette* song sung at the dance that June night left little room for interpretation about the images that the ILGWU wanted enforced concerning working-class women, hegemonic heterosexuality, and femininity. The song "Nos Midinettes" described the daily lives of seamstresses as they rushed to work in the factories where their deft fingers churned out coats, jackets, and dresses all day and every day. The refrain, however, suggests that at the end of a long day, the young *midinette* can still command the attention of a young man:

> And now the day has ended.
> Under cover, she powders herself.
> Allow me, miss, to help you avoid getting wet?
> Gosh! It's raining, she crosses a creek
> At first, indignant, she blushes!
> She turns around, he is handsome, she smiles.
> Oh! How happy she is that he finds her pretty,
> Our little worker.

Trying to take cover from the rain, the young *midinette* is forced to jump over a puddle until a polite and chivalrous young man fortuitously rescues her. The shy *midinette* blushes and then turns away with a smile, happy that her Prince Charming is handsome and a gentleman.[69] According to this popular song, at the end of a hard day at work, young garment workers would encounter their white knight, who, with the prospect of marriage, would whisk them away from the drabness of their work lives. The image of the blushing *midinette* points to the feminine reaction expected of young women when strange but handsome young men approached with offers of assistance and protection. Demure feminine behaviour was praised as one of the proper signs of a respectable lady.

In 1948 the first Reine des Midinettes was crowned at the Bal des Midinettes, starting the tradition of an annual beauty contest. At the height of its popularity, the ball and the beauty contest boasted a list of influential guests such as provincial and federal ministers of labour, the mayor of Montreal, television personalities, the president of the Canadian Labour Congress, and newspaper editors. As the dance and the beauty contest grew, they cultivated working-class sociability and collectivity in the guise of a white, middle-class event, as well as providing Montrealers with an opportunity to be seen by leaders of the business and political communities. The Reine des Midinettes was not only a moment of display; it also became a symbol of prestige. It should be noted, however, that although the Reine des Midinettes contest offers an opportunity to illustrate a version of settler femininity within a francophone context, the beauty pageant featuring duchesses in the annual Carnaval de Québec is another example of how settler logics about beauty, bodies, and nation can be analyzed in Canada.[70] Again, little has been written about one of the Carnaval de Québec's key attractions, but there is no doubt that discourses of race, white supremacy, and settler nationalism have figured prominently since its founding in 1955. For instance, the mascot of the event is a seven-foot snowman, the Bonhomme, wearing a *ceinture fléchée*, similar to the one worn by Miss Canada in the nineteenth-century cartoons mentioned in the Introduction, as a symbol of Quebec's settler fantasy about its heritage and culture.

By appropriating the beauty contest model, the ILGWU encoded proper standards of gender and sexuality within the context of a predominantly working-class culture, coded white. The actual beauty queen distilled the image or icon of what the ideal working-class union sister should look like and how she should behave. In fact, the majority of women who made up the ILGWU were either married immigrant women who spoke little English or French or long-time union activists such as Yvette Charpentier, Léa Roback, and Rose Pesotta, women who dedicated their lives to the service of high-ranking ILGWU officials like Bernard Shane and David Dubinsky. Yet the image of ideal settler femininity offered to the working-class community was the image of a nineteen-year-old, French Canadian, single "girl." With this one event, the leaders of the ILGWU promoted the union as wholesome, fresh, and energetic, associating it with the best of Canadian youth.

The emphasis placed on the wholesome image of the French Canadian seamstress is even more apparent when we consider the role played by female union officials. Rose Pesotta, vice-president of the ILGWU, organized over 10,000 workers in the mid-1930s. When she came to Montreal to assist Bernard Shane and Claude Jodoin (who eventually served as president of the Canadian Labour Congress), Pesotta recalled that she faced a "Fascist-minded government," a conservative press, a hostile Catholic Church, and reluctant dressmakers.[71] Pesotta pointed to the Catholic League of the Needle Workers of Quebec as the ILGWU's greatest threat.[72] The historically strong religious tradition in Quebec, coupled with a conservative and anti-communist provincial government headed by Maurice Duplessis, proved to be a formidable source of opposition to the ILGWU's efforts in Montreal. Against these odds, in 1937 the ILGWU called a general strike that lasted for three weeks. At the end of those three weeks, Montreal's female garment workers were victorious and won reductions in hours, an increase in salary, and a "closed shop" clause.

Except for Rose Pesotta, most of the leaders and top-level union bureaucrats at the ILGWU were men. The directorship of the educational services that the ILGWU provided for its members, however, was a position historically held by a woman. Sexist attitudes among union officials were rampant. Dubinsky and Shane, for example, were known for constantly referring to female garment workers as "girls." Sociologist Elaine J. Leeder suggests that Pesotta's eventual loss of influence in 1942 resulted from her objection to the way that the male-dominated union leadership treated women and from the secondary role that women played in the union. Pesotta publicly denounced Dubinsky's style of leadership, insisting that "no baby kissing, pretty girl photos, trophy for sports or banquets can give the membership more aid and comfort than feeling that elected leadership is honest, efficient, and sincerely rendering a service."[73] However, her outcry against the union leadership did little to change the course of labour organizing in the postwar era. The union became less of a political force and support system for the garment workers and more of a facilitator of recreation that occasionally organized a union drive. By the late 1950s and throughout the 1960s, the ILGWU's claim to fame was its union label campaign promoted with the help of the Mlle Étiquette Syndicale/Miss Union Label beauty contests.[74] Pesotta's vision of the union as a site for women's empowerment was overshadowed by societal ideals about women's proper roles as exemplified by the beauty contest.

The Queen of the Dressmakers beauty contest, however, did coincide with Dubinsky's agenda. It promoted the ILGWU as a respectable and conservative union that served the interests of the Montreal garment industry. It highlighted the need to elevate the low-paid and exploited white garment worker to the higher status of respectable young woman while maintaining traditional values concerning gender and sexuality. The Reine des Midinettes became an official public figure with her own ambassadorial functions, representing the union and her fellow *midinettes*.

The union newspaper sentimentalized the lives of female garment workers by using patronizing language and metaphors: "It is true that a *midinette* is a very hard little worker, but she is also a ray of sunshine in the workshop, the factory, the street, and the home."[75] By comparing garment workers to rays of sunshine, the union placed the responsibility for working toward a "better life" on the individual. This metaphor was central to capturing the meaning behind the ILGWU's beauty contest as the "symbol of hope and energy."[76] Although very few of these garment workers would have labelled themselves a "little worker" (*petite ouvrière*), they certainly would have considered themselves to be "hard-working" (*laborieuse*). The majority of garment workers performed tedious work in dreary conditions. They received low wages and were easily exploited by their employers, especially in the case of immigrant women who did not speak the language and remained ignorant of their rights. Hopes of advancement, more money, better working conditions – other than clean bathrooms and ventilation – were usually inconceivable. The idea that they would someday own a factory was even harder to imagine. Indeed, such dreams were usually reserved for the men who worked in what was defined as skilled labour: cutters and designers. Few of these women had high school diplomas, which further undermined any hope that they might have had of finding work in other fields. In a sector where low wages and a steady supply of labour were the norm, this individualistic approach to ameliorating the workplace environment meant that union bureaucrats were saved from having to challenge the employers to combat low morale among the rank and file.

ILGWU officials also used the union's newly established newspaper, *Justice*, to communicate standards of white settler femininity. Its woman's page, called "Le Coin de la Femme," first appeared in the September 1937 issue. Léa Roback, a formidable union activist, was the first editor of "Le Coin de la Femme." Born in turn-of-the-century Montreal to Polish Jewish immigrants, Roback joined the Communist Party in early adulthood and in 1936 joined Rose Pesotta in the struggle to unionize garment workers. She was asked by the organizers of the ILGWU to establish educational services for its members. Her career as education director, however, was short-lived. By May 1939, pressures from the internal anti-communist witch hunt had led to her political demise in the ILGWU.[77]

Between 1937 and 1939, Roback published articles for the woman's page that perpetuated ideals of femininity and domesticity. In her first issue, Roback encouraged readers to write her if they needed help solving family, love, or work problems.[78] In the same issue, a new column entitled "Votre beauté Madame" featured an article on the latest makeup products and application techniques for eyes that warned about the importance of using the "right" colours to accentuate the natural colour of the eyes. Another article offered advice on foot care, suggesting that "if your feet are not at ease in your shoes, it will show on your face," with a further warning that the improper care and treatment of feet was usually the cause of the premature appearance of wrinkles.[79] After taking care of their feet, women in the ILGWU could turn their attention to reducing those "unsightly" big thighs.[80] In keeping with the theme of the ideal feminine figure, advice on remaining trim and svelte made many appearances on the woman's page.

Along with "practical advice" on how to put out a grease fire or how to remove stains, regular features of the woman's page included recipes, cooking tips, fashion notes, and death, birth, and marriage announcements. In its November 1937 issue, "Le Coin de la Femme" also announced a list of the courses provided by the ILGWU's education department. Among the offerings were a music course featuring lessons in French theatre, a gym class that would allow *les jeunes filles* to accomplish their work in the factories with "energy and courage," a course on the art of public speaking, and finally a course called Le Bilinguisme geared toward people who could speak neither French nor English.[81] In the following year, courses on the history of the working class and trade unions also graced the ILGWU's educational program, only to disappear after Roback was removed as education director in 1939. History courses on the Canadian labour movement, the ILGWU, and international workers' struggles did not return until 1950, after which they remained constant features of the program.

The courses offered by the ILGWU's education department were supposed to prepare these young, unmarried women to become graceful brides and devoted wives. In 1950 two new courses called "Charme et Personalité" and "Arts Domestiques" – a cooking class – joined psychology, "Culture Physique" (aimed at women), language, singing, bowling, and ballet on the roster of classes in the curriculum. "Charme et Personalité" was so popular that in order to accommodate the enthusiasm, the education department started a column in *Justice* where the beauty culture teacher, Gisèle Desrosiers, answered questions about beauty and maintenance (as in maintaining body weight).[82] This class, renamed "Charme et Féminité" in 1963, aimed to teach working-class garment workers "maintenance, posture, physical culture, modern and expressive dance, make-up, elegance, etc." Union sisters could also take a 1957 course called "Culture Générale" where students brushed up on general issues that, the director claimed, would improve their "personality." The course consisted of lessons in "grammar, phonetics, diction, good manners, etiquette, etc."[83]

The "Culture Générale" class was integral to the process of becoming cultured and middle-class. This course provided lessons that would help union sisters to carry on conversations on general topics and to improve their grammar and pronunciation, the implication being that these qualities would add to their general attractiveness. The early public-speaking courses developed by Roback in the late 1930s, originally designed to enhance union members' self-esteem, were replaced with a course that would make Montreal dressmakers – at least the single, white, French Canadian garment workers – less conspicuous in middle-class circles. The language of instruction for these charm and culture classes was French, which effectively excluded immigrant women who were not fluent. Indeed, most immigrant women confronted language barriers that created bigger challenges than learning how to balance a book on their head.

These classes and the gender and sexual codes that they perpetuated tried to erase traces of working-class or ethnic mannerisms or traits. To show what took place in these classes and to entice new students, the union newspaper published pictures of young female students in shorts balancing books on their heads or the beauty culture teacher applying makeup to a volunteer in order to demonstrate proper technique. Emulating middle-class charm and posture meant behaving in a feminine and sophisticated manner. In a sense, the charm and personality courses that continued to be offered well into the early 1970s were justified in view of the perception held by most people that working-class women were "rough around the edges." The notion that charm equalled beauty and a good personality made the course a prerequisite for any garment worker who wanted to participate in the annual beauty contest.

Yet the reality for many garment workers fell well outside the romantic ideals posited by the union's charm courses. Sociologist Charlene Gannagé's book on Toronto garment workers in the 1980s examines the personal lives of the working-class women she interviewed in order to establish their role in the union and their ability to assume leadership roles. She concludes that because most women who worked in the Toronto clothing industry were married or single mothers, they experienced what some scholars call a "double day."[84] Female garment workers performed two jobs, one in the factory and the other in the home. Immigrant women's absence from union meetings and from the upper managerial levels of the union bureaucracy was caused by a lack of childcare facilities and language barriers rather than by any unwillingness to participate in union politics.[85] Gannagé suggests that men's ability to take language courses in the evening or to congregate in various social halls and taverns where union business was discussed informally was possible because their wives were at home providing childcare and managing the home. Not surprisingly, male garment workers assumed leadership of the union meetings, whereas female garment workers remained on the margins and were unable to move out of the union rank and file.

The ILGWU beauty contests illustrated how the ethnic and linguistic hierarchy that existed among garment workers was replicated through the public images that the union portrayed to the Montreal community. The Montreal dressmakers' beauty contest continued to enjoy support well into the mid-1980s. According to Gannagé, the ILGWU offered charm classes and cooking lessons that perpetuated the idea that a woman's role was ultimately in the home as wife and mother.[86] Instead of instituting policies that established support services for their female union members, such as childcare facilities, the union continued to use the beauty contest as a rallying force for union loyalty.

The invisibility of ethnic and racial differences in relation to familial duties helped to solidify the constructed images of beauty, white settler femininity, and class status in the ILGWU. Most of the women who attended charm classes and cooking lessons were those who did not have to rush home after work to tend to children, husbands, and homes. This was not necessarily the case for unmarried and childless immigrant women who worked in the garment industry. For them, daily life included a strong attachment to family responsibilities regardless of marital status and was characterized by familial hierarchies that included extended family members. Some of the heteropatriarchal values that persisted throughout the 1950s and 1960s were magnified in ethnic communities, where young women stayed home in the evening to help with chores, whereas their male siblings were allowed to engage in social lives outside the immediate familial circle. Union meetings or even courses were inaccessible to these immigrant women simply because they were not allowed to leave the watchful eye of their parents in the evening.

In a November 1961 issue of *Justice,* Yvette Charpentier wrote an editorial on the patron saint of seamstresses, Saint Catherine:

> We must not forget that November 25 is associated with the old tradition in France where young, single women under the age of twenty-five don bonnets in honour of Saint Catherine. This saint's day was associated with seamstresses because the common practice in those days was that around the world the young girls of this industry did not marry except in very small numbers. Today, this situation happily does not exist ... For all of us in the fashion industry, tradition has designated Saint Catherine as our patron saint. In honouring our patron saint on this day, we are in fact celebrating each other. We honour our work and our profession as seamstresses. We celebrate our patron saint with pride, and what pride. Because this pride truly exists in our work.[87]

Women who worked as seamstresses or dressmakers took this tradition of wearing bonnets and lace veils to honour their patron saint quite seriously. Various union locals sponsored plays that depicted Saint Catherine's life.[88] To celebrate November 25, the ILGWU and many of its locals organized and sponsored dances in honour of Saint Catherine. Indeed, the Bal des Midinettes was organized specifically to commemorate the patron saint of the *midinettes.*

Eight hundred people gathered at the Arsenal des Fusiliers Mont-Royal for the first Bal des Midinettes in 1938. Politicians and business representatives of the Montreal garment workers were among the honoured guests who also attended the event. Soon the Bal des Midinettes and the celebrations associated with the patron saint of seamstresses merged into one event. By the mid-1940s, the Bal des Midinettes occurred close to November 25 in honour of Saint Catherine.[89] Whereas the Bal des Midinettes was, in fact, an opportunity for the Montreal garment industry to display its products through the popular fashion show, the dance was constructed as an event that represented the pride and cultural values of the ILGWU. The union newspaper explained,

> The Bal des Midinettes is therefore more than a dance with some attractions; it is a demonstration of our union's accomplishments and brings

attention to our workers. In turn, the city benefits from the quality products of their International Ladies' Garment Workers' Union. It is with this notion that we come together to forget our tiring and monotonous work by straightening our backs and lifting our heads high, like all free and independent human beings fully realizing the joy of life, on such a magnificent evening of shared solidarity.[90]

The beauty contest that emerged from the Bal des Midinettes in 1948 was considered an extension of this union pride in the same manner that the annual Labour Day parade and picnic historically reinforced a sense of solidarity among union members.[91] However, the logic of white settler femininity meant that the beauty contest could not successfully fulfill its role to instill solidarity precisely because it was based on competitiveness, individualism, and personality culture. Here, the beauty contest was promoted as another means of solidarity building by union organizers, but it served only to enhance the benefits of settler nationalism for white and immigrant women while deepening racial and ethnic divisions.

The first announcement of an ILGWU beauty contest was for an event to be held at the union's annual Labour Day picnic at Montreal's Belmont Park in 1938. Apparently, the competition was so stiff that in order to save the judges from any embarrassment, "it was decided by the organizers that the beauty contest would be cancelled – to the chagrin of the male union members."[92] The Queen of the Dressmakers beauty contest, in contrast, was a success from the beginning. In November 1948, the first Reine des Midinettes was crowned in front of 1,500 people. Nominated by the women who worked in their respective shops, seventeen contestants competed, with Berthe Jacques winning the Reine des Midinettes title in 1949. During the competition, the candidate did not represent her local but rather the company that employed her. The process of selecting candidates was standardized in 1954.

The ILGWU beauty queen and her princesses (usually the two runners-up but in some years an entire royal court of five or six) received gifts for their victory that ranged from bracelets to weekend wardrobes and $100 cheques. These gifts were not as noteworthy as some of the prizes awarded to Miss Canada or Miss America, but the prize itself was not presented as the focus of the ILGWU beauty contest. Instead, the fame that accompanied the title seemed to be more significant than any prize because selection by a panel of "expert" judges from the business and entertainment communities in Montreal meant instant celebrity status. For working-class women, the notion of being more than just another low-paid and exploited garment worker held more meaning than any prize. Winning a beauty contest broke the trap of anonymity, especially since the Reine des Midinettes was the official "ambassador" of Montreal seamstresses and, as such, represented the ILGWU at as many public functions as possible. After 1948 the ILG-WU's float for the Labour Day parade was garnished with huge pincushions and an even larger bobbin. This bobbin was the new throne of the Reine des Midinettes. By fashioning the beauty queen's crown, sceptre, and throne to reflect the tools of the trade, the union's beauty contest represented pride in garment workers' occupational skills. Such interlacing of the tools of the trade with the spectacle of the parade demonstrates that the meaning of the beauty contest went beyond showcasing feminine beauty. For a number of years in the 1950s, the ILGWU won first prize for the best float in the parade.

As a public figure, the Reine des Midinettes was invited to represent the union at orphanages, especially when the union donated money, or she opened the newest union building. Her functions included presiding over the openings of the annual "revues" and attending the variety shows at the end of the school year that were established and organized by Yvette Charpentier during her reign as education director, as well as being the first union member to register for the charm classes. She was also an active participant in union drives. The Reine des Midinettes served as the centrepiece of a 1964 union campaign to recruit 5,000 nonunionized garment industry workers in Montreal. As part of that campaign, the ILGWU assembled a travelling caravan featuring the Reine des Midinettes and a couple of her royal attendants to raise awareness among nonunionized workers regarding the benefits of unionization.[93]

Reine des Midinettes 1951, Marielle Sicotte, had a particularly busy reign. Not only did Sicotte have the opportunity to star in a National Film Board (NFB) documentary on female garment workers in Montreal titled *Midinette* – or *Needles and Pins* for the English audience – but she was also invited to a banquet organized by the mayor of Montreal to welcome Princess Elizabeth and her husband, Prince Philip, Duke of Edinburgh.[94] This invitation was heralded as a coup for the ILGWU. Notwithstanding the political undertones of the invitation, the notion of having an audience with a *real* princess made being the Reine des Midinettes more than just a dream come true.

The NFB documentary *Midinette*, seen by millions of Canadians throughout the late 1950s and early 1960s, was yet another opportunity used by the ILGWU to show how wonderful life could be if all working-class women in the garment industry took the necessary steps to improve themselves. Indeed, this was the message of the documentary, one wholeheartedly encouraged and endorsed by the top union officials. *Justice* kept its readers abreast of the film's progress and production schedule, encouraging a romantic view of life as an actor by including pictures of Sicotte surrounded by camera and lighting equipment:

> Just like in Hollywood, here is a camera, a director, cameramen, technicians, and a pretty girl. The film personnel and the equipment belong to the National Film Board. The pretty girl, as you know, is Marielle Sicotte, Montreal's former Reine des Midinettes, who is starring in a documentary being filmed by the National Film Board on the seamstresses of this Canadian metropolis.[95]

Although the NFB and the ILGWU claimed that the documentary centred on the lives of seamstresses in Montreal, Canadians were offered only a glimpse into the reality of what it was like to be a garment worker and, by extension, a working-class woman in Montreal in the 1950s. By 1955 the documentary was no longer about Montreal seamstresses and was eventually advertised as "a film on a garment worker with the aim to show aspects of her social and professional life."[96]

In 1958 the NFB's first documentary on garment workers in Montreal was a twenty-minute film on the transformation of an apathetic working-class French Canadian "girl" into a "beautiful" pageant queen:

> The film shows how, thanks to her union, Marielle becomes more assured and builds her self-confidence by learning how to dance, express herself in public, sing, and understand economic concepts and issues concerning management-labour relations. These new horizons have dispelled Marielle's apathy and shyness, making room for confidence, grace, beauty, and a better understanding of life.[97]

This "caterpillar to butterfly" motif ignored a much larger reality of the life of female garment workers and working-class women. Themes that did not make it to the screen were the linguistic, racial, ethnic, and childcare issues that single and immigrant women experienced on a daily basis. Instead, the images captured by the NFB focused on Sicotte's apathy toward life and her indifference toward what the ILGWU could offer. The film employed images of the beauty contest, including contestants dressed in white gowns made by their fellow workers to typify the life of a seamstress in Montreal. The message here was that if you were "ugly," bored, and alienated as a working-class woman, you had only yourself to blame.

In 1962 the ILGWU celebrated its twenty-fifth anniversary. In honour of the event, the union organized La Semaine des Midinettes. The week's activities were crowned with a special version of the beauty contest. That year, Queen of the Dressmakers would be a national event with candidates from Toronto, Vancouver, and Winnipeg. According to an article in *Justice,* the responses from these cities were quite positive.[98] In Toronto seventeen women finally had an opportunity to compete in the now famous Queen of the Dressmakers contest and to defend their city's colours.[99] The winner of the contest in 1962 was an eighteen-year-old Montreal woman, Liliane Simard. Her story is particularly interesting because it gives us some insight into what was considered an ideal *midinette.* "Liliane 1st," as she was called after her coronation, was a

> very pretty young girl, a little shy, who wears her crown in the shape of a thimble with the right amount of cockiness. Liliane 1st is truly happy with her victory, and her joy at having been chosen by her fellow workers as one of the candidates who could represent the 20,000 ILGWU members reached its peak at the annual banquet on November 24, where she blushed, her eyes glistening with tears and her voice choking, as she thanked her new subjects.[100]

What made Simard an ideal choice, other than the fact that she was single, white, and young, was that she was a member of a longstanding unionist family. *Justice* took great pride in this story and used it to promote a sense of solidarity among its readers. To establish a sense of history and continuity, one article recounted how Simard's grandmother worked as a seamstress in conditions that were unfathomable to Simard. Her mother's experience in the fur industry had been equally difficult, but Simard's mother, Adrienne St. Laurent, was an active member of her union and one of the key players in the struggle to improve working conditions in the sector. At the time of the story's publication, St. Laurent was still active in her union and worked in the union's business office. Simard's aunt, also a seamstress, remained an active member of the ILGWU for many years, and her uncle was an active member of the International Cement Workers' Union.

Simard was an ideal Reine des Midinettes because she demonstrated in the interview segment with the judges her strong sense of "general knowledge, posture and beauty, good taste, and a good personality,"[101] as well as a family history of union activity. In other words, as an official representative of the union, Simard showed her enthusiasm and effort to "improve" herself, with the added bonus that she portrayed an excellent example of a dedicated union sister. Like Marielle Sicotte, Liliane Simard pulled herself out of her lower-class existence and habits, proving that she was a committed union member by taking charm and ballet classes. As a platform to achieve some form of socio-economic uplift through appearances only, the Queen of the Dressmakers beauty contest was all the more alluring for some French Canadian garment workers. Although beauty and "a good personality" were cited as the primary reasons why Simard was selected as the Reine des Midinettes, the ability of the ILGWU to promote her as a union sister to a larger Quebec audience made her all the more attractive.

The title of ILGWU queen further reinforced the ideal of submissiveness and compulsory heterosexuality. Articles announcing the weddings of ILGWU beauty queens littered the pages of the union newspaper.[102] These stories trumpeted the marriages of ILGWU beauty queens as success stories, thus creating the illusion that the Reine des Midinettes had found her Prince Charming and true vocation, just like the song promised. The marriage announcement of Denyse Martineau, Reine des Midinettes 1954, in *Justice* proclaimed that the *midinettes'* queen was giving up her royal title to be "Queen of the Home."[103] Eleven years later, Nicole Coutu, Reine des Midinettes 1965, was also said to be giving up her title for the more important role of wife, with the added bonus of marrying a union brother.[104] When Sicotte and another former queen, Lise Blanchet, both gave birth to baby boys in 1962, *Justice* ran an article titled "From Royalty to Maternity," complete with pictures of the former beauty queens and their new babies, who were "too young to realize that they have royal blood running through their veins."[105] By anchoring the former beauty queens as having achieved heterosexual marital bliss and doing their duty, the ILGWU maintained an ideal of working-class women as wives and mothers while downplaying their lives as workers.

Conforming to traditional codes of motherhood and marriage was considered to signal the logical transformation of an unsophisticated working-class "girl" into a graceful princess. The candidates for the Queen of the Dressmakers beauty contest wore white dresses with long satin gloves made from employer-donated material. The white dress (required attire for all contestants from the inception of the ILGWU beauty contest to 1976) seemed to reinforce the Cinderella motif. Whereas Miss Civil Service contestants wore office clothing to capture the ideal of the typical government girl, the white dresses worn by the ILGWU beauty contest candidates amplified a more complex goal, reminiscent of those underlying the cotillion and the debutante ball. Again, the idea was to have at least one night when they could *feel* like they were part of another socio-economic stratum. Young textile workers who became contestants enacted roles designed to replicate their transformation into women worthy of donning a glamorous white gown. The reaction of Michelle Tisseyre, one of the judges of the ILGWU beauty contest, upon first seeing a young *midinette* in the white dress conformed to the intended effect:

> When the first candidate entered the room in which the jury had been assembled, my heart skipped a beat. How charming was this young girl approaching us in her white gown! A graceful curtsy, a little shyness, but soft-spoken with a manner of speech that was deferential, simple and friendly. Her appearance was in such contrast to my mental picture of a little factory worker that I could hardly believe my eyes. I don't recall whether we gave the crown to her or to one of her rivals, but I do remember that 18 were presented to us, most of them as charming as the first.[106]

The judges chosen to sit on the jury were for the most part personalities from the entertainment community, but they also included influential players from Montreal's newspaper and business communities. Not only did the judges lend legitimacy to the beauty contests as "experts" on issues of beauty and grace, but they also attracted both participants and spectators to the beauty contest event. In some instances, judges from the entertainment community would also agree to perform at the Bal des Midinettes, thus increasing the prestige of the dance as well as selling more tickets. More importantly, however, these celebrities heightened the illusion of glamour and stardom that became associated with the Reine des Midinettes, as reinforced by the making of the *Midinette* documentary. The ILGWU pageant became a spectacle offering escape from the drab and boring lives that most working-class women may have experienced.

Beauty culture practices, rituals, and institutions such as beauty contests permeated the workplace as women's presence in paid labour became an inevitability. Employers saw the beauty contest as another vehicle through which to boost sales, attract customers, contain proper occupational roles in the workplace, enhance morale, and even promote patriotism and the war effort. What made the beauty contests so versatile was their adaptability to the internal needs of a given industry, regardless of the product or concept to be marketed. Consumer culture and entrenched cultural beliefs about female images and women's bodies created a societal predisposition to beauty contests that heightened their potential as educational or advertising tools. Employers who adopted the beauty pageant format to suit their interests were rarely disappointed. Beauty contests thrived as accepted and popular events that succeeded in reaching the minds and hearts of the people who embraced them as spectators or participants, thus extending their usefulness beyond employers' promotional concerns and into boosting workers' solidarity.

The lowest-paying industries in Montreal – dressmaking, textile milling, tobacco manufacturing, and shoemaking – were the very industries where women predominated. The exploitation associated with the garment industry meant that women's status was crystallized in their role as the cheapest labour. The resurgence of traditional gender and sexual roles in the postwar era made it possible for unions such as the ILGWU to establish a beauty contest, which provided an excellent promotional tool, an opportunity to impose conventional ideology concerning women's roles by reinforcing white settler femininity, and an event that boosted solidarity among garment workers. Although these results may seem contradictory, they actually demonstrate the complex relationship between class, gender, race, and sexuality as well as the sense of belonging to a settler version of citizenship that developed in the garment workers' community.

Historians of working-class culture have identified various cultural phenomena as sites for community, solidarity, and resistance.[107] Beauty contests for working-class women afforded them an opportunity to be part of a world different from their own. In the pageant setting, one could be less anonymous, more glamorous, and maybe even win something. Although they were organized by employers and were still competitions, the Miss War Worker, Miss Civil Service, and Miss Secretary of Canada contests may have had the additional result of creating an atmosphere of shared values among workers because contestants competed in work clothing. The Queen of the Dressmakers contest, for example, was constructed as a benevolent event catering to multiple purposes, including workers' solidarity, even though it excluded large numbers of nonwhite women, most of them immigrants. The nature of workplace beauty contests meant that female workers negotiated myriad cultural messages regarding occupational status, being white, and sexuality, but it also presented them with opportunities to break out of the anonymity that attended these low-skill jobs. Most women willingly participated in these competitions; they wanted these pageants to exist. Beauty contests were also used to promote business and community interests defined by the employers, community leaders, and union officials who linked the contests to the beauty industrial complex. Ultimately, the workplace beauty pageant evolved as a pivotal component of settler nationalism and imaginings from the 1940s to late 1960s. Yet the possibility for working-class white women, Indigenous women, and Black women to subvert and destabilize settler logics of femininity was present even as these bodies may have emulated the performance of settler femininity or seemed to be acceptable as representations of this settler fantasy. In the next chapter, we encounter the Miss Malta of Toronto, Miss Black Ontario, Miss Caribana, and Indian Princess contests, where immigrant, Black, and Indigenous bodies interacted with settler colonialism along differing historical and affective trajectories, thus offering a critical opportunity to nuance the uses and intentions of performing femininity through the beauty contest model.

4

Contesting Indigenous, Immigrant, and Black Bodies

Communities of all varieties adopted the beauty contest model. Highly adaptable and easily modified, pageants enjoyed a reputation as harmless and fun, but they also afforded an opportunity to showcase and advance community values. Some examples from the 1950s and 1960s included Miss Tip Topper, a pageant organized by the Tip Toppers Club, a social club for tall women and men, and Miss Goodwill, a pageant where the contestant had to have one American and one Canadian parent to be eligible for competition.[1] Here, the titleholder's main responsibility was to promote *goodwill* – that is, cross-border trade and tourism – between the United States and Canada. Gay and transgendered communities also used beauty contests to promote community pride.[2] Mr. Leather, Miss Gay America, Miss Gay Canada, and Miss Gay Universe, although commercialized and driven by small-business and corporate interests, emerged as community-based beauty pageants that served as entertaining charitable events especially for fundraising purposes during the HIV/AIDS crisis in the 1980s and 1990s. In 2019 Black women won the three major US beauty queen titles, namely Miss USA (Cheslie Kryst), Miss Teen USA (Kaliegh Garris), and Miss America (Nia Franklin). Instead of using this moment to discuss the history of Black beauty pageants within the long history of these contests in the United States, an *Essence* magazine article chose to focus on what the author described as Black women's original "crown," their hair.[3]

As symbolic representations, beauty queens carry visual codes of what a nation and its communities highlight as ideal and valuable. Addressing the powerful meanings amplified by national allegory as signifying "an analogical story that is repeatedly incorporated into the nation's self-defining narratives," Daniel Coleman further explains that the tropes of these national allegories, such as the beauty queen, function as a "tense pedagogy, meant to inculcate authoritative values yet always destabilized by the non-identity between the values they idealize and the signifying figures that are meant to perform or demonstrate these values."[4] In this chapter, immigrant, Indigenous, and Black women's bodies play out this "tense pedagogy" through the beauty contest as they both replicate and destabilize the discourses of settler femininity.

In the case of Canada, the multicultural policies instituted in the early 1970s redirected the political and social criteria regarding citizenship questions and belonging, shaping how beauty contests could be used to further those symbolic representations befitting a white settler society. Sociologist Sunera Thobani argues that these multicultural policies offered Canada a "successful transition from a white settler colony to a multiracial, multiethnic, liberal-democratic society," adding that the "adoption of multiculturalism helped stabilize white supremacy by transforming its mode of articulation in a decolonizing era."[5] This shift and the accompanying drive to rearticulate racial hierarchies constitutive of settler fantasies about nation drew on the politics of tolerance and diversity. The tolerance embedded in multiculturalism provided a new platform for beauty pageants to deliver white female bodies as a symbolic representation of the nation, whether in national competitions such as Miss Canada or community-based contests such as Miss Chinatown.

How did beauty contests function as cultural products in the reification of both the white settler and the multicultural imaginary nation at the local and national levels in Canada? How did Black or Indigenous women negotiate white settler codes of feminine respectability through the beauty contest model? White settler femininity is predicated on the colonial and sexual violence perpetrated against Black and Indigenous bodies, including understanding these bodies as primitive, savage, and morally vacant. Indeed, although the Miss Malta of Toronto, Miss Black Ontario, Miss Caribana, and Indian Princess contests discussed below centre the bodies of immigrant, Black, and Indigenous women as performing a version of settler femininity, these bodies occupy a threatening position in settler societies. Specifically, Black and Indigenous bodies impede settler futurity and the fantasy of corporeal elimination and territorial expansion because these bodies continue to exist. Beauty contests as a corporeal curriculum work to discipline these lingering, persistent bodies that are considered outside what Lorenzo Veracini calls settler normativity because of their unruliness and excessiveness.[6] Despite the fact that the winners of these contests enjoyed similar financial and socio-cultural rewards as the winners of contests like Miss War Worker and Miss Civil Service, their ability to successfully portray respectability and wholesomeness was compromised not by their efforts but by the way their bodies continued to be imagined, gendered, and sexualized. Still, the women who participated in immigrant, Black, and Indigenous beauty pageants did so for a variety of reasons that were often either linked to community pride or seen as a way to create opportunities that bolstered careers or gave them the ability to maintain their positions in the workplace.

Benedict Anderson argues that the invention of community is the linchpin of the nation and that community is formed based on the cohesiveness of traditions, rituals, "cultural products," and language.[7] Symbols are also central to the project of imagining a community and, as we have seen with the figures of Marianne and Britannia in other settings, women's bodies serve as cultural artifacts in the formation of nation. Communities represent themselves via symbols and figures that reflect a shared set of values about the imagined nation. Imagining a nation involves the production of symbols or other cultural products to solidify a shared consciousness and to engage citizens (or those who are considered to be included in the nation) in a communal sense of belonging across time and space. In the Canadian national imagination, this sense of "community" is anchored by a white settler vision of the colonized nation, and through the notion of diversity and multiculturalism, it is grounded in the racialized other. The colonized and racialized body that this national imagination has fostered is, in turn, reenacted and reified in the beauty contest.

When Indigenous communities in Canada, historically constructed as other and positioned literally and metaphorically beyond the boundaries of the nation, embraced the beauty contest model "to educate" the white population, the beauty pageant's role as a legitimate cultural conduit was obvious. Indigenous leaders recognized the beauty queen's body as a potential vehicle through which to communicate messages about race and culture even as racial stereotypes were reified. Recognizing that institutions like beauty pageants conveyed the imagined nation as white, female, and youthful, the Indian Princess Pageant, for example, offered not only an alternative but also a rearticulation of beauty, femininity, and belonging.

It is perhaps no accident that most immigrant, Black, and Indigenous communities established their beauty contests in the 1960s, a time when nationalist debates in Canada were prominent. Considered an apolitical platform, beauty contests approached these debates about ethnicity and race without provoking major discomfort or concern because they were entertaining. When they were the topic of national or local attention, it usually involved some kind of controversy. The 1960s were a time of turmoil and upheaval when Cold War dramas, anti-war and student protests, the burgeoning Red Power movement, and debates on gender, race, and class inspired by the Royal Commission on the Status of Women and the Royal Commission on Biculturalism and Bilingualism, along with Quebec's Quiet Revolution and the rise of the sovereignty movement, reshaped how nationalism was defined and redefined.[8] As the federal government attempted to broker competing national visions throughout the 1960s, celebrations like the state-sponsored Centennial Year in 1967 were deployed to galvanize settler national pride at a time when the residential school system was firmly in place and Indigenous families were subjected to the forced removal of their children in what is called the Sixties Scoop. In addition to these events, Pierre Elliott Trudeau's Liberal government issued the 1969 White Paper, authored by future prime minister Jean Chrétien, then minister of Indian Affairs and Northern Development. This Liberal policy was designed to assimilate Indigenous and First Nations peoples by making them "equal citizens" through the elimination of their Indian status. The White Paper proposed to abolish legal documents that guaranteed treaty rights, including the 1876 Indian Act, to convert reserve land to private property, and to dismantle the Department of Indian Affairs and Northern Development. The 1960s marked the coming of age of a settler futurity concretized by racial hierarchies and systemic efforts to continue the settler logics of elimination and expansion.

This chapter uncovers how beauty rituals and settler femininity are used as effective tools for disciplining racialized bodies in white settler nations. As gendered and racialized projects, beauty pageants at both the national and community levels function to institutionalize discipline through the celebration of white, middle-class, wholesome femininity. The process of improving immigrant, Black, and Indigenous bodies in specific contexts, what interdisciplinary scholar of Black and Indigenous studies Tiffany Jeannette King calls "spaces of inclusion," is part of the disciplinary practices embedded in beauty contests.[9] The chapter features four examples of pageants invested in this improvability: Indian

Princess, Miss Malta of Toronto, Miss Black Ontario, and Miss Caribana. All four of these beauty contests were either directly or indirectly connected to the Centennial Year celebrations. The sections that discuss these pageants serve two purposes. First, they demonstrate how white settler fantasies about Indigenous and Black bodies as well as immigrant subjectivities maintained the racialized practices of the colonial past through gender and sexuality in the contemporary period. Second, the main objective of these beauty contests, and almost all beauty pageants that featured women from Indigenous, Black, or immigrant communities, was to make claims about citizenship within the white settler nation precisely because racialized bodies were envisioned as outside the bounds of nation.

This chapter also includes a section on how the Centennial Commission, a Crown corporation created by the secretary of state in 1963 to celebrate Canada's centennial in 1967, played an interesting role in imagining and inventing a pan-Canadian nation unified in its diversity. The Centennial Commission considered mounting a Miss Centennial contest. Utilizing the beauty contest model was not a new idea in bureaucratic circles. For example, the Miss Civil Service contest, discussed in Chapter 3, was in full force by the 1960s. The potential messages that could be read on the beauty queen's body functioned to reinforce the Centennial Commission's version of the settler fantasy of a white settler community, but the idea of a Miss Centennial contest was also a way to work through and possibly circumvent the popularity of the Indian Princess Pageant, which was also sponsored by the Centennial Commission. Considered together, contests such as Miss Black Ontario, Miss Caribana, Indian Princess, and Miss Malta of Toronto are examples of how particular communities attempted to legitimize their place in debates about the settler nation, citizenship, and the narrative known as Canada through the bodies of beauty queens.[10]

Racializing and Gendering the Modern Settler Nation

Definitions of what is feminine, beautiful, ugly, white, or charming derive from social hierarchies based on gender, class, sexuality, and race. Bodies read as "Black," "Asian," or "Native" immediately represent cultural meanings that are problematized as morally or physically inferior, or othered. In her book on Black womanhood, beauty, and the politics of race, sociologist Maxine Leeds Craig shows that by problematizing the bodies of racialized women, the dominant culture mounts a discourse that perpetuates their exclusion from definitions of femininity and beauty:

> Exclusion from the dominant beauty ideal did not mean that black women had been spared objectification in either dominant or minority culture. On the contrary, whether facing disparagement of their bodies in dominant cultural images or the mixture of appreciation (where alternative standards prevailed) and ridicule (where dominant standards prevailed) within African American communities, black women were diminished when their general worth was determined by their physical appearance.[11]

Craig outlines how the "general worth" of Black women's bodies is framed in reference to white bodies. Although *all* bodies are racialized, white bodies tend not to be read as such. Although racialized bodies can be improved, that improvability is limited and ensures the downplaying of their worth.

Racializing bodies involves positing women of colour as the ugly other or concretizing their "wholesale definition as non-beauties."[12] Definitions of ideal beauty were recast through the establishment of local beauty salons, magazines, cosmetics, and beauty contests that catered to Black women. Socio-political deployments such as the "Black is beautiful" movement in the 1960s demonstrated that Black womanhood was worthy of celebration.[13] The hair-straightening and skin-bleaching practices of the first half of the twentieth century made way for an articulation of beauty where the so-called "natural Black look" prevailed. By reversing an earlier association of "dark skin, kinky hair, and African facial features with ugliness, comedy, sin, or danger," "Black is beautiful" was a deliberate refutation of white beauty and the white erotic gaze as a reference point.[14]

Feminist scholar Margot Francis suggests that the actors of the Garden River First Nation, near Sault Ste. Marie, Ontario, who performed in the play *Hiawatha*, based on Henry Wadsworth Longfellow's 1855 poem *Song of Hiawatha*, used their staging as a form of resistance, especially since their version enabled them to engage in storytelling and dancing "officially discouraged or forbidden" in the 1930s.[15] Although they performed white settler appropriations and fantasies of the noble savage, the actors interviewed by Francis recounted that they had known they were "playing Indian" for white audiences, but the opportunity to preserve the Anishinaabe language system and to perform Anishinaabek legends, songs, and dances, for example, created a "play within a play."[16] Like the minstrel show of the early nineteenth century and the Garden River First Nation's performance of

Hiawatha, the beauty pageant encouraged cultural efforts toward "corporeal containment" that could be challenged, subverted, and rearticulated to elicit fear or fascination from the white settler in the context of the erotic gaze.

The notion of racial uplift was another cultural discourse used to satisfy white settler ideals of femininity and beauty. Racial uplift involved a discourse of representation based on the cult of character, respectability, and the idea of racial dignity. Black leaders' exhortations for Black women to behave in a way that enhanced racial pride were meant to quiet the "slurs of white racists." The "good character of the race" was inscribed on the bodies of Black women.[17] In the case of women, however, "good character" was connected to certain white-defined ideals of femininity, beauty, and domesticity.[18] Embracing beauty practices and products enforced racial uplift, with the added caveat that although white women had to maintain a certain degree of morality in regard to gender codes and sexuality, nonwhite women had to be even more vigilant.

Racial ideology and white supremacy demand the containment and regulation of racialized bodies so that they become acceptable and safe. As sites of (dis)order, female bodies and, in particular, nonwhite female bodies historically conjured up social anxieties and sexual dangers. Nonwhite female bodies are represented regularly as exotic, unknown, desirable, and feared because they fall beyond the confines of "a discourse of whiteness that works to authenticate the identity, respectability, sexuality, morality, grace, and femininity of white women."[19] Given that white female bodies have been contained and regulated by a history of beauty rituals designed to have them occupy as little space as possible, bodies read as nonwhite have had an even greater distance to travel to reach normative ideals propagated by white settler society. For example, Rochelle Rowe's work on Jamaica's "Ten Types–One People" beauty contest, established to commemorate Jamaica's 300th anniversary as a British colony, examines how the celebration of the racialized female body as constructed by a multiracial Jamaican identity included references to how these same bodies were invented by colonizers.[20] In the "Ten Types" beauty contest, "the history of (en)gendering race through the bodies of Caribbean women, particularly of African decent," took a similar path as the Indian Princess Pageant and its association with the Centennial Commission.[21] The race work in both of these pageants cannot escape the coloniality of the sexualized and racialized female body.[22] White settler femininity, another form of race work, reinforces and maintains this coloniality in the historical present partly through the liberalizing process of multicultural discourses that include claims of tolerance and the politics of recognition.[23] We see this fantasy of multiculturalism's "unity in diversity" discourse played out again in the Miss Malta of Toronto contest and the Miss Canada Pageant, especially throughout the 1970s.

Miss Centennial: The Controversy of Citizenship and the Spectacle of the Settler Nation

The 1967 centennial celebrations were pivotal to the project of imagining and reinventing Canada during a period of heightened debates over national identity and within a flourishing consumer culture. Canada's centennial and Expo 67 afforded the federal government a unique opportunity to market a particular narrative of Canadian national history through symbols, songs, and monuments; at the same time, particularly through the post-Expo exhibition *Man and His World*, the Liberal government under Lester B. Pearson produced a vision of Canadian settler futurity designed to appeal to the international corporate community as well as to Canadians themselves.[24] Officials in the pageant community recognized the centennial and Expo 67 as ideal venues for Canadian beauty contests. The potential to connect the existing national icon of white settler femininity, Miss Canada, with the nationalist fever awakened by the centennial celebrations seemed a perfect opportunity to expand national support for the Miss Canada Pageant.

Although the Centennial Commission decided to abandon the idea of a beauty contest as a central pillar of the nationwide centennial celebrations, it is noteworthy that the same Crown corporation funded and supported other beauty contests, such as the Indian Princess Pageant. Theoretically, when the chair of the Indian Princess Pageant Committee, Jean Cuthand Goodwill, requested funding to support the initiative, the Centennial Commission should have declined due to the controversial nature of beauty contests and the deplorable history of appropriation and erasure of Indigenous people by the Canadian state. However, the Centennial Commission's support of the Indian Princess Pageant dovetailed with its mandate to offer a white settler version of Canada and explains its ability to reject the idea of a Miss Centennial title and embrace the "native womanhood" of an Indian princess.[25]

Pageant organizers understood that ensuring the long-term survival of the Miss Canada Pageant depended on Canadians associating the pageant with a sense of national pride, so they proposed the centennial celebrations as an ideal platform to sell Miss Canada as a symbol of the nation. Miss Canada officials sent the Centennial Commission's public relations department a marketing package that included a brief profile of Miss Canada 1967, Barbara Kelly, and a "schedule of rates" and costs for using Miss Canada and her title. In an obvious effort to convince potential sponsors that using a beauty queen would increase revenues by boosting interest in their events, the author of the release made this pitch:

> The combined efforts of the Canadian Centennial Commission with Expo '67 have generated a new excitement and created a "go-ahead" image for Canada. There is a new awareness of advertising which is constructed with Canadian content. The association with MISS CANADA '67 is a natural one ... THINK! ... product endorsements, conventions, sales meetings, merchandising, television and radio commercials, newspaper, magazine and billboard advertising, trade show exhibits, ribbon-cutting and personal appearances.[26]

The "natural" association referred to the commercialism attached to both Miss Canada and the centennial celebrations. Embracing nationalist ideals and promoting Canada on the national and international scene were at the core of the celebrations. Under its new management, the Miss Canada Pageant had also acquired an international reputation, further explicated in Chapter 5.

The idea for a Miss Centennial contest began in 1963, when Centennial Commission executives met with Don Toppin, national director of the Canadian Council for Programmed Learning, who wanted to solicit a corporation, industry, or association to take responsibility for "organizing and financing a nation-wide contest in late 1966 or early 1967 with the final judging to take place at the World's Fair in Montreal on July 1st, 1967."[27] Although the Centennial Commission would not provide any monies for the event, all present "agreed that the selection of an outstanding Canadian girl as winner would have a very important role to play in the 1967 celebrations."[28] The commission even went so far as to acquire patents for the titles Miss Centennial, Miss Centenary, and Miss Canadiana. According to the advertising agency that acquired the patents, Miss Centennial would look to the future.[29] Situating Canada as a major player in economic and technological advancements in the international community was another key aim of centennial celebrations, so promoting the nation to the world through the body of a young woman looking to the future was embraced as an option that deserved further exploration.

Discussions about whether to integrate a beauty contest into the celebrations were also influenced by the broader framework within which the Centennial Commission worked. John Fisher, the centennial commissioner, and his top bureaucratic officials had to juggle competing goals.[30] On the one hand, the centennial celebrations and Expo 67 were politically sensitive events and, as such, required careful orchestration in order to optimize Canada's image on the world stage. On the other hand, cross-country celebrations for Canada's 100th anniversary had to be fun and patriotic while still selling a state-defined pan-Canadian settler nationalism to a citizenry that was mired in ongoing debates over the country's future.

As debates over the beauty contest idea unfolded, some members of the Centennial Commission expressed doubt about the merits of using a beauty contest title. In mid-June 1965 the commission asked John R. Markey, an employee of the Toronto-based public relations and advertising company Collyer Advertising, to provide a "personal report" on the Miss Dominion of Canada and Miss Canada Pageants. Mackey reported that the Miss Dominion of Canada Pageant had a reputation for "exploiting the girls involved" and that this was "further complicated with an intense antagonism between" the Miss Canada and Miss Dominion of Canada Pageants. Markey advised that the negative image of these pageants outweighed the potential they might have to promote Canadian nationalism:

> It is my opinion that it would be most dangerous for the Centennial Commission to be in any way involved with either of these organizations. I think it could lead to extremely poor press. As they are both highly commercial, to say the least, in their methods, any public criticism of or questionable action by either group would naturally reflect on the Commission.[31]

However, Markey did not dismiss the idea of a beauty queen representing the Centennial Commission's interests. He suggested a Miss Centennial contest as an alternative. Indeed, Mackey believed in the "natural logic" of a "Miss Canadian Centennial" contest and offered the following as an example of how it might be organized:

> The contestant from let us say, Penticton, B.C., would become "Miss Centennial-Penticton" and would then, through the Provincial Committee, enter again for example – the "Miss B.C. Centennial" contest. As each provincial contest reached a final a winner would then be eligible to enter the "Miss Canadian Centennial" National Contest, which obviously should be

at the peak period of Expo. This would call for the community contests to be held in the spring of 1967, the provincial contest in June or July and preferably the national contest at Expo sometime in August.[32]

Fisher agreed with Markey's assessment and instructed his staff to devise a "feasibility report" for the concept of a Miss Centennial.[33]

A document prepared by Peter Aykroyd, director of public relations and information, and circulated to all members of the management committee outlining the feasibility of a Miss Centennial contest listed twelve items for consideration, including a final recommendation of what the Centennial Commission's position should be. Under the item "Public Opinion," Aykroyd said that although the public generally accepted the idea of beauty contests, many Canadian women did not consider them to be a "worthwhile activity for young Canadians." He noted that "the reputation and public acceptance of these contests have not been good partly because they have been exploited commercially and partly because of the reported open disagreements between promoters, judges and contestants."[34] In the end, Aykroyd recommended that the Centennial Commission not involve itself officially with any Miss Centennial contest and that anyone seeking the Centennial Commission's involvement should be informed of this policy.

Although they recognized that a beauty queen could have many promotional benefits, concerns over the exploitative and commercial nature of beauty contests kept the Centennial Commission at a distance. Ultimately, the commission's apprehension about the public's negative perception of beauty contests and their potentially damaging effects on the centennial celebrations sounded the death knell for Miss Centennial. In 1967 the Miss Canada Pageant was barely climbing out of a series of controversies that were highly publicized, with the same being true south of the border for the Miss America Pageant. The debate about organizing a Miss Centennial contest speaks to the many contradictions and tensions that lie at the heart of beauty pageants as sites of contestation over citizenship, racial identity, and nationalism. In this particular case, the decision of the commission to forgo the Miss Centennial contest also illustrates the complications of promoting nationalistic versus corporate interests and pursing domestic versus international agendas.

The malleability of beauty contests created endless possibilities for the rearticulation of beauty and feminine ideals among communities. Whether the community in question was national or local or based on racial and ethnic identities, beauty contests constructed women's bodies as cultural products to be consumed by the settler nation. The idea of a Miss Centennial contest to promote Canada's 100th birthday reverberated with government officials because of a longstanding tradition of using women's bodies to sell and support nationhood both at home and abroad. Even though the Centennial Commission did not initiate a national pageant, it was willing in principle to support other contests that it felt fit comfortably with the version of white settler nationalism that it wanted celebrated. Although these contestants emulated and performed what was considered a modern femininity in the context of the 1960s, their *place* in the version of settler femininity that captured the fantasy of settler nationalism was tenuous at best.

Pocahontas, Pauline Johnson, and the Indian Princess Pageant

Violent and sexualized Eurocentric representations and images of Indigenous women are at the heart of white settler nationalism. Fur traders, missionaries, and settlers were joined by anthropologists, filmmakers, and photographers in creating the racialized and gendered images of Indigenous peoples that persist to this day, particularly the racist images of the Indian princess, noble savage or wise elder, and "squaw."[35] Such iconography adorned posters, cigarette and cigar cartons, cereal boxes, postcards, films, and a host of other media, including beauty contests.[36] The Indian Princess Pageant discussed here is not the first beauty contest of its kind. Both historians Katherine G. Morrissey and Cecilia Morgan point to other examples, such as Miss Spokane and John Ojijatekha Brant-Sero's participation in the Folkestone male beauty contest in "full native dress, with feathery headgear."[37] In each of these cases, the beauty contestants followed what became a tradition of performing "Indian" subjectivities as they were depicted in frontier communities, or what is often understood as the Hollywood version of the Wild West. In frontier societies, Indigenous women were constructed in opposition to respectable, white, European women. Historian Sarah Carter notes that the incessant practice of contrasting representations of white and Indigenous femininity expressly "articulated racist messages that confirmed cultural difference" to *prove* the inferiority of Indigenous women as well as to uphold the need for repressive policies that disciplined and contained their bodies.[38]

Importantly, the presence of Indigenous women as the racialized other created opportunities for white settler women to reject Eurocentric gender ideals, as occurred with the birth of the "cowgirl."[39] Cowgirls were white settler women "who opted for the masculine freedoms that 'playing Indian' accorded them, and who were not re-patriated into white society ... Eventually, they were cast in the same terms as the sexual/racial outlaw of the earliest adventure novels."[40] White women who transgressed the codes of femininity dictated by European standards were marginalized as racially other in settler society. Because cowgirls wore pants, swore, chewed tobacco, and rode astride a horse, they were discursively produced as sexually deviant like Indigenous women. These cowgirls, who played at being "Indian," bypassed the supposedly passive femininity of the white settler women and found a subversive space in their appropriated subjectivity. What made these cowgirls dangerous was the way that they modified the invented discourse of the "Indian maiden." The idea of the "Indian maiden" remains a popular one. For example, the Miss Indian World contest is an international event that enjoys an enormous following. Although I focus on the Canadian Indian Princess Pageant organized in the 1960s, beauty contests featuring Indigenous women continue to proliferate:

> The title of Miss Indian World is the highest and most prestigious cultural pageant title to be held by a young native woman. The pageant attracted 20 contestants from all over the United States and Canada representing their tribes and tribal nations. Her role and duty as Miss Indian World is to bridge the cultural gaps between Indian and non-Indian people worldwide. She also represents all native people and serves as an ambassador to all cultures.[41]

Like her predecessors, Miss Indian World functions to play out the colonizer's idea of the Indigenous woman, reifying the homogenization often associated with white settler stereotypes of Indigenous women while educating the colonizer, including the cowgirl with her gendered and racialized performance, about what it means to be Indian.

The image of the Indian princess dates back to the invented story of Pocahontas, the young Indigenous woman who sacrificed her life to save the life of a white man and to marry another.[42] In her article on Carrier women and residential schools in British Columbia, anthropologist Jo-Anne Fiske refers to Pocahontas as the "'intolerable metaphor' of native womanhood" who came to symbolize "feral squaw and salvaged virtue."[43] Fiske connects this metaphor to what she calls "patriarchal exoticization," which "thrusts native women into the reality of a racially or ethnically divided world of misrepresented sexuality and underrepresented social reality."[44] The white settler erotic gaze usually associated with beauty contests was accentuated in the Indian Princess Pageant because of patriarchal exotica. Images of Indigenous womanhood reverberated with what folklore scholar Rayna Green calls the "Pocahontas perplex," or the dichotomy between the Indian princess and the "squaw," a racialized version of the Madonna-whore duality.[45] In this moral configuration, Indigenous women are constructed either as slaves to their sexuality and licentious prostitutes or as a female version of the noble savage. As we shall see, the Indian Princess Pageant was careful not to perpetuate this dichotomy, a strategy that was central to its credibility.

The epithet "squaw" was widely used by white settlers to describe Indigenous women, but its effectiveness as a derogatory term was based on the image of the noble Indian princess: "Where the princess was beautiful, the squaw was ugly, even deformed. Where the princess was virtuous, the squaw was debased, immoral, a sexual convenience. Where the princess was proud, the squaw lived a squalid life of servile toil, mistreated by her men."[46] Carter argues that by characterizing Indigenous women's behaviour as morally suspicious, Indian Agents and members of the North West Mounted Police (predecessor of the Royal Canadian Mounted Police) could place constraints on their activities and movements.[47] The sexual commodification embedded in the term "squaw" created two strikes against Indigenous women. First, it was a term that implied a sexual object who was subjected to exploitation simply because she was a woman. Second, the term had an added value for white settlers because the sexual domination of Indigenous women was imbued with racial overtones about primitivity critical to the colonization project. The image of the Indian princess as pure and dignified existed only in the colonizer's fantasy precisely because of the sexual commodification communicated through the term "squaw."

In the Canadian settler context, the story of E. Pauline Johnson (Tekahionwake) embodies a discourse of Indigenous womanhood, specifically that of the Indian princess.[48] Her widespread popularity enabled her to capture the imaginations of Canadians intent on mythological ideas of Indigenous culture and femininity. Johnson was also a forerunner of the racial performance inherent in the role of the Indian Princess beauty queen. Born in 1861 on the Six Nations Reserve near the Grand River, southeast of Brantford, Ontario, Johnson was known as one of Canada's notable entertainers until her death in 1913 in Vancouver, British Columbia. Her father, George, H.M. Johnson (Onwanonsyshon) became chief of the Six Nations in 1853 and worked as the Crown interpreter for the Six Nations. Johnson's public debut as a poet and performer occurred at the age of thirty in 1892 in Toronto, launching her career and a series of tours across the country until she settled in Vancouver in 1908.[49]

As a poetess, a performer, and a woman of mixed Haudenosaunee and British heritage, she defied the image of the "squaw." Perceived as resembling both a genteel white woman and a female version of the "noble savage," Johnson was emblematic of the Indian princess myth. Like Pocahontas, Pauline Johnson was both a tolerated version of Indigenous womanhood *and* a symbol of white settler nationhood. Pocahontas and Pauline Johnson were part of the reconstitutionalization of the colonial myth-making process:

> Pauline Johnson represented a shining example of Indian womanhood for her non-Native audiences, who saw in her the personification of Pocahontas, the Indian princess ... The romantic story of Pocahontas inspired countless works of art, both low and high, idealizing the image of the Indian woman ... The original Miss America, Pocahontas came to represent the beautiful, exotic New World itself. Her story provided a model for the ideal merger of Native and newcomer.[50]

Historian Mark Cronlund Anderson and art historian Carmen L. Robertson argue that Johnson's status as an Indian princess "did not demand racial purity" and that her hybrid status made her "simultaneously a process as well as an end product."[51] As process and end product, Johnson could be upheld as part of the settler fantasy about the elimination and possession of Indigenous bodies and culture. Colonizers could not establish themselves as superior and the rightful inheritors of the land without the dual process of annihilating the colonized culture while reconstituting an ideal of the other. What made Johnson and perhaps the Indian Princess titleholders different from the image of Pocahontas was their ability to reclaim Indigenous subjectivity by re-enacting racial performance on their own terms. Morgan argues that Johnson used First Nations dress "to make a political point."[52] Aware that her performances and clothing posed problems of authenticity, Johnson redoubled her efforts by drawing on "European fantasies" of Indigenous life. The question of cultural authenticity played a major role in Johnson's ability to "sell" herself to white settler audiences as respectable. In particular, she succeeded by using her body and clothing as spectacle, such as changing her wardrobe during her recitals. Appearing first in a costume designed to fulfill white expectations of so-called Indian clothing and then in

European-style evening gowns, Johnson exposed the artificiality of clothing and the contested space of her body by portraying authentic discourses of neither Indigenous nor white womanhood.[53]

Fabricating stories of cultural authenticity is pivotal to imagining a nation. Indigenous peoples in Guatemala also played with authenticity and appropriation in order to promote their community and place in the nation.[54] Just like the Indian Princess Pageant in Canada, the contest in Guatemala used distinctive clothing, traditions, language, and history to separate the cultural uniqueness of the female Mayans from the Ladinas, women of mixed European and Indigenous descent. Establishing this distinctiveness within the context of the beauty contest model enabled the Mayan contest and the Indian Princess Pageant to use white signifiers and rituals to educate and to promote the Native community's values and ideals regarding beauty to a predominantly white audience.

The Indian Princess Pageant offers a telling example of how beauty contests contained and regulated racial subjectivities within settler societies and also provided a platform for staging and controlling a version of Indigenous femininity. The Indian Princess Pageant was only a small part of the long tradition of inventing and imagining the idea of Native womanhood. What made the pageant unique was its ability to challenge white settler discourses of beauty and femininity while appropriating an institution based on Eurocentric beauty rituals. Moreover, and perhaps most interestingly, the pageant reappropriated the cultural fictions invented by white settlers, past and present. The practice of performing or playing Indian can be traced to frontier society, where the genocide of Indigenous peoples and cultures allowed for a new cultural identity based on invented Native traditions, dress, and behaviours,[55] all of which were complicated further by discourses of Native womanhood. The ideal of the Indian princess, steeped in racial and sexual imagery, informed much of that discourse and crystallized the central metaphor of the pageant organized in Canada in the mid-1960s. The myth of Pocahontas and the legacy of Pauline Johnson served as foundations of that metaphor. Their stories contributed to the cultural memory of the Indian princess and its eventual reappearance in the mid-twentieth-century pageant.

The Indian Princess Pageant originated in 1964 in connection with the annual conference of the National Indian Council held at the Garden River First Nation Reserve.[56] It was a grand success, leading council members to ask the government for a grant to cover the contestants' travel expenses. The Centennial Commission was informed of this pageant through a letter written to John Fisher by Jean Cuthand Goodwill, chair of the Indian Princess Pageant. This letter briefly introduced the pageant to Fisher, stating that it "involves many of our young women across the country who demonstrate potential leadership qualities which would be a benefit both to our Indian people and the Canadian society in general."[57] In her attempt to entice the centennial commissioner to see the pageant as advantageous to his political interests, Goodwill suggested that it would be a "tremendous opportunity" for the commission to use the pageant as part of its 100th anniversary celebrations. This correspondence was the first step toward a budding relationship between the federal government and Indigenous women in the context of beauty pageants.

However, the Indian Princess Pageant of the mid-1960s was not the first instance in which Indigenous communities in North America organized beauty contests. As early as the 1950s, young Indigenous women could compete for the Miss Totem title.[58] The common thread between the Miss Totem contest and the Indian Princess Pageant is that both were meant to use culture and the idea of beauty as a source of pride and to build a sense of community. In her treatment of the Miss Indian America contest, visual art scholar Wendy Kozol discusses how, from the 1960s to 1970s, the US Bureau of Indian Affairs used photography as a public relations visual strategy to showcase the success of the bureau's programs for improving Native American inclusion in the state apparatus.[59] The 1966 Maniwaki Winter Carnival featured two beauty queens: a Carnival Queen (Pearl Tenascon) and a Sport Queen (Theresa Morin).[60] There is also some evidence that Indigenous women actively participated in Centennial Queen competitions, especially in the Ontario region.[61] In all of these examples, contestants and winners were supposed to exemplify the imagined authenticity of the Indian princess within the framework of settler femininity. As part of the beauty industrial complex, Indian princess beauty contests also flourished in the context of the rodeo, a sport and entertainment spectacle that focuses primarily on romanticizing male bodies.[62] Re-enacting Wild West fiction, rodeos like the Calgary Stampede often featured an Indian Princess alongside the official Rodeo Queen.[63]

The Indian Princess Pageant ostensibly was designed to stimulate awareness of Indigenous peoples in the white settler community. In particular, the National Indian Princess Committee (NIPC) endeavoured to

> promote the culture of Indian peoples of Canada and their expression as a
> people, instill pride in the Indian peoples of Canadian society as a whole

[regarding] the history of the Indian and their contributions to Canada, create an understanding of the present environment of the Indian people of Canada, create a better understanding between Indian and non-Indian peoples, create an opportunity for further development of Indian people through the planning of local, provincial, territorial and national Indian Princess Contests and through the development of Indian girls, themselves, and project a new image of Indian people through the personality of the contestants.[64]

The beauty contest and the bodies and personalities of the contestants became terrains on which racial pride and the "new image of Indian people," however imagined, would be defined and showcased. Anderson and Robertson discuss the coverage of Indigenous women and beauty contests in Canadian newspapers, demonstrating how the Indian princess trope was used to hearken to the past and present by showing images of Indian princesses against a skyline of high-rise buildings, thus magnifying "the noble savage frozen in a modern, civilized cityscape."[65] These images and the discourses used throughout the media coverage of various beauty contests over a ten-year period shored up the settler fantasy of the ever-present yet improved Indigenous body. Aware of negative stereotypes, the contestants of the Indian Princess Pageant heralded what was considered a proactive approach to modernizing the self-image of Indigenous youth.

The "hostesses" of the Indian Pavilion at Expo 67 were another example of embodied racial uplift. Janet Morris, who was Miss Indian Affairs 1965 and competed in the Miss Civil Service/RA Queen contest (see Chapter 3), was chosen as one of twelve women who would be sent to Expo 67. In the official announcement of the chosen twelve, the *Indian News* described her as a "tall, pretty, Micmac maiden" who was "frightened at the prospect of being a representative of her people but the more she thought of it, the more she realized it opened the window to the world; that the Indians exist as a proud and noble race of people."[66] The Indian Pavilion hostesses and the contestants in the Indian Princess Pageant were made to exemplify a pan-Indigeneity framed in the trope of the noble "maiden" – and in Morris's case, her role as Miss Indian Affairs made her a logical choice for Indian Pavilion hostess. As Miss Indian Affairs, she already occupied a version of racialized and respectable femininity.

For the NIPC and the officials of the Indian Princess Pageant, packaging and extrapolating on an older version of the noble savage/maiden was one way to develop a public image of Indigenous people and to create better

Indian Princess 1964 Pageant contestants. | Library and Archives Canada, C147300.

relations between Indigenous people and white settlers. The winner of the Indian Princess Pageant became the spokesperson for all things noble, good, and dignified, as perceived and constructed by the organizers of the contest. She also became an advocate against racial discrimination, an issue that was seen as paramount to the success of any given Indian Princess's reign. Using beauty, or more importantly, a beauty queen, to help promote racial pride enabled the NIPC to show that Indigenous people were good, trustworthy, and beautiful, as well as to combat racist ideas.

The first Indian Princess titleholder, appointed in 1963, was kahntinetha Horn,[67] a member of the Mohawk Wolf Clan of the Kahnawake Mohawk Territory in Quebec, a working model, and a university student in Montreal. At the time of her appointment, Horn was already known for her political views as an activist in the Red Power movement. A mother of four girls and employed by the government, Horn worked tirelessly as an activist for the Mohawk Nation, especially for her community in the Kahnawake Mohawk Territory. By 1990 Horn was one of the key activists, warriors, and Indigenous leaders defending the sacred lands of her ancestors by barricade during the Oka Crisis, a historical event where members of the Mohawk Nation fought against members of the Sûreté du Québec, the Royal Canadian Mounted Police, and the Canadian Armed Forces to protect their rights and lands.[68]

Horn continued her activism even as Indian Princess, using the position to promote a political "platform" that challenged "Euro-Canadian stereotypes both of 'Indians' and of women."[69] Indigenous studies scholar Kahente Horn-Miller writes that her mother used her beauty strategically, arguing that it was employed "as a weapon and [that] she learned early on how to wield it with panache."[70] kahntinetha Horn's critique of federal policies and legislation against Indigenous communities, especially in the context of the centennial celebrations, caused the sort of publicity that the National Indian Council and commission officials did not welcome, but that was the point.[71] Although Horn satisfied the standards of white settler beauty, her position as an activist who spoke out against Canadian racism and Eurocentrism was grounded in a need to represent the issues and challenges being faced by her people. Horn's acts of resistance demonstrate how the politics of beauty can work as potential sites of counternarratives for Indigenous and Black bodies. In settler societies, these bodies negotiate beauty culture, fashion, and cosmetics as a political act and to create narratives that counter the discourses of whiteness and settler femininity.[72] In the logic of the settler fantasy, although Horn oozed the modern, confident, mid-twentieth-century idea of settler femininity coveted by so many, her refusal to behave in a demure and submissive fashion tarnished her crown. As a compromised beauty queen, Horn was dethroned by the organizers of the Indian Princess Pageant in the summer of 1964. Clearly, Horn's political agenda did not fit the NIPC's criteria for creating "a better understanding between Indian and non-Indian peoples." Horn's radicalism and her challenge to the existence of "Canada" were incongruent with the vision of settler nationalism endorsed by the Centennial Commission and the Liberal government of the day, positioning her as a killjoy.

Feminist scholar Sara Ahmed explains how discursive figures such as the happy housewife, the angry Black woman, and the feminist killjoy were deployed for their affective power throughout second-wave feminist history. For Ahmed, feminists "kill joy" because "they disturb the very fantasy that happiness can be found in certain places."[73] The feminist killjoy, then, is an "affect alien" not only because she is a source of disturbance, trouble, or joylessness but also because her feminist unhappiness is understood as her own envy of those who have achieved the happiness that she has failed to achieve.[74] Ahmed's theoretical configuration of the feminist killjoy as "the troublemaker ... who violates the fragile conditions of peace" by "not finding the objects that promise happiness to be quite so promising" is based on the rejection of what Ahmed calls "happy objects" or "scripts."[75] Ahmed does not invoke the beauty queen as an affective power, but I do so here because of this figure's similarities to the happy housewife. The figure of the beauty queen, therefore, affectively personifies a willingness "to meet up over happiness."[76] Her affective power is based on the good and happy feelings connected to the attributes of the beauty queen: wholesomeness, white settler values, beauty, poise, and orchestrated sexual innocence. Horn was eventually perceived as a killjoy, whether she identified as a feminist or not, because she asserted her agency in refusing to play the Indigenous "happy object."

At the first national contest in October 1964, Irene Seeseequasis (later Tootoosis) was deemed a better choice as Indian Princess, especially after she told the *Regina Leader Post*, "I don't wish to be a controversial figure. It is important to avoid friction if anything is to be accomplished."[77] Tootoosis and the other seven beauty contestants travelled to the Wikwemikong Pow-Wow on Manitoulin Island in Ontario, and then the titleholder visited the Sioux Pow-Wow at Fort Qu'appelle in Saskatchewan.[78] Funding for the Indian Princess Pageant came as a grant from the Centennial Commission in 1965 and was orchestrated by the national chair, Jean Cuthand Goodwill. Indian Princess 1965 won her title at the National Indian Council's annual conference.

In her final report and financial statement to the Centennial Commission, Goodwill described the 1965 pageant as a "colourful event with the candidates being presented on stage in their traditional Indian costumes and judged for poise, personality, and charm."[79] The overall format of the pageant did not differ from other national contests such as the Miss Canada Pageant, but a main difference was that contestants did not compete in bathing suits. Indeed, in the case of the Indian Princess Pageant, maintaining an exaggerated sense of propriety was part of projecting a "new image" of Indigenous women as respectable. In keeping with the pageant's objective to promote culture, the contest's talent segment included a showcasing of the contestants' performances of "folk" songs and dances.[80] In addition, each participant was asked to deliver a "five minute talk on her views of the Canadian Indian's hope and future."[81] Prizes included an "Indian Shawl," roses, and a cash prize from the Hudson's Bay Company. As part of her responsibilities, Indian Princess winner Jeanette Corbiere – who would later assume a central role in challenging the discriminatory provisions of the Indian Act that stripped Indigenous women of their status if they married non-Indigenous men[82] – then travelled to Fort Qu'appelle and to the Canadian National Exhibition in Toronto to visit the *Famous Canadian Indians* exhibition.

The commercialization of the event increased as Indigenous communities embraced it.[83] By 1966 the pageant was seen as a major event, especially with continued funding from the Centennial Commission. At the National Indian Council's annual conference in Calgary, the competition included nine contestants. The winner, Marlene Jackson (Plains Cree), visited Australia and nine countries in Europe and participated in the half-time show at the Canadian Football League's Grey Cup championship in Vancouver.[84] The NIPC's chair, Marion Meadmore, was particularly resourceful in soliciting business and national support due to her working connections with Canadian Pacific Airlines and the members of the Women's Editor Association, which helped to publicize the Indian Princess Pageant. The pageant's integration into the Pan-Am Games held in Winnipeg in 1967 catapulted the contest onto the international stage, making it a point of interest for various business interests. Joan Palmantier (Chilcotin), Indian Princess 1967, and the provincial representatives experienced a hectic itinerary that included attending functions at Fort Alexander, Manitoba, and Fort William, Ontario, in Ottawa, Montreal, and the Kahnawake Mohawk Territory, and at the Wikwemikong Pow-Wow and Expo 67, where she appeared at the All Indian Lacrosse Tournament and the Indian Pavilion.[85] Ironically, Vivian Ayoungman (Blood), Indian Princess 1968, is featured posing with Minister of Indian Affairs and Northern Development Jean Chrétien, author of the assimilationist and racist 1969 White Paper.[86]

The pageant's connection with the Centennial Commission and other government officials went beyond visits to Expo 67 and reveals a much closer association with the commission's project of constructing a celebratory story of Canada and its white settler heritage. At the 1966 Indian Princess Pageant, the stage was decorated with National Indian Council, Centennial Year, and Canadian flags, reinforcing a discourse of political affiliation between the NIPC and the Centennial Commission.[87] As part of the pageant's aim to promote "goodwill and friendship," a trip to British Columbia was designed to help that province and its cities to celebrate the centennial. For example, Marlene Jackson and the provincial delegates received centennial medallions at Victoria's Centennial Square.[88] Throughout the four years that the Indian Princess Pageant was sponsored by the

Centennial Commission, the titleholder visited cities and reserves promoting the celebrations.

Indigenous organizers themselves took pains to situate the Indian Princess Pageant within the Centennial Commission's version of Canadian national history: "Canada's heritage and past should not be lost in the hectic pace of the space age ... The Princess Canada Pageant is a welcome reminder of our heritage and most certainly does bring pride and interest to the Canadian INDIAN!"[89] The successful relationship between the Centennial Commission and the NIPC was based on carefully articulated regulations and policies that further entrenched racial and sexual discourses of Native womanhood.[90] Particularly important, these rules were intended to establish the Indigenous beauty queen as the mouthpiece of both the national and provincial or territorial organizational committees. Her job was not an easy one. She was expected to be at the complete disposal of her sponsors and pageant organizers. Proof of "Indian descent," marital status, and an age limit were included in the roster of rules. Other rules covered the possibility of using the runner-up to step in when the reigning Indian Princess was otherwise indisposed due to illness or "studies," as well as the number of chaperones that would travel with the contestants.

Moral and sexual concerns were a mainstay of beauty pageant regulations, and contestants in the Indian Princess Pageant encountered similar constraints. One of the regulations stipulated that "a girl who fails to live up to her obligations as a result of misconduct or marriage will be asked to relinquish her title (provincial, territorial and national)." Beauty pageant organizers often used vague and ambiguous wording to justify disqualification based on a direct reference to *sexual* misconduct. Although marriage was seen as a viable option and sometimes as an obligation of women between the ages of eighteen and twenty-five, marriage justified disqualification precisely because it created a dilemma regarding a beauty queen's sexual status. In the case of the Indian Princess, already presented as a symbol of hope, possibility, and dignity, maintaining the illusion of virginity heightened the viability that the titleholder had sexual *potential*. The role of contest chaperones was crucial in this regard because their presence confirmed that measures were in place not only to protect the beauty contestant but also to ensure the maintenance of sexual purity.

Another mainstay of beauty pageant regulations and policies, one closely related to the rule of sexual purity, was that "contestants must be of good character, well groomed, poised and have a pleasing personality." I call this the charm rule because the organizers were attempting to capture a concept central to the beauty pageant ideal of beauty – that is, that women who are good-natured, submissive, compliant, and wholesome exude good character or have a pleasing personality. Grooming and poise are important components of this idea of charm because they present the image of pride in one's public self. The charm rule is often overshadowed as a component of settler femininity because of the historical significance placed on denigrating Indigenous women's sexuality and making it the source of their inferiority to white settler women. However, this idea of "good character" forms a centralizing force behind the reification of race at the heart of settler femininity. Performing settler femininity in the mid-twentieth century demanded not just moral respectability but also the ability to embody the values of personality culture, such as charm and being "pleasing" or the "happy object."

In an article reporting on the proceedings of the Indian Princess Pageant Committee held in the spring of 1968 in Winnipeg, it was revealed that committee members had discussed the "present and future plans for the National Pageant."[91] Offering highlights of the more popular Indian Princesses, such as Irene Seeseequasis in 1964 (Cree), Jeanette Corbiere in 1965 (Anishinnaabe kwe), and Marlene Jackson in 1966, described as "a true ambassador for the Indian people throughout Canada, the U.S., Europe and Australia," the article also reported that the committee members agreed that "the main purpose of holding these pageants was to provide another means of creating a better image of Indian people and thereby fostering a greater understanding among other Canadians. Judging by the response received in the past by the Indian people, the general public, the press and TV coverage across Canada, the committee felt their objective had been realized."[92] Promoting a "better image of Indian people," even if it meant calcifying a different version of the noble savage through the body of the Indian Princess Pageant's winner, was a central aim of the contest. For the committee, the "educational value" provided by the beauty contest was well worth any compromises or misrepresentations that the contestants had to enact.

In the Indian Princess Pageant, moral and sexual purity, in addition to charm, take on different meanings. Persistent colonial vestiges of the sexually promiscuous "squaw" had to be counteracted because of this trope's perennial association with Indigenous women in the white settler imagination. The performance of femininity by Indigenous beauty queens destabilized settler femininity while selling an image of diversity and racial pride that clashed with centuries of systemic racism. The body of the Indian Princess titleholder, therefore, became more than a modernized symbol of Indigenous youth and femininity. It became the site where the white settler gaze confronted the enduring image of Indigenous people but this time on slightly different terms. The focus on Indigenous women's bodies became an even more contentious issue as the Indian Princess Pageant began to be staged less regularly and as the changes to the Indian Act regarding marriage and status began to surface. Indigenous studies scholar and activist Leanne Betasamosake Simpson has analyzed the uses of Indigenous bodies and the logic of colonial violence, recounting her own experience of trying to make sense of "why the words *squaw, dirty Indian,* and *stupid* have so much power over me."[93] Her response to this question captures the epistemic violence at the core of settler fantasies that inform performances of settler femininity: "We must understand that colonizers saw Indigenous bodies – our physical bodies and our constructions of gender, sexuality, and intimate relationships – as a symbol of Indigenous orders of government and a direct threat to their sovereignty and governmentality."[94] Indigenous women magnified the symbolic significance of Indigenous governance by their critical place as leaders with a role in maintaining Indigenous culture and by their reproductive power. The threat they posed needed to be eliminated or, at the very least, tamed.

Miss Malta of Toronto: Beauty and Belonging

Discourses of race, sexuality, gender, and colonial violence at the forefront of settler logics and anxieties surrounding Indigenous women's bodies played out differently across immigrant women's bodies, which were considered adaptable and easier to assimilate. Various immigrant communities organized beauty contests to promote ethnic subjectivities while maintaining wider citizenship and settler nation discourses. Although this section focuses mainly on the Miss Malta of Toronto beauty contest, evidence exists that other immigrant communities in Canada organized beauty pageants, such as Miss Estonia in Manitoba and Miss Chinatown in Vancouver.[95] Research on the Miss Chinatown USA beauty contest by historian Judy Tzu-Chun Wu illustrates how an analysis of the contest enriches our understanding of "Chinese American efforts to construct both gender and ethnic identity during the post-World-War-II era."[96] For Wu, ethnic beauty pageants provide scholars with the opportunity to examine the ways that "idealized versions of womanhood reflect broader concerns about power and culture."[97] This understanding allows historians of beauty contests to regard ethnic pageants as a component of identity formation at the local, regional, and national levels. Ethnic beauty contests reflect community identity and culture and function as venues through which to respond to the pressures and ideals of ethnicity and gender imposed by white settler culture.

The Miss Ao Dai beauty pageant, established as part of festivals organized by Vietnamese immigrant communities in the United States, unravels the complex ways that a Vietnamese traditional dress symbolizing femininity and beauty existed in relation to Vietnamese immigrants' use of the beauty contest model to "negotiate the process of assimilating into bourgeois American culture while remaining ethnically Vietnamese."[98] This particular project formed the core of establishing the Vietnamese "imagined community" within the confines of the American ideals of the settler nation. By using a cultural symbol such as the *ao dai,* a national costume comprised of a long silk tunic over pants, the Vietnamese community created the illusion of respectability even though the contestants were wearing what scholar Nhi T. Lieu has described as a "form-fitting dress, often made with transparent fabrics ... For a flattering fit, a woman must have a thin, slender, yet curvaceous body."[99]

The ubiquity of ethnic beauty pageants demonstrates that immigrant communities were well aware of the advantage of combining female bodies with ideals of settler nationhood and an imagined community. Immigrant community leaders were often encouraged to organize such pageants, especially as discourses of tolerance and multiculturalism created opportunities to promote the notion of community pride. The Maltese of Toronto welcomed the chance to showcase their community and to use the beauty contest model as a platform while ensuring that non-Maltese also participated in the event. Officials in the media, business, and government external to the Maltese community were honoured guests at the Miss Malta of Toronto contest and participated annually either as spectators or as judges in the years showcased below. Through such contests, immigrant groups sought to establish themselves as distinctive but active participants in the cultural and political discourse of multiculturalism even though these events complied with white settler nationalism.

The Miss Malta of Toronto contest represented many of the ideals identified by scholars of beauty pageants based in immigrant communities.[100] The Maltese immigrant community in Toronto established its contest to function in very much the same way as the Miss Chinatown and Miss Ao Dai contests. These beauty contests celebrated community pride while affording various businesses and social organizations the opportunity to advertise and sell their products. Organizers and beauty contestants recognized the powerful images and messages that beauty contests offered and sought to avail themselves of the political and social opportunities that these contests presented. Ethnic beauty contests were used as a venue to ease cultural and identity tensions between immigrant communities and the white settler culture, but they also succeeded in solidifying racialized and gendered representations of belonging that were central to the making of multicultural subjectivities and nation.

The organizers of the Miss Malta of Toronto contest, however, took this political compromise to its logical conclusion. They dispensed with traditional formal wear and made no effort to position the contest as an event within a larger cultural festival. Rather, the contest itself was *the event* for staging respectable femininity. The pageant was divided into three stages – "Sunday Dress," "Bathing Suits," and "Formal Dress" – but none of these stages included any form of traditional Maltese costume.[101] Downplaying the inclusion of so-called traditional ethnic clothing in the pageant proceedings, a feature that positioned ethnic beauty contests as distinct from non-immigrant pageants, may have been an attempt to show that the community was prepared to relinquish outward displays of cultural distinctiveness and to embrace a version of white, middle-class femininity associated with the settler nation. However, this tactic did not extend to other criteria of the pageant. According to the rules, contestants had to be Maltese or of Maltese descent, single, between the ages of seventeen and twenty-three, and no less than 5'1", and they had to compete in one-piece bathing suits with straps.[102] Although the overall form of the Miss Malta of Toronto contest conformed to the Miss Canada Pageant, the singing of the Maltese national anthem and other folk songs played by the Maltese Canadian Society of Toronto Band stood as Maltese cultural signifiers. The careful balancing of business interests and community pride guaranteed the overall success of the Miss Malta of Toronto beauty contest as a performance of multicultural citizenship and drew on the pride that Maltese Canadians felt about their community, their host country, and their homeland.

Discussing Sephardic beauty contests in Los Angeles, interdisciplinary studies scholar Stephen Stern describes a community's appropriation of the pageant model as a way to "promote honor, virtue, and ethnic pride."[103] Stern also suggests that beauty contests, as civic modes of presenting ethnic values, were used to negotiate "the tension between the centripetal forces of ethnic community – with its tendencies toward enveloping its members – and the centrifugal forces of individualism."[104] The discourse of ethnic pride in the context of Canadian multiculturalism was driven by these same centripetal and centrifugal forces, such that members of ethnic minority groups could never embrace either identity completely. Canada's political tradition of bestowing its immigrant communities with the "right" to promote their distinctiveness within a set of predefined parameters set forth in the 1971 Multiculturalism Act helps to explain beauty pageants such as Miss Malta of Toronto and their role in shaping ethnic subjectivities as *part of* white settler national identity. Central to displaying the bodies of young Maltese women in the late 1960s and 1970s was the goal of establishing Maltese immigrants as valued members of the Canadian settler nation while maintaining their status as members of a contained immigrant community. Such was the disciplinary power of the multicultural project.

Since the Maltese comprise one of the smaller ethnic communities in Canada, very few scholarly studies exist on the history of their immigration.[105] Maltese immigrants arrived in Upper Canada as early as 1836, but the two significant phases of emigration from Malta occurred from 1918 to 1920 and from 1946 to 1955.[106] According to a 1948 article in the *Times of Malta*,[107] the first Maltese immigrants who arrived in Halifax were 131 building workers. These immigrants were characterized as the "advance guard" of 500 men, and their arrival in Canada was "authorized" by the government as a means to "recognize in a tangible way the magnificent wartime accomplishments of Malta." Recognition of Malta's contribution to the war effort was cited as the official reason for the authorization of Maltese immigration to the country, but it should be noted that in the period following the Second World War, Canada opened its doors to many immigrants in order to facilitate the postwar economy.[108] In fact, massive emigration from Malta was due to severe unemployment caused by "postwar demobilization of many dockyard workers." These immigrants' experience in the construction trades was seen as valued expertise in Canada (and Australia). As a result, the Canadian government wanted the Maltese to work mostly as general labourers.[109]

The socio-economic realities of the Maltese in Canada placed them in the working or lower-middle class when they first arrived. In a 1965 report on the Maltese community, Toronto officials found that the majority of the Maltese were young and had public school education, although the report could not determine how this education compared with Canadian standards. Many were unskilled or semi-skilled at best. Several had experience in trades at Malta's naval dockyard, which helped them to find employment other than factory labour, a sector where many new immigrants worked. Although the Maltese showed a strong reluctance to work outdoors, especially in the winter, few found themselves unemployed because they were willing to engage in any available labour.[110]

At the height of the Miss Malta of Toronto contest in the 1960s, there were approximately 12,000 Maltese Canadians living mostly in Ontario. As construction workers and small-business owners, the Maltese in Toronto gathered in the Dundas West area of the city. The cultural, recreational, and social activities of the community centred on the church, the *Maltese Forum* (a quarterly carrying cultural, educational, and historical information on Malta), soccer clubs, a band, the Knights of Malta, the Malta Government Trade Commission and Consulate, and various aid associations such as the Maltese Canadian Society of Toronto (MCST).[111] Founded in 1922, the MCST was the community-based organization that established the Miss Malta of Toronto contest, and it played the same role as the United States Junior Chamber in the organization of local and regional beauty contests. The MCST's purpose was "to assist new immigrants in making a smooth transition to their new life in Canada, while helping them preserve their cultural identity."[112] The pageant was the MCST's main cultural activity and set it apart from other clubs and associations, especially since it garnered attention from government officials and members of the business community. The beauty contest, however, was just one of many cultural activities sponsored and organized by the MCST and the Maltese community in Toronto. Other activities included the Fiera Maltija (a type of country fair), the Carnival Dance, outings to shrines, picnics, children's Christmas parties, and annual displays promoting Malta at Toronto's new city hall.

As with the national beauty contests, municipal, provincial, and federal politicians were invited to attend the beauty competition as honoured guests.[113] Their presence both promoted the event in the eyes of the community and created an opportunity for politicians to maintain voter loyalty in the next election. Local businesses donated prizes and money and in return had their names and company logos printed in the official pageant program. Consequently, the winner of the Miss Malta of Toronto contest received prizes ranging from a return trip to Malta (the grand prize) to jewellery and a health club membership. These prizes were considered valuable incentives for the participants, many of whom reflected the working-class realities of the larger Maltese community. Most contestants were students at Toronto-based vocational/technical schools or worked as receptionists, secretaries, tellers, seamstresses, or factory workers at companies such as Ontario Hydro, Toronto Plastics, Northern Electric, National Knitting Mills, DuPont, the Bank of Commerce, and the Canadian National Railway.[114]

The victory of Margaret Tonna, Miss Malta of Toronto 1968, as Miss Ontario that same year was a source of immense pride for the Maltese community. Through her victory, the Maltese community demonstrated that it had "passed the test" of citizenship. Tonna's win was considered evidence that a member of the Maltese community could represent Ontario, a white, anglophone stronghold, at the national level. This kind of recognition of belonging served to buttress inclusion of the Maltese in the settler narrative and as an immigrant success story. Tonna's story adhered to the logic of the 1971 multicultural policy adopted by the federal Liberal government, specifically its twin strategy of encouraging ethnic pride while solidifying the identification of new populations with the white settler nation. The Miss Malta of Toronto titleholder embodied her community's ethnic integration into the Canadian fantasy of settler nationhood and an anchoring of ethnic subjectivities to ease socio-political tensions. These themes were repeated in the case of the Miss Black Ontario and Miss Caribana contests held in roughly the same period as the Miss Malta of Toronto contest, except that Black women's bodies did not reproduce the same resonance with the racial hierarchies propagated by settler futurity.

Miss Black Ontario and Miss Caribana: Beautifying Racial Uplift in the 1970s

The first Miss Black Ontario beauty pageant was organized in the summer of 1976.[115] Diane Fenton, representing La Fay's of Jamaica Beauty Salon, captured the crown that year. According to an article in *Spear* magazine, one of Toronto's most prominent Black periodicals, the pageant was a popular and well-attended event: "It was 1:40 am. The large ballroom in Toronto's Downtown Holiday Inn was quiet. The tension-filled air sat heavily on the shoulders of the more than 900 guests and the 10 semi-finalists shifted nervously as the envelopes containing the name of the first Miss Black Ontario and her runners-up was opened."[116] The ten semi-finalists, chosen from a group of twenty-nine contestants representing Black-owned businesses in the Toronto area, included Miss Continental Hairstylists, Miss Terrylon Travel, Miss Vernon's Upstairs Shop, Miss Mally Fashions, and Miss Stan James Auto Repairs.[117] Black businesses in Toronto served as sources of community pride, especially with the growth of the Black middle class during the late

1960s. Beauty pageants were a way to showcase socio-economic viability, but they also served as meeting points for community planning and formation. Historian Tiffany M. Gill's work on beauty shops demonstrates the central role that Black female entrepreneurs in the salon and cosmetic industries played in community formation and activism throughout the twentieth century but especially during key periods such as the era of the civil rights movement.[118] These spaces were used as mobilizing nodes – places where members of the community congregated to discuss issues pertaining to all matter of things, including racial discrimination. Gill's research also reveals how the beauty culture industry enabled Black women to "embrace some of the trappings of modern life as well as provided an opportunity for Black women to gain an economic benefit in the process."[119] Black beauty pageants could be placed within this larger context of advancements made through the maintenance of gender codes and physical appearance.

The format and sponsorship of the Miss Black Ontario contest echoed the structure of most queen pageants, placing it in a long history of such events. Unlike the Miss Black America contest, established in 1968 in Atlantic City, the motivation behind Miss Black Ontario was not directly a protest statement against segregation rules. Instead, the Miss Black Ontario contest was established to promote Black pride in Toronto. Contestants in Miss Black Ontario came to embody racial uplift as part of beauty culture practices and community values. Anchored in the larger Black liberation movement, Miss Black Ontario, Miss Caribana, and Miss Montreal Carnival used the beauty pageant format to present a positive image of Black beauty and Black women's bodies even as these bodies negotiated the violence of settler nationalism. The production of Blackness in settler societies breaks the racial binary created by the settler-Indigenous split. This binary, argues King, is conceptualized in terms of "naturalized/'just is' spaces [that] simultaneously depend on the productive and reproductive labor of Black women as well as [their] erasure."[120] With few exceptions, scholars and historians have played a crucial role in silencing Canada's long history of slavery, which included African and Indigenous bodies.[121] Settler narratives that consistently erase the history of slavery in Canada and its place in the transatlantic slave trade solidify the settler-Indigenous binary by placing Black bodies outside the boundaries of what King calls "settler humanness," meaning that these bodies cannot make "settled space."[122]

Both in the United States and in Canada, racial uplift played a formidable role in advancing the position of the Black middle class in settler society. At the turn of the nineteenth century, efforts by the Black middle class to transform the social and political circumstances of Black people were answered by violence in various forms, from political and legal strategies such as Jim Crow laws to lynch mobs and eugenics. Racial uplift demanded negotiating and manipulating the settler values of individualism, personal achievement, respectability, heteropatriarchy, and class hierarchies while being continuously read as the other.[123] Beauty pageants were but one way to translate these values in the form of racial uplift and Black femininity. For Black women, racial uplift did not only mean embracing heteropatriarchy and motherhood; it also meant performing chastity, moral character, and sexual purity in order to demonstrate respectability. The growing legitimacy of beauty contests as a tool of settler femininity became a platform that the Black middle class could use to perform racial uplift.

Karen Tice has documented how university-based beauty pageants "rescripted and revitalized" these competitions as a way to promote "discourses of achievement, leadership, upward mobility, cultural education, and professional development," especially for Black female co-eds from the 1930s to 1990s.[124] Tice reformulates the use of the word "platform," which usually refers to a contestant's community service project, such as raising AIDS awareness, by introducing the concept of "platforming" to describe the project of "self-making, sculpting, and performing normative class, race, and gender competencies – on stage and off."[125] Platforming played a critical role in the lives of Black women not only because it demanded body discipline but also as a mechanism to "refute structural racism." Destabilizing or challenging racial ideals of beauty through platforming functioned to "counter the panoptic white gaze."[126] Black Torontonians used the beauty pageant format to promote Black pride through community networking and to educate members of the Black and non-Black communities about Black history and achievements.

The Miss Black Ontario contest was no different from the Black campus pageants in providing the rationale that beauty pageants presented the possibility to launch careers in the beauty and entertainment industries:

> The Miss Black Ontario Pageant was born of the need to provide exposure for young Black women in the province, especially those who are looking forward to a public oriented career such as in modelling, acting or entertaining. It was felt such a Pageant could encourage pride and self-confidence and at the same time give the public at large a chance to see the talent, elegance, beauty and poise of Ontario's Black women.[127]

In the context of the "Black is beautiful" movement, equating pride and self-confidence with beauty and poise within the format of a beauty contest was appropriate. Despite this connection, the Miss Black Ontario contest did face controversy since some Black activists located in Toronto did not consider it to be an exercise in racial uplift. Discussing her experiences in the 1970s and her move toward feminist activism in that period, Dionne Brand says,

> The whole community thought this was an uplifting event, but we organized a protest at the Sheraton Hotel. We got about three other women to come with us and we made a huge banner and put out a manifesto. Our leaflet said we didn't have to imitate the degradation of white women. The community was aghast, but we had so much fun.[128]

For Brand, imitating institutions historically understood as enclaves of white femininity was considered to be a form of degradation; however, these statements do point to the ways that upholding white beauty practices was used as a path toward social and cultural currency in certain segments of the Black community in Ontario, especially among small-business communities.

The Miss Black Ontario contest was only one of several beauty pageants organized by Black communities in Toronto. Miss Caribana (also referred to as Queen of Caribana) was crowned at the Caribana Ball, usually the Friday evening of the massive cultural event celebrated annually in Toronto since 1966. The first Miss Caribana competition was held in 1975, a year earlier than Miss Black Ontario, and was hosted at the Constellation Hotel. The winner of the title that year was Jennifer Shaw, an aspiring professional model who also worked as a typist at a Toronto-based insurance company and was sponsored by the Underground Railroad Restaurant. Shaw's story was showcased within the larger context of racism and the modelling industry as well as her identification with the women's liberation movement. Described as a "women's libber" in an interview with *Contrast*, a Toronto Black community weekly, the journalist used Shaw's victory as an opportunity to inquire about her views on women's liberation, abortion, marriage, and job availability for Black models.[129]

Beauty contestants in the 1970s, including those competing in national contests such as Miss Canada, were confronted regularly with questions about marriage or women's liberation. Shaw's responses did not differ from those given by others. She offered answers that were strategic, trying to

Tonya Maxine Williams, Miss Black Ontario 1977. | Photograph by Jeff Goode, *Toronto Star,* gettyimages.com.

balance a progressive tone with the need to remain eligible given the pageant's parameters: "Issues like equal pay for equal work, and equal opportunities for advancement in all fields of employment, I support fully but I think there are certain values a woman must retain, values like being a good wife and mother, a good homemaker and being able to keep her home and family clean."[130] In this interview response, Shaw reinforced her status as a beauty queen by reassuring readers that family values and wifely duties must be upheld by all women, but she also signalled a turn toward liberal ideals of equality. In another interview, Shaw sidestepped a question about her "future plans" concerning marriage by stating that her main goals were to establish her career as a model and perhaps to start a modelling school.[131] Her views on abortion aligned with her views about a woman's duty: "One of the greatest gifts God gave a woman is the ability to give birth, why then abuse that gift?" She added that an abortion should take place only if a woman is raped or if "it can be proved scientifically that the child will be born deformed or with diseases."[132]

Despite the fact that debates about abortion and disability rights circulated with some frequency in the 1970s given the Abortion Caravan's successful campaign and growing knowledge of the thalidomide controversy, Shaw's comments on the systemic racism at the heart of the modelling industry grabbed *Contrast's* sole attention.[133] *Contrast's* Claudio Lewis focused on the numbers of Black "girls" who flocked to the industry and spent considerable funds at modelling schools but, in contrast to their white counterparts, were unable to translate their enthusiasm and acquired skills into job opportunities.[134] The purpose was to highlight white supremacy in the industry by pointing to both systemic racism and the wider issue of "offending" white Canadians: "Several of them admit the agencies, designers and fashion photographers are constantly rejecting the talents of Black models. Added to this manufacturers refuse to use these girls for fear of offending their customers."[135] Without revealing the manufacturer's name, the article also mentioned that one model had been told that using Black models was "not allowed."[136] Like Black beauty contestants who participated in beauty contests, Black female models were no strangers to the politics of assimilation/tokenism at the heart of settler society and its narratives of tolerance and belonging. Especially in the 1970s the politics of tokenism were a key factor in sustaining the status quo through policies such as multiculturalism and discourses of belonging. This tokenism and the pull toward assimilation were played out again but in different ways in the Miss Canada Pageant throughout the 1970s and 1980s. I discuss how including the occasional woman of colour helped to reassure settlers that the project of multiculturalism was a success because it espoused liberal notions of diversity while sustaining inequality.

Indigenous, immigrant, and Black communities adopted the beauty contest model for several purposes. Beauty contests and beauty queens promoted cultural heritage, especially the history, dress, and language of the community in question, but they also created opportunities for socioeconomic advancement and, in some cases, were used as a vehicle to work for political change. This seemed to be the case for Indigenous and Black women who participated in beauty pageants. As Horn's experiences demonstrate, the Indian Princess Pageant could also be used to dislodge the dominant discourse of nationalism, replacing it with alternative visions of Indigenous sovereignty. However, the beauty contests discussed in this chapter also differed from contests such as the Miss Canada and Miss

Dominion of Canada Pageants in other ways. In the context of white settler society, the messages transmitted by national contests such as Miss Canada reified already "understood" cultural discourses about white beauty and femininity that Indigenous, Black, and immigrant beauty pageants had to prove. Adopting the beauty contest format served – even if unintentionally – to cement the reminder that elimination, dispossession, and erasure were not complete. More to the point, settler femininity was not a universal trope easily applied and assimilated, at least not in the case of Indigenous and Black bodies. As bodies outside the bounds of settler normativity or the eventual coding of whiteness, Indigenous and Black women could only hope to improve; they could never quite fit into the civilizing project of settler futurity. Indigenous and Black beauty contestants did use the beauty pageant as a meaning-making platform in a variety of areas, including the possibility of participating in the Miss Canada Pageant. The next chapter returns to the national stage.

5

Miss Canada, Commercialization, and Settler Anxiety

The Miss Canada Pageant souvenir programs included a brief vignette about the Miss Canada crown. The longstanding crown, called the Tears of Joy, designed by Universe Trading/Majorica International of Montreal, was replaced in 1973 by the Sarah Coventry jewellery firm. To heighten the supposed mysticism and symbolism of this headpiece, the 1972 Miss Canada souvenir program included the "inspirational challenge" behind its fabrication. The narrative highlighted in this vignette was based on the goddess Aphrodite's reaction to a beautiful young maiden being honoured as a queen, whereupon the goddess's tears of joy turned into "sparkling diamonds and fine pearls that fell upon the crown."[1] Reinforcing the myth that Miss Canada was a queen and that Canadians were her subjects, Sarah Coventry continued the tradition of such language as late as the 1980s:

> When designers were first approached with the project of creating a crown for Miss Canada, they knew their design must reflect the history of the nation she represents, while at the same time displaying a contemporary image of Canada's future. The crown worn by Miss Canada is a regal one, befitting such an important title. As the spotlights focus on this year's newly crowned Miss Canada, this multi-faceted crown will capture all the glamour and excitement of the evening. Icy blue chatans and hundreds of glittering rhinestones combine in a regal design for that precious crowning moment.[2]

In an effort to give an aura of myth to the Miss Canada title, the connection between the "history of the nation" and the bejewelled crown was intended to make Canadians believe that the bearer of this crown was worthy of wearing it only if she could embody white, middle-class, wholesome femininity as defined in a settler society such as Canada. The winner of what we are supposed to believe is a coveted title, like the crown, becomes the proverbial crowning jewel in the racial fantasy of settler colonialism as a gendered logic.

Televising the Miss Canada Pageant redefined the pageant on the national and international stages. By 1963 Miss Canada titleholders were touring the country and travelling the world, opening up new entertainment and business opportunities. This shift meant that the pageant adopted a corporate discourse where Miss Canada was simultaneously promoted both as a wholesome and charming Canadian "girl," placing white feminine bodies firmly at the centre of settler society discourse, and as a profitable advertising tool. Despite the changing nature of settler femininity associated with beauty contests since the 1920s, beauty contestants and queens continued to play a role in entrenching the symbols, codes, and images of the settler fantasy while attempting to quell anxieties over the shift in women's place in Canadian society.

The pageant reflected white settler anxiety connected to the political, social, and linguistic concerns influencing discourses of citizenship and national identity by the late 1960s. The strategies applied to quell these anxieties were designed to systematically erase and subvert issues related to racial hierarchies, gender, class, poverty, colonialism, and nonheterosexual sexualities. The interview segment of the Miss Canada Pageant played a pivotal role in this shift. The questions asked by pageant officials and the responses given by the contestants reveal the level of anxiety caused by the dominant political and social discourses of the late 1960s to 1980s. Chapter 5 focuses on how beauty pageants attempted to deal with changes to settler nationalism and with fantasies of finally "resolving" the reminders of colonialism's unfinished project: the continued presence of Indigenous and Black bodies, the growing reality of cultural and linguistic differences, and the ongoing need for efforts at dispossession. National beauty contests like Miss Canada were in conversation with contests such as Miss War Worker, La Reine des Midinettes/Queen of the Dressmakers, Indian Princess, and Miss Black Ontario while they negotiated the shifting character of settler nationalism. Although these pageants were distinct events, they were all battling for a stake in emulating, challenging, or destabilizing settler femininity.

The beauty industrial complex enveloped the Miss Canada Pageant once the competition grew in stature as a national institution. However, interest in the pageant was somewhat lukewarm and sometimes truncated. In 1959 the Kiwanis Club of Hamilton sponsored the Miss Canada Pageant, but it was the Pepsi-Cola Company's financial assistance that elevated the pageant's credibility. That same year, Pepsi-Cola donated $6,000 worth of scholarships.[3] In total, the nineteen-page souvenir program distributed in 1959 contained twenty-six ads for various local and regional businesses. It also included a page describing the institutional history of the Pepsi-Cola Canada Company, biographies of the six judges, twenty-two passport-size pictures of the contestants for the Miss Canada Pageant in 1960, and an innovation from previous years: a blank voting page where members of the audience could rank the contestants.

The Miss Canada Pageant was in transition. Although the pageant had always maintained a close relationship with business interests and the entertainment industry, this connection expanded in importance. In the 1961 souvenir program, Edna Weaver wrote a small piece titled "What It Means to Be Miss Canada." She suggested that being Miss Canada involved both glamour and discipline: "Being Miss Canada is NOT an easy job. Constantly being in the public eye imposes many restriction[s]. You will be separated from family, friends, and familiar places for periods of [time and will meet new] types of people. You will learn much."[4] This insistence that the Miss Canada title was a "job" speaks to the intimate relationship between the pageant and big business. By the early 1960s, part of Miss Canada's duties involved touring the country to promote the pageant and its sponsors. This undertaking was characterized as a "priceless prize" due to the many contacts that Miss Canada could make. Her role in selling products was linked to the title, and as Miss Canada was "THE representative of our Canadian girls to all with whom you come in contact," her reign was acknowledged as both a tool to establish the title as a cultural institution and an advertising vehicle.[5]

The relationship between the Miss Canada Pageant and national business interests still depended on the image of the pageant, but this relationship was under strain at the beginning of the 1960s. A bomb scare and yet another major controversy concerning the winner in 1962, Connie-Gail Feller, exacerbated tensions and tarnished the pageant's already dubious reputation.[6] After only a month and a half as Miss Canada, Feller was dethroned. The president of the Miss Canada Pageant, Dr. Allan Hollinrake (husband of managing director Frances Hollinrake) told the media that Feller had "failed to abide by the rules and regulations of the pageant as set out in a signed contract."[7] The official reasons cited for her dethronement were failure to meet commitments and parental interference. The controversy surrounding Feller had various layers to it, including "rumours of religious prejudice on the part of the pageant officials" (Feller was Jewish).[8] Furthermore, some journalists highlighted the contradiction between the comments of S. Radcliffe Weaver and Edna Weaver about Feller's being one of the best Miss Canadas ever and the abrupt end to her reign, as well as reporting that the Weavers offered inadequate accommodations and unqualified chaperones.[9] After the announcement of Feller's dismissal, Helen (Nina) Holden, the first runner-up, assumed the crown and received the $1,000 scholarship that originally had gone to Feller.

By this time, the pageant's financial difficulties had increased, and its legitimacy problems had escalated. No pageant was held in 1962 to crown a Miss Canada 1963, which meant that Holden held the title for twenty-two months. During her reign, negotiations took place between the Weavers and the new owners of the title. Six months after she received the crown, Holden became disenchanted and threatened to abdicate her throne. In a television interview on April 13, 1962, Holden explained the reasons for her change of heart and announced the new ownership of the Miss Canada Pageant:

INTERVIEWER: Miss Canada, you almost abdicated your throne. What made you change your mind?

HOLDEN: I almost abdicated my throne because of the lack of organization within the Miss Canada Pageant, but MCP Productions made me change my mind.

INTERVIEWER: And as of now, they will be running future pageants?

HOLDEN: They certainly will.

INTERVIEWER: Would you do it all again?

HOLDEN: Yes, I think I would because the experiences I have learned during the past six months have really made it worthwhile.

INTERVIEWER: Has being Miss Canada made your life miserable in any way?

HOLDEN: I wouldn't say miserable. I would say a little hard to cope with but not miserable.

INTERVIEWER: What changes would you recommend for future pageants?

HOLDEN: I would like to see, through television, Canadian people taking an active part in the choosing of their Miss Canada, and instead of saying, "Who is she?" or "What does she do?" or "How did she become Miss Canada?" they will know through television.[10]

Although Holden's ability to admit to her unhappiness while continuing to participate in the pageant may have seemed contradictory, it fit the logic of the beauty pageant world. If the end justified the means, then one's emotional state was less important than access to contacts in the business and entertainment fields. Her "recommendation" was a scripted response, designed to introduce Canadians to the fact that the pageant would now be televised, another important step toward making the title enticing to business.

MCP Talent Associates was responsible for mounting the first televised production of the Miss Canada Pageant after it changed hands in 1962 from S. Radcliffe Weaver to G. Walter Pasko. Taking a cue from their American counterpart, the new owners knew that a major source of

FASHION CANADA . . . MISS CANADA . . . AIR CANADA—

—working together to promote Canada

Following a cross-country tour of Canadian fashion, Fashion Canada, a branch of the Federal Department of Industry, Trade and Commerce, invited Miss Canada to draw the winning ticket for an Air Canada trip for two. Assisting Donna Sawicky in this task is her chaperone and constant companion for the past year, Air Canada stewardess Mrs. Jolanta Loewen.

Donna Sawicky, Miss Canada 1972, promoting Air Canada products for an ad sponsored by Fashion Canada. | Innovation, Science and Economic Development Canada.

revenue from beauty pageants was payments from companies using the trademarked title to advertise products, and television played a major role in selling those products. In November 1963, Pasko and his associates partnered with Tom Reynolds, national sales manager at CFTO-TV, to realize their vision. Reynolds was the president of both Cleo Productions and MCP Talent Associates. Pasko and Reynolds wanted to transform the pageant into an internationally recognized contest with support from government, corporate money, and another key element: television.[11] The officials of the "new" Miss Canada Pageant wanted to elevate the competition to the celebrity status of the Miss America Pageant. But success was still out of reach: Miss Canada 1964, Carol Ann Balmer, took her $1,000 scholarship and continued her studies as a first-year physical education student at the University of Toronto. Thus she did not comply with pageant officials' requests to book her for official engagements, which usually involved endorsement and publicity engagements with corporate and government sponsors. Balmer, however, was within her right to refuse their demands since her contract did not oblige her to commit time to the pageant's promotional ventures.[12]

Adamant that this would never happen again, Reynolds left his job at CFTO-TV, purchased Cleo Productions, and made absolutely certain that the Miss Canada contract obliged the holder of the title to honour all engagements and commitments made by the company. The second most important step Reynolds took was to hire a full-time personal manager for Miss Canada, the label "chaperone" being dropped. For this position, Reynolds made the strategic choice of June Dennis, one of the first women radio announcers, who was single and experienced in the area of public relations.[13]

The new structure proved promising for Cleo Productions. Miss Canada 1965, Linda Douma, became the first "full-time" Canadian beauty queen and travelled the world. Consequently, she was the first Miss Canada to establish the pageant as a viable, reliable partner for business. Douma proved to be an excellent choice for the "new" Miss Canada Pageant, at least as far as Reynolds was concerned. She travelled to Hawaii, Japan, India, South America, and the United States, meeting diplomats, executives, and politicians, as well as visiting hospitals and United Nations troops in Cyprus and Gaza, charming everyone she met.[14] What made Douma a popular choice was her ability to combine "friendliness" and "dignity," traits "necessary for a Miss Canada."[15] Her performativity of settler femininity encased in wholesomeness and charm with a touch of elegance solidified Cleo

Productions' ability to sell the pageant to corporate donors. She embodied another shift in settler femininity that maintained respectability, whiteness, and a sensuality that could be marketed.

A promotional booklet featuring Linda Douma's year as Miss Canada shows the lengths to which Cleo Productions used the national ideals of youth, beauty, and settler femininity as a commodity.[16] The booklet showcases the many newspaper articles from around the world trumpeting Douma as "Canada's Sweetheart" and commenting on her talents. The organizers called the pageant "a unique, all-Canadian institution" with "tremendous merchandising and promotion potential."[17] "Happy advertisers" such as the Canadian Travel Bureau, the Department of Trade and Commerce, the Department of Defence, Canadian Inns, Canadian Pacific Airlines, the Canadian Restaurant Association, the Clairtone Sound Corporation, the Fur Fashion Council, Henry Morgan and Company, Loblaws, Samsonite of Canada, and the Brown Shoe Company of Canada were included in the booklet.

According to one of the many articles included in the promotional booklet, Linda Douma's victory "put Sidney [British Columbia] on the map."[18] The beauty queen's traditional visit to her hometown after winning the title initiated her year of official engagements. It was also the moment when the reality of what the title entailed set in. Waiting for her as she descended from the plane were her parents, grandparents, and siblings. Lieutenant Governor George Pearkes, Sidney chairman A.A. Cormack, and Saanich's member of the Legislative Assembly, John Tisdalle, also greeted her, alongside "Mounties in red serge in her honour."[19] A parade through the town of Sidney, complete with a police car, Chinatown's Drum and Bell Corps, and Majorettes and Lions Club members, reached Sancha Hall, where the North Saanich High School band played.[20] Douma promised that as she toured Canada and the world, she would not only be a representative of Canada but also be a personal delegate from Sidney.

Douma's trip back home was only the beginning. In early December she landed in the middle of the crisis in Cyprus, where Canadian United Nations troops were stationed. As part of the CBC's live show *Cyprus Showcase*, the new Miss Canada's primary job was to entertain the troops along with other Canadian singers, dancers, and a baton twirler. In her capacity as an entertainer and a national symbol, Douma and the Miss Canada title were presented as a welcome respite for the soldiers engaged in a violent war. In the midst of a crowd of soldiers who were far from home, a representative of young, white, Canadian womanhood reassured them that

Centennial commissioner John Fisher ("Mr. Canada") and Linda Douma, Miss Canada 1965. | Library and Archives Canada, 147254.

their presence in Cyprus was warranted and justified: the "danger" they faced by participating in this war was "worth it." A soldier offered the following official welcome to Douma, verbalizing the importance placed on white women's bodies as legitimate grounds for protecting the settler fantasy of nation through violence: "You represent our wives, our mothers, our sweethearts, our daughters and our sisters."[21] Douma personified the fantasy of settler femininity and *home* that these men desired, figuratively and literally. Her presence in Cyprus functioned as a booster for the military, but it also served another purpose for the Miss Canada Pageant: through Douma, the pageant could be considered a "concerned citizen," ready to do its part to support "our boys," thus showing corporations that the Miss Canada Pageant was "not just a beauty contest" but a viable player on the international stage.

After her trip to Cyprus, Douma was sent on a two-week "vacation" in Hawaii. An article written by June Dennis for the *Peel-York Shopper,* a community newspaper in Toronto, included a front-page story about Douma's duties in Hawaii, where she was invited to a United States Navy reception at Pearl Harbor to honour the arrival of two Canadian destroyers, HMCS *Fraser* and HMCS *Qu'Appelle.*[22] Although not as overtly political as her trip to Cyprus, Hawaii set the stage for an ongoing ambassadorial role that Miss Canada was supposed to embody. However, the invitation from the United States Navy and Douma's "inspection" of a Canadian destroyer continued the themes already visited in Cyprus. In this moment, Miss Canada's standing as an "ambassador" and the pageant's association with the Canadian military took on new meaning. Miss Canada's participation in her country's so-called peacekeeping efforts elevated the beauty queen from mere entertainer to patriotic booster. In a not so subtle manner, the seductively co-opted white, respectable female body became the extension of white settler nationalism through its performance of patriotism.

The internationalization of the Miss Canada title and its version of white settler nationalism was not limited to the military milieu. Douma's successes in Cyprus and Hawaii translated into unprecedented financial support from both government and business circles. For example, Douma's trip to Japan, courtesy of the Canadian government and Canadian Pacific Airlines, promoted Canada as a tourist destination, the first such promotional attempt, but it was also used as an opportunity to strengthen political and economic ties with Japan through the creation of yet another beauty pageant title.[23] Her first duties in Japan were to attend an Airlines Ball at the Hilton in Tokyo and to open a Canadian Products Week at a department store.[24] During her many appearances on this junket, she also promoted another important sponsor, Samsonite of Canada. As part of this promotion, Miss Canada 1965 would give special packing demonstrations using Samsonite luggage products.

In addition to using a Canadian beauty queen to promote a recalibrated idea of Canada to the Japanese, the Canadian government also sponsored a beauty contest to choose a Miss Japan-Canada Friendship. This strategically chosen title and venture cost the Department of Trade and Commerce $40,000.[25] The Miss Japan-Canada Friendship contest was purely an advertising gimmick orchestrated by the Canadian government. In her first visit to Toronto, Hiroko Koba, the winner of the title, wore geisha costume, but she said that she preferred wearing Western dress at home.[26] Of course, Koba would have had little choice but to wear what was imagined as traditional clothing for Japanese women since her performativity as the other in this fantasy of Orientalism was pivotal to accommodating the white settler gaze. Her comment about what she wore "at home," away from the public's prying eyes, underlined that although Koba embodied the racialized gendered performance of the backward other, her nod toward "Western dress" signalled that Japan had moved on from its repressive, traditional customs and embraced the advanced and modern ways of the West. In effect, Japan was redeemed as an acceptable political and economic ally even as it retained its status as other.

India and Buddhism in particular became the focus of Douma's Orientalism. After her reign, Douma returned to Victoria to finish the third year of her bachelor of arts degree. As she explained to Shirley Culpin, a reporter for the *Sidney Review*, "when I visited the Orient during my year as Miss Canada ... I'd been tremendously attracted to the culture and the Zen temples there."[27] She said that in India she felt a "sense of peace and gentleness that is in that land" and decided to visit a "Buddhist temple when I was out exploring one day, and I immediately felt at home there."[28] Douma's transformation from a beauty queen to a Buddhist living in a hut in Nepal constituted a rejection of all that the Miss Canada Pageant represented. Seemingly, Douma was pushing back at the beauty mystique, the feminine ideal, commercial consumerism, and the so-called charm and poise that gave her access to a world full of financial opportunities. She refused to engage in the corporate culture that the title was supposed to foster and did not embark on a career in show business, modelling, or public relations. This differed from her many predecessors who viewed the beauty contest as a stepping stone to careers in the movies and television, singing, acting, and the theatre.[29] Their subsequent successes in these various pursuits bolstered the cachet of the title for potential contestants and for the audiences who gazed upon them.

Douma may not have been dazzled by the glamour and money of the pageant world, but Reynolds was not to be deterred. After all, Douma's decision meant that she could no longer perform settler femininity for post-reign engagements as a former and popular Miss Canada. In his tireless efforts to attract potential sponsors to the Miss Canada Pageant, Reynolds convinced the editors of the *Monetary Times* to publish an article on the advantages of using the Miss Canada image to sell a product. He told the reporter that his primary focus was to "upgrade the image of Miss Canada."[30] Although local communities interested in sending a representative to the national finals had to pay between $500 and $1,500 for rights to the Miss Canada franchise, the money collected from sponsors amounted to $50 an hour, $250 a day, or $1,000 a week.

According to Reynolds, sponsors had much to gain from forging a relationship with Miss Canada: "We are commercial, and with no apologies ... Commercially, too few concerns have capitalized [on] the potential of Miss Canada, on her ability to draw crowds, attract attention. A beautiful, intelligent, charming girl, who has been named Miss Canada with 2½ million people watching has tremendous drawing power."[31] Clairtone's public relations director, Gloria Collinson, agreed with Reynolds. Hiring Miss Canada seemed more reliable than using a professional model or an entertainer for promotional purposes because of the performativity of settler femininity embodied in the pageant's winner. As a disciplined and regulated modern body, Miss Canada would "be there on time, do what she's expected to do, react well in any situation, and not disappear with a client or a customer."[32]

Diane Landry, Miss Canada 1966, exemplified this disciplined body by proving herself to be the epitome of dependability and wholesomeness; she was a public relations dream. Not only was Landry bilingual, but she was also born in Manitoba rather than Quebec, thus keeping controversies over regional preferences and Canadian nationalism at bay, a particular concern in the mid-1960s. She was the youngest child in her family, and her trip to Toronto for the national finals in November 1965 was the first time she had left St. Boniface, Manitoba. Landry's popularity was further augmented by her piety. The highlight of her reign was meeting Pope Paul VI on her visit to the Vatican.[33] Landry's religious beliefs were a bonus, as they bolstered her image as virtuous. However, Reynolds knew that this image could easily harm his ability to exploit Landry as a marketable product. As a beauty queen, Landry had to find the right balance between virtuousness and sexual availability, the formula that was needed to sell lots of products. Fortunately, Landry was equipped to do just that based on her talent as a singer and entertainer. Landry's future aspiration was to work in opera or theatre. In April 1966, Landry was engaged to promote the opening of a home show in Montreal. Interviewed by radio reporter Louise Langlois, Landry spoke of the "excitement" she continued to feel as Miss Canada and how it would greatly assist her as a singer in the future because "now people recognize my name."[34] In November 1969, Landry would sit on the Miss Canada 1970 panel of judges, and in late 1971, playing the role of beauty queen expert, she co-hosted the Miss Canada 1972 broadcast along with Jim Perry and Barbara Kelly, Miss Canada 1967.

Another first for the Miss Canada Pageant was the victory of Carol MacKinnon, Miss Canada 1968. MacKinnon, crowned in a regional preliminary

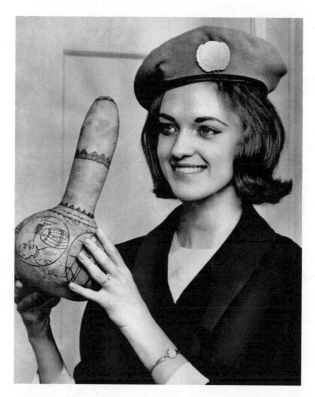

Linda Douma, Miss Canada 1965, wearing a United Nations beret on return from a trip to Cyprus in support of Canadian troops. | Photograph by Harold Whyte, *Toronto Star*, gettyimages.com.

contest sponsored by the Summerside Lobster Festival and Livestock Exhibition, was the only Miss PEI to win the title. For her performance in the talent competition, MacKinnon astutely chose to read a speech on patriotism in both French and English.[35] This demonstration of settler nationalist pride was particularly important when competing during the centennial year, helping to entrench the myth of bilingualism. In a postvictory interview, MacKinnon said that she felt like Cinderella and that she "never really expected a small town girl like me to win a big city contest like this."[36] Although MacKinnon lived in a small town at the time, her experiences had made her far more sophisticated than she revealed. Her father was a member of the Royal Canadian Air Force, and his assignments had taken her family to various countries in Europe.[37] During her reign, MacKinnon would visit Germany (to entertain Canadian troops stationed there), Czechoslovakia, and Japan. Her family background meant that she was well suited for the new international role of Miss Canada, a fact that would not have been lost on the judges or the Miss Canada Pageant organizers.

The globetrotting adventures of Miss Canada continued in the 1970s and 1980s. The required tour with the Canadian Armed Forces to entertain the troops remained until the early 1980s. The countries that Miss Canada visited were selected for their potential tourist market, especially since funds from sponsors such as Yamaha, Sea Queen, Canadian Pacific Airlines, Samsonite of Canada, and British Airlines depended on such advertising. Of course, while visiting places such as Germany, Italy, Spain, Mexico, Sweden, England, the Bahamas, or Niagara Falls in Ontario (a mandatory Canadian stop), Miss Canada herself became the tourist. Indeed, for many winners of the title, their trips overseas were the first time they left Canada. While in London, England, for example, many of the Miss Canadas visited the classic tourist destinations like Buckingham Palace, Tower Bridge, and Trafalgar Square. Although her main function overseas was to promote "Canadian heritage" and products supplied by her sponsors, playing tourist was part of the experience. However, Miss Canada's ultimate success as an advertising tool was measured by her ability to emulate white settler nationalism through her body and her words – to sell a homogeneous version of what it meant to be Canadian – something that proved increasingly problematic as Canadians entered the politically and socially turbulent 1960s and 1970s.

The Spectacle of Beauty, White Settler Femininity, and Race

The talent and interview segments of the Miss Canada Pageant's broadcasts existed to justify the pageant as an exercise beyond scoring femininity and beauty. It was nerve-racking for the contestants but necessary to legitimize the pageant's claims to be concerned with intelligence and poise or, in an earlier period, "good character." The talent and interview segments showcased more than just public-speaking skills or artistic ability.[38] Indeed, Sarah Banet-Weiser argues that in the context of the "larger spectacle of the pageant," these segments or "competitions" served "as the architecture for the construction of the contemporary ideal female subject."[39] In the case of Miss Canada, the performances chosen by the contestants to demonstrate their talent and their responses during the interview resonated with settler nationalism, multiculturalism, and liberal feminism. In all probability, the contestants constructed their answers based on what they thought the judges, pageant officials, and audience wanted to hear. My intention is not to ascribe motivations that I cannot support, but even the orchestration of responses tells us how important replicating the settler script was in the competition. These issues were of paramount importance from the late 1960s to 1980s in Canada and became a centrepiece of the pageant.

The talent and question segments provided contestants the opportunity to construct themselves as patriotic, mainstream, and "all-Canadian." Responses reflected the political, social, and cultural narratives popular at the time, while offering the impression that the contestants were fundamentally unique individuals who harboured a special vision. With 5 million Canadians tuned in to watch the ninety-minute broadcast of the Miss Canada 1969 Pageant, this special vision had to reflect the fantasies about gender, race, class, and culture within Canada while quelling any anxieties emblematic of white settler societies around these categories.[40] The interviews determined the contestants' "intelligence, personality and those inner qualities that a Miss Canada must have." Pageant officials suggested that the answers to the questions were "not too important ... but her sincerity, good taste, poise and dignity will give the judges and the audience conclusive proof she is truly a Miss Canada."[41]

Pageant officials insisted that there were no right answers, but there were definitely wrong ones, especially when a particularly leading question was asked. For example, Miss Canada 1970, Julie Maloney, was asked this question prepared by Kate Reid, one of the judges: "You are pretty girls who have become a finalist in the Miss Canada Pageant. Does your beauty help you to get a husband or do you hope that by winning the Miss Canada title it will enable you to do something that will help your country?" In the context of the 1970s, when the influence of the women's movement was quite palpable, a question of this sort was highly political: what *was* the right or wrong answer? Maloney's response was that she did not intend to use her title to secure a husband because such a title was "too important." For her, it meant "travelling across your country and trying to meet your fellow Canadians, not searching for a man."[42] Was it the correct answer because it dovetailed with emerging liberal feminist thought that women should not have to depend on marriage to lead fulfilling lives or because she performed the expected amount of discretion and national sentiment? Responding that she would indeed use the title to find a husband would clearly have been the

Miss Canada 1967 *(sitting)*, Miss Canada 1966, and first runner-up Miss Muskoka Vacations. | Photograph by Frank Lennon, *Toronto Star*, gettyimages.com.

wrong answer or at least self-serving. Maloney's answer was effective: her retort resonated with settler nationalist pride and with the liberal feminist ideal of the liberated woman while signalling her willingness to take on the public relations task of travelling the country central to her role as Miss Canada. In this example, we encounter a shift in how settler femininity was perceived and performed. Maloney did not perform a wholesale, conservative, and duty-bound version of settler femininity reminiscent of the postwar Miss Canadas discussed in Chapter 2.

With national unity issues now at the forefront of the political and cultural landscape, the Miss Canada Pageant began to struggle with its ability to reflect the new and competing visions of this narrative articulated and reinforced by intellectuals and politicians. The adoption of the Canadian flag, the Quiet Revolution, the rise of the Parti Québécois, the Royal

Commission on Biculturalism and Bilingualism, the centennial celebrations, the 1970 October Crisis in Quebec, the War Measures Act, emerging multi-cultural policies, the 1969 White Paper, and the Charter of Rights and Freedoms all impacted institutions that claimed to represent the white settler nation.[43] It was impossible for the Miss Canada Pageant to ignore the dramatic cultural and political shifts from the 1960s to 1980s. These changes encouraged contestants to choose a talent that showed their adaptability to these shifts or to use the talent segment of the pageant to discuss contemporary political, social, and cultural issues. Although contestants in the 1970s and 1980s still insisted that their hobbies consisted of cooking, sewing, reading, or sports such as tennis, skiing, horseback riding, or swimming, they were increasingly asked questions that specifically dealt with white settler nationalism.

During the broadcast of the Miss Canada 1972 Pageant, Miss Oktoberfest, Miss Saskatchewan, Miss Mississauga, and Miss Thunder Bay fielded questions about their life experiences and hobbies, but host Jim Perry asked Denise Poirier, Miss Quebec City, about her views concerning Canadian national unity.[44] Poirier spoke little English. Guest celebrity Pierre Lalonde, a popular Quebec pop singer and host of the television show *Jeunesse d'aujourd'hui* until 1971, was asked to translate:

> PERRY: From the information that you have given us, we understand that you have definite views on Canadian national unity. Please tell us them.
> POIRIER: [long pause] I cannot say very much now ...
> LALONDE: It's a little bit hard for her to answer, it's a little difficult.
> PERRY: All right. Thank you, Denise.
> LALONDE: She's still a beautiful girl!
> PERRY: She is indeed a beautiful girl!
> LALONDE: [turning to the audience] Come on now!
> [The audience starts to clap, and Lalonde escorts Miss Quebec City back to her seat.]
> PERRY: [to Miss Quebec City] Vous avous [sic] – vous avis [sic] repondu trés bien.[45]

Needless to say, this debacle did not bode well for Miss Quebec City. However, it stands as a testament to the importance placed on questions of settler national unity and to the awkward and inadequate ways that the Miss Canada Pageant tried to address these questions in an attempt to remain germane as an arbiter of white settler nationalism. The pageant

was broadcast in November 1971, only seven months after the repealing
of the War Measures Act, and Canadians, especially in Quebec, were
still reeling from the aftermath of the October Crisis.[46] Using Poirier as
the voice of Quebec youth to speculate on an issue that divided policy
makers and academics seems absurd, but it also points to the pageant
organizers' feeble attempts to maintain its status as a relevant national
institution.

Questions about nationalism and national unity persisted throughout
the 1970s. Whereas Blair Lancaster, Miss Canada 1974, was asked what
"concept or theory" of life she possessed, Miss Calgary, Helen Cutler, was
asked a question framed to elicit nationalist sentiments.[47] Perry asked her
an "open" question about what she felt Canada's greatest improvement was
in 1973:

> I feel the greatest improvement in Canada today has been the increase in
> nationalism. Not only has there been an increase in both radio and tele-
> vision, especially in the amount of Canadian content that we have increased
> too. There has been greater improvement in the support of athletics as well
> as the increase in popularity for national bilingualism. Someday I would
> like to be bilingual and it would please me to be in France or Quebec espe-
> cially and be able *to speak the language of Canada* – not only English but
> also French.[48]

Like most Canadians, Cutler would have been bombarded with debates and
discussions concerning multinationalism and bilingualism that were centred on the question of two founding nations and languages. Cutler's embrace of French and English as the "language of Canada" completed the
narrative of white settler fantasies focused on nationalist pride since it was
the final acknowledgment of the erasure of Indigenous languages and a signalling to immigrants that their inclusion was grounded in their ability to
work and communicate in English and French, unlike the national subject.
The "language of Canada" became a totalizing force used to help perpetuate
class and racial ideology.

Eventually, the interview segment functioned almost exclusively as a platform to showcase nationalist sentiment or tackle political issues. In 1976 finalists were given a list of questions in advance so that they could prepare and
memorize their answers, thereby increasing their chances of delivering more
coherent responses. However, they also had to demonstrate that they were
thinking on their feet, just as they would be expected to do in the presence of

the media when performing a "rehearsed spontaneity."[49] When Miss Oakville 1975, Leslie Mitchell, was asked what her favourite season of the year was and why, she skirted the questions and instead delivered this sentimental tribute to a fictive ideal of the Canadian landscape and the changing seasons:

> My favourite season of the year would have to be autumn. The Rockies take a mystical quality about them, the Prairies are golden with the harvest of wheat, Ontario and Quebec are both colourful with the fall of leaves, the Maritimes are glazed with the mists from the sea and I love to walk down a wooded street and feel the crisp, cold leaves beneath my feet. I feel that this is when Canada shows its true beauty.[50]

Orchestrated to elicit particular sentiments about the untainted "wilderness" of Canada, Mitchell's poetic description showcased an iconic and fundamental narrative used in white settler evocations linking space, sovereignty, and ownership framed in denial and a lack of recognition of land dispossession. This rendition of Canada's geographical attributes from coast to coast reiterated the mythology of the land as empty, vast, virginal, and untouched. A seemingly innocuous response reinforced a basic precept of settler colonialism: the fantasy of an uninhabited country ready for the taking.

The spectacle of settler nationalism that played out on the television screen during the interview segment of the show entrenched racial hierarchies through white female bodies. Questions that focused on Canada's wilderness, bilingualism, and nationalism were about testing contestants on their ability to deal with potential public relations nightmares as they faced journalists and reporters ready to use the Miss Canada title as a way to gauge commentary on the major political and cultural debates of the late 1960s and 1970s. The skills being tested were only partly about poise and charm. Pageant organizers knew that advertisers wanted a Miss Canada who could sell their products because she represented a homogeneous, sanitized, and "enjoyable" version of white settler nationalism. An important part of this seductive co-optation was the ability to be perceived as tolerant, which was increasingly considered an indispensable skill for anyone aspiring to the Miss Canada title.

Miss Canada, White Bodies, and the Myth of Tolerance

The Royal Commission on Biculturalism and Bilingualism solidified the idea of two founding nations, effectively "reproducing the colonial erasure" of Indigenous peoples through bureaucratic discourse.[51] In her extensive study of the commission, theorist Eva Haque shows the colonial, class, and racial logics underpinning the commission's results and conclusions, which were written by eleven white men and one white woman.[52] But the commission was more than just another example of the "old boys' club" mentality; it was also a systematic attempt to entrench logics that kept power in the hands of a privileged few even in the face, or in spite, of the growing numbers of immigrants. Building on the commission's mandate to recalibrate racial ideology through the mantra of two founding nations, the adoption of multiculturalism as a national policy created a new approach to nation building where "Canadians whose origin was non-French, non-British, and non-Aboriginal" were officially recognized by the federal government.[53] The government of Pierre Elliott Trudeau tabled the Multicultural Policy in 1971, formed the Multicultural Directorate in 1981, and entrenched the notion of a pluralistic ethnocultural society in the Charter of Rights and Freedoms in 1982. A foundational component of this multicultural trope was that "it disguised the persistence of white supremacy and power in a new constitution of whiteness as signifying 'tolerance.'"[54] These federal and legislative initiatives, coupled with sociologist John Porter's coinage of the word "mosaic" to describe Canada's ethnic diversity, may have forced institutions that claimed to represent the nation to adapt their delivery of the core values of settler nationalism.[55] The Miss Canada Pageant was affected by these developments. Not surprisingly, questions that focused on "other cultures" seeped into the interview segment. Although the pageant attempted to reproduce the trope of multiculturalism by showcasing ethnicity through spectacle, it remained a largely anglophone and Eurocentric institution. The Miss Canada Pageant helped to maintain the idea that the national space was still basically white even though it now embraced the fraudulent tolerance of "diversity" as a cultural mechanism to absolve itself of responsibility for its white supremacist past.[56]

Discussions of ethnicity and race were anchored in a language that promoted and amplified such differences as regional. When footage of the Miss Oktoberfest contest was showcased during the 1972 telecast, it was described as an example of "the colour, pageantry and enthusiasm that surrounds a regional contest." Later in the broadcast, Miss Oktoberfest 1972, Donna Sawicky, was crowned Miss Canada 1972. This same discourse resurfaced in the 1974 pageant, this time in relation to Clara Anderson, an Indigenous woman representing the National Indian Princess Pageant (not the same as the Indian Princess Pageant discussed in Chapter 4). Using the words "colour" and "pageantry" erased racial or ethnic differences between contestants and replaced them with what sociologist Himani Bannerji calls a "feeling of brightness, brilliance, or vividness, of a celebration of a difference which was disconnected from social relations of power."[57] Bannerji argues that the discourse of "official multiculturalism" helped to hide and enshrine power relations based on race and ethnicity by imparting "a naturalized political language even to the rest of Canadian society."[58]

However, some contestants did use the pageant as a platform to perform othered ethnicity or race, attempting not to threaten the celebratory discourse and "pageantry" associated with nationalist institutions such as the Miss Canada title but to use the spectacle and entertainment value of the competition to showcase what Sara Ahmed has called the "acceptable stranger" version of the immigrant other in Canada.[59] The performance of the acceptable stranger, the immigrant other who has successfully assimilated and does not challenge the racial ideology of white settler nationalism, became key to establishing the pageant as an active participant in official multiculturalism and settler nation building. These tactics and strategies used by bodies outside of settler normativity, with only some limited improvability, challenged the ability of settler femininity to deliver settler futurity. Indigenous and Black bodies disrupted the white settler narrative and were a reminder that the erasure of racialized bodies was incomplete.

The celebratory language of multiculturalism was especially apparent in the questions posed to contestants during the interview segment. Miss Saskatoon, Barbara Borycki, third runner-up in the Miss Canada 1974 Pageant, was asked, "In what ways do the many ethnic origins of Canadian people affect Canada?" Interpreting the question as referring to immigrants, Borycki said that all the "wonderful ethnic things" that immigrants contributed to Canada, such as food and religion, made the country an "original place."[60] The notion of uniqueness or originality stemmed from the cultural differences that immigrants embodied, thereby situating ethnicity and race as culture. For Sunera Thobani, this linkage between the immigrant, or racialized subject, and culture underlines multicultural policy, which "advocated that their [immigrants'] strangeness was not only to be tolerated but also was to be preserved and made cannibalistically available for the nation's sustenance and enrichment."[61] The immigrant subject and the acceptable stranger are tolerable in white settler societies as long as they can perform a version of ethnicity and race that helps to add cultural "colour." It was this vein of spectacle and tolerance that allowed Borycki to use her white body to reiterate the racial ideology of white settler nationalism.

In an example of the inclusionary-exclusionary discourse of multiculturalism, Silvana Benolich and Bess Assimacopoulos, competing as Miss Lethbridge and Miss Kitchener-Waterloo, presented this short piece by way of an introduction during the Miss Canada 1986 Pageant:

BENOLICH AND ASSIMACOPOULOS [IN UNISON]: We're roommates.
ASSIMACOPOULOS: She's Italian.
BENOLICH: And she's Greek.
ASSIMACOPOULOS: I like souvlaki.
BENOLICH: I like spaghetti.
ASSIMACOPOULOS: I like Ouzo.
BENOLICH: I like Sambuca.
ASSIMACOPOULOS: But what's the difference?
BENOLICH AND ASSIMACOPOULOS [IN UNISON]: Canada's a free country![62]

This verse, videotaped prior to the Miss Canada Pageant and then viewed by audiences, enacted the immigrant subject as the acceptable stranger, with the added twist that it posed the question "What's the difference?" and responded by stating that "Canada's a free country!" Miss Lethbridge and Miss Kitchener-Waterloo captured the essence of multicultural policies instituted in white settler societies, where celebratory and harmless examples of cultural difference, such as food and drink, become absorbed as part of the zeal for homogeneity wrapped in the guise of democracy and equality at all costs. In effect, the question and answer component of their verse rendered Miss Lethbridge and Miss Kitchener-Waterloo both inside and outside the national body, allowing them to "wash away" their so-called differences and make themselves whole – an acceptable representation of national identity in the eyes of the tolerant national subject.

The discourse of multiculturalism was also used against Janet Jonathan, Indian Princess 1975, one of the ten finalists of the Miss Canada 1975 pageant.[63] Although Indian Princess delegates did not regularly participate as contestants in this national competition, Jonathan's presence and standing in the 1975 contest permit a glimpse into how the politics of diversity deployed particular problems for alterior bodies. Jonathan was asked about the advantages of Canada's multiculturalism. Positioned as an ideal of Indigenous femininity, Jonathan acknowledged Canada's multiculturalism but seemed skeptical about the commitment to inclusion: "Yes, I do feel that Canada has advantages in being a multicultural country. Each of us can learn from the other nationalities that come to Canada. We can, if we want to, learn the nationality's art, history, culture, and languages. If we are willing to learn them. This would make us a better Canada."[64] In an attempt to push for a deeper recognition of heterogeneity, Jonathan tries to move beyond defining difference as a culinary experience by invoking the *willingness* to learn more about culture through art, history, and language. Signalling the condition of needing to be committed to heterogeneity – "if we are willing to learn them" – Jonathan used the interview platform to signal some doubts about the "advantages" of multiculturalism.

"I'm not a feminist but ... "

The feminist movement in the early 1970s, comprised of mostly white settler women, created new problems for the Miss Canada Pageant. Pageant officials must have felt that contestants had to answer questions that addressed women's changing status. The inauguration of International Women's Year (IWY) in 1975 meant that the Miss Canada Pageant could no longer ignore the vast changes in Canadian society, and questions about women and careers were common. These questions reflected a discourse of settler femininity and the "liberated woman" emerging from a liberal feminist framework that did little to sufficiently challenge the racial, class, and colonial logics entrenched in Canadian society. The failure of white settler feminists of this era to interrogate the settler state's policies, tactics, and laws systematically benefited those women who reflected the values associated with whiteness. Despite their critiques of the gender inequality and oppression of heteropatriarchy, unlike Black and Indigenous feminists, white settler feminists were implicit in the making of settler logics that sustained settler femininity coded as legitimate womanhood.

White settler feminism's complicity in upholding the settler state, even in its critiques, protests, and attempts to transform policy, underscored some of the main feminist political endeavours in the late 1960s and throughout the 1970s. In addition to International Women's Year, the tabling of the report of the Royal Commission on the Status of Women in 1970, with its 167 recommendations concerning mostly equality rights for women, created new problems for institutions such as beauty contests. Attempting to shield itself from feminist criticism, the Miss Canada Pageant did not miss the opportunity to question potential titleholders on issues that dealt directly with women's status in society. Terry Meyer, Miss Canada 1975, was asked what measures would improve the status of women in Canada. In perfect sync with liberal feminist ideology, Meyer brought the judges' and the audience's attention to the Royal Commission on the Status of Women:

> I don't believe I can go into all the measures that are needed immediately in Canada to improve the status of women. I believe the primary focus would be to implement the recommendations of the Royal Commission on the Status of Women. As well, I believe we have to start at the ground level in education, effecting legislation, and in trying to influence the attitude so that not only can women fulfill themselves to their true potential but men themselves can be rounded people.[65]

Continuing her strategy of offering vague responses, Meyer did not mention the word "feminism," was careful to de-emphasize the need for rapid change, and did not offer criticisms about silence on the discrimination experienced by racialized women, women living with disabilities, or lesbians in Canada during her farewell speech at the broadcast of the Miss Canada 1976 Pageant. Terry Meyer was positioned by the pageant as a role model of the liberated, white woman who could continue to be read as wholesome, middle-class, and respectable. Her response could not push beyond these borders since doing so would put advertising dollars in jeopardy. Sponsors banked on the idea that Miss Canada still appealed to the white settler values of heteropatriarchy.

However, like the women reformers of the 1920s and 1930s, settler feminist protesters of this era had other ideas in store for the Miss Canada Pageant. The first sentence of a 1975–76 editorial in the Toronto feminist newspaper *The Other Woman* read, "We are against Miss Canadas, Miss Worlds, Miss Universes, Miss Teenage Canadas, Miss Grey Cups ... All these beauty contests are a constant reminder that we have a role to fulfill, that we have to all the time set ourselves up to be judged."[66] The editorial responded to the protest and disruption of the Miss Canada 1976 Pageant by ten settler feminists who had formed a collective from two feminist organizations in Toronto: the Toronto Women's Anarchist Group and the Radical Lesbian Feminist Group.[67] Coverage of this disruption was widespread, which included attention to the fact that all ten women were lesbian, supposedly creating a narrative that ran counter to the one upheld by the women who competed in the Miss Canada Pageant.

This particular editorial supported the disruption of the Miss Canada Pageant but condemned the tactics used by the protesters. It elaborated upon the disagreements in Toronto within women's groups on issues of strategic practice, stating that "militancy definitely has its place within feminist struggles but we must carefully examine its context and resort to it only under sympathetic conditions." In particular, *The Other Woman* maintained that this action would fail to achieve long-term change and be dismissed as just another "splashy one-shot action."[68] This action was critiqued as levelling more harm than good due to the press coverage, which reiterated the stereotype that all feminists were so-called man-hating lesbians. For instance, two articles published in the *Toronto Sun* in the days following the protest made this association. In an attempt to describe the events of the evening, the *Sun* reported that "minutes before Sylvia McGuire of Halifax was named Miss Canada two of the demonstrators – one a short-haired hefty woman – jumped on stage screaming and waving their arms."[69] Another article published in the *Sun* perpetuated the notion that the demonstrators were man-haters by echoing comments made by Miss Canada 1976 during a press conference: "They really turned me off ... I don't think the Miss Canada pageant is the place to do that. I'm not sure what they stand for. Somebody said they weren't against the contestants, but men. They called it a 'meat market,' did they? Well, I wouldn't be in the contest if I agreed with that."[70]

Unlike the protest of the Miss America Pageant in 1968, the action against Canada's premier beauty contest was neither a highly organized nor a coordinated affair. Initiated by the New York Radical Women, the now infamous protest of the Miss America Pageant in 1968 remains one of the defining moments of feminist activism in North America. Approximately a hundred women's liberationists descended on Atlantic City from New York, Boston, Detroit, Florida, New Jersey, and Washington, DC, carrying signs and a manifesto:

> *Miss America as Big Sister Watching You.* The Pageant exercises Thought Control, attempts to sear the Image onto our minds, to further make women oppressed and men oppressors; to enslave us all the more in high-heeled, low-status roles; to inculcate false values in young girls; to use women as beasts of buying; to seduce us to prostitute ourselves before our own oppression.[71]

The theatrics of the protest attracted national coverage, which generated both myths and facts about the event that are legendary to this day. From the "invented" story of women burning their bras in the "Freedom Trash Can"[72] to the real story of the crowning of a sheep, the protesters drew enormous attention. Some protesters "chained themselves to a life-size Miss America puppet to emphasize women's enslavement to 'beauty standards.'"[73] The protesters also succeeded in disrupting the pageant during the broadcast. One of the organizers, Alix Kates Shulman, purchased sixteen tickets. This allowed some of the protesters to enter the hall and unfurl a large banner that read "Women's Liberation." This part of the action was quite effective, as it caused the audience to turn its attention away from the pageant proceedings. It certainly destabilized Miss America herself, to the point of reducing her to tremors and stutters.[74] These actions caused the producers to contemplate the possibility of broadcasting the pageant without a live audience.

The national attention that the Miss America Pageant protest attracted not only put white settler feminism on the map but also transformed beauty contests. From the outset, beauty contests were controversial and subject to critique from women's organizations. However, the 1968 protest of the Miss America Pageant was different. It challenged the institution's exalted position as the arbiter of American female ideals by focusing on the sexual objectification of female bodies. Notably, this massive and foundational protest did not necessarily dislodge the idea that respectability and femininity were core attributes of white bodies or the place of these white bodies in settler narratives of superiority. Conversely, the Miss Black America 1968, taking place near the Women's Liberation Front action and the Miss America Pageant, was organized as a protest-contest and as a direct response against the exclusionary racial politics of the Miss America pageant. It was only in 1970 that the first Black woman competed in the Miss America Pageant, fifty-one years after its inception.[75] Starting in 1968, it *was* the ideological clashes between the feminist movement and beauty contest organizers, producers, supporters, and participants, not internal controversies, that made the news. The shifting narrative of beauty pageants was not whether they could *adapt* to the modernization of society as they had in the early part of the century but whether they could continue to enforce settler nationalism through white, docile, respectable female bodies unchecked.

In many ways, the same was true of the action orchestrated by feminists against the Miss Canada Pageant. According to an interview that they granted to *The Other Woman*, the protesters first arrived in taxis in an effort to look like just another group arriving to enjoy the show. This attempt to act "natural" failed, and instead they called attention to themselves. As they drove to the CFTO-TV gates, the taxi driver told the security guard that his passengers had a bomb. They were turned back and decided to try a different tactic. They returned from their initial meeting place to the television station, got past the first security officer, and ran toward Studio 6 with other officers in pursuit.[76] As they ran into the studio, they threw leaflets at the audience that said "Happy IWY and Smash Sexism." They arrived precisely at the moment when the announcer was introducing Terry Meyer. Raising their fists and denouncing big business, two of the protesters managed to get on stage. The others physically fought with the security guards and police officers who struggled to reach the protesters on the stage. In an interview with *The Other Woman*, protester Adrienne Potts said that she approached the contestants standing on stage as an honour guard for the departing Miss Canada 1975, telling them "we are not attacking you."[77]

The Other Woman interview also revealed that although their decision to storm the pageant was spontaneous, each member of the coalition had her own reasons for participating. As anarchists, radical lesbians, and socialist feminists, the ten women passionately believed that by disrupting a beauty contest they could effectively communicate their dissatisfaction with the tone of International Women's Year, specifically their concern that the women's movement was losing its radicalism by developing partnerships with the state without questioning the colonial logics that sustained the state's political power and legitimacy. In their minds, the women's movement was being "co-opted."[78] But at least one of the women who participated in the protest did so because she wanted to use the action as a springboard to finally come out as a lesbian.[79] Ann Russell, a member of the Wages for Housewives group, said that she had been "fantasizing" about this protest in the same way that she had fantasized about "walking down the street and beating up pricks."[80]

This incident highlights the tensions that were surfacing throughout the movement ideologically and strategically in the mid-1970s. In a study of the Canadian women's movement, settler feminist scholars have recorded the internal schism that developed in the middle of IWY, a momentous event for feminists around the world who wanted to bring women's issues to the forefront of political, social, and economic agendas. As the movement grew, the grassroots factions began to move in a different direction from the largely white and middle-class institutional feminists, who were quickly being established as the legitimate voice of women's liberation issues in Canada.[81] Radical feminists, especially those who protested the Miss Canada 1976 Pageant, partly resisted this association between the feminist movement in Canada and the legitimization of institutional feminists as the only "true" voice of women.

For lesbian and radical feminists, heterosexism in society and within the feminist movement itself was increasingly prominent. Although the controversial presence of lesbians in the US feminist movement was hotly and openly debated, their impact on the Canadian movement was less detrimental and destabilizing.[82] Yet lesbian feminists were more likely to push for debate and change around issues of sexuality and gender. The protest of the Miss Canada 1976 Pageant on November 3, 1975, must be situated as part of this larger debate between radical and liberal/institutional feminists regarding the role of heterosexism in the oppression of women and within a feminist politics.

The core reason for the 1975 action was to expose what the protesters saw as tactics initiated by government and big business to "pacify" feminists with funding strategies and partnerships during International Women's Year.[83] The protesters considered the strategies and activities associated with IWY, such as the Local Initiative Programme, Opportunities for Youth, and Wages for Housework, to be extensions of the patriarchal and capitalist system without including a critique of how this system was made possible by slavery and colonialism. For the protesters, the purpose of the women's liberation movement was to change the heteropatriarchal structure of Canadian society, not to engage in partnerships with male-dominated institutions. More precisely, it was the idea of the liberated woman that created the most consternation for the protesters, who understood "the liberated woman" to be a new catchphrase for the movement as it struggled to gain public acceptance.[84]

The critique against the liberated woman was based on settler feminists' belief that the ultimate goal of IWY was to promote a liberal ideal of the liberated woman or "woman on the move" as a "product."[85] The protesters saw the initiatives behind IWY as instrumental in commodifying not only women but feminism as well. By focusing on the liberated woman as the new, legitimate construction of Canadian women, the media were creating a consensus that excluded women who did not fit into this settler narrative. It was for this reason that the action against the Miss Canada 1976 Pageant was so crucial to the protesters' project of bringing the women's movement back to what they saw as its original purpose. After all, the liberated – or professional – woman did not represent "working women, housewives, women on welfare, sole-support mothers, native women, black and third world women."[86] Rather, she represented the values that radical feminists saw as implicit in liberal capitalist democracies; for her, the needs of white, wealthy, and educated individuals trumped the collective good, justifying her refusal to critique the commodification of women's bodies and femininity.

The protesters' conceptualization of the liberated woman was congruent with the way that media and corporate interests packaged Miss Canada. In their press release, the protesters stated that the action was taken "to protest the degrading and sexist nature of the Miss Canada Pageant. We were not attacking the contestants but the big business practice of making economic gains through the exploitation of women, the winning women in the Pageant [who] are given prizes or rewards for satisfying their judges."[87] Like the crown for which the contestants competed, "liberation" was something for women to "live up to, to buy, to compete for," a situation that the protesters blamed on the pressure to conform to male-identified ideas about what constituted success.[88]

The press release submitted to the media included a quotation from Meyer, who after the disruption offered these words as part of her farewell speech: "I have in the past year had an opportunity, as a woman, to express my views to thousands of people and I hope that I have been able to convey to these people that the Canadian woman is intelligent, motivated, aware and very much on the move."[89] With these words, Meyer underlined the link between Miss Canada and the liberated woman, a woman ready to tackle the challenges that the world presented but with a feminine edge. It was this liberated but feminine image that so disturbed radical feminists, for this construction quickly emerged as the public face of (white) feminism in Canadian culture. However, this was precisely what the pageant organizers wanted. This image could be used both as evidence that the pageant was modern and as proof that it could continue to deliver the message of settler nationalism through white bodies. Employing this adaptation of a feminist platform, the beauty queen appropriated the language of rights and choice that led many to be convinced that the act of participating in beauty contests constituted a kind of feminist action.[90] In such a rationalization, competing for a beauty queen crown, the media suggested, would exemplify the lives of "ordinary" women in ways that the latter did not.

For the protesters, the liberated woman discourse smacked of sexism and capitalist exploitation, rendering their action against the Miss Canada 1976 Pageant all the more justified. Contestants were regarded as women trying to survive in a world hostile to women's needs and aspirations, even if these women were coded white. In their analysis, systemic sexism prevented women from making choices that did not involve the exploitation or objectification of their bodies. Activists accused contestants of being victims of false consciousness. Such a characterization, however, opened radical feminists to the reciprocal accusation that they were guilty of perpetuating patronizing attitudes by offering enlightenment, protection, and salvation to their duped sisters. Certainly, beauty pageant contestants often argued that such feminist critiques and protests couched in terms of the need to "show them the light" were condescending and insulting. They regarded themselves as taking informed decisions about how to use *their* bodies, completely aware of the consequences. Many of these pageant contestants identified as feminists or at least argued that they embodied some version of feminism, never questioning that this feminism was racialized white and that their ambitions to use the beauty contest for more profitable careers in the entertainment business were just as legitimate as the aspirations of other (white) feminists.

It seems highly appropriate that at the height of the largely white women's movement in this period, one of the clashes between radical and liberal feminists occurred over the bodies of the beauty queens. Radical feminists evaluated their actions after the fact, sometimes resulting in critiques from within the movement that caused a reassessment of their efforts. Liberal feminists and some sectors of the media wasted no time in pointing to the flaws in these actions, perpetuating the myth that the protesters were "anti-woman" and shifting attention away from the real motives behind the protests. Whatever their affiliation or position, feminist protesters of beauty pageants were also implicated in sustaining white settler femininity by not critiquing these contests for the racial, class, and colonial logics that they maintained. Their argument consistently centred on the objectification and heterosexism enforced through the beauty pageant format without making any connections to the white settler fantasy that racialized the white female body as the referential marker of womanhood.

Predictably, most of the questions in the Miss Canada 1977 Pageant focused on career and education issues, and the media focus on the discourse of women's "balancing act" was deployed to help demonstrate the potential impact of feminism on heteropatriarchy. For example, Yvonne Foster, Miss Canada 1977, was asked whether she thought a woman should take her husband's name after marriage; Louise Mondeau, Miss Montreal, was asked why she chose a teaching career; and Deborah Fernandez, Miss Toronto, was asked how important a career was to the Canadian woman. The career theme continued in the second phase of questions after the four finalists were selected. Foster and Mondeau both chose to speak about careers. In her prepared statement, Foster declared her strong support for women's participation in the workforce, suggesting that "by having a career in television broadcasting I would be contributing something as a woman to our country ... I feel that having a career would make me a better person and that I will learn more about people and places around me."[91] Mondeau's theory of women and careers took a slightly different turn, touching on what was considered the controversial issue of balancing a family and a career. Mondeau said that women were "lucky" in the opportunities they now had but that they must never forget that they are "made of love" and must not miss their chance to have a family and children for the sake of personal fulfillment.[92] The implication that women chose their careers or their personal fulfillment over their *duty* to become mothers and wives underscored the critique that liberal feminists were selfish and posed a threat to core family values.

The invocation of this sentiment as part of the broadcast of the Miss Canada 1978 Pageant would have struck a chord with Canadians increasingly destabilized by white feminist challenges to the heteropatriarchal system of power. The idea that women should place their families before their careers remained a standard response. When asked her views on working mothers, Miss Bathurst 1978 said that women's first duty was to their husbands and their children.[93] A contestant in the Miss Canada 1983 Pageant said that she chose dentistry as a profession because it would allow her time to establish a family in the future.[94] Such responses were less an indication of the liberal feminist movement's success or failure than examples of the contestants' inability to banish white settler heteropatriarchal notions of femininity and women's proper place. These responses also coincided with a neoconservative backlash against the feminist movement in the 1980s that focused on the supposed harm to families caused by career-minded women.[95] However, the "working women" under scrutiny were not Black, working-class, or immigrant women; the feminist backlash centred on a deep anxiety to reconstitute the gender and racial supremacy of white women as the reproductive force behind the white settler nation. The familial challenges faced by racialized women who had families and participated in the labour force were rarely mentioned, if at all.

For the next thirteen years, only one other contestant would champion women's independence as a source of strength. Sandy Doverling, Miss Oakville 1981, believed that a woman in the 1980s "should be strong and healthy and stand on her own two feet" and that by doing so "she can enter into a pageant such as this [and] get out and enjoy life."[96] These theories on women's role, although continuing in the tradition of the liberated, white woman, were in the minority as the pageant entered its last full decade, which coincided with the mounting backlash against feminism in the 1980s.

Making It to the Top of the World: The Miss Canada and Miss Universe Pageants

The 1980s were similar to the 1970s in terms of the format and structure of the Miss Canada Pageant. One important difference was Miss Canada's standing in the Miss Universe Pageant and therefore the image of settler femininity and nation that she would project.[97] When Karen Baldwin, Miss Canada 1982, won the Miss Universe Pageant in Lima, Peru, in the same year, the national contest experienced a boost at home and on the international stage. Baldwin's victory put the Miss Canada Pageant back into the spotlight as a legitimate beauty contest and especially as a viable business venture. It also solicited congratulatory messages from Governor General Edward Schreyer and Prime Minister Pierre Elliott Trudeau. Schreyer congratulated Baldwin on behalf of "all Canada," whereas Trudeau tempered his words with a telegram stating that she "must feel justifiably proud in being the first Canadian to receive this recognition."[98] In the House of Commons, the Liberal member of Parliament for the Ontario riding of London West, Jack Burghardt, received all-party support for a motion to congratulate her.[99] As an exemplar of the wholesome, white girl next door from a city in southern Ontario and a middle-class family, Baldwin captured the trope most treasured in a modern version of settler femininity.

Baldwin's road to success at the Miss Universe Pageant was paved by her performance during the Miss Canada 1982 Pageant. Broadcast a year after the Quebec referendum on sovereignty, contestants placed the nation at the forefront of their comments. Alena Patrak, Miss Kitchener-Waterloo, a semi-finalist in the Miss Canada 1982 Pageant, did not mince words. Patrak said that Canadians "tend to complain too much. I realize that we have political and economical problems, but we must never forget that this is still a wonderful country that we call our home, and I wish we could regain some of the patriotic pride that we have lost over the years."[100] Baldwin, taking a different strategy, used her prepared statements to share her philosophy of life. She said that she felt it was important for

an individual to have goals in his [sic] life. I feel that life is beautiful and time is precious and we shouldn't be doing things that we feel is a waste of time and we aren't enjoying doing. In order to obtain these goals, we have to realize our potential, and I feel the greatest ambition or the greatest goal in life is to be happy.[101]

Her victory was due to a combination of her first-place standing in the swimsuit competition and this idealism, which could have been a shrewd political ploy. Regardless, she struck the balance between sensuality and innocence considered essential in a beauty queen. In the impromptu question segment, Baldwin said that her favourite ballet was *Swan Lake* because it expressed so much "emotion." None of the four finalists were asked questions dealing with a political issue or controversy. The result was that their answers focused on music, happiness, and feelings, but it was also the first time that a contestant was asked a question in her preferred language, which in this case was French.

Baldwin's win in Lima made an enormous difference for the telecast ratings of the Miss Canada 1983 Pageant. The broadcast took every available minute to pay tribute to Baldwin as the outgoing Miss Canada 1982 and reigning Miss Universe. The Miss Canada orchestra composed songs and music in her honour.[102] Clips of her homecoming in London and her victory walk at the Miss Universe Pageant were featured. When Baldwin was finally introduced, she appeared in her Miss Universe crown and sash on a red velvet throne flanked by an honour guard of the Royal Canadian Mounted Police (RCMP). The connection between the RCMP and the national police force formerly known as the North West Mounted Police, which was established in 1873 and used by the Canadian government as a tool of colonial violence against Indigenous peoples, would have been lost on Canadians. On the contrary, most would have seen this use of the RCMP as entirely appropriate, maybe even patriotic. In this viewing moment, the racial fantasy of the settler nation, where white settlers can refashion their history in order to forget and deny past colonial violence while ensuring that they continue to benefit from it in the historical present, was televised. Baldwin was fashioned into a national treasure.

In a *Chatelaine* magazine article published in 1992, the same year that the Miss Canada Pageant was cancelled, Susanne Kelman blamed feminists, financial problems, poor programming quality, withdrawal of the swimsuit segment, and a changing, more "urban" society for the death of the pageant.[103] Kelman argued that the cynical audiences of the early 1990s could no longer digest the pageant's "fairy-tale" narrative constructed from the late 1940s to the early 1980s. Indeed, beauty pageants on national and global stages suffered a period of malaise: they were considered boring television viewing, and more importantly, pageant organizers did not modify the external messaging surrounding pageants but dealt only with changing fashion trends. The only exciting moment in the Miss Canada Pageant was when Juliette Powell, Miss Laurentian 1989, famed for her television appearances on the MuchMusic channel and in the *Electric Circus* show, won the title.[104] As the first and only Black Miss Canada, Powell created a slight tremor but not enough to help the Miss Canada Pageant's profit line. Other than the usual announcement in newspapers, Powell's win went largely unnoticed, probably because the distinction of being the first Black woman to win a national pageant had already been bestowed upon Vanessa Williams, Miss America 1984. Moreover, the scandal that had caused Williams to resign her title ten months later meant that Powell's victory was just part of pageant history. Of course, I do not deny that, for Williams and Powell, these victories were significant given their placement outside of settler futurity. What made Williams noticeable was the *Penthouse* magazine scandal and jittery sponsors. Powell's story was less dramatic both because her limited improvability made her an acceptable representation of nation and because there was no public controversy associated with her; she was a poised, studious, and respectable young person. How do we account for Kelman's arguments then? Well, Kelman was only partially right. She correctly pointed to cynicism as a possible reason for the pageant's failure to inspire Canadians. As I have traced in previous chapters, beauty contests have been dogged by controversies of every possible variety from their inception, yet they linger.

As a "goodwill ambassador," Miss Canada had to reconcile her image as a wholesome "girl next door" with her job as a public relations model. Miss Canada was both a national icon and an advertising tool. When white settler societies begin to endure gut-wrenching discussions about national unity, multiculturalism, and the status of women, the fragility of pageants as viable institutions is revealed. For some decades, the Miss Canada Pageant enjoyed popular and business support, but it could not survive political and social changes from the late 1960s onward as the gender, class, and racial ideology of settler nationalism came increasingly under attack. Global decolonial movements, resistance from immigrant organizations, protests against heteropatriarchy from anti-racist and radical feminists, and anti-war campaigns from peace and leftist groups forced beauty contests to be in a constant state of redefinition. Beauty contestants had to perform more than a charming disposition in order to be construed as a defender and representation of white settler nationalism and heteropatriarchy. Unlike the Miss

America Pageant, which seems to have adapted almost seamlessly to shifts in white settler political and social discourses, Miss Canada retained its ideals of wholesome, white Canadian womanhood for a little too long.

Was the pageant at least a profitable commercial success? That depends on whom you ask. As early as 1967 the Centennial Commission did not seem to think that Miss Canada could promote the image and values needed to sell the idea of Canada. However, companies like Yamaha, which had donated a baby grand piano and money to the Miss Canada Pageant for over fifteen years, may have answered that question differently.[105] Tom Reynolds defended the pageant's legitimacy in the following manner: "Look at the people who work with us – the judges, the CTV network, the big businesses and the government departments who employ Miss Canada's services – if it weren't legitimate they wouldn't work with us. If it weren't successful, they wouldn't repeat their associations with us."[106]

The legitimacy referred to by Reynolds was inextricably linked to the ability of the white bodies of Miss Canada contestants to represent certain ideals about gender, class, and race that would appeal to the white settler gaze. The Miss Canada Pageant, however, had begun to lose money and audience support by the mid-1970s. Miss Canada's 1982 victory in the Miss Universe Pageant garnered some support for the Miss Canada Pageant that year, but in 1983 the show's ratings took a turn for the worse. At the end of 1992, the Miss Canada Pageant was shut down. Nicole Dunsdon of Summerland, British Columbia, was the last reigning Miss Canada.

Different tactics were used to sustain audience support, including RCMP honour guards, celebrity judges, and making stronger connections with new and established Canadian fashion designers, but the pageant seemed "out of step with the changing times."[107] On January 3, 1992, the CBC broadcast a story announcing the end of the pageant's run, which included a comment from Joseph Garwood, a top executive at Cleo Productions, now a subsidiary of Baton Broadcasting, who said, "It's time to present Canadian youth in a more contemporary fashion."[108] Of course, there was no elaboration on exactly what shape this representation would take. Representing a feminist voice, Judy Rebick, under the banner of the National Action Committee on the Status of Women, said that "beauty pageants are a symbol of the exploitation and oppression of women."[109] Again, no account was offered of the extent or character of this exploitation or oppression. Indeed, this standard feminist argument was often evoked as *the* critique of beauty contests and was often made in reference to the sexist character of beauty contests, especially the way that they objectified woman – a rallying cry used as early as the protest against the Miss America Pageant in 1968. No reference was made to the way that the pageant entrenched racial and elitist hierarchies. In the same CBC broadcast, Dominique Dufour, Miss Canada 1981, who hailed from Laval, Quebec, lamented the pageant's imminent closure by emphasizing that Canadians were about to lose a national event that brought Canadians together, making a point to reference Quebec participation.[110] In the absence of a clear and cogent explanation for the pageant's closure, Canadians were left to their own conclusions. Perhaps the relative indifference that followed this announcement was due to the fact that Canadians *knew* that beauty pageants – as a spectacle, entertainment, and a white settler fantasy – were far from over.

Conclusion

In a personal account of the virtues of being beautiful published in a 1931 *Chatelaine* magazine article titled "I Would Rather Have Beauty Than Brains," Nan Robins asked, "What chance has a star when the sun comes out?"[1] The answer in the 1930s, more often than not, was "not a very good one" because beauty ideals increasingly involved standards set by corporate interests and personality culture. By this time, beauty practices were daily, ritualized affairs, and in order to be labelled "feminine," women needed to adhere to beauty codes popularized by beauty contests, the entertainment industry, media, and the rise and fall of the modern woman with her attitudes toward style, sex, and the performance of femininity. Although all of these social, cultural, economic, and political components contributed to what was defined as feminine and beautiful in Canada from the 1920s to 1980s, beauty pageants played a key role in institutionalizing beauty practices and shaping norms and expectations of femininity. As both public spectacles and a cornerstone of the beauty industrial complex, beauty contests relied on women's bodies to represent the nation and perform rituals of citizenship. Beauty scholars have documented how, despite being dismissed as frivolous events, beauty pageants serve as effective vehicles through which to convey the complex interplay among beauty, gender, modernity, class, race, sexuality, and nation. We do this by contesting, for example, discourses of beauty or sexuality, but settler societies are built on racial and gender hierarchies tied to colonial violence. Thus, along with contesting beauty, gender, and race, we must also contest the violent formation of nation through white colonial power structures such as heteropatriarchy. Beauty contestants, then, whether they participated in spectacles that were organized along ethnic or racial lines, or initiated by their employers or unions, or funded by media and corporate partners were not merely feminized and racialized representations of nation; their role was to embody the value of settler femininity and systematically entrench the ideals of settler nationalism in the twentieth century.

Robins's account of her experience of beauty discourse in a society where one's appearance became a criterion in defining the self also speaks to the changing nature of the performance of settler femininity. Gone was the era when a good character and a wealthy father, no matter what one's physical appearance, would secure a husband. Indeed, Robins's 1930s commentary offered observations on the hierarchy between beautiful, "plain," and ugly women to tease out the new relationship between ideals of beauty and a woman's ability to attract the opposite sex. She described her roommates, Mabel and Sonia, as being particularly blessed because one was beautiful and the other "mysterious."[2] Robins painted Mabel as a superficial woman whose most pressing concern was "keeping her dates from getting mixed up, and having them find out about each other."[3] Mabel enhanced her physical advantages by "chumming" with her friend Beth, who was "so plain," but "any boy lucky enough to get her would be getting one of the finest girls in the world." In contrast, Sonia commanded male attention because of her "long languid eyes of a queer shade of blue," which, in Robins's opinion, gave Sonia a kind of mystery that intrigued men. In Robins's hierarchy of beauty, one's face counted as cultural capital, a theme on which the beauty industrial complex banked.

Interestingly, Robins used the word "plain" to describe women who belonged somewhere between the Mabels and Sonias of the world and the "ugly."[4] Although we are supposed to focus on this hierarchy and politics of appearance, we are also supposed to assume that all of these women are white – whether they are beautiful, plain, or ugly. Here, Robins's remarks reflect a discourse of settler femininity and beauty infused with the culture of personality, a modern concept, which holds that supposedly the majority of women might successfully perform white femininity and beauty if only they secured the proper instruction. The ability to access outside help is framed in the language of hope. Such hope made the beauty pageant and cosmetic industries successful enterprises that helped to create and institutionalize the belief that learning how to be beautiful and feminine by reading beauty manuals, exercising, dieting, or taking charm courses could make even the most plain among us beautiful. Invariably, the winners were celebrated as beautiful because of what they represented, not necessarily because they embodied a single, homogeneous ideal of beauty. Plain white women could dream about becoming beauty queens, too, and could achieve success with the right work ethic and consumer products. In fact, that was the point of the beauty industrial complex: it banked on the contradictions at the heart of beauty discourses that called for the natural look or moral codes of respectability, which were supposedly effortless, while selling products and rewarding (literally, with prizes) those women among us who also worked for it.

From the 1920s to 1940s, the wholesome or all-Canadian girl was more likely than a sophisticated professional model to win a beauty contest title. As early as 1923, Miss Canada personified settler femininity through a mixture of modernity and a touch of old-world Victorianism. The flapper, or modern woman, with her fashion flair, ambiguous sexual status, and taste for independence, was too risky a representative for the settler nation. The feminized version of the racial and gendered fantasy of nation had to straddle the shift from the cult of character to personality culture and also to incorporate the rise of consumer culture. Beauty queens became both better versed in promoting the nation as dynamic and energetic and better able to project themselves as beautiful but sexy, thus embodying the pageant paradox when business interests became more prominently involved as sponsors.

Although the entertainment, fashion, and cosmetic industries had a continuous relationship with beauty contests throughout their history, endorsements by other business ventures such as soft drink, furniture, or automobile companies and the inclusion of new competitive elements such as the swimsuit segment encouraged a wider audience, particularly among men. By the mid-twentieth century, selling a product required advertisers to grab consumers' attention, tap into their desires, and appeal to a shared set of settler values about racial and gender hierarchies.[5] Beauty queens who had a winning personality and just enough sex appeal (but not too much!) were ideal advertising tools. Most beauty queens were not photographed sprawled on the hood of car clad in a bikini but instead stood next to donated cars, usually in an evening gown, with the sponsoring company's logo prominently displayed. Even Robins recognized the power of sex appeal when she remarked that "there are girls, pretty ones, plain ones, fat ones, thin ones ... No matter [what] they look like, or how much brains they have or lack, if they have a little [sex appeal] they don't need to depend upon anything else."[6] Nevertheless, like most settlers, Robins maintained the erasure of Indigenous, Black, and immigrant women in her assessment.

Understanding the history of beauty contests is relevant for analyzing contemporary settler society, where developments in the beauty industrial complex have taken new and arguably absurd turns.[7] Consider the reality show *The Swan*, produced by the Fox network from April to December 2004, in which women agreed to undergo plastic and dental surgery, fitness training, and therapy in the hope that they could be transformed from an "ugly duckling" into a "beautiful swan."[8] In the final episode of the series, certain lucky participants returned to compete for the title of Ultimate Swan. Indeed, pageants such as the Miss Plastic Surgery contest held in China in 2004 and *The Swan's* beauty contest offered plastic surgeons a unique and powerful venue through which to sell their skills to millions of viewers.[9] It is important to remember that the practice of "enhancing" oneself with cosmetic surgery has been an accepted and constant feature of beauty pageants; the Ultimate Swan and Miss Plastic Surgery contests simply exposed a long-hidden practice. Certainly, these examples underscore the message that beauty can be made. Their existence also proves that although these *new* beauty contests may be regarded as less relevant than their predecessors as signifiers of national (settler or not) discourses, they still maintain their importance as cultural signifiers and profit-generating ventures.

Nevertheless, beauty pageants are mostly linked to individual countries and, as a result, remain at least formally associated with the ideas of nation; however, their relationships with the beauty industrial complex, too, are intact. Although a historical study of Miss Canada's participation in international beauty contests is yet to be written, the ongoing performance of settler femininity in the global context is no less pertinent, even if it has been modified. After the Miss Canada Pageant folded in 1992, several Miss Canada titles surfaced claiming to represent the nation at the numerous international pageants held annually.[10] One of the most widely publicized was Miss Canada International, a pageant established in 1995 by its president and CEO, Sylvia Stark.[11] Miss Canada International gained notoriety through a series of scandals. Three particularly noteworthy controversies increased its media profile: the assault by Danielle House, Miss Canada International 1996, of her ex-boyfriend's girlfriend at Memorial University's student pub; the role of Lynsey Bennett, Miss Canada International 2002, in the Nigerian protests of the Miss World Pageant; and the victory of Russian immigrant Natalie Glebova, Miss Universe Canada 2005, at the Miss Universe Pageant.[12]

Performances of settler femininity continue at global beauty competitions, especially at the Miss Universe Pageant.[13] The Miss Universe Pageant includes a national costume or national dress segment, which is usually quite popular with audiences and offers an opportunity for the contestants to capitalize on national pride. There are several examples that demonstrate how beauty contestants from Canada still promote a modern version of settler femininity in the twenty-first century at this international event. Although it would be fascinating to explore the ways that other settler nations, such as the United States and Australia, represented their versions of modern settler femininity in this segment of the Miss Universe Pageant, I will focus my analysis on the Miss Universe Canada contest and the national costumes showcased to represent the Canadian nation at the Miss Universe Pageant.

These examples are not meant to be exhaustive, but they do confirm how invested beauty contest organizers are in femininity as a signifier of the settler nation. What is slightly different also in this version of settler femininity is that some of the beauty queens representing Canada at the Miss Universe Pageants were part of immigrant diasporas. Miss Universe Canada 2008, Samantha Tajik, is of Iranian heritage; Miss Universe Canada 2013, Riza Santos, claims a Filipino heritage; Miss Universe Canada 2015, Paola Núñez, traces her roots to the Dominican Republic; and Miss Universe Canada 2017, Adwoa Yamoah, is of Ghanaian heritage. Despite the inclusion of these nonwhite bodies within the discourse of acceptable settler femininity as representative of the white Canadian nation, these bodies continue to reinforce the foundational fantasy of the settler nation as inclusive, tolerant, and expandable enough to accept racialized bodies that adhere to the ideals of whiteness and that are prepared to benefit from the history of colonial violence without questioning it.

The costumes worn both by Samantha Tajik, Miss Universe Canada 2008, and by Chelsae Durocher, Miss Universe Canada 2011, were examples of cultural appropriation. Tajik wore a beaded buckskin bikini and a full headdress of fake eagle feathers. Durocher also wore a full headdress as well as a dress aiming to "commemorate" the Haida Nation.[14] Paola Núñez, Miss Universe Canada 2015, wore a totem pole costume, explaining that it was not meant as an insult to Indigenous peoples but was a "Dominican-inspired" totem pole.[15] Riza Santos, Miss Universe Canada 2013, wore a red tunic evocative of the Royal Canadian Mounted Police (with cleavage showing), black tights, brown leather riding boots, and the iconic Stetson hat, while brandishing a Canadian flag. Chanel Beckenlehner, Miss Universe Canada 2014, wore a hockey-themed costume that included a bulky score board as head gear, fanned hockey sticks emanating from the back, and an eighteenth-century-styled skirt split in the middle to reveal thigh-high plaid stockings. Finally, Adwoa Yamoah, representing the title of Miss Universe Canada 2012 at the Miss Universe 2012 pageant, wore a fanned-out dress whose bottom half was made of stitched flags from various nations. This dress was meant to celebrate the narrative of multiculturalism and liberal tolerance in Canada.

The Miss Universe Canada and Miss Canada International contests constitute contemporary examples of the enduring impact of beauty pageants on the national and international political landscape – and they are not going away. They also confirm the continuing history of national beauty contests' deployment of the female body as a marker of culture and the settler nation.[16] As the predecessor to Miss Canada International, the Miss Canada Pageant reflected the political and cultural issues that unfolded during its tenure and used women's bodies as sites of moral regulation and cultural containment while promoting a specific narrative of Canadian gender, ethnic, race, and class identities. When Natalie Glebova was crowned Miss Universe 2005, the Canadian media accentuated the fact that she was an immigrant, attempting to reinforce the discourse of ethnic diversity. The question of diversity took a new turn with the disqualification of Jenna Talackova, one of the ten finalists for the title of Miss Universe Canada 2010, because she had broken the rule that one must be a "'natural born' female" to qualify for the pageant.[17] As a trans woman active on the global beauty contest circuit, Talackova's status introduced yet another challenge regarding not just the relevancy of beauty pageants in the twenty-first century but also how they will respond to new contestations of femininity, citizenship, gender, and the settler nation.

The most recent controversy in the pageant world, one that underlines the power of the fantasy of settler femininity, was occasioned by the 2019 Miss India contest. On May 27, 2019, the *Times of India* published a photo spread of the contestants in that year's competition, all of whom appeared to share fair skin tones.[18] The news of this controversy managed to reach a global audience because of London-based pop culture commentator Samira Sawlani's Twitter feed. In an interview with *CBC News*, Sawlani said that she found this depiction of Indian femininity problematic because "we are still seeing this Eurocentric beauty ideal being held up to us. This is some kind of colonial hangover that we seem to have."[19] As one of the most blatant examples of settler femininity, this episode in the Miss India contest highlighted the temporal reach of settler futurity. Although the articles I consulted did not mention the ways that the caste system undoubtedly shaped the ability of women to even participate in the competition, this example does exemplify the magnitude and force of the relationships between racial hierarchies, settler nationalism, and the politics of beauty.

This contestation of femininity, citizenship, and nation is further brought into relief in the examples of beauty competitions organized and established by various communities based on racial, ethnic, and class divisions. The Indian Princess Pageant, Miss Black Ontario, Miss Malta of Toronto, and the many workplace beauty pageants discussed in Chapter 3 that were organized by government departments, companies, and unions, such as Miss War Worker, Miss Civil Service, and La Reine des Midinettes/Queen of the Dressmakers, together illustrate how communities challenged, appropriated, and embraced settler nationalism throughout the twentieth century. In some cases, these beauty contests functioned to boost community pride, to "educate" Canadian society, as with the Indian Princess Pageant, or to foster multicultural tolerance without once mentioning the many-faceted ways that these contests reinforced the erasure of difference. In the context of growing discontent from both Quebec and the left during the 1960s and 1970s, the federal state relied on the language of national unity and multiculturalism to promote a brand of allegedly inclusive settler nationalism. Beauty contests organized by the government, unions, companies, and racial and ethnic communities furnished perfect venues through which to promote banal nationalism and the values of inclusiveness and diversity.

The use of beauty contests to bolster belonging in a settler society was partly the project behind the Mrs. Chatelaine contest, established by the editors of *Chatelaine* magazine in 1960. In this case, the community in question was Canadian homemakers.[20] Historian Valerie J. Korinek argues that although this pageant was organized to celebrate "all homemakers living in Canada," it was a "contest that rewarded a middle-class, heterosexual and, ultimately, extremely conservative vision of Canadian women. The contest rules explicitly or implicitly excluded single women, working wives and mothers, older women, working-class women and lesbians."[21] What could be more banal and frivolous than a contest for homemakers? Yet, as Korinek shows, this beauty contest was highly relevant as a platform to promote heteropatriarchal values for a particular audience. But these values were also critical to entrenching, through yet another cultural mechanism, this time a popular women's magazine, the logic of settler femininity and its link to nationalism. This version of the ideal homemaker, ready to serve her husband and children in a spotless house, was challenged by what Korinek calls "anti-contestants," *Chatelaine* readers who rejected the unrealistic and elitist image that the winners of the Mrs. Chatelaine contest portrayed. Again, the anti-contestants did not contest the notion of nation or its formation. Indeed, in a lively critique of the contest, readers suggested a "Mrs. Slob" contest as a counterbalancing and less exclusionary version of the stereotypical homemaker but never mentioned the possibility that we should eliminate beauty contests altogether as institutionalized vehicles connecting a mythic narrative of nation to women's bodies, even to the body of the anti-contestant.[22]

Critical resistance to the Mrs. Chatelaine contests, however, was emblematic of a much larger movement against beauty contests in the 1960s and 1970s. Although *Chatelaine* received thousands of entries over the course of the pageant's sixteen-year tenure, feminists in Canada actively organized against beauty contests – not just because they excluded working-class homemakers but also because of what they perceived to be an exploitative and degrading institution. In the late 1960s feminists organized against the Miss Canadian University Pageant just as Bettie Hall, Mrs. Chatelaine 1969, became the first working mother to win *Chatelaine*'s contest, a gesture that was supposed to show recognition of the changing realities in Canadian women's lives. These realities, however, were complicated by feminist critiques of the corporate and sexist character of beauty pageants and by the debates between liberal and radical factions within the women's movement in Canada.

In a 1997 retrospective featured in *Chatelaine*, Sarmishta Subramanian contends that by the end of the Mrs. Chatelaine contest in 1976, winners of the title were "liberated" and "independent," the very claim that inspired the radical feminist protests of beauty contests in the 1970s.[23] Indeed, even before the 1976 action against the Miss Canada Pageant, feminists of the Vancouver Women's Caucus had sent a protest contestant to the Miss Canadian University 1970 Pageant, a contest that had been organized by the Waterloo Lutheran Winter Carnival Committee since 1960.[24] At that protest, Janiel Jolley, Miss Simon Fraser University, asked the contestants not to be manipulated into profiting those who "oppressed them the most, cosmetic and fashion corporations."[25] The protesters of the Miss Canadian University Pageant were most definitely the women Subramanian evoked. Similarly, the feminist protest of the Miss Canada 1976 Pageant focused on critiquing the notion of the "liberated woman" as romanticized by Subramanian. Increasingly situated as a representative of the modern, liberated woman, beauty queens in the 1970s and into the 1980s became easy targets for feminists who believed that the women's movement was being co-opted by liberal and capitalist values as dictated by government and corporate interests. It is difficult to say with any certainty that feminists' protests against the Miss Canada Pageant precipitated the pageant's downfall in 1992. After Karen Baldwin was crowned Miss Universe 1982, the Miss Canada Pageant, although still relevant as a cultural discourse, lost ground as a highly visible part of the beauty industrial complex in the Canadian context. What has made beauty pageants resistant to feminist attacks in the long term is their ability to modify their messaging, much like the enduring logic of white settler femininity.

Notes

Introduction

1 Beauty pageants occupy a tenuous position in the twenty-first century. The beauty pageant format endures and is still used by organizations, universities, and businesses to sell products or entrench gender, sexual, and racial values, but their significance on the cultural landscape does not have the same amplification as in the twentieth century, whereas reality shows are influential and have surpassed the beauty pageant or freak show in popularity and reach. See Banet-Weiser and Portwood-Stacer, "'I Just Want to Be Me Again!'"

2 The literature on body history is vast. For Canadian examples, see Nicholas, *Modern Girl;* and Gentile and Nicholas, eds., *Contesting Bodies.* I use the concept of "bodies" extensively in this book. Although it is often used as an abstract or objectifying placeholder, it is my intent to use it simultaneously as a metaphor and a way to foreground a subjectivity based in materiality, performance, and becoming. I am in no way suggesting, for example, that bodies are divorced or exist in abstraction from embodied experiences of race, gender, class, colonialism, sexuality, and able-bodiedness in historical and contemporary contexts.

3 I use the terms "pageants," "contests," and "competitions" interchangeably. I also refer to contestants as "participants," "delegates," and "representatives," terms used by various organizers.

4 See Barman, "Taming Aboriginal Sexuality."

5 See Van Kirk, *Many Tender Ties.* For a literary analysis of settler feminism in Canada, see Henderson, *Settler Feminism.* On the domestic sphere as a contact zone, see McPherson, "Home Tales."

6 Pickles and Rutherdale, eds., *Contact Zones*, is divided into three sections, which deal with dress and performance, regulation and sexuality, and bodies in everyday contact.

7 Billig, *Banal Nationalism*.

8 Coleman, *White Civility*.

9 Tuck and Gaztambide-Fernández, "Curriculum, Replacement, and Settler Futurity," 73. See also Tuck and Yang, "Decolonization Is Not a Metaphor."

10 Veracini, *Settler Colonialism*, 75. On whiteness and settler society, see Erickson, "Phantasy in White." Finally, for the most recent and exciting work on the connections between slavery and settler colonialism, see King, *Black Shoals*.

11 Banet-Weiser, *Most Beautiful Girl*, 8. Banet-Weiser offers the most thorough treatment of the Miss America Pageant to date. For the first scholarly work on the Miss America Pageant, see Riverol, *Live from Atlantic City*. For an anthology on Miss America, see Watson and Martin, eds., *"There She Is, Miss America!"* See also Watson and Martin, "Miss America Pageant."

12 King-O'Riain, *Pure Beauty*, 60–61.

13 See Nakamura, "'Miss Atom Bomb' Contests"; and Roberts, "New Cure for Brightleaf Tobacco."

14 Smith, "Indigeneity."

15 Ibid., 68, also Figure 4.2 and the related explanation.

16 Wolfe, "Race and the Trace of History," 285.

17 Coleman, *White Civility*.

18 For more on the Royal Canadian Mounted Police, see Dawson, *Mountie*.

19 The information on Johnny Canuck is taken from Lefolii, *Canadian Look*, 10. Johnny Canuck stood for Canada in the same way that Uncle Sam and John Bull represented the United States and England respectively. Apparently, English-speaking Canadians coined the name "Canuck" as early as 1830 in reference to their French-speaking counterparts.

20 On Niagara Falls, see Dubinsky, *Second Greatest Disappointment*. For more on the Canadian National Exhibition, see Walden, *Becoming Modern in Toronto*. On the historical myth of Laura Secord, see Coates and Morgan, *Heroines and History*.

21 Veracini, *Settler Colonialism*, 77.

22 Nielson, "Caricaturing Colonial Space," 479.

23 Lefolii, *Canadian Look*, 10.

24 Ibid. See also "When Miss Canada Was Pure, Plump and Proud," *Weekend Magazine*, December 3, 1966, 30–31.

25 On Marianne, see Agulhon, *Marianne au combat*; and Segalen and Chamarat, "La Rosière et la 'Miss.'" How the "female savage" image used to depict America evolved into the goddess exemplified by the Statue of Liberty is discussed in Higham, "Indian Princess."

26 For a particularly useful deconstruction of how colonizers depicted bodies of Indigenous women, see McClintock, *Imperial Leather*. In her chapter "The Lay of the Land: Genealogies of Imperialism," McClintock argues that the female body was "figured as marking the boundary of the cosmos and the limits of the known world," which allowed colonizers and Europeans to situate the Americas and Africa in "porno-tropics" – that

is, the projection of forbidden sexual desires and fears through a specific and deliberate image of the female body (22). For a historical analysis of the colonizers' gaze and the "savage" body in the context of the representation of Amerindians in the early sixteenth century, see Dickason, *Myth of the Savage*. In addition to providing several pictures demonstrating the hairy female body, Dickason also suggests that the "concept of savagery reveals that ... it involved the well-known Renaissance folkloric figure of the Wild Man; early Christian perceptions of monkeys, apes, and baboons; and the classical Greek and Roman tradition of the noble savage" (63).

27 Nielson, "Erotic Attachment," 103.

28 The literature on the early representations of Miss Canada is still scant but growing. For a valuable account of the all-Canadian girl and the world of political cartoons, see Burr, "Gender, Sexuality, and Nationalism." It is important to note that Christina Burr's discussion is largely focused on the nationalist views of political cartoonist and social reformer John Wilson Bengough, who used his "chalk" to "articulate his vision of nation in the context of anti-colonial struggles, conflicts about race and creed, and the emergence of French Canadian nationalism during the latter part of the century" (506). He often did this by using "Miss Canada" as a satirical representation to voice his political concerns. Lastly, Burr argues that Bengough's cartoons "contributed to the creation of an image of communion, or 'imagined community,' necessary to the building of a national identity" (515). On Miss Canada as "a patchwork image of ancient, imperial, and national symbols whose image reflected the ongoing tensions around gender, progress, and modern life," see Nicholas, "Gendering the Jubilee," 269. See also Nicholas, *Modern Girl*, esp. ch. 4. For a more general look at the construction of national identity, multiculturalism, and images in popular culture, see Mackey, *House of Difference*.

29 Burr, "Gender, Sexuality, and Nationalism," 506.

30 Ibid., 516.

31 For more on the connections between the concept of the North and settler colonialism, see Baldwin, Cameron, and Kobayashi, eds., *Rethinking the Great White North*. See also Grace, *Canada and the Idea of North*.

32 Banet-Weiser, *Most Beautiful Girl*, 7–8.

33 Nahoum-Grappe, "Beautiful Woman," 94. In a sense, the erotic gaze takes its theoretical cue from Karl Marx's conceptualization of commodity fetishism.

34 Banet-Weiser, *Most Beautiful Girl*, 24.

35 Peiss, *Hope in a Jar*, 4, passim; Burstyn, *Rites of Men*, 103, passim.

36 Peiss, *Hope in a Jar*, 99. For more on American beauty culture, see Blackwelder, *Styling Jim Crow*; and Conor, *Spectacular Modern Woman*.

37 Peiss, *Hope in a Jar*, 99, 130.

38 Burstyn, *Rites of Men*, 17.

39 Ibid.

40 Ibid., 142. Despite the fact that we all engage in beauty rituals, beauty queens and professional models are cultural exemplars due to their dedication and discipline in taking those rituals to the level of institutional spectacle.

41 Although my focus is on how beauty contest scholars *contest* beauty and bodies as representations of nation while seeming to forgo an analysis that interrogates nation

as a concept marked by colonial violence, the same rigour needs to be applied to how we use the terms "modernity" and "modern." Scholars who research fashion, beauty, modelling, beauty pageants, and advertising, which are often argued to be products of modernity, should turn their attention to theoretical research that has done this work, such as Dussel, "Eurocentrism and Modernity"; Quijano, "Coloniality and Modernity/Rationality"; Mignolo, *Darker Side of Western Modernity;* and Lugones, "Heterosexualism." Essentially, these scholars argue that modernity is invented as a temporal space marking the beginning of world history and rational thought but that its existence is possible because of a dialectical relationship with what Dussel calls its "non-European alterity" (65). In other words, modernity, coded as progressive and civilized, also heralds the logic of colonial genocide and elimination.

42 On the culture of personality, see Susman, *Culture as History*, xxii and esp. ch. 14. For more on the erotic gaze, see Matthews Grieco, "Body, Appearance, and Sexuality"; and Nahoum-Grappe, "Beautiful Woman."

43 Susman, *Culture as History*, xxvii. In the US context, consumerism has been defined as "the belief that goods give meaning to individuals and their roles in society." Cross, *An All-Consuming Century*, 1. Comparative work for Canada has yet to be written, but for important studies that explore consumer culture, see Owram, *Born at the Right Time*, esp. ch. 4; Parr, *Domestic Goods;* Dummitt, "Finding a Place for Father"; Belisle, *Retail Nation;* and Warsh and Malleck, eds., *Consuming Modernity.*

44 Susman, *Culture as History*, 280.

45 Cross, *All-Consuming Century*, 2. Cross's thesis on the role of consumer culture, class, and race hierarchies is problematic in that it ignores the political, legal, and social apparatuses that continued to promote and maintain these hierarchies, effectively nullifying the "liberatory" function of consumer culture. However, his point about the democratization or equalizing effects of mass consumerism is useful given that the capacity to purchase consumer goods – irrespective of an individual's economic status – is designed to create the illusion of equality.

46 On beauty culture with a focus on bodies, see Nicholas, "Beauty Advice"; and Nicholas, "Representing the Modern Man."

47 Throughout the 1970s and 1980s, the Miss Canada Pageant featured a segment known as the Miss Canada Fashion Revue, where the pageant contestants modelled the latest fashions created by up-and-coming fashion designers. These segments were usually choreographed and were considered the high point of the show.

48 "City Gives Miss Canada Check for $500, Suggests an Advisory Committee," *Daily Telegraph*, February 17, 1923, 14.

Chapter 1: Beauty Queens and (White) Settler Nationalism

1 See Vigarello, *Histoire de la beauté*. For more of his work, see Vigarello, *Le corps redressé;* and Vigarello, *Le propre et le sale*. See also Nahoum-Grappe, *Beauté, laideur;* Suleiman, ed., *Female Body;* Flandrin and Phan, "Les métamorphoses"; and Shorter, *History of Women's Bodies*. The only deviation from this interpretation is Marwick, *Beauty in History*. For a historiographical essay examining work on the body and sexuality in the eighteenth century, see Harvey, "Century of Sex?"

2 This argument is developed especially in Nicholas, *Modern Girl*, ch. 4.
3 Matthews Grieco, "Body, Appearance, and Sexuality," 46. The religious, political, and social upheavals of the Middle Ages generated much suspicion over the place of the body in people's spiritual salvation. Various religious reform movements created confusion and dogma regarding the body by suggesting that it – especially the female body – was Satan's vessel. Women, as the daughters of Eve, could not reach heaven because of their "wicked" bodies unless they remained virgins or reinvented themselves as such.
4 Ibid., 47.
5 Nahoum-Grappe, "Beautiful Woman," 88. For Nahoum-Grappe, "female identity manifested itself as beauty, and beauty in turn, by activating the tautological association of physical presence with sexual identity, pointed up the menace of femininity" (90).
6 Matthews Grieco, "Body, Appearance, and Sexuality," 55.
7 For more on a later interpretation of plumpness and class, see Walden, "Road to Fat City." For a discussion on the connection between thinness, ugliness, and poverty, especially its depiction in art and literature, see Eco, *Storia della bruttezza*.
8 Matthews Grieco, "Body, Appearance, and Sexuality," 56.
9 Ibid., 57. Matthews Grieco credits the Neoplatonist school of thought for this shift in beauty discourse, where the beauty of the soul was connected with the physical appearance of the person.
10 Ibid., 58.
11 Ibid., 61.
12 McClintock, *Imperial Leather*, 61.
13 Nahoum-Grappe, "Beautiful Woman," 94. Nahoum-Grappe also speaks of the "aesthetic mask" that men and women use as a component of communication (91).
14 *Toilettes* were social events where an aristocratic woman invited an audience into her home while she painted herself and engaged in various beauty practices in a "conscious construction of a seductive public personality." Matthews Grieco, "Body, Appearance, and Sexuality," 63.
15 Vigarello, *Histoire de la beauté*, 138.
16 Susman, *Culture as History*, 274.
17 Segalen and Chamarat, "La Rosière et la 'Miss,'" 44. All translations from this article are mine.
18 Ibid., 46. By the nineteenth century in England, the May Day festivities had disappeared – "a casualty of industrialization" – to be replaced by the Catholic symbolism of the Virgin Mary in the role of May Day queen. Banner, *American Beauty*, 250.
19 Segalen and Chamarat, "La Rosière et la 'Miss,'" 46.
20 Banner, *American Beauty*, 254.
21 For more on Barnum, see Barnum, *Colossal P.T. Barnum Reader*. See also Dennett, *Weird and Wonderful*.
22 For more on prostitutes, clothing, and social-sexual discourse, see Valverde, "Love of Finery"; and Bell, *Reading, Writing, and Rewriting*. For more on the

role of clothing in the lives of middle-class Victorian women, see Roberts, "Exquisite Slave."

23 Banner, *American Beauty*, 256.

24 Ibid., 257; Savage, *Beauty Queens*, 15.

25 Cited in Grout, *Force of Beauty*, 144.

26 Ibid.

27 Archives of Ontario (AO), Library Collection, PAMPH 1891, no. 61, *The Ladies' Guide to Health, Etiquette and Beauty and General Household Knowledge* (Windsor, ON: J.S. Labelle & Co.), 11. Other such manuals read by Canadians and geared toward a female audience include *Beauty Hints*, published by the Lydia E. Pinkham Medicine Company of Cobourg, Ontario, in 1920, and Grandma Nichols's *The Great Nineteenth Century Household Guide*, originally published in 1894 by J.L. Nichols Company Limited and reprinted by Coles Publishing Company in 1978. *Beauty Hints* was in essence an advertising pamphlet for Lydia E. Pinkham's Vegetable Compound, which was promoted as a "medical" aid for beauty. Beauty aids then – as now – were often couched in scientific discourse to heighten credibility. In this particular pamphlet, we encounter testimonials of women who have used the Vegetable Compound and had their beauty and health restored miraculously and instantaneously. "The ideal woman," according to the pamphlet, was "strong, healthy and beautiful in form and feature with a happy disposition" (12). *The Great Nineteenth Century Household Guide* was closer to a beauty manual in form, with entries on how to preserve the figure, beauty, cosmetics, cheerfulness, physical culture, taking life as it comes, complexion, and skin troubles (153–66). *The Household Guide* stated that although charm was difficult to describe, it was "beauty of expression ... that cannot exist where there are low, sordid feelings" (158).

28 AO, Library Collection, PAMPH 1891, no. 61, *The Ladies' Guide to Health, Etiquette and Beauty and General Household Knowledge* (Windsor, ON: J.S. Labelle & Co.), 11.

29 Grout, *Force of Beauty*, 28.

30 AO, Library Collection, PAMPH 1891, no. 61, *The Ladies' Guide to Health, Etiquette and Beauty and General Household Knowledge* (Windsor, ON: J.S. Labelle & Co.), 12.

31 Grout, *Force of Beauty*, 190.

32 A good example of the connection between the entertainment business and the cosmetic industry is the story of Max Factor, "the make-up artist to the stars." Peiss, *Hope in a Jar*, 154. With a cultural emphasis on celebrities and the mass production of magazines, beauty culturists were able to profit from the emergence of the new woman. For more on the legitimate display of women and their relationship with industry, see Peiss, *Hope in a Jar*, ch. 4; and Nicholas, *Modern Girl*, chs. 2 and 6.

33 For more on the links between female nudity, bathing suits, and beauty contests, see Latham, "Packaging Woman." Although the arguments in this article are not entirely developed, Latham successfully shows that it is not a coincidence

that the Miss America Pageant took place on the beach and that Margaret Gorman won the 1921 title in a "modern" bathing suit.

34 Material on body theory is extensive. For some examples, see Foucault, *Discipline and Punish;* Foucault, *History of Sexuality,* vol. 3, esp. part 4; Butler, *Bodies That Matter;* Baudrillard, "Finest Consumer Object"; Shilling, *Body and Social Theory;* Gallagher and Laquer, eds., *Making of the Modern Body;* Canning, "Body as Method?"; Gilman, *Making the Body Beautiful;* McNally, *Bodies of Meaning,* esp. ch. 5; Bordo, "Feminism"; Gatens, "Corporeal Representations"; Mohanram, *Black Body;* Bynum, "Why All the Fuss?"; and Nicholas, *Modern Girl.*

35 See Valverde, "Social Purity."

36 For more on the eugenics movement in Canada, see McLaren, *Our Own Master Race;* Dyck, *Facing Eugenics;* Malacrida, *Special Hell;* and Strange and Stephens, "Eugenics in Canada."

37 For only a sampling of examples, see Vertinsky, "Social Construction"; Todd, "Bernarr Macfadden"; Schwartz, *Never Satisfied;* Stearns, *Fat History;* and Macdonald, *Strong, Beautiful and Modern.* For Canadian examples, see Walden, "Road to Fat City"; and Nicholas, "'I Was a 555-Pound Freak.'"

38 I found this reference to the Miss Nippon contest in Shissler, "Beauty Is Nothing," 108. However, Shissler's information is based on Robertson, "Japan's First Cyborg?"

39 See Comacchio, *Nations Are Built of Babies.*

40 "Toronto Child Won Palm for Beauty," *Montreal Gazette,* January 4, 1923, 13. The winner, Doris Elizabeth Hyde of Toronto, was interviewed ten years after her victory. She was four at the time of her crowning. For a brief interview, see Library and Archives Canada (LAC), ISN 276212, "Galloway's Gallery Back in '22 and '23," hosted by Bill Galloway, audiovisual, November 7, 1980.

41 "Little Beauties Strut Their Stuff at Rotary Party," *Niagara Falls Evening Review,* April 20, 1949, 10.

42 LAC, ISN 175964, "CBC News Filmpack," narrated by Peter Jennings, audiovisual, September 3, 1962. For a discussion on "better babies" contests and agricultural fairs in early-twentieth-century America, see Stern, "Beauty Is Not Always Better"; and Roberts, *Pageants,* 119–22.

43 Savage, *Beauty Queens,* 33.

44 Creating a space for children to participate as spectators at pageants also ensured an intergenerational and future market for beauty queens.

45 For an example of this phenomenon, see Savage, *Beauty Queens.*

46 On colonialism as a structure, not an event, which explains the continuing violence of colonialism past the period of the imperial project, see Wolfe, *Settler Colonialism.*

47 Lugones, "Heterosexualism," 190. It is important to note that Lugones uses a slash between the words "colonial" and "modern" in the title of her article in order to emphasize that decolonial theorists see structures as two sides of the same coin.

48 Lugones's work is especially critical to this argument, but other such work includes Smith, "Queer Theory"; and Rifkin, "Erotics of Sovereignty."

49 For a fascinating discussion of the link between modernism and fashion shows in France and the United States, see Evans, *Mechanical Smile*. There is no shortage of scholarly material on the flapper, but for a Canadian perspective, see Nicholas, *Modern Girl*, esp. ch. 3. Finally, historiographical research on the modern girl exploded with the publication of Weinbaum et al., eds., *Modern Girl around the World*.

50 Alan Feuer, "Still Smiling for the Troops, However Solemn Their Mission," *New York Times*, August 28, 2005, A19.

51 Billig, *Banal Nationalism*, 45.

52 This is especially the case for the first decades of the Miss America Pageant. For more on some of the controversies plaguing the grandmother of the modern beauty contest, see Watson and Martin, "Miss America Pageant."

53 For more on the history of the Miss America Pageant, see Riverol, *Live from Atlantic City*.

54 Synnott, "Truth and Goodness – Part I," 608.

55 Synnott, "Truth and Goodness – Part II," 55.

56 For example, see Eco, *Storia della bruttezza*; and Bettella, *Ugly Woman*.

57 For more on the history of freak shows, see Bogdan, *Freak Show*; Thomson, ed., *Freakery*; Nicholas, "Debt to the Dead?"; and Nicholas, *Canadian Carnival Freaks*.

58 Braunberger, "Revolting Bodies," 3.

59 Klein, "Fat Beauty"; Rothblum, Solovay, and Wann, eds., *Fat Studies Reader*.

60 Dow, "Feminism," 134.

61 For an example of how people of colour politicized beauty, see Walker, "Black Is Profitable." For more on Black beauty contests, see Tice, *Queens of Academe*; Roberts, *Pageants*; and Craig, *Ain't I a Beauty Queen?* On lesbian bodies, see Cahn, "From the 'Muscle Moll.'"

62 Brownmiller, *Femininity*, 8.

63 For evidence of how African American women used skin-whitening products, see Peiss, *Hope in a Jar*. These products sold in the millions, and women were exposed to ads extolling their virtues even though their "benefits" were hotly contested by experts.

64 The Miss Canada Pageant used the title Miss Friendship, whereas the Miss America Pageant used the title Miss Congeniality. I use the Miss Friendship title to mean both unless otherwise specified.

65 The Miss Canada Pageant always announced the accounting firm that it had on site to calculate the results submitted by the judges. This served to legitimize the judging process. For several decades, this accounting firm was Clarkson Chartered Accountants.

66 Susman, *Culture as History*, 276.

67 Ibid.

68 Ibid., 274, emphasis in original.

69 Welter, "Cult of True Womanhood."

70 Cermer Mada, "Personal Beauty and Some of Its Canadian Characteristics," *Saturday Night*, March 17, 1888, 3.

71 Ibid.
72 Ibid.
73 Ibid.
74 Ibid.
75 Susman, *Culture as History,* 276, 278. Susman first articulated the nuances between the cult of character and the culture of personality, but other scholars have dealt with this conceptualization. For example, see Warren, "Shift from Character to Personality," which explores the ideas explicated by Susman as they relate to religious thought, psychoanalysis, and Christian realism. See also Nicholson, "Gordon Allport."
76 Susman, *Culture as History,* 277, emphasis in original.
77 Susman uses the modern motion picture as another indicator of the prominence of the culture of personality. With this development emerged a new profession: the movie star. Susman, *Culture as History,* 282–83.
78 Ibid., 280.
79 Tice, *Queens of Academe,* 25–26.
80 Ibid., 43.
81 A scholarly treatment of charm schools has yet to be written; however, for an exploration of army regulations on hairdos, clothing, and lady-like behaviour as a way to ensure that women in the military remained charming, see Davidson, "'Woman's Right to Charm and Beauty." See also my discussion of the physical culture courses offered to Miss Civil Service beauty contestants during the 1960s in Gentile, "Searching for 'Miss Civil Service.'"
82 LAC, ISN 116393, "On the Spot: School for Charm," hosted by Fred Davis, audiovisual, 1950. This show was in some ways an earlier version of programs available on television today, such as *Extreme Makeover* and *The Swan.*
83 Ibid.
84 These women, referred to as "the gentler sex," were described variously as "gentle and alluring" and as a "smooth, slick specimen that pleases our eyes." This segment of the show implied that women who were particularly successful in being charming and thus beautiful were veritable "sirens" capable of leading the innocent (i.e., men) into irrational behaviour.
85 LAC, ISN 116393, "On the Spot: School for Charm," hosted by Fred Davis, audiovisual, 1950.
86 Ibid.
87 Ibid.
88 Ibid.
89 For a discussion of Donald Trump's role in the Miss USA Pageant, see Perlmutter, "Miss America." Indeed, Trump makes no pretence about his investment in the Miss USA and Miss Universe Pageants. He understands the function of these institutions as money-making enterprises.
90 North York Centre Public Library, "Miss Dominion of Canada Beauty Pageant," souvenir program, July 1, 1968, 1. The quoted phrase is part of a short message written by Bruno describing the aim of the pageant.

91 The Miss Dominion of Canada Pageant affiliated itself with several international beauty pageants, but the Miss World, Miss Universe, and Miss International Pageants seem to be the contests that were regularly attended by its winner. Other international beauty pageants on Miss Dominion's roster included the Miss Globe, Queen of the Pacific (Australia), and Miss Teen Intercontinental Pageants. Needless to say, Miss Dominion's reign was exhausting.

92 Today, Canada is represented at the Miss Universe Pageant by the winner of the Toronto-based beauty contest Miss Canada International and/or by Miss Universe Canada. These beauty competitions are discussed in the Conclusion.

93 Fenton Griffing, *How to Be,* 73.

94 Alexander Ross, "Limelight: Next Chore for Our Courts: Judging Beauty Contests," *Maclean's,* December 14, 1964, 2.

95 Ibid.

96 Lavenda, "'It's Not a Beauty Pageant!'" 31. See also Lavenda, "Minnesota Queen Pageants."

97 Lavenda, "Minnesota Queen Pageants," 169.

98 Lavenda, "'It's Not a Beauty Pageant!'" 40.

99 For an interesting approach to the history of debutantes and their connection to beauty pageants in Texas, see Haynes, *Dressing Up Debutantes.* For the only treatment of debutantes in Canada, see Chenier, "Class."

100 Lavenda, "Minnesota Queen Pageants," 174.

101 Gordon Sinclair, "Beauty Contests Are the Bunk," *Maclean's,* October 15, 1949, 16. Sinclair was a controversial radio journalist. He was also host of *Let's Be Personal,* a daily broadcast on CFRB Toronto (1942–84) and a regular panel member of the CBC's weekly *Front Page Challenge* in the 1960s and 1970s. He is famous for a 1973 passionate defence of the United States titled "The Americans," which was entered into the US congressional record.

102 Ibid., 45–46.

103 Ibid., 46.

104 Ibid., 17.

105 Ibid., 16. Sinclair was aware that his condemnation of beauty contests was "tardy." Even so, twenty years was a long time to wait to "blow the whistle" if they were indeed so awful.

106 Ibid.

107 Ibid., 46.

108 There are many examples of these beauty queen manuals, but see especially Fenton Griffing, *How to Be a Beauty Pageant Winner;* and Burwell and Bowles, *Becoming a Beauty Queen.* Beauty pageant manuals had a dual purpose. First, they gave aspiring beauty contestants information on the multitude of contests available, complete with addresses and a list of criteria. Second, and most importantly, they contained virtually the same information as in earlier beauty manuals, with sections on how to walk, talk, sit, exercise, dress, apply makeup, and so on.

Chapter 2: Miss Canada and Gendering Whiteness

1　In his article on beauty contests and Italian national identity in the immediate post-1945 period, historian Stephen Gundle also argues that Italians were forging a new collective identity and used traditional feminine beauty to help create a "unified cultural matrix." Drawing heavily on American iconography, the Miss Italia contest was used to help quell the tensions between moderate and Catholic forces, on the one hand, and the left led by the Communists, on the other. Gundle, "Feminine Beauty," 359. For Canadian examples that illustrate the connections between the Canadian citizen, nation building, and commercialization, see Menzies, Adamoski, and Chunn, "Rethinking the Citizen"; and Purdy, "Scaffolding Citizenship." A classic treatment is Razack, *Race, Space, and the Law.*

2　There is no shortage of research on the conscription crisis during both world wars in Canada. One of the more interesting rifts that it caused is explored in Theobald, "Divided Once More." Lionel Groulx was a priest with political influence whose ardent criticism of Confederation was equalled only by his nationalist sentiment, laced with racism, for French Canadian sovereignty. See Bock, *Nation beyond Borders.*

3　The push toward independence as a colony culminated in the signing of the Balfour Declaration at the 1926 Imperial Conference. There is very little critique of this event in Canadian historiography, but one essay worth reading is Barnes, "Bringing Another Empire Alive?" This historical event figured prominently in solidifying Canada's status as a nation and dovetailed with O.D. Skelton's appointment as minister of external affairs by Prime Minister Mackenzie King in 1926. King's directive to Skelton included the expansion of Canada's role in global political and economic affairs. On Skelton, see Hillmer, *O.D. Skelton.*

4　On the history of treaties in Canada, see Miller, *Compact, Contract, Covenant,* esp. ch. 7.

5　There is no shortage of scholarly work on the new woman and modern girl. Scholars interested in these tropes of femininity and womanhood argue either that the new woman should be regarded as the "mother" of the modern girl or that these representations should be considered in a more fluid relationship. For a short but effective summary of this debate, see Weinbaum et al., *Modern Girl around the World,* ch. 1, and esp. 9 and 10.

6　For a discussion of the Miss Canada 1927 contest, won by Madeline Woodman, which was sponsored by Famous Players Lasky and held in theatres across western Canada, and for an analysis of the Miss Canada 1923 contest, won by Winnifred Blair, see Nicholas, "Catching the Public Eye," esp. ch. 3. From 1923 to 1946, businesses and event organizers used the Miss Canada title for various purposes, but these contests did not constitute nationally organized pageants such as the one held in 1923 and those held in 1946 and afterward. Although the Miss Canada 1927 title examined by Nicholas is notable, it did not have the same cross-country representation as the other Miss Canada titles.

7 "Miss Halifax Has Reached Montreal," *Montreal Gazette*, February 3, 1923, 4.

8 "Twenty-Six Girls Have Been Chosen," *Montreal Gazette*, January 18, 1923, 5. Other groups included Stanley Presbyterian Church, the City of Outremont, the Getogether Club, and the Strathcona Academy.

9 Cited in ibid. In their commentary on Fitzgerald's judging criteria, some in the media suggested that "the judges for this title will be governed largely by the ability of the entrants to act with poise, dignity and charm in whatever attitude or atmosphere she may be placed." "Miss Halifax Has Reached Montreal," *Montreal Gazette*, February 3, 1923, 4.

10 "Twenty-Six Girls Have Been Chosen," *Montreal Gazette*, January 18, 1923, 5.

11 The finalists for the Miss Canada title in 1923 were Leona McIntosh (Miss Edmonton), Pearl Miller (Miss Regina), Muriel Harper (Miss Winnipeg), Gabrielle Rivet (Miss Montreal), Gwendolen Shaw (Miss Sainte-Anne-de-Bellevue, a suburb of Montreal), Eileen Hawkins (Miss Sherbrooke), Anna Lois Walsh (Miss Quebec), Winnifred C.I. Blair (Miss Saint John), and Ora Doherty (Miss Halifax).

12 "Souvenir Journal for Miss Montreal," *Montreal Gazette*, January 9, 1923, 6.

13 "Supper and Dance for Miss Winnipeg," *Montreal Gazette*, February 1, 1923, 4.

14 "'Miss Quebec' Entertained," *Montreal Gazette*, February 2, 1923, 3. Anna L. Walsh, the only contestant chaperoned by her mother and sister, was the Miss Canada candidate representing the *Quebec Telegram*.

15 "Spirits of Amity with Fair Rivals," *Montreal Gazette*, February 5, 1923, 6.

16 Ibid. The original erroneously said, "Miss St. John," whereas Saint John, New Brunswick, was meant.

17 Ibid.

18 "Keys of City for Fair Contestants," *Montreal Gazette*, February 6, 1923, 5.

19 "Spirits of Amity with Fair Rivals," *Montreal Gazette*, February 5, 1923, 6.

20 "Are Noncommittal Regarding Judges," *Montreal Gazette*, February 7, 1923, 4.

21 "Judges Incognito until Saturday," *Montreal Gazette*, February 8, 1923, 8.

22 "What Qualities for 'Miss Canada'?" *Montreal Gazette*, February 9, 1923, 5.

23 "Five Judges to Pick 'Miss Canada,'" *Montreal Gazette*, February 10, 1923, 4. The judges were Donat Raymond, president of the Windsor Hotel and chairman of the Winter Sports Committee; J.F. Sayer, president of the Montreal Amateur Athletic Association; C.F. Notman, president of William Notman & Sons, photographers; George F. Driscoll, general manager of Trans-Canada Theatres Limited; and A.L. Caron, involved with the National Amateur Athletic Association and a member of the Winter Sports Committee.

24 Ibid.

25 Ibid.

26 "What Qualities for 'Miss Canada'?" *Montreal Gazette*, February 9, 1923, 5.

27 Ibid.

28 For a comprehensive look at the history of women and sport in Canada from the late nineteenth century to the 1990s, see Hall, *Girl and the Game*. Hall does not use the term "sports girl," nor does she refer to the Miss Canada 1923 contest. She does, however, make reference to "la belle neige," which she translates

as "the sports queen," when recounting the role that some women played in a marathon snowshoe race held in Montreal in the 1930s. She suggests that as the idea became more popular, and thanks to the media, sports queens were increasingly associated with men's sports clubs and associations (92).

29 Ibid., 90.

30 Lowe, *Looking Good*, 105. See also Hall, *Girl and the Game*, 88–93.

31 For example, the question of breeches became increasingly important in this era, further loosening Victorian clothing conventions. "City Gives Miss Canada Check for $500, Suggests an Advisory Committee," *Daily Telegraph*, February 17, 1923, 14.

32 Lowe, *Looking Good*, 104. Lowe argues that by the post–First World War period, the sexualized female body had already emerged thanks to the influence of working-class women and girls at the turn of the twentieth century. For a US example, see Peiss, *Cheap Amusements*, which discusses "charity girls" (110). For an Australian example, see Conor, "'Blackfella Missus.'"

33 "What Qualities for 'Miss Canada'?" *Montreal Gazette*, February 9, 1923, 5.

34 Ibid.

35 Ibid.

36 Hamlin, "Bathing Suits and Backlash," 30.

37 Ibid., 41.

38 Ibid., 44. Of course, by the time that the Depression hit in 1929, the pageant's continued cancellation may have been due to economic factors. For more on the Miss America Pageant in the 1920s, see Riverol, *Live from Atlantic City*.

39 I use the term "women reformers" to designate political and social perspectives taken by the women's movement at the turn of the twentieth century. In the case of beauty contests, it was not only women reformers who critiqued pageants but also socialist feminists. I refrain from using the term "first-wave feminism" since the wave theory of feminist history reinforces a periodization that focuses on the achievements and struggles of largely white, middle-class women. The history of feminist action in unions, women's immigrant groups, and the Black women's community tends to be ignored and silenced with the wave approach to writing about feminist history.

40 At its foundation, *The Woman Worker* was the mouthpiece of the Canadian Federation of Women's Labour Leagues and spoke to both class and gender oppression, a double-edged issue not always dealt with by the Communist Party of Canada. For the argument that *The Woman Worker* was "serious" about what was known as the "woman question" and should be regarded as "highly significant in the history of Canadian socialist-feminism," see Hobbs and Sangster, eds., *Woman Worker, 1926–1929*, 8. *The Woman Worker*'s last publication was in April 1929, with the death of its leader and editor, Florence Custance. For more on this important chapter in women's history, see Sangster, *Dreams of Equality*, esp. ch. 2. For a general introduction to material on women and reform in Canada, see Kealey, ed., *Not Unreasonable Claim*.

41 By the turn of the century, women's suffrage was taking hold as a major international issue. Canada could not ignore the tides of change. With strong lobby-

ing in Britain and the United States, Canada was hard-pressed to continue to categorize women as non-citizens. For more on the Canadian suffrage movement, see Prentice et al., *Canadian Women;* and for a classic, see Cleverdon, *Woman Suffrage Movement in Canada.* For new insight on the suffrage movement, among other issues, see Valverde, *Age of Light, Soap, and Water.*

42 Political organizing started some time before the First World War. The Woman's Christian Temperance Union was intensifying its political activities and endorsed women's suffrage as early as 1891. The Toronto-based Canadian Women's Suffrage Association was also a major proponent of extending the franchise for women, starting as early as the 1880s. It was in 1883 that the National Council of Women of Canada, established by Lady Aberdeen, became the umbrella group representing these women's organizations. However, it was only with Prime Minister Robert Borden's decision to grant the vote to women in 1917 under the Wartime Elections Act that some Canadian women were able to vote in the federal election. In 1918 the passing of the Women's Franchise Act gave all Canadian women the right to the vote if they satisfied the qualifications for citizenship.

43 Hobbes and Sangster, eds., *Woman Worker, 1926–1929,* 7.

44 "Beauty Contests," *The Woman Worker,* September 1926, 5, cited in Hobbs and Sangster, eds., *Woman Worker, 1926–1929,* 111.

45 Hobbs and Sangster, eds., *Woman Worker, 1926–1929,* 111.

46 Ibid.

47 My analysis conflicts with an argument put forward by historians Margaret Hobbs and Joan Sangster, who suggest that "communist women were fearful that preoccupation with personal beauty could be a frivolous distraction for working-class women from serious issues like the class struggle, and their opposition to beauty pageants can be read in this light" (ibid., 103). The evidence clearly shows that the editorial staff at *The Woman Worker* did not see the engagement with beauty rituals as "frivolous" and were more worried about the exploitation of women's bodies for profit. Hobbs and Sangster do argue, however, that the same materialist argument used against the exploitation of working-class women's bodies in the sex trade greased the protest machine against beauty contests (103).

48 "Toronto Local Council of Women Protest against Beauty Contests," *The Woman Worker,* February 1927, 6, in ibid., 118.

49 Archives of Ontario (AO), Attorney General Central Registry Criminal and Civil Cases, RG 4-32, "A.L. Smythe, National Council of Women, Query on Legislation to Stop Beauty Contests," Letter to William Herbert Price from Agnes Lind Smythe, February 26, 1927.

50 AO, Attorney General Central Registry Criminal and Civil Cases, RG 4-32, "Letter from Mr. Bayly to Mrs. R.G. Smythe," March 5, 1927. For more on Section 208, see Government of Canada, *Criminal Code,* part 5, ch. 36, s. 208. The individuals guilty of this offence could expect as punishment imprisonment for one year, with or without hard labour, or a $500 fine. On this form of entertainment in the early twentieth century, see Ross, *Burlesque West,* which otherwise deals with the burlesque scene after the Second World War.

51 AO, Attorney General Central Registry Criminal and Civil Cases, RG 4-32, "Letter from Mr. Bayly to Mrs. R.G. Smythe," March 5, 1927.

52 AO, Attorney General Central Registry Criminal and Civil Cases, RG 4-32. "Memorandum from Mr. Bayly, Deputy Attorney General, to Mr. Price, Attorney General," March 9, 1927.

53 Ibid.

54 AO, Attorney General Central Registry Criminal and Civil Cases, RG 4-32, "Letter to Mrs. Smythe from Mr. Price," authored by Edward Bayly, March 9, 1927.

55 AO, Provincial Council of Women fonds, F 798-1-1, MU 2342, Minute Books, Provincial Council of Women, subheading "Toronto Resolution," June 3, 1927, 114.

56 This section provided brief vignettes of every province's actions on moral issues, including abortion, illegitimate births, the feeble-minded, prostitution, age of consent, and suitable housing for "girls." For more, see AO, Provincial Council of Women fonds, F 798-1-1, MU 2342, Minute Books, Provincial Council of Women, *Proceedings of the Thirty-Fourth Annual Meeting of the National Council of Women of Canada Held in Stratford, Ontario, October 4–7, 1927*, unpaginated.

57 Ibid.

58 AO, Provincial Council of Women fonds, F 798-1-1, MU 2342, Minute Books, Provincial Council of Women, subheading "June 7, 1928 10 am meeting – re Beauty Contests," June 7, 1928, 153.

59 Historical scholarship on the regulation of female sexuality and agency abounds, but for some Canadian examples, see Dubinsky, *Improper Advances;* Lévesque, *Making and Breaking the Rules;* and Strange, *Toronto's Girl Problem.* For a US example, see Peiss, *Cheap Amusements.*

60 The term "civilized morality" belongs to Sigmund Freud, but D'Emilio and Freedman, *Intimate Matters,* esp. 172–73, borrow it to describe attitudes toward sexuality in late-nineteenth-century America. Like Peiss, *Cheap Amusements,* they argue that in the 1920s women were creating new ways to interact with each other and with men, thus shaking the foundations of "civilized morality."

61 For more on the Border Cities Local Council of Women's resolutions and petitions, see AO, Provincial Council of Women fonds, F 798-1-1, MU 2342, Minute Books, Provincial Council of Women, subheading "Resolution from Border Cities Local Council," September 14, 1935, 62; AO, Provincial Council of Women fonds, F 728-2-2, Annual Meeting File 1933–1935, subheading "Resolutions Passed by the Ontario Provincial Council of Women in Session at the Semi-Annual Meeting Held in St. Catharines, Ont., for Presentation to the Ontario Provincial Government," May 16–17, 1935; and AO, Provincial Council of Women fonds, F 798-1-1, MU 2342, Minute Books, Provincial Council of Women, subheading "November 21, 1935 – Annual Meeting," 8.

62 Miss Canada 1927, Madeline Woodman, also participated in the Miss World Pageant held in Galveston, Texas, which was also organized by Famous Players. Nicholas, "Catching the Public Eye," 150.

63 See also Gentile, "Blair, Winnifred C."
64 "Miss St. John Won Miss Canada Title," *Montreal Gazette*, February 12, 1923, 4. The announcement came at 12:40 a.m. at a ball attended by a large crowd. This article estimated the number of people attending the ball at between 400 and 500. A front-page article in the *Saint John Daily Telegraph*, however, claims the number was closer to 1,000. "St. John Girl Chosen Miss Canada at Montreal Carnival," *Daily Telegraph*, February 12, 1923, 1.
65 "Miss St. John Won Miss Canada Title," *Montreal Gazette*, February 12, 1923, 4.
66 Cited in "City Gives Miss Canada Check for $500, Suggests an Advisory Committee," *Daily Telegraph*, February 17, 1923, 14.
67 Ibid.
68 Ibid.
69 As Miss Imperial, Blair had entered a contest held by the *St. John Times-Star* for the selection of the Carnival Queen and the crowning of Miss Saint John, thus becoming the representative of the Imperial Theatre, owned by Walter H. Golding. As part of the latter's efforts to promote his theatre, he asked Blair to participate in the contest, which she did reluctantly.
70 "City Gives Miss Canada Check for $500, Suggests an Advisory Committee," *Daily Telegraph*, February 17, 1923, 14.
71 Ibid. For more on Blair's life after her reign, see Goss, "Fairest Girl."
72 "Miss Canada Left for Maritime Home," *Montreal Gazette*, February 12, 1923, 6.
73 "Miss Winnifred C.I. Blair Now Hailed from Atlantic to Pacific as Miss Canada," *Daily Telegraph*, February 12, 1923, 1.
74 "Thousands Throng Station to Greet Successful Candidate," *Daily Telegraph*, February 13, 1923, 10.
75 "Carnival Spirit Has Seized the Citizens of Staid Saint John," *Daily Telegraph*, February 13, 1923, 1; "Thousands Throng Station to Greet Successful Candidate," *Daily Telegraph*, February 13, 1923, 10; "Miss Winnifred C.I. Blair Now Hailed from Atlantic to Pacific as Miss Canada," *Daily Telegraph*, February 12, 1923, 2.
76 "Miss Canada a Life Member of Club," *Daily Telegraph*, February 19, 1923, 4.
77 "St. John to the Front," *Daily Telegraph*, February 12, 1923, 6.
78 "Miss Canada Is Unspoiled by the Homage of Her Court," *Daily Telegraph*, February 23, 1923, 4 (reprint of *Toronto Star* article).
79 Ibid.
80 Ibid.
81 Filey, *I Remember Sunnyside*, 94. According to Filey, a total of 475 applicants were interested in competing for the title. Jean Tomie, winner of Miss Toronto 1926, was the first Miss Toronto crowned at Sunnyside. She was accepted as a contestant in the Miss America Pageant but was excluded from the finals because of her citizenship. She did, however, win the Miss Congeniality title (95). See Nicholas, "Catching the Public Eye," ch. 3, for a detailed discussion of Miss Toronto 1926, especially the connection between public morality, swimsuits, beauty contests, and the motivations of the Sunnyside organizers.

82 Library and Archives Canada (LAC), ISN 196206, "Take 30: Hard Times," hosted by Ed Reid, audiovisual, May 26, 1975.

83 For more on women's experience of the Depression, see Srigley, *Breadwinning Daughters.*

84 For the suggestion that this healthy body culture had an "empire-wide character," see Macdonald, *Strong, Beautiful and Modern,* 12.

85 Ibid., 18.

86 Ibid., 152. .

87 The page-two story about Pauline Francoeur's (Miss Quebec) and Pauline Mignault's (Miss Montreal) multiple convictions for vagrancy, being found in a "disorderly house," and being a "flaneur de nuit" was accompanied by a photo of the two women in gowns and sashes shaking hands and by photos of their police booking shots. The article created a sensation and was covered in newspapers across the country as well as in New York City. To make matters worse, the contests for these titles were organized by the League of Public Welfare (La Ligue du Bien Public), a social hygiene organization established as a result of a "clean-up" campaign against night clubs and other venues in Quebec cities. See "Deux filles publique iront-elles représenter la province de Québec à un concours national de Beauté," *Le Devoir,* July 5, 1947, 2. Francoeur and Mignault sued the newspaper for libel and defamation. See "Beauty Winners Suing Le Devoir for $30,000," *Montreal Gazette,* July 26, 1947, 1.

88 From the outset, the Miss Canada pageant was steeped in controversy. The dispute centred on the copyright for the Miss Canada title itself. According to an article in the *Hamilton Spectator,* Toronto photographer C.C. Milne challenged the Hamilton Centennial Committee's right to organize its beauty contest under that title. After consultation with lawyers on both sides, the Hamilton Centennial Committee decided to proceed, while insisting that it was not breaking any copyright laws since its contest was called the "Centennial beauty contest to choose Miss Canada." For more on this legal battle, see "Stage Contest Despite Threat," *Hamilton Spectator,* June 22, 1946, 7.

89 "Victory Thrill to Miss Canada," *Hamilton Spectator,* July 6, 1946, 7.

90 "Ontario Beauty Crowned Queen," *Hamilton Spectator,* July 5, 1946, 5.

91 Ibid.

92 Marilyn Reddick, "My, uh, Dazzling Career as Miss Canada," *Maclean's,* September 15, 1954, 19.

93 Under Slaughter's directorship (1935–67), the Miss America Pageant underwent drastic and lasting changes. She spearheaded the introduction of the scholarship program in the early 1940s as well as the talent segment of the pageant. She was the director responsible for instituting rules designed to ensure the moral fortitude of the contestants, including age restrictions, no smoking and drinking, and curfews. In addition, she instituted Rule 7, which stipulated that "contestants must be of good health and of the white race" (Tice, *Queens of Academe,* 31). She also convinced members of Atlantic City's social elite to volunteer as chaperones, thereby increasing the pageant's social and cultural legitimacy. For more on Slaughter, see Banet-Weiser, *Most Beautiful Girl,* ch. 1.

94 Ellen Fairclough served as the chair of the Hamilton Trust and Savings Corporation until 1972, when Dr. Murray H. Robertson replaced her. In her institutional history of Ellen Fairclough's career and life, historian Margaret Conrad briefly mentions Fairclough's participation in the corporation, suggesting that these were the "happiest years of her business career." Conrad, "'Not a Feminist, But ...,'" 22.

95 James McHardy, "Something New Has Been Added to Beauty Contest Criteria," *Saturday Night,* September 27, 1947, 31.

96 Banet-Weiser, *Most Beautiful Girl,* 74. For more on bathing suits and beauty contests, see Latham, "Packaging Woman"; and Hamlin, "Bathing Suits and Backlash."

97 Latham, "Packaging Woman," 80.

98 Marilyn Reddick, "My, uh, Dazzling Career as Miss Canada," *Maclean's,* September 15, 1954, 18.

99 Ibid., 19. Miss Canada 1952's father was a singer for a novelty quartet, the Commodores. During her reign, Reddick's father acted as her manager. She received between $50 and $100 for her public appearances during her twelve-month contract.

100 Ibid., 106. Reddick recounts that when she arrived four hours late to entertain Canadian troops stationed in Hanover, Germany, one soldier had gotten so drunk while waiting for her that "he kept coming up to me and crying and saying I reminded him of his wife."

101 Ibid.

102 These problems have mostly been financial. See Vancouver Public Library (VPL), Special Collections, Beauty Contests: Clippings file, "Promotional Flop Robs B.C.'s Miss Canada of Her Awards," *Vancouver Sun,* c. 1949.

103 VPL, Special Collections, Beauty Contests: Clippings file, Kathy Archibald, "Here's How It Felt to Be Miss Canada," *B.C. Magazine,* December 4, 1954, 10–11, 20.

104 Ibid., 10.

105 "That 'Miss Canada' Contest," editorial, *Kingston Whig-Standard,* July 23, 1953, 4.

106 LAC, ISN 323613, "Archibald, Kathy and Evelyn Webster – Interview," interview by Bob Lewis and Arthur Harnett, CJON Radio, audio recording, October 8, 1953, transcribed by author.

107 Ibid.

108 For a deeper understanding of the intersections between white supremacy and the political and legal systems, see Backhouse, *Colour-Coded.*

109 LAC, ISN 224294, "CBC Newsmagazine," audiovisual, July 15, 1956.

110 Ibid.

111 Adams, *Trouble with Normal,* 42.

112 LAC, ISN 224294, "CBC Newsmagazine," audiovisual, July 15, 1956.

113 Moreau was twenty-six years old when she won the title and was the first bilingual Miss Canada.

114 Queen's University, Stauffer Library, Special Collections, "Miss Canada Pageant 'Melody of Beauty,'" souvenir program, 1957, unpaginated.

115 Ibid.
116 Ibid.
117 Ibid.
118 See especially Pickles, *Female Imperialism,* ch. 7.
119 Queen's University, Stauffer Library, Special Collections, "Miss Canada Pageant 'Melody of Beauty,'" souvenir program, 1957, unpaginated.
120 Ibid. In the souvenir program, the brief biography of W.J. Deadman, the new president of the Miss Canada Pageant, described the Hamilton Homemakers Club as the "backbone" of the pageant. No word sketch or highlights of its contributions were featured in the souvenir program.
121 Ibid.

Chapter 3: Labour of Beauty

1 Library and Archives Canada (LAC), ISN 218605, "Tabloid," hosted by Dick MacDougall, audiovisual, October 9, 1956. *Tabloid* was a public affairs CBC program hosted by Dick MacDougall, Percy Saltzman, Norman Kihl, and Barbara Franklin and produced by Ross McLean. Mary Ann Lenchuk was also Miss Tea Bag '56. It is entirely possible that Lenchuk was one of the "professional" beauty queens mentioned by Gordon Sinclair, as discussed in Chapter 1. Gordon Sinclair, "Beauty Contests Are the Bunk," *Maclean's,* October 15, 1949, 45–46.
2 LAC, ISN 218605, "Tabloid," hosted by Dick MacDougall, audiovisual, October 9, 1956.
3 Lake, "Female Desires," 432. In her article on the construction of femininity in postwar Australia, Marilyn Lake argues that the emphasis on sexual allure in advertising reflected a modern discourse of femininity born in the 1930s. See also Reichert, *Erotic History of Advertising.* For Canadian examples, see Belisle, "Sexual Spectacles"; Cook, *Sex, Lies, and Cigarettes,* esp. ch. 5; and Warsh and Marquis, "Gender, Spirits, and Beer."
4 Cobble, "'Spontaneous Loss of Enthusiasm,'" 28. Cobble mentions an ad campaign in which a flight attendant says, "Hi, I'm Linda, and I'm going to FLY you like you've never been flown before." For more on the history of flight attendants, see Nielsen, *From Sky Girl.*
5 Sugiman, *Labour's Dilemma;* Sangster, *Earning Respect;* Strong-Boag, "Canada's Wage-Earning Wives"; Parr, *Gender of Breadwinners;* Forestell, "Necessity of Sacrifice"; Davis and Lorenzkowski, "Platform for Gender Tension."
6 Cited in Bruce, *Back the Attack!* 58.
7 Bruce, *Back the Attack!* 116.
8 Smith and Wakewich, "'Beauty and the Helldivers.'" Can Car was a Montreal company established in 1909. The owners reopened the Thunder Bay plant in 1937 to manufacture aircraft for wartime use. It quickly became an important munitions factory. Smith and Wakewich's study includes a history of Can Car's workplace culture and its impact on notions of community, family, and nation.

See also Smith and Wakewich, "Trans/Forming the Citizen Body." For more on postwar US containment culture, nation, and the family, see May, *Homeward Bound*.

9   Smith and Wakewich, "'Beauty and the Helldivers,'" 81–82.

10 On pin-ups and "girlie pictures," see Meyerowitz, "Women."

11 Klausen, "Plywood Girls," 199.

12 Ibid., 208. Klausen suggests that although the female-dominated labour force at Alberni Plywoods created an opportunity to eliminate gender-specific work, the absence of a feminist consciousness meant that this chance was lost (211).

13 The brief details of the contest are taken from *Harmac News*, cited in ibid., 223.

14 Pierson, *"They're Still Women."* Following in Pierson's footsteps, Van Vugt, "Beauty on the Job," expands on the relationship between beauty, femininity, and women during the Second World War. This work includes a section on Miss War Worker.

15 Pierson, *"They're Still Women,"* 142. For more on wartime propaganda, femininity, and advertising, see also Bland, "Henrietta the Homemaker." Military historian Jeff Keshen takes issue with feminist interpretations positing that wartime propaganda "trivialized" women's work. Keshen argues that these campaigns could also be "interpreted as reassuring a woman that she need not sacrifice her sexual appeal by taking on physically demanding, typically male jobs." Keshen, *Saints, Sinners, and Soldiers*, 151, also chs. 6 and 7.

16 The phrase "beauty as duty" is taken from Kirkham, "Fashioning the Feminine," 166.

17 John Inglis, a metalworker and patternmaker, and his partner, Daniel Hunter, founded the company Inglis & Hunter in the early 1860s. After the departure of Hunter in 1887, Inglis renamed his company John Inglis & Sons, which was reincorporated as the John Inglis Company Limited in 1913. For more on Inglis, see Sobel and Meurer, *Working at Inglis*.

18 City of Toronto, Metro Archives, SC 297, Inglis Company fonds, subseries A, General Correspondence, 1941–44, box 14 (196602), file: "Beauty Contest," Memorandum: A.L. Ainsworth to B.A. Trestrail, A.L. Scott, F.J. Baldwin, and G.A. McLeod, July 2, 1943.

19 Ibid.

20 Ibid.

21 "Beauty Contest Held at Inglis Girls' Club: Labour-Management Committees Sponsor and Direct Gigantic Affair," *The Shotgun*, August 7, 1943, 1.

22 The judges included Controller F. Hamilton; Commander A.W. Baker, RCNVR; Coup Captain J.S. Scott, MC, AFC, RCAF; Colonel J.W.H.G.H. Van den Berg, DSO, Commanding 32nd (Res.); Mary Moon, editorial staff, *Globe and Mail*; Mary-Etta MacPherson, editor, *Chatelaine Magazine*; and Glenda Farrell and Dean Norton, Toronto theatre actors (ibid.). The Commercial Division of the company contributed the prizes for the competition. The winner received a bond worth $100, and the runners-up got $50 bonds (ibid., 6).

23 Ibid., 1.

24 It is not clear from the archival material how Pattison could win via nomination given the presence of judges and the selection of finalists. For a picture of June Pattison being crowned by Archer Lee Ainsworth, see Sobel and Meurer, *Working at Inglis*, 75. In an interview conducted by Sobel and Meurer, Pattison said that after winning the pageant, she was told to wear makeup to work every day (75).

25 Pierrick Labbé's research on munitions manufacturing in Quebec and Ontario offers one of the few scholarly treatments on women's work in Quebec-based munitions plants. However, although he discusses women and munitions work, he does not include information about recreational activities such as beauty contests or other beauty culture programs. Labbé, "L'Arsenal canadien," ch. 6.

26 Archives of Ontario (AO), Robert Hamilton Papers, [General Engineering of Canada], F 2082-1-1-18, box 4, file: "History of Scarboro 1941–45," 2.

27 Brand, "'We weren't allowed,'" 182. See also Jones, *Labor of Love*, ch. 7; and Mullenbach, *Double Victory*, ch. 1.

28 Payne, *Official Picture*, 91.

29 AO, Robert Hamilton Papers, [General Engineering of Canada], F 2082, box 3, file: "Employee Magazine," "Attention All Ye Maidens Fair Fame and Fortune Ye May Share," *The Fusilier*, June 20, 1943, 2.

30 AO, Robert Hamilton Papers, [General Engineering of Canada], F 2082, box 3, file: "Employee Magazine," "K. Russell, Finalist in Beauty Contest: Scarboro Group Makes Fine Showing – Much Favourable Comment," *The Fusilier*, August 1, 1942, 1.

31 Boyer, "'Miss Remington,'" 203. Boyer points to the existence of a Miss Remington in 1910 (208).

32 Ibid., 203.

33 "Miss Civil Service Meets Miss Canada," *RA News*, September 1954, 20.

34 *RA News* was the official organ of the Recreation Association of the Public Service of Canada and catered to the employees of the Canadian federal government.

35 Tom Coughlin, "Editorial," *RA News*, May 1965, 2.

36 See *RA News*, January 1966, 16.

37 Dave Burton, "RA Queens Past and Present Got Together," *RA News*, August 1966, 10.

38 "A Million Dazzling Tulips Kick Off Tourist Season," *Ottawa Citizen*, May 18, 1963, 5, photograph. The *Ottawa Journal*, May 18, 1963, 18, had a picture of the RA Queen 1963 flanked by Alberta premier Ernest Manning and the national leader of the Social Credit Party, Robert Thompson.

39 Alan Phillips, "The Government Girl," *Maclean's*, January 15, 1953, 25.

40 "Do You Know Miss Civil Service?" *RA News*, February 1952, 2.

41 LAC, Indian Affairs and Northern Development fonds, RG 22, vol. 614, file 853-3, "Miss Resources Beauty Contest," Memo from W.J. Bottomley to Mr. A.C.L. Adams, February 25, 1953.

42 LAC, Indian Affairs and Northern Development fonds, RG 22, vol. 614, file 853-3, "Miss Resources Beauty Contest," Memo from Len Law to T.R. Reid, President, Resources Recreation Club, January 20, 1954.

43 LAC, Indian Affairs and Northern Development fonds, RG 22, vol. 614, file 853-3, "Miss Resources Beauty Contest," Irene Baird to Miss Pelletier, February 14, 1955. In 1953 the judges for this department preliminary included an executive of the T. Eaton Company and a producer at the National Film Board. LAC, Indian Affairs and Northern Development fonds, RG 22, vol. 614, file 853-3, "Miss Resources Beauty Contest," Department of Resources and Development, March 13, 1953.

44 See Phyllis Bright, "DPW Selects Queen for 1962," *Dispatch,* Spring 1962, 7–8. Peter Jennings went on to become the anchor of ABC's *World News Tonight.* Angelo Mosca became a wrestler following his football career. The third judge for the 1962 competition was Joyce Unsworth, a local businesswoman who owned two beauty salons. The following year, the judges for Miss Public Works included the owner of an Ottawa finishing school and officials of two radio shows, CFRA and CBOT. For more, see "Miss Public Works Selected for 1963," *Dispatch,* Spring 1963, 8. *Dispatch* was the federal Department of Public Works internal newspaper.

45 "Inside Information," *RA News,* May 1961, 8.

46 LAC, Department of External Affairs fonds, RG 25, vol. 8253, file 9241-H-40, part 1.1, "RA Queen of the Year Contest," c. 1959. These procedures and rules continued into the 1960s, except that married women, originally barred from the contest, were able to compete by 1961.

47 Ibid.

48 "This Time She Really Is!" *Indian News,* July 1965, 1. Morris also participated in the Miss Micmac beauty contest when she was fourteen as the delegate from the Eskasoni First Nation. Morris is mentioned in McCallum, *Indigenous Women,* 113.

49 Alexander, *Guiding Modern Girls,* 9.

50 "This Time She Really Is!" *Indian News,* July 1965, 2.

51 Ibid., 1, 2.

52 According to Betty Shelton, the head of the Miss Civil Service Committee, "we barred married women from the contests three years ago. But there was such a whoop and holler – about half the girls in the service are married – that we had to reinstate them." Cited in "Tomorrow Miss Civil Service Will Open the National Tulip Festival," *Ottawa Journal,* May 17, 1962, 3. For the article announcing Gitten's victory, see "D.O.T. Belle Is RA Queen," *RA News,* June 1962, 1.

53 Suzanne Perry, interview with author, Ottawa, June 20, 1996.

54 Pat McMullen, "The Zublinsky Report," *RA News,* May 1952, 10. "The Zublinsky Report" was an article written for male readers that offered advice on how to find a girlfriend. It gave advice on what "persons" a man should pursue depending on the "type of girl" he wanted to date. See also Gentile, "'Government Girls, Ottawa Men.'"

55 Fran Jones, "Fashion Note," *RA News,* June 1959, 12. Jones did not mention names but did make comments such as "only one wore a dress that was out of keeping with the idea," making it easy to identify the transgressor.

56 Ibid.
57 "RA ASKS ... What Constitutes Charm?" *RA News,* September 1957, 16.
58 Ibid.
59 "G' Girls ... You Can Become Miss Secretary of 1960," *RA News,* May 1960, 13.
60 Ibid.
61 Ibid. The employer of the national finals winner also received a Statesman typewriter.
62 Ibid.
63 Ibid.
64 Ibid.
65 Boyer, "'Neither Forget nor Remember,'" 221.
66 Ibid.
67 "Notre 'Bal des Midinettes,'" *Justice,* May 1, 1938, 1.
68 "Le 'Bal des Midinettes,'" *Justice,* July 1, 1938, 1, 2.
69 "Et voilà la journée terminée/En cachette, elle s'est vite repoudrée/Croe! Il peut, elle traverse un ruisseau/Permettez-moi, mam'selle, que j'vous préserve de l'eau?/Tout d'abord, indignée, elle rougit!/Elle se r'tourne, il est bien, elle sourit./Oh! comme elle est heureuse quand on la trouve jolie,/La petite ouvrière ici." "Nos Midinettes," *Justice,* June 1938. Unless otherwise noted, translations are my own.
70 A documentary of the Carnaval's beauty contest was filmed by Robert Favreau. See Favreau, dir., *Le soleil a pas d'chance.* For a history of the Carnaval de Québec, see Bisson, "L'esprit du Carnaval." Bisson writes that the beauty contest began in 1955 and ended in 1996 because it was losing popularity as a tourist attraction for the winter festival. See also Bisson, "La 'Revengeance' des duchesses."
71 Pesotta, *Bread upon the Waters,* 253. For more on Rose Pesotta's role in the ILGWU and her personal life, see Leeder, *Gentle General;* and for a brief account of Pesotta's role in the Montreal organizing drive in 1937, see Gagnon, "Rose Pesotta."
72 For an account of the rise and fall of Catholic unions in Quebec from the 1930s to 1980s, see Palmer, *Working-Class Experience,* 257–64.
73 Cited in Leeder, *Gentle General,* 83. This statement was part of a letter that Pesotta wrote to Dubinsky voicing her concerns about the union's direction. For more on sexism and the role of women in the ILGWU, see Schofield, "Uprising of the 20,000."
74 The union's newspaper, *Justice,* did not publish many articles on the Mlle Étiquette Syndicale, but it did publish a picture of the winner for 1964. See *Justice,* September 1964, 5. The union label campaign was promoted by having *jolie midinettes* hand out pamphlets on Montreal streets while wearing short dresses.
75 "Une midinette, c'est une petite ouvrière très laborieuse c'est vrai, mais c'est aussi un rayon de soleil dans l'atelier, la manufacture, la rue, le foyer." "Ici l'on chante," *Justice,* October 1949, 4.
76 Ibid.

77 Demczuk, "Léa Roback," 229. Interestingly, an article in *Justice* announcing that Léa Roback was stepping down as education director failed to mention the internal strife in the ILGWU and her role in it. It cited "health problems" as the reason for her abrupt departure. See the announcement in *Justice*, April 8, 1939, 2. Grace B. Wales replaced Roback as education director.

78 Léa Roback, "Le Coin de la Femme," *Justice*, September 1, 1937, 7.

79 "Si vos pieds ne sont pas à l'aise dans vos chaussures, l'apparence de votre visage s'en ressentira. Les pieds mal chaussés, c'est à-dire chaussés de chaussures soit trop larges ou trop étroites sont la plupart du temps la cause de rides prématurés." "Votre beauté Madame," *Justice*, October 1, 1937, 3.

80 For more on advice to reduce cellulite in thighs, see an article that appeared on the woman's page entitled "Pour l'amincissement des hanches," *Justice*, February 1, 1938, 3.

81 "Nos cours d'études," *Justice*, November 1, 1937, 4.

82 "Bonne nouvelles aux midinettes," *Justice*, October 1950, 3.

83 Yvette Charpentier, "Notre cours nouveau de culture générale," *Justice*, October 1957, 1.

84 For more on how immigrant women experience the "double day," see Gannagé, *Double Day, Double Bind*, esp. 55–62. Gannagé's book takes a sociological approach to the issue of working-class women's experience in the garment industry and the union.

85 On issues concerning child care responsibilities, see ibid., 56–65; and for more on the effects of language barriers on women's access to union meetings and leadership, see ibid., 180–85.

86 Ibid., 177.

87 "Toutefois, il ne faudrait pas que le 25 novembre soit associé uniquement à cette vieille tradition de France qui veut que le 25 novembre de chaque année les demoiselles célibataires au-dessus de 25 ans coiffent le bonnet de la bonne Ste. Catherine. D'ailleurs, cette fête patronale a été associée aux midinettes parce qu'il était presque reconnu que les jeunes filles de cette industrie dans tout le monde, ne se mariaient qu'en très petit nombre. Aujourd'hui, cette situation n'existe plus comme tel, et c'est bien tant mieux ... Pour nous tous de l'industrie de la couture, la Ste. Catherine c'est la fête d'une patronne que la tradition nous a désignée. En fêtant cette patronne, c'est nous tous que nous devons fêter. C'est notre travail; notre métier de couturière. Nous la célébrons avec fierté, et quelle fierté. Parce qu'elle existe vraiment cette fierté de notre travail." Yvette Charpentier, "Editorial," *Justice*, November 1961, 2.

88 See the picture of two fully costumed cast members in "Deux charmantes Catherinettes," *Justice*, December 15, 1943, 1. See also "Le local 112 célèbre la Sainte Catherine," *Justice*, December 1946, 3.

89 "Bal des Midinettes," *Justice*, November 1946, 1.

90 "La Bal des Midinettes est donc plus qu'une simple danse avec d'autres attractions, c'est une démonstration praticable des accomplissements de notre Union et attire l'attention des ouvriers, et la ville en général bénéficie des biens dérivés de leur Union internationale des ouvriers du vêtement pour dames ...

C'est avec cette idée que nous nous rassemblons, pour oublier le travail fatiguant et monotone, en nous redressant le dos et nous levant la tête, comme des êtres humaines libres et indépendantes réalisant pleinement la joie de vivre, que nous nous rassemblons pour une soirée magnifique de camaraderie en commun." "Grande parade de modes pour le Bal des Midinettes," *Justice*, October 1947, 1.

91 For more, see Heron and Penfold, "Craftsmen's Spectacle."

92 "La compétition étant trop forte – et pour sauver les juges de l'embarras du choix, il a été décidé par les autorités compétentes qu'il n'y aurait pas de concours de beauté – au grand regret de nos membres masculins." "L'ILGWU dans le cortège de la fête de Travail," *Justice*, September 1, 1938, 1–2.

93 "Syndicat en roulotte," *Justice*, November 1964, 5. The article includes a picture of Reine des Midinettes 1964 and her attendants waving to a large crowd of people while sitting in a horse-drawn carriage.

94 While researching my doctoral dissertation, completed in 2006, I did not come across Michael Denning's short analysis of the popular Broadway show *Pins and Needles* in his 1997 book *The Cultural Front: The Laboring of American Culture in the Twentieth Century*. The comedy revue was performed by ILGWU workers at the beginning of the Second World War. I cannot find a connection between this revue and the NFB documentary, but the reversal of words in the title of the Canadian documentary – that is, *Needles and Pins* instead of *Pins and Needles* – should be noted here. Joan Sangster has also written on Queen of the Dressmakers. See Sangster, "'Queen of the Picket Line'"; and Sangster, *Transforming Labour*, ch. 3.

95 "Comme à Hollywood, voici une caméra, un metteur en scène, des cameramen, des techniciens et une jolie fille. Le personnel et l'équipement sont ceux de l'Office National du Film. La jolie fille, vous l'avez reconnue, c'est Marielle Sicotte, ancienne reine des midinettes de Montréal, qui est en vedette d'un documentaire que vient de tourner l'Office National du Film sur les midinettes de la métropole canadienne." "Silence on tourne," *Justice*, September 1954, 1.

96 "Midinette," *Justice*, January 1955, 3.

97 "Le film en question montre comment grâce à son union, Marielle finit par avoir plus d'assurance et plus de confiance en elle-même, comment elle apprend à danser, à s'exprimer en public, à chanter, à comprendre les grandes lignes de la vie économique et des relations patronales-ouvrières. Ces nouveaux horizons qui s'ouvrent pour Marielle dissipent en elle la méfiance et la timidité, pour faire place à la confiance, à la grâce, à la beauté et aux connaissances les plus diverses." "La vie d'une Midinette de notre union portée a l'écran," *Justice*, January 1955, 2.

98 "Premier concours national," *Justice*, November 1962, 6. See also the picture of two Toronto garment workers who participated in national beauty contests accompanying the article.

99 Ibid. Of the seventeen women who competed in Toronto, two candidates were selected to represent their city, Gosette Blockine (Local 199) and Maria Kuchling (Local 72).

100 "très jolie jeune fille, un peu timide, qui porte sa couronne en forme de dés à coudre avec juste un bien de suffisance. Liliane 1ière est vraiment heureuse de son titre et toute la joie d'avoir été choisie par ses compagnes de travail pour être candidate et peut-être représentante des 20, 000 membres de l'UIOUD atteint son sommet lors du grand banquet le 24 novembre, alors que rougissante, ses jolis yeux étincelant de larmes, elle remercie ses nouveaux sujets d'une voix émue." "Sa Majesté Liliane 1ière, jeune et jolie est issue d'une famille syndicale," *Justice*, December 1962, 8.

101 Ibid.

102 For more on weddings as cultural institutions and industry, see Ingraham, *White Weddings*.

103 "Reine d'un foyer," *Justice*, September 1954, 3.

104 "Notre jolie reine épouse un membre de l'union," *Justice*, November 1965, 3.

105 "Les compagnes Marielle Moore et Lise Blanchet ont bien voulu accueillir notre photographie qui vous offre, plus bas, les deux mignons qui, trop jeunes encore, ne réalisent pas qu'ils ont dans les veines du sang royal." "La Royauté à la Maternite," *Justice*, September 1962, 13.

106 Cited in Bantey, *Les Midinettes/The Midinettes*, 105.

107 For Canadian examples, see Morton, *Ideal Surroundings*; and Marks, *Revivals and Roller Rinks*.

Chapter 4: Contesting Indigenous, Immigrant, and Black Bodies

1 According to the footage I viewed, there were several of these clubs all over North America. See Library and Archives Canada (LAC), ISN 216455, "Canadian Cameo Spotlight #2," narrated by Lamont Tilden, audiovisual, June 1950. On Miss Goodwill, see LAC, ISN 176430, "CBC News Filmpack," narrated by Frank Stallery, May 2, 1963.

2 No comprehensive history of gay beauty contests has been written. I am currently researching beauty contests organized by the leather and drag communities in Toronto, Ottawa, and Montreal. In her history of Cherry Grove, anthropologist Esther Newton mentions Miss Fire Island, a pageant organized by the gay community. Newton, *Cherry Grove*, 135. For more on gay male pageants, see Johnson, *Beauty and Power*, which explores transgender pageants in the South Philippines.

3 Davis, "Our Crowns, Our Glory."

4 Coleman, *White Civility*, 40.

5 Thobani, *Exalted Subjects*, 144, 146.

6 King, "In the Clearing," 24, focuses on the postplantation Black female body as unruly and excessive space and thus disruptive of settlement; however, I include Indigenous women's bodies as posing similar anxious feelings for settlers by their continued existence.

7 Anderson, *Imagined Communities*, 37.

8 I refer to the Royal Commission on the Status of Women and the October Crisis in Chapter 5, but for more information on the Indigenous rights

movement, see Miller, *Skyscrapers Hide the Heavens;* Manuel and Derrickson, *Unsettling Canada;* Simpson and Ladner, *This Is an Honour Song,* which discusses the Oka Crisis; and Crosby and Monaghan, *Policing Indigenous Movements.*

9 King, "In the Clearing," 157.

10 Officials of the Indian Princess Pageant also referred to it as the Princess Canada Pageant or the Canadian Indian Princess Pageant.

11 Craig, *Ain't I a Beauty Queen?* 6.

12 Ibid., 5.

13 For an examination of the "Black is beautiful" movement, see ibid., ch. 2, but it is also useful to refer to Walker, "Black Is Profitable."

14 Craig, *Ain't I a Beauty Queen?* 24. For a Canadian example of these practices, see Mire, "Skin-Bleaching."

15 Francis, *Creative Subversions,* 135. For more on the play, see Chapter 5.

16 Ibid., 133.

17 Craig, *Ain't I a Beauty Queen?* 31.

18 On femininity, domesticity, and character, see Llewellyn, "Teaching June Cleaver."

19 Kinloch, "Rhetoric of Black Bodies," 99.

20 Rowe, "'Glorifying the Jamaican Girl,'" 37.

21 Ibid.

22 The term "coloniality of power" was coined by Quijano, "Coloniality and Modernity/Rationality," 171–72. It is a theory that forges the interconnection between the material, epistemological, and historical legacy of European colonialism and imperialism, insisting that the racial hierarchies created in the historical past are present in modified forms in the historical present. The best treatment of gender and the coloniality of power is Lugones, "Heterosexualism." For a more theoretical assessment of coloniality, see Alcoff, "Mignolo's Epistemology of Coloniality."

23 The scholarship critiquing the politics of recognition as a worthy pursuit is growing. For some of best work in this field, see Simpson, *Mohawk Interruptus;* and Coulthard, *Red Skin, White Masks.*

24 See Berton, *1967: Canada's Turning Point.*

25 Fiske, "Pocahontas's Granddaughters," 671.

26 LAC, Centennial Commission fonds, RG 69, vol. 177, file 4-1-59, emphasis in original.

27 LAC, Centennial Commission fonds, RG 69, vol. 185, file 4-3-6, internal memo from Robbins Elliot to John Fisher, August 6, 1963.

28 Ibid.

29 LAC, Centennial Commission fonds, RG 69, vol. 185, file 4-3-6, vol. 1, letter from Don Toppin to J.F.D. Sampon, Vice-President, Junior Chamber of Commerce, June 22, 1964.

30 John Fisher was appointed the centennial commissioner by Secretary of State Judy LaMarsh in 1963. By 1967 he had become synonymous with the nickname "Mr. Canada" as a tribute to his love for Canada. An ardent nationalist and

federalist, Fisher was labelled Mr. Canada from his days as the CBC's "roving reporter" and due to his work beginning in 1943 with the radio show *John Fisher Reports*. In 1961 he became a special assistant to Prime Minister John Diefenbaker. According to freelance journalist Charles Enman, Fisher's "nationalism was born during the Depression," another moment in the formation of Canada's invented community. Charles Enman, "'Mr. Canada' Loved His Country," obituary, *Ottawa Citizen*, December 15, 1999, A6.

31 LAC, Centennial Commission fonds, RG 69, vol. 177, file 4-1-59, vol. 1, report for Peter Aykroyd from John R. Markey re "'Miss Dominion of Canada,' i.e. Miss Universe, and 'Miss Canada,' i.e. Miss America, Beauty Pageants," June 14, 1965.

32 Ibid.

33 LAC, Centennial Commission fonds, RG 69, vol. 177, file 4-1-59. The reference to preparing a feasibility report was sent to Aykroyd by one of Fisher's assistants on a handwritten memorandum dated October 25, 1965, and attached to the Markey public relations report on a "Miss Centennial Contest."

34 LAC, Centennial Commission fonds, RG 69, vol. 177, file 4-1-59, "Miss Centennial Contest" document prepared by Peter Aykroyd for management committee, September 23, 1965.

35 Historian Robin Fisher has written extensively on Indigenous history, and his study of Europeans' ideas of the "Indian" shows that they tended "to believe the worst about [them]." Most of the historical writing was saturated with racial generalizations and argued that the eventual demise of Indigenous peoples was based on their inferiority. Fisher, "Image of the Indian," 78. See also Steele, "Reduced to Images." For useful contemporary accounts of these issues, see Bird, "Gendered Construction"; and Anderson and Carmen, *Seeing Red*, ch. 10.

36 Scholarly work on the use of racialized images in popular culture abounds, but some excellent examples include Valaskakis and Burgess, *Indian Princesses and Cowgirls*; Lears, *Fables of Abundance*; as well as those dealing with Black images, such as Manring, *Slave in a Box*; and Jewell, *From Mammy to Miss America*.

37 On Miss Spokane, see Morrissey, "Miss Spokane." For a brief mention of the Folkestone male beauty contest, see Morgan, "'Wigwam to Westminster.'"

38 Carter, *Capturing Women*, 160.

39 Valaskakis and Burgess, *Indian Princesses and Cowgirls*, 65. See also LeCompte, *Cowgirls of the Rodeo*.

40 Valaskakis and Burgess, *Indian Princesses and Cowgirls*, 69. According to Valaskakis and Burgess, there is some evidence that the first emergence of the cowgirl in dime novels – specifically in a novel titled *A Hard Crowd, or Gentleman Sam Sister*, written by Philip S. Warne in 1878 – can be considered the "prototype for the stereotypical butch lesbian" (65).

41 Tony Fitzgerald, "Miss Indian World from Canada," *Hamilton Spectator*, May 6, 2002, C12.

42 For my purposes here, I rely on what other scholars have written on the Pocahontas myth to help explicate the connections between the racialized

version of womanhood so central to the legend of Pocahontas and its impact on our understanding of the Indian Princess Pageant. For more on the topic, see Green, "Pocahontas Perplex."

43 Fiske, "Pocahontas's Granddaughters," 671. The term "intolerable metaphor" belongs to Green, "Pocahontas Perplex," 714.

44 Fiske, "Pocahontas's Granddaughters," 672.

45 Green, "Pocahontas Perplex."

46 Francis, *Imaginary Indian,* 121–22. Carter, *Capturing Women,* makes reference to the use of the term "squaw man" in the 1880s to refer to a man of the lowest social class (184).

47 Carter, "Categories and Terrains," 178; Carter, *Capturing Women.*

48 Pauline Johnson's life and works have been the topic of several histories and interpretations. For an analysis of Johnson as an example of a "plastic shaman," see Francis, *Imaginary Indian,* 109. For a closer reading of Johnson's "hybridity," see Strong-Boag and Gerson, *Paddling Her Own Canoe;* Strong-Boag, "'Red Girl's Reasoning'"; and Anderson and Robertson, *Seeing Red,* esp. ch. 5. A more recent biography of Johnson is Gray, *Flint and Feather.*

49 Anderson and Robertson, *Seeing Red,* 104.

50 Francis, *Imaginary Indian,* 120–21.

51 Anderson and Robertson, *Seeing Red,* 111.

52 Morgan, "'Wigwam to Westminster,'" 323.

53 Ibid., 331. The idea of cultural authenticity and Indigenous beauty contests is also explored in Schackt, "Mayahood through Beauty," whose discussion of beauty contests in Guatemala shows that clothing and tradition were central to the invention of "Indianness" in the Rab'in Ajaw (literally "Indian princess" or "king's daughter") contest during the late 1960s. McAllister, *Beauty Queens,* makes a similar argument.

54 Schackt, "Mayahood through Beauty," 273.

55 On images of "Natives" in frontier society, see Deloria, *Playing Indian;* Francis, *Creative Subversions;* Bridger, *Buffalo Bill;* Francis, *Imaginary Indian;* Wall, "Totem Poles"; and Burbick, "Romance."

56 LAC, Centennial Commission fonds, RG 69, vol. 430, file 4-23-2-22, memorandum from Robbins Elliot, Director of Planning, Centennial Commission, to Stan Zybala re National Indian Council–Annual Indian Princess Canada Pageant, July 23, 1965. The National Indian Council was founded in 1961 largely through the efforts of prairie Indigenous leaders. According to historian J.R. Miller's account of "Indian-white" relations in *Skyscrapers Hide the Heavens,* the council's highpoint was its activities with the Indian Pavilion at Expo 67, which attracted "international attention" (232).

57 LAC, Centennial Commission fonds, RG 69, vol. 430, file 4-23-2-22, letter from Jean Cuthand Goodwill to John Fisher, July 18, 1965. This correspondence was on letterhead of the Indian and Metis Friendship Centre.

58 LAC, ISN 190667, "Miss Totem Selected," Universal Pictures, 1957. This video clip of the Miss Totem contest shows a brief glimpse of its particulars. The footage I viewed was black and white and silent. It began with about ten women

dressed in white dresses and white sashes walking past a panel of judges. The video also showed a contestant speaking to the audience while the other contestants waited their turn. As part of the ceremony, two Indigenous men were filmed in full costume while holding eagle feathers and drumming. The last clip showed the winner of the contest on a turning stage while holding a trophy and wearing a traditional white A-line dress. Instead of a tiara, her "crown" was a headdress. I do not believe this contest is the same as the one mentioned in a chapter on beauty culture in McCallum, *Indigenous Women*, which refers to "the Miss Totem Princess Beauty Contest, run at the All-Indian Buckskin Gloves Boxing Tournament in Vancouver" (110).

59 Kozol, "Miss Indian America," shows how the staging of the pictures that featured the beauty queens suggested that the gaze of these subjects created a visual knowledge about citizenship and difference, emphasizing how identities and experiences of marginalization and citizenship are relational and mutable.

60 *Indian News*, April 1966, 4. See the picture at the bottom of the page with the caption "Algonquin Beauties." The picture also includes Shirley Whiteduck, who was the presiding princess of the Maniwaki Winter Carnival.

61 I believe that the Centennial Commission funded these queen pageants since there seems to be little evidence that this title existed prior to or after Canada's centennial. However, archival research in this area is needed. For examples of two Indigenous centennial queens, see "Centennial Queen Chosen," *Indian News*, April 1967, 3; and "Northern Beauty Earns Southern Holiday," *Indian News*, December 1967, 4.

62 On the eroticization of male bodies in rodeos and for some examples of Indian princesses, see Burbick, "Romance," 126; and Kelm, "Manly Contests." For a more general treatment of settler colonialism and masculinity, see Erickson, *Westward Bound*. Some work has been undertaken on the topic of rodeo queens, such as Laegreid, "Rodeo Queens"; Laegreid, *Riding Pretty*; and Rutledge Shields and Coughlin, "Performing Rodeo Queen Culture." For a preliminary history of Indigenous women, beauty practices, and Canadian sport, see Hall, "Toward a History."

63 On beauty contests and the Calgary Stampede, see Hamblin, "Queen of the Stampede"; and Jourdrey, "Expectations of a Queen." Recent scholarly treatments on Canadian rodeos are Kelm, *Wilder West;* and Clapperton, "Naturalizing Race Relations."

64 Archives of Ontario (AO), Department of Travel and Publicity fonds, RG 5-7, box 32, series A-4, file 5.16, "Department of Tourism and Information 1967–1969."

65 Anderson and Robertson, *Seeing Red*, 199.

66 "Charm, Grace, and Beauty to Greet Expo Visitors," *Indian News*, April 1967, 6. See also "Hostesses Arrive for Expo," *Indian News*, February 1967, 3; and a picture of Philomène Desterres modelling the hostess uniform in *Indian News*, April 1967, 6. On decisions related to the clothing and styles worn by the Indian Pavilion hostesses, see Kirkman, "Fashioning Identity."

67 In her forthcoming article about her mother's "celebrity" as a model and beauty queen, Kahente Horn-Miller writes that the correct spelling of her mother's name is not the commonly used "Kahn-Tineta" but rather "kahntinetha." See Horn-Miller, "My Mom, the 'Military Mohawk Princess.'" I am grateful to Kahente for sending me an advance copy of her paper.

68 The Oka Crisis is one of Canada's most important historical events but is rarely included as part of the national narrative and/or taught in schools. For two important documentaries, see Obomsawin, dir., *Kanehsatake;* and Welsh, dir., *Keepers of the Fire.* See also Alfred, *Heeding the Voices;* and St. Amand, *Stories of Oka.*

69 Kicksee, "'Scaled Down to Size,'" 199. Here, Kicksee discusses the public image of the "Indian" and the centennial celebrations. See also Rutherdale and Miller, "'It's Our Country.'"

70 Horn-Miller, "My Mom, the 'Military Mohawk Princess,'" 7.

71 Kicksee, "'Scaled Down to Size,'" 199.

72 For such arguments, especially in regard to the way that Indigenous and Black women used hair trends and styles as well as the cosmetics industry to respond to larger discourses about beauty as white, see McCallum, *Indigenous Women;* and Gill, *Beauty Shop Politics.*

73 Ahmed, *Promise of Happiness,* 66.

74 Ibid., 49.

75 Ibid., 60–61, 65, 59.

76 Ibid., 65.

77 Cited in Kicksee, "'Scaled Down to Size,'" 200.

78 Both the Wikwemikong and Sioux Pow-Wows were events that received funding from the Centennial Commission. As "invented traditions," these events have been described as "entertainment spectacle put on for Euro-American tourists" and "an important commercial venture" for the inhabitants of these reserves. Kicksee, "'Scaled Down to Size,'" 181, 183.

79 LAC, Centennial Commission fonds, RG 69, vol. 430, file 4-23-2-22, "Final Report – 1965."

80 As part of the National Indian Princess Pageant in Yellowknife during the Centennial Year celebrations, contestants had to demonstrate "historical knowledge" by celebrating moccasins, bows, baby carriers, and headbands, as well as the ability to survive in a harsh environment. Watson, "Reification of Ethnicity," 457.

81 Ibid.

82 For an analysis of the role of Corbiere (by 1971 also known as Lavell) in what would become a major court challenge in 1973, see Anderson and Robertson, *Seeing Red,* 206–7.

83 For example, in 1966 the New Brunswick delegate for the Indian Princess Pageant competed as part of a three-day event that included 3,000 people comprising Cree and Mohawk from Quebec, Sioux from Saskatchewan, and Mik'maq from Nova Scotia and New Brunswick. See "Maliseet Beauty Becomes Indian Princess of New Brunswick," *Indian News,* December 1966, 4.

84 The Miss Grey Cup contest was inaugurated in 1951 as part of the Grey Cup Festival, which included a parade, a ball, and the pageant. Each contestant represented a franchise of the Canadian Football League. The festival itself was a promotional ploy born in 1948 and was described in one of the Grey Cup official souvenir programs as a "football Mardi Gras." The Miss Grey Cup contest lasted for almost forty years and enjoyed the same status as the Miss Canada Pageant as a national institution. For more on the history of the Miss Saskatchewan Roughrider beauty contest, see Jozic and Staniec, "No Ordinary Life."

85 AO, Department of Travel and Publicity fonds, RG 5-7, box 32, series A-4, file 5.16, "Department of Tourism and Information 1967–1969"; Indian Princess Canada, National Indian Princess Canada Pageant Committee Meeting, January 6–7, 1968, Winnipeg, Manitoba.

86 For the photograph, see "Princess Meets the Minister," *Indian News,* October 1968, 3. The White Paper proposed the abolishment of the Indian Act and erected policies that would make Indigenous peoples "equal" to all Canadians. Opposition and resistance to the 1969 White Paper by Indigenous leaders across Canada led to its failure. For more on the 1969 White Paper, see Turner, *This Is Not a Peace Pipe,* esp. ch. 1.

87 LAC, Centennial Commission fonds, RG 69, vol. 430, file 4-23-2-22, "Final Report – 1966." For more on First Nations and centennial celebrations in British Columbia, see Dawson, *Selling British Columbia,* 211–16.

88 LAC, Centennial Commission fonds, RG 69, vol. 430, file 4-23-2-22, "Final Report –1966."

89 LAC, Centennial Commission fonds, RG 69, vol. 430, file 4-23-2-22, "Report to Centennial Commission for 1967."

90 The full list of regulations can be found in AO, Department of Travel and Publicity fonds, RG 5-7, box 32, series A-4, file 5.16, "Department of Tourism and Information 1967–1969."

91 "Indian Princess Pageant Committee Achieves Objectives," *Indian News,* April 1968, 5.

92 Ibid.

93 Simpson, *As We Have Always Done,* 102.

94 Ibid., 104.

95 For footage of Miss Estonia, see LAC, ISN 175833, "CBC News Filmpack," narrated by Jim Chorley, audiovisual, 1962. Miss Estonia 1962, Ann Pahatil, a secretary working for Hydro Ontario, was crowned by the previous year's winner, Ann Talvik. I found footage of Miss Chinatown 1957, but this contest continued into the 1960s, 1970s, and 1980s. The souvenir programs for the Miss Vancouver Pageant consistently show pictures of the Miss Chinatown entrants sponsored by Vancouver's Chinese Chamber of Commerce. For more, see LAC, ISN 224345, "Newsmagazine," hosted by Patrick Keatley and William Stevenson, audiovisual, 23 February 1958; and Vancouver Public Library, Special Collections, souvenir programs. For another Canadian example of an ethnic beauty pageant, see Fielding, "Changing Face of Little Italy."

96 Wu, "'Loveliest Daughter!'" 5. Wu's article is one of the best treatments of ethnic beauty pageants in the San Francisco area.
97 Ibid., 6.
98 Lieu, "Remembering 'the Nation,'" 129.
99 Ibid., 135.
100 The literature on this topic is not extensive, but it is quite solid. See Wu, "'Loveliest Daughter!'"; Lieu, "Remembering 'the Nation'"; Barnes, "Face of the Nation"; Stern, "Ceremonies of 'Civil Judaism'"; Clowes, "'Are You Going to Be?'"; and Gray, "Which among Our Polish Women?"
101 LAC, Maltese Canadian Society of Toronto fonds, MG 28, vol. 11, part 7, file: "1968 – Miss Malta Beauty Contest." This information was taken from the official pageant program.
102 LAC, Maltese Canadian Society of Toronto fonds, MG 28, vol. 11, part 7, file: "1968 Miss Malta of Toronto Contest Rules and Entry Form." There are eleven items that also deal with the winner's obligations to the organization during her reign, as well as with her care and responsibility for the society trophy, crown, coronet, and sceptre.
103 Stern, "Ceremonies of 'Civil Judaism,'" 107.
104 Ibid., 105.
105 George Bonavia, a Maltese immigrant who arrived in Canada in 1948, has written a history of the Maltese Canadian community in Canada. Commissioned by the Department of Multiculturalism, the study was based on research that Bonavia conducted as an immigration officer and on his experiences as a journalist and broadcaster with the Canadian Broadcasting Corporation. Much of the information I use to help contextualize Miss Malta of Toronto is taken from Bonavia, *Maltese in Canada*. Crawford, "Maltese Diaspora," is dedicated to the official and unofficial reasons for Maltese emigration but does not include a cultural analysis of the Maltese community in Canada.
106 See Bonavia, *Maltese in Canada*, 6; and Government of Ontario, "Maltese."
107 LAC, Maltese Canadian Society of Toronto fonds, MG 28, vol. 11, part 7, file: "Maltese Immigrants of Canada – Press Clippings 1948–1972."
108 Canada's immigration policy of the 1920s featured racist restrictions on immigrants from eastern and southern European countries similar to those in the later part of the nineteenth century under Minister of the Interior Clifford Sifton. The Maltese were among the immigrant groups specifically targeted by these restrictions, along with the Chinese and Italians. This policy meant that immigrants from Malta were scant between 1923 and 1948. See Crawford, "Maltese Diaspora," 26. For a general overview of Canada's post-Confederation immigration policy, see Whitaker, *Canadian Immigration Policy*.
109 Bonavia, *Maltese in Canada*, 13–14. There is much research to be conducted on the experiences of Maltese immigrants upon arrival. Most were promised jobs in their respective fields only to find that they were offered work in factories or as labourers. As a result, some Maltese asked to be sent back to Malta. In fact, from what I can surmise, most of the history of the Maltese Canadian

community is a story of "failed immigration," and high percentages of people returned to their homeland.

110 Ibid., 40.

111 Ibid., passim.

112 "Maltese-Canadian Society of Toronto," MaltaMigration.com, http://www. maltamigration.com/settlement/associations/ca/mcst1.shtml. See also Cumbo and Portelli, "Brief History of Early Maltese."

113 LAC, Maltese Canadian Society of Toronto fonds, MG 28, vol. 11, part 7, file: "1968 – Miss Malta Beauty Contest." Some of the names included Toronto mayor William Dennison, federal minister of transport Paul T. Hellyer, and Senator Paul Martin, leader of government in the Senate.

114 Ibid. This list of professions and the companies or schools that the contestants of 1969 attended or worked at was part of the information that contestants added to their entry forms.

115 Black beauty pageants were organized in different provinces. In the 1970s Black community centres and associations in British Columbia, Alberta, and Manitoba sponsored and organized these contests. In 1975 the *Edmonton Journal* reported that Manitoba had held a Miss Ebony contest as early as 1973 and that the Miss Black British Columbia contest, organized by the BC Association for the Advancement of Coloured People, was getting ready to celebrate its second year in existence. See Jim Bentein, "Black Like Being Invisible," *Edmonton Journal,* May 7, 1975, 29. The article featured an interview with Patricia Thomas, one of the founding members of the Cultural Association for Black People and of the Miss Black Alberta contest. Thomas explained that although a costly affair, the pageant was aimed at fighting against the treatment of Black people as invisible. The Miss Black Alberta contest received money from provincial and federal programs. For more on this contest, see "They're Out to Prove Black Is Beautiful," *Edmonton Journal,* July 8, 1975, 28.

116 "Beauty and Talent Show: First Black Ontario Pageant Brings Out the Best in Our Girls," *Spear,* July 1976, 12.

117 Ibid., 14–15.

118 Gill, *Beauty Shop Politics,* esp. ch. 3.

119 Ibid., 35.

120 King, "In the Clearing," 142.

121 Notable scholars who have written extensively about the slave trade in the Canadian context include Winks, *Blacks in Canada;* and Cooper, *Hanging of Angélique.*

122 King, "In the Clearing," 156.

123 There is no shortage of scholarship on racial uplift. For an excellent introduction, see Gaines, *Uplifting the Race.*

124 Tice, *Queens of Academe,* 13.

125 Ibid., 15.

126 Ibid., 46.

127 "'The Isle of Spice' Will Be the Host of Miss Black Ontario 77," *Spear,* June 1977, 23.

128 Included in Rebick, *Ten Thousand Roses,* 132.
129 Claudio Lewis, "Jamaican Beauty Crowned Miss Caribana '75," *Contrast,* August 8, 1975, 16.
130 Claudio Lewis, "Modeling Career Is Not Easy Says Miss Caribana," *Contrast,* August 22, 1975, 9.
131 Claudio Lewis, "Jamaican Beauty Crowned Miss Caribana '75," *Contrast,* August 8, 1975, 16.
132 Claudio Lewis, "Modeling Career Is Not Easy Says Miss Caribana," *Contrast,* August 22, 1975, 9.
133 For a thorough examination of the Abortion Caravan, see Palmer, "Choices and Compromises"; and on thalidomide in Canada, see Chisholm, "Curious Case of Thalidomide."
134 Claudio Lewis, "Modeling Career Is Not Easy Says Miss Caribana '75," *Contrast,* August 22, 1975, 9; Claudio Lewis, "Job Discrimination against Black Models," *Contrast,* September 5, 1975, 1, 3.
135 Claudio Lewis, "Job Discrimination against Black Models," *Contrast,* September 5, 1975, 3.
136 Ibid., 1.

Chapter 5: Miss Canada, Commercialization, and Settler Anxiety

1 Vancouver Public Library (VPL), Science Reference Compact. "Miss Canada 1972 Pageant," souvenir program. This so-called legend is probably a combination of several myths from Ancient Egypt, Greece, and India. However, the pearl has been associated with Aphrodite, brides, and purity.
2 VPL, Science Reference Compact, "Miss Canada 1980 Pageant," souvenir program.
3 Queen's University, Stauffer Library, Special Collections, "Miss Canada Pageant 1959," souvenir program. The pageant was postdated after 1957 so that the pageant took place in the year prior to the winner's reign.
4 Queen's University, Stauffer Library, Special Collections, "Miss Canada Pageant 1959," souvenir program. For more on this theme, see Queen's University, Stauffer Library, Special Collections, "Miss Canada Pageant 1961," souvenir program.
5 Queen's University, Stauffer Library, Special Collections, "Miss Canada Pageant 1959," souvenir program.
6 Library and Archives Canada (LAC), ISN 175225, "CBC News Filmpack," narrated by Frank Herbert, audiovisual, August 12, 1961. This newscast announced both Feller's victory and the bomb scare incident.
7 VPL, Special Collections, Beauty Contests: Clippings file, "Miss Canada Dethroned," *Vancouver Sun,* September 23, 1961.
8 Reference to "religious prejudice" can be found in Joyce Fairbairn, "Pageant under Fire: Connie Gail Was Ready to Quit," *Ottawa Journal,* September 25, 1961, 1. This article also includes a complete copy of Feller's press release explaining her side of the story. The *Ottawa Citizen* reported that a public

consultant company hired by the Weavers to assist with the pageant claimed that the Weavers "complained that Connie's observance of Jewish holidays forced cancellation of commitments." "Victoria Girl Replaces Ottawa Beauty Queen," *Ottawa Citizen*, September 25, 1961, 1.

9 Indications that S. Radcliffe Weaver, the pageant organizer, was delinquent in paying his bills are discussed in "Controversy Nothing New to Pageant's S.R. Weaver," *Ottawa Citizen*, September 25, 1961, 3. For other articles that covered Feller's dethronement, see Paul M. Duna, "Connie-Gail Dethroned as Miss Canada," *Ottawa Citizen*, September 25, 1961, 3; "Officials Were Justified in Decision – 1961 Queen," *Ottawa Citizen*, September 25, 1961, 3; "Connie Gail and Other Winner May Go on TV," *Ottawa Citizen*, September 27, 1961, 7; and Joyce Fairbairn, "Miss Canada 1959: Lauds Courage of Connie Gail," *Ottawa Journal*, September 25, 1961, 3.

10 LAC, ISN 175743, "CBC News Filmpack," narrated by Earl Cameron, audiovisual, April 13, 1962.

11 For more on the history of television, see Rutherford, *When Television Was Young*; Peers, *Public Eye*; and Nolan, *CTV: The Network*.

12 LAC, June Dennis fonds, MG 31, D191, vol. 1, "Courier," c. 1967, 1.

13 June Dennis was one of the few female radio personalities in Canada in the 1950s. She had various careers, including as a novelist (*A Mike for Marion*, 1962, and *TV Career Girl*, 1964), a publicist, and a personal manager for two reigning Miss Canadas.

14 LAC, June Dennis fonds, MG 31, D191, vol. 1, "Linda Douma – Miss Canada, 1965," in "The 1966 Miss Canada Pageant," souvenir program, 5.

15 Ibid.

16 LAC, Centennial Commission fonds, RG 69, vol. 177, file 4-1-59, "Miss Canada Pageant," promotional booklet.

17 Ibid., 4.

18 "Best Part Is Coming Home to You," in ibid. The second part of the promotional booklet in the Centennial Commission fonds includes several newspaper clippings reprinted as a collage showcasing the media attention and publicity that Douma garnered. These pages were not numbered. The clipping that I am highlighting here was accompanied by a picture of Douma sitting on the hood of a car complete with her Miss Canada sash and roses while waving to the camera, as well as by a picture of the 300 people who attended her welcome home party.

19 Ibid.

20 Ibid.

21 "'Turkey Rose' Taunts Troops," in ibid.

22 "Canada's Sweetheart," in ibid.

23 LAC, June Dennis fonds, MG 31, D191, vol. 1, "Courier," c. 1967, 4. The trip to Japan and Hong Kong was part of the trade-travel mission, but this document also lists the Canadian Travel Bureau, the Department of Trade and Commerce, and the Canadian Tourist Bureau as sponsors of the Miss Canada Pageant in this period.

24 LAC, June Dennis fonds, MG 31, D191, vol. 1, "Linda Douma – Miss Canada, 1965," in "The 1966 Miss Canada Pageant," souvenir program, 5. See also LAC, Centennial Commission fonds, RG 69, vol. 177, file 4-1-59, "Girl with One Blue and One Green Eye," promotional booklet.

25 "Trade Department Seeks Japanese Beauty," *Ottawa Journal*, February 5, 1965, 10.

26 For a picture published in the *Globe and Mail*, April 1, 1965, W6, see LAC, Centennial Commission fonds, RG 69, vol. 177, file 4-1-59, "Miss Canada Pageant," promotional booklet. I was unable to locate any other winners of this title in subsequent years. However, it is entirely possible that the title could have been resurrected as the need arose since its function was to solidify Canadian and Japanese economic interests on "friendlier" terms.

27 Shirley Culpin, "Future Path for Ex-Beauty Queen May Lead Back to India," *Sidney Review*, September 12, 1979, 5.

28 Ibid.

29 For a good illustration of this outlook, see Marilyn Reddick, "My, uh, Dazzling Career as Miss Canada," *Maclean's*, September 15, 1954, 18–19, 104–7. For a much more scathing account of the commercialism behind the Miss Canada Pageant and the unattainable "dreams" that it fostered, see Valerie Miner Johnson, "Meet Miss Canada; or, the Rape of Cinderella," *Saturday Night*, February 1973, 15–16, 18–20.

30 "Miss Canada Cleans Up," *Monetary Times*, May 1966, 41.

31 Ibid., 42.

32 Ibid. Clairtone was a manufacturer of music sound systems and electronics.

33 LAC, June Dennis fonds, MG 31, D191, vol. 1, "Courier," c. 1967, 7.

34 LAC, ISN 163182, "Présent (Société Radio-Canada)," hosted by Ellio Lumbroso and Harvey Paradis, audio, 14 April 1966. Louise Langlois interviewed Diane Landry in Montreal at the opening of the home show Le Salon de la Maison Moderne. The radio interview was in French. Transcribed and translated by author.

35 VPL, Special Collections, Beauty Contests: Clippings file, "The Future of Miss Canada," *Vancouver Province*, November 16, 1967; VPL, Special Collections, Beauty Contests: Clippings file, Cyril Robinson, "A Tomato from Potato Country," *Weekend Magazine*, December 23, 1967. Unfortunately, I was unable to transcribe this speech because I did not have access to the telecast of the Miss Canada 1968 Pageant. Robinson does offer one quotation from MacKinnon's speech: "I just wanted to get a general message across to the people and tell them we should all be proud to be Canadian ... and that everything that divides us isn't as important as everything that unites us."

36 VPL, Special Collections, Beauty Contests: Clippings file, Cyril Robinson, "A Tomato from Potato Country," *Weekend Magazine*, December 23, 1967.

37 VPL, Special Collections, Beauty Contests: Clippings file, "The Future of Miss Canada," *Vancouver Province*, November 16, 1967.

38 Banet-Weiser, *Most Beautiful Girl*, 88.

39 Ibid.

40 See CTV Private Archives, CTV Special Presentation, *Miss Canada 1969 Pageant,* November 3, 1968. By 1969, Cleo Productions had been bought by Baton Broadcasting and CTV. Tom Reynolds started a new company, MCP Productions, which organized the Miss Teenage Canada contest. The new president of Cleo Productions was E.J. Delany, who was also president of Baton.

41 VPL, Science Reference Compact, "Miss Canadian 1972 Pageant," souvenir program.

42 CTV Private Archives, CTV Special Presentation, *Miss Canada 1970 Pageant,* November 10, 1969.

43 For more on the centennial celebrations, see Berton, *1967: Canada's Turning Point.* On Canada's flag, see Matheson, *Canada's Flag;* and Fraser, "Canadian Flag for Canada." For a brief exploration of the various debates in the early twentieth century over the adoption of a Canadian flag, see Vachon, "Choosing a National Flag." Scholarly work on the Royal Commission on Bilingualism and Biculturalism abounds, but for a look at its impact on language debates and Canadian federalism, see Jedwab, "To 'Bi' or Not to 'Bi'"; Balthazar, "Quebec and the Ideal"; and Oliver, "Impact of the Royal Commission." For an inside look at the commission's proceedings as well as a discussion of Quebec nationalism, see Laurendeau, *Journal tenu pendant la Commission royale.* On the Quiet Revolution in Quebec, see Cuccioletta and Lubin, "Quebec Quiet Revolution"; and Carel, "Le révolution tranquille en paradigme." For a wonderful and extensive bibliography on the Parti Québécois and the sovereigntist movement, see Boilard and Lajoie, *Le Parti québécois.* For analyses, see Fraser, *René Lévesque;* Leger, *Le Parti québécois;* and McRoberts, *Quebec.* For essays that focus primarily on the Charter of Rights and Freedoms, see James, Abelson, and Lusztig, eds., *Myth of the Sacred.* See also Cairns, *Reconfigurations.*

44 CTV Private Archives, CTV Special Presentation, *Miss Canada Pageant 1972,* November 8, 1971.

45 Ibid.

46 There continues to be a gap in the number of scholarly sources on the October Crisis, but there are some notable books and essays with a solid approach to the topic. For example, see Fournier, *F.L.Q.;* Cardin, *Comprendre octobre 1970;* Whitaker, "Apprehended Insurrection?"; Laurendeau, *Les Québécois violents;* and Mills, *Empire Within.*

47 In her farewell speech during the broadcast of the Miss Canada 1975 Pageant, Blair Lancaster said that once she returned to Burlington, she would open "Blair Lancaster's Finishing School." This elicited laughter from the audience, but Lancaster did continue to participate in the beauty culture industry, establishing a business venture called the Modelling and Fashion Agency in Burlington, Ontario. Gillian Judkins, "Preteens Parading in Pageants," *The Gazette* (University of Western Ontario), February 11, 1997.

48 CTV Private Archives, CTV Special Presentation, *Miss Canada 1974 Pageant,* November 5, 1973, emphasis added.

49 Banet-Weiser, *Most Beautiful Girl*, 89. Banet-Weiser argues that this "rehearsed spontaneity" was an essential feature of the interview competition in the Miss America Pageant.

50 CTV Private Archives, CTV Special Presentation, *Miss Canada 1975 Pageant*, October 29, 1974.

51 Thobani, *Exalted Subjects*, 144.

52 Haque, *Multiculturalism within a Bilingual Framework*.

53 Abu-Laban and Gabriel, *Selling Diversity*, 105.

54 Thobani, *Exalted Subjects*, 160.

55 Porter's analysis in *The Vertical Mosaic* is focused on social power.

56 See Brown, *Regulating Aversion*.

57 Bannerji, "Paradox of Diversity," 545.

58 Ibid.

59 For a thorough analysis of the "acceptable stranger," see Ahmed, *Strange Encounters*, ch. 5, 95. Ahmed coined this term.

60 CTV Private Archives, CTV Special Presentation, *Miss Canada 1974 Pageant*, November 5, 1973.

61 Thobani, *Exalted Subjects*, 164.

62 CTV Private Archives, CTV Special Presentation, *Miss Canada 1986 Pageant*, November 8, 1985.

63 I was unable to determine definitely Jonathan's nation. It is also not clear to me that her title is a continuation of the Indian Princess Pageant organized as part of the centennial celebrations discussed in Chapter 4. Jonathan could have easily won her title in a queen pageant organized as part of an event and then received funding, or she may have been sponsored to attend the Miss Canada 1975 Pageant.

64 CTV Private Archives, CTV Special Presentation, *Miss Canada 1975 Pageant*, October 29, 1974.

65 Ibid. For more on the Royal Commission on the Status of Women, see Bégin, "Royal Commission on the Status of Women," an article written by its director of research.

66 Canadian Women's Movement Archives (CWMA), "Beauty Contests," editorial, *The Other Woman*, December 1975–January 1976, 2. According to sociologist Becki Ross, *The Other Woman* was one of the most widely read Canadian feminist newspapers. *The Other Woman* was a popular and important voice of grassroots feminism in Toronto. It is also of note that the editorial staff of *The Other Woman* were against International Women's Year, seeing it as a patriarchal and capitalist ploy. Ross, *House That Jill Built*, 60. On *The Other Woman*, see also Adamson, Briskin, and McPhail, *Feminist Organizing for Change*.

67 The Miss Canada Pageant took place on November 3, 1975, and the coverage of the protest by *The Other Woman* was a follow-up on those events. Although the Toronto Women's Anarchist Group and the Radical Lesbian Group were the main organizations involved, protester Adrienne Potts mentioned in an interview with *The Other Woman* that the ten women who protested included members of other groups. She may have been referring specifically to Wages

Due Lesbians and Wages for Housewives. CWMA, "Interview," *The Other Woman,* December 1975–January 1976, 3.

68 CWMA, "Beauty Contests," editorial, *The Other Woman,* December 1975–January 1976, 2.

69 "Lesbians Storm Beauty Pageant," *Toronto Sun,* November 4, 1975, 20.

70 Cited in Bruce Blackadar, "A Kiss for One and All," *Toronto Sun,* November 5, 1975, 18. Protesters in the 1968 demonstration against the Miss America Pageant were also exposed to this coverage. See Dow, "Feminism," 143.

71 Cited in Gosse, *Movements of the New Left,* 127, emphasis in original. According to historian Alice Echols, the Miss America protest "marked the end of the movement's obscurity because the protest – the movement's first national action – received extensive press coverage." Echols, *Daring to Be Bad,* 93. See also the "Manifesto" of the 1968 protest of the Miss America Pageant in Atlantic City – entitled "No More Miss America!" – in Morgan, ed., *Sisterhood Is Powerful,* 584–88.

72 Morgan, ed., *Sisterhood Is Powerful,* 585. The objects tossed into the "Freedom Trash Can" included high-heeled shoes, bras, girdles, typing books, curlers, false eyelashes, and copies of *Playboy, Cosmopolitan,* and *Ladies Home Journal.* The contents of the "Freedom Trash Can" were supposed to be burned, but the protesters were forbidden to do so by city officials in order to prevent a potential fire. Morgan says that there was no bra-burning ceremony, noting that "bra-burning was a whole-cloth invention of the media."

73 Echols, *Daring to Be Bad,* 93.

74 Ibid., 94.

75 Watson and Martin, "Miss America Pageant," 111. For more on the Miss Black America 1968 protest-contest, see Welch, "Up Against the Wall Miss America."

76 The *Toronto Star* reported that this guard had broken ribs as a result of the protesters' forced entry, but I have no evidence to support or dispute this story. See "Feminists Storm Stage at Miss Canada Contest," *Toronto Star,* November 4, 1975, A3.

77 CWMA, "Interview," *The Other Woman,* December 1975–January 1976, 3.

78 Ibid. There are two versions of the interview that I mention in the text. The long version is an interview conducted by Pat Leslie of *The Other Woman,* which I transcribed for my purposes here. The short version is in some ways radically different, not only because it is a truncated version but also because the reorganization of the interview by Leslie or the editors of the feminist newspaper changed the tone of the original taped version. For the taped version, see CWMA, Sound Recording 11/13, Pat Leslie, "Interview of the Women Who Protested the Miss Canada Pageant 1975, *The Other Woman*."

79 CWMA, *The Other Woman,* December 1975–January 1976, 3. The woman identified in *The Other Woman* was Audrey Donaldson.

80 Ibid.

81 Adamson, Briskin, and McPhail, *Feminist Organizing for Change,* 54. These grassroots factions included radical feminists, lesbian feminists, and socialist feminists. As the decade progressed, issues integral to the survival of immigrant,

Indigenous, and Black women were also affecting the ability of the Canadian women's movement to claim one unified voice.

82 Ibid., 58.

83 Press release written by the coalition of protesters, reprinted in *The Other Woman*, December 1975–January 1976, 3. See also CWMA, Sound Recording 11/13, Pat Leslie, "Interview of the Women Who Protested the Miss Canada Pageant 1975, *The Other Woman*."

84 Press release written by the coalition of protesters, reprinted in *The Other Woman*, December 1975–January 1976, 3. The Miss Canada protest seems to have started an internal debate, at least based on an editorial written by *The Other Woman* coalition. In the same issue, the editors remarked that although they were "against" all types of beauty pageants and that they "agree" with "the disruption of the Miss Canada Pageant," they "question their [the protesters'] tactics." In the editor's view, "splashy one-shot actions only result in press distortion." See "Beauty Contests," *The Other Woman*, December 1975–January 1976, 2.

85 "The Other Woman Speaks to the Miss Canada Pageant Protestors," *The Other Woman*, December 1975–January 1976, 3.

86 Ibid.

87 Ibid. The connection between the pageant and sexism was central to the action.

88 Ibid.

89 Press release written by the coalition of protesters, reprinted in *The Other Woman*, December 1975–January 1976, 3. The quotation that they submitted was not entirely accurate. The press release included the words "For the benefit of our newly-arrived guests," which was a reference to the protesters. I made a transcription of the show from the original videotapes, and I have included here what Meyer actually said.

90 Dow, "Feminism," 137.

91 CTV Private Archives, CTV Special Presentation, *Miss Canada 1977 Pageant*, November 16, 1976.

92 Ibid.

93 Ibid.

94 CTV Private Archives, CTV Special Presentation, *Miss Canada 1983 Pageant*, November 1, 1982.

95 The most famous book on the backlash against the women's movement is Susan Faludi's national bestseller *Backlash: The Undeclared War against American Women*. Faludi dedicates Chapter 8, "Beauty and the Backlash," to the beauty industry's role in this backlash. Faludi was not the first to write about this cultural issue. See also Rush, "Many Faces of Backlash." For a more recent discussion of this "undeclared war" from a Canadian socio-historical perspective, see Hamilton, *Gendering the Vertical Mosaic*, esp. ch. 5.

96 CTV Private Archives, CTV Special Presentation, *Miss Canada 1981 Pageant*, November 3, 1980.

97 The Miss Dominion of Canada Pageant stopped sending its title winners to the Miss Universe Pageant in 1978. Instead, Andrea Eng, the first runner-up in the Miss Canada 1978 Pageant, was sent. Terry Mackay, Miss Canada 1980, was a

finalist in the Miss Universe 1980 Pageant, thus beginning a string of victories for Canada at the competition in the first half of the decade. The next year, Miss Canada 1981, Dominique Dufour, a bilingual professional model from Laval, Quebec, created a huge stir when she captured the first runner-up spot at the Miss Universe Pageant. By 1983 Dufour had replaced Barbara Kelly as the beauty queen "expert" co-host and had started her career as a broadcaster and entertainer.

98 "Miss Universe Earns Praise of Canadians," *London Free Press*, July 28, 1982, A15.

99 Ibid.

100 CTV Private Archives, CTV Special Presentation, *Miss Canada 1982 Pageant*, November 2, 1981.

101 Ibid.

102 CTV Private Archives, CTV Special Presentation, *Miss Canada 1983 Pageant*, November 1, 1982.

103 Susanne Kelman, "Who Killed Miss Canada?" *Chatelaine*, August 1992, 39–41, 77–78.

104 Powell said that she never wanted to be Miss Canada and only decided to enter the contest to "prove" a point that Black women could win. Beam, "Juliette Powell."

105 See, for example, LAC, Centennial Commission fonds, RG 69, vol. 177, file 4-1-59, vol. 1, report for Peter Aykroyd from John R. Markey re "'Miss Dominion of Canada,' i.e. Miss Universe, and 'Miss Canada,' i.e. Miss America, Beauty Pageants," June 14, 1965.

106 Cited in "Miss Canada Cleans Up," *Monetary Times*, May 1966, 41.

107 Steven Paikin, "1992: Farewell, Miss Canada," *The National*, January 3, 1992, https://www.cbc.ca/archives/entry/1992-farewell-miss-canada.

108 Ibid.

109 Ibid.

110 Ibid.

Conclusion

1 Nan Robins, "I Would Rather Have Beauty Than Brains," *Chatelaine*, February 1931, 56. According to the article, Robins was twenty-four years old and worked in an office.

2 Ibid.

3 Ibid.

4 Ibid.

5 For more on the fetishization of goods and the techniques used to entice consumers, see Reichert, *Erotic History of Advertising*, chs. 1 and 4.

6 Nan Robins, "I Would Rather Have Beauty Than Brains," *Chatelaine*, February 1931, 57.

7 The murder of JonBenét Ramsey is perhaps the most sensational example of how beauty pageants continue to be a major part of our lives. JonBenét started

competing in beauty pageants as early as age four. Her death in 1996 turned a spotlight on child beauty contests, forcing North Americans to take stock of this multi-million-dollar industry, which includes pageant promoters, dress designers, agents, and pageant coaches. Indeed, the number of pageants available to children is staggering. Notably, Ramsey's death did not necessarily diminish the number of beauty pageants, nor did it create a sustained debate on the sexualization of beauty contests. What was clear was that beauty contests themselves were not fundamentally problematic but that the sexualization of children in these events was an issue. I argue that this debate was more likely a consequence of the circumstances around Ramsey's death – there was conclusive evidence that she was sexually assaulted before she was strangled – than a serious exploration of the world of beauty pageants and their alleged impact on the sexualization of girl's bodies. For more on JonBenét Ramsey, see Jerry Adler, "The Strange World of JonBenet," *Newsweek*, January 19, 1997, 43–47; and Ann Louise Bardach, "Missing Innocence," *Vanity Fair*, October 1997, 324–30, 372–78. For an "inside" look at this branch of the beauty pageant industry, see Susan Orlean, "Beautiful Girls," *New Yorker*, August 4, 1997, 29–36.

8 One major feature of this show is that the participants are barracked in a house without mirrors. The show premiered on April 7, 2004, but is no longer on the air. See "The Swan."

9 "China to Hold Fake Beauty Pageant," *BBC News*, August 4, 2004, http://news.bbc.co.uk/2/hi/asia-pacific/3533680.stm. The pageant was established when the winner of the Miss Intercontinental contest was dethroned after it was discovered that she had undergone several thousand dollars worth of surgery. A history of beauty contests in China has yet to be written, but they were abolished in 1949 with the rise of the People's Republic. China's relationship has shifted, however; the Chinese government agreed to host the Miss World Pageant in 2003.

10 Some examples include Miss Canada International, Miss Universe Canada, and Miss World Canada.

11 Sylvia Stark has come under fire in the courts for her tactics regarding the Miss Canada International contest. See David Rider, "Contestants Starved, Lied to, Angry Beauty Queens Allege," *Globe and Mail*, August 2, 2003, A4; and Hayley Mick, "Pageant Organizers Face Suit," *Globe and Mail*, August 2, 2003, A3.

12 For some examples of the coverage regarding Danielle House, see "Charged Beauty Queen Speaks," *Globe and Mail*, October 30, 1996, A4; Jan Wong, "A Dethroned Beauty Queen Confronts the Naked Truth," *Globe and Mail*, November 13, 1997, D1; and Patrick Graham, "Power House," *Saturday Night*, June 1998, 35–41. The incident that brought House into the spotlight took place on October 18, 1996. House later posed as *Playboy's* December 1997 centrefold. On the Miss World protests in Nigeria, see Tertsakian, "Nigeria." This study is based on interviews and print research of the riots and argues that the Miss World fiasco was the result of decades of civil unrest between ethnic and political groups in Kaduna and only secondarily about the religious

comments made by journalist Isioma Daniel in *Thisday* regarding the Prophet Muhammad and the Miss World beauty contestants. Nevertheless, Daniel was forced to flee for her life because of a fatwa issued against her and now lives in Norway as an exile. For a television documentary on her experience and the Miss World riots, see Off and Shprintsen, "Of Fatwas and Beauty Queens." For more media coverage, see "Ottawa Tried to Rescue Miss Canada from Nigeria," *Globe and Mail,* November 23, 2002, A1; "Miss Canada Was First to Urge Nigerian Pageant Be Cancelled," *Globe and Mail,* November 25, 2002, A3; "Miss World Fallout Envelops Two Lives," *Globe and Mail,* November 26, 2002, A1, A14; "They Died for Beauty," editorial, *Globe and Mail,* November 26, 2002, A17; and "Bennett Likes Life in the Spotlight," *Globe and Mail,* November 27, 2002, A11. On Natalie Glebova, see Rosie DiManno, "Here It Is: The Picture You Weren't Allowed to See," *Toronto Star,* June 1, 2005, A2.

13 Miss Canada International seemed to change hands in 2003 and came under the umbrella of the Beauties of Canada organization, which also founded and ran Miss Universe Canada. In various years, the winner of one of these pageants represented Canada at the Miss Universe Pageant, owned by future president of the United States Donald Trump.

14 For an image of the national costume worn by Chelsae Durocher, see "Oh, (Miss) Canada."

15 Tristin Hopper, "'There's Been a Tremendous Misunderstanding': Miss Universe Canada Carved over Totem Pole Outfit," *National Post,* December 21, 2015, http://nationalpost.com/news/canada/unfortunately-theres-been-a-tremendous-misunderstanding-miss-universe-canada-carved-over-totem-pole-outfit.

16 Another example of the female body being used to bolster the rise of the modern nation is Turkey's affair with beauty contests in the 1930s under President Mustafa Kemal Atatürk. Anthropologist A. Holly Shissler argues that in Turkey beauty contests "were exercises in nationalism and the projection of a 'modern', positive national image. From the beginning they had a distinctly nationalist content and were supposed to help promote an image of Turkey as a 'civilized' nation." Shissler, "Beauty Is Nothing," 112. For more on Turkey and gender, see Göle, *Forbidden Modern.* Iran also experienced a similar Westernized view regarding beauty, women, and nation under Prime Minister Reza Shah Pahlavi during the 1920s and 1930s. For an account of the influence of consumerism and ideals of nation in Iran, see Amin, "Importing 'Beauty Culture.'"

17 Niamh Scallan, "Transgendered Contestant's Ouster from Miss Universe Canada Sparks Outrage over 'Natural Born' Rule," *Toronto Star,* March 27, 2012, https://www.thestar.com/life/2012/03/27/transgendered_contestants_ouster_from_miss_universe_canada_sparks_outrage_over_natural_born_rule.html.

18 "Who Will Be Crowned Miss India This Year?" *Times of India,* May 27, 2019, https://epaper.timesgroup.com/olive/ODN/TimesOfIndia/shared/ShowArticle.aspx?doc=TOIM/2019/05/27&entity=Ar02501&sk=5F24CEB3&mode=text#.

19 Cited in Zulekha Nathoo, "Snapshot of Miss India Finalists Renews Debate over Fair Skin Infatuation," *CBC News*, June 1, 2019, https://www.cbc.ca/news/entertainment/miss-india-finalists-fair-skin-1.5158878.

20 The Mrs. Chatelaine contest was one of many beauty contests organized by magazines. We have already encountered the *National Home Monthly*'s "Glamour Girl" in Chapter 3, but other references include *Drum*'s "Mr. Africa" in Johannesburg, South Africa. For more on "Mr. Africa," see Clowes, "Are You Going to Be?'" A treatment of the Mrs. Chatelaine contest can be found in Korinek, "'Mrs. Chatelaine' vs. 'Mrs. Slob.'" Reference to this pageant is also included in Korinek, *Roughing It in the Suburbs*, 87.

21 Korinek, "'Mrs. Chatelaine' vs. 'Mrs. Slob,'" 251, 252.

22 Ibid., 266. Beatrice Maitland of Chatham, New Brunswick, was the first to suggest a "Mrs. Slob" contest in 1961.

23 Sarmishta Subramanian, "Mrs. Chatelaine Grows Up," *Chatelaine*, April 1997, 77–80, 140. This article is a "then and now" account of some of the winners of the Mrs. Chatelaine contest. Interestingly, the author includes the story of Carole Anne Soong, the only visible minority to win the title, having done so in 1973. Soong was an "active" member of the BC Status of Women Coordinating Committee, which became the Vancouver Status of Women. Subramanian points to Soong's successful efforts to change the Mrs. Chatelaine title to Ms. Chatelaine as another example of the pageant's nod to the influence of the feminist movement.

24 For more on the Miss Canadian University Pageant protests as well as other campus protests against pageants, see Gentile, "Queen of the Maple Leaf," 240–55.

25 Simon Fraser University Archives and Records, F73, Marg Hollibough Scrapbooks, 1970, "Janiel Jolley Shows 'Em the Way," *The Peak*, February 4, 1970.

Bibliography

Archival/Special Collections

Archives of Ontario (Toronto)
Canadian Women's Movement Archives (Ottawa)
City of Toronto, Metro Archives (Toronto)
CTV Private Archives (Toronto)
Library and Archives Canada (Ottawa)
North York Centre Public Library (North York)
Queen's University, Stauffer Library, Special Collections (Kingston)
Simon Fraser University Archives and Records (Burnaby)
Vancouver Public Library, Science Reference Compact (Vancouver)
Vancouver Public Library, Special Collections (Vancouver)

Newspapers, Magazines, and Periodicals

B.C. Magazine (*Vancouver Province*)
Chatelaine
Contrast (Toronto)
Daily Telegraph (Saint John)
Dispatch (Department of Public Works, Government of Canada)
Edmonton Journal (Edmonton)
The Fusilier (General Engineering of Canada)
The Gazette (University of Western Ontario)
Globe and Mail

Hamilton Spectator
Harmac News (Alberni Plywoods)
Indian News (Department of Indian Affairs)
Justice (International Ladies' Garment Workers' Union)
Kingston Whig-Standard
Le Devoir (Montreal)
London Free Press
Maclean's
Monetary Times (Toronto)
Montreal Gazette
National Post
Newsweek
New Yorker
New York Times
Niagara Falls Evening Review
The Other Woman (Toronto)
Ottawa Citizen
Ottawa Journal
RA News (Recreation Association of the Public Service of Canada)
Saturday Night
The Shotgun (John Inglis Company)
Sidney Review
Spear (Toronto)
Times of India
Toronto Star
Toronto Sun
Vancouver Province
Vancouver Sun
Vanity Fair
Weekend Magazine

Secondary Sources

Abu-Laban, Yasmeen, and Christina Gabriel. *Selling Diversity: Immigration, Multi-culturalism, Employment Equity, and Globalization.* Toronto: Broadview, 2002.

Adams, Mary Louise. *The Trouble with Normal: Postwar Youth and the Making of Heterosexuality.* Toronto: University of Toronto Press, 1997.

Adamson, Nancy. "Feminists, Libbers, Lefties, and Radicals: The Emergence of the Women's Liberation Movement." In *A Diversity of Women: Ontario, 1945–1980*, ed. Joy Parr, 252–80. Toronto: University of Toronto Press, 1995.

Adamson, Nancy, Linda Briskin, and Margaret McPhail. *Feminist Organizing for Change: The Contemporary Women's Movement in Canada.* Toronto: Oxford University Press, 1988.

Agulhon, Maurice. *Marianne au combat.* Paris: Flammarion, 1979.

Ahmed, Sara. *The Promise of Happiness.* Durham, NC: Duke University Press, 2010.

–. *Strange Encounters: Embodied Others in Post-Coloniality.* New York: Routledge, 2000.

Alcoff, Linda Martin. "Mignolo's Epistemology of Coloniality." *CR: The New Centennial Review* 7, 3 (2007): 79–101.

Alexander, Kristine. *Guiding Modern Girls: Girlhood, Empire, and Internationalism in the 1920s and 1930s.* Vancouver: UBC Press, 2017.

Alfred, Gerald R. *Heeding the Voices of Our Ancestors: Kahnawake Mohawk Politics and the Rise of Native Nationalism.* Toronto: Oxford University Press, 1995.

Amin, Camron Michael. "Importing 'Beauty Culture' into Iran in the 1920s and 1930s: Mass Marketing Individualism in an Age of Anti-Imperialist Sacrifice." *Comparative Studies of South Asia, Africa and the Middle East* 24, 1 (2004): 79–95.

Anderson, Benedict. *Imagined Communities: Reflections on the Origin and Spread of Nationalism.* London: Verso, 1983.

Anderson, Mark Cronlund, and Carmen L. Robertson. *Seeing Red: A History of Natives in Canadian Newspapers.* Winnipeg: University of Manitoba Press, 2011.

Backhouse, Constance. *Colour-Coded: A Legal History of Racism in Canada, 1900–1950.* Toronto: University of Toronto Press, 1999.

Baldwin, Andrew, Laura Cameron, and Audrey Kobayashi, eds. *Rethinking the Great White North: Race, Nature, and the Historical Geographies of Whiteness in Canada.* Vancouver: UBC Press, 2011.

Ballerino Cohen, Colleen, Richard Wilk, and Beverly Stoeltje, eds. *Beauty Queens on the Global Stage: Gender, Contests, and Power.* New York: Routledge, 1996.

Balthazar, Louis. "Quebec and the Ideal of Federalism." *Annals of the American Academy of Political and Social Science* 538, 1 (1995): 40–53.

Banet-Weiser, Sarah. *The Most Beautiful Girl in the World: Beauty Pageants and National Identity.* Berkeley: University of California Press, 1999.

Banet-Weiser, Sarah, and Laura Portwood-Stacer. "'I Just Want to Be Me Again!': Beauty Pageants, Reality Television and Post-Feminism." *Feminist Theory* 7, 2 (2006): 255–72.

Banner, Lois W. *American Beauty.* New York: Alfred A. Knopf, 1983.

Bannerji, Himani. "The Paradox of Diversity: The Construction of a Multicultural Canada and 'Women of Color.'" *Women's Studies International Forum* 23, 5 (2000): 537–60.

Bantey, Edward. *Les Midinettes/The Midinettes, 1937–1962.* Trans. Gisèle Lebeuf. Montreal: International Ladies' Garment Workers' Union, 1962.

Barman, Jean. "Taming Aboriginal Sexuality: Gender, Power, and Race in British Columbia, 1850–1900." *BC Studies* 115–16 (Autumn–Winter 1997–98): 237–66.

Barnes, Felicity. "Bringing Another Empire Alive? The Empire Marketing Board and the Construction of Dominion Identity, 1926–1933." *Journal of Imperial and Commonwealth History* 42, 1 (2014): 61–85.

Barnes, Natasha B. "Face of the Nation: Race, Nationalisms and Identities in Jamaican Beauty Pageants." *Massachusetts Review* 35, 3–4 (1994): 471–92.

Barnum, Phineas T. *The Colossal P.T. Barnum Reader: Nothing Else Like It in the Universe.* Ed. James W. Cook. Chicago: University of Illinois Press, 2005.

Baudrillard, Jean. "The Finest Consumer Object: The Body." In *The Consumer Society: Myths and Structures*, 129–50. London: Sage, 1998.

Beam, Liane. "Juliette Powell: Working Her Way to the Top." n.d. http://faze.ca/juliette-powell-working-her-way-to-the-top.

Bégin, Monique. "The Royal Commission on the Status of Women in Canada: Twenty Years Later." In *Challenging Times: The Women's Movement in Canada and the United States*, ed. Constance Backhouse and David H. Flaherty, 21–38. Montreal and Kingston: McGill-Queen's University Press, 1992.

Belisle, Donica. *Retail Nation: Department Stores and the Making of Modern Canada*. Vancouver: UBC Press, 2011.

–. "Sexual Spectacles: Saleswomen in Canadian Department Store Magazines between 1920 and 1950." In *Feminist History in Canada: New Essays on Women, Gender, Work, and Nation*, ed. Catherine Carstairs and Nancy Janovicek, 135–58. Vancouver: UBC Press, 2013.

Bell, Shannon. *Reading, Writing, and Rewriting the Prostitute Body*. Bloomington: Indiana University Press, 1994.

Berton, Pierre. *1967: Canada's Turning Point*. Toronto: Seal Books, 1998.

Bettella, Patrizia. *The Ugly Woman: Transgressive Aesthetic Models in Italian Poetry from the Middle Ages to the Baroque*. Toronto: University of Toronto Press, 2005.

Billig, Michael. *Banal Nationalism*. London: Sage, 1995.

Bird, S. Elizabeth. "Gendered Construction of the American Indian in Popular Media." *Journal of Communication* 49, 3 (1999): 61–83.

Bisson, Anne-Florence. "La 'Revengeance' des duchesses: Une mise en scène carnavalesque hors Carnaval." *Ethnologies* 34, 1–2 (2012): 113–32.

–. "L'esprit du Carnaval de Québec: Entre participation citoyenne et fréquentation touristique." MA thesis, University of Laval, 2015.

Blackwelder, Julia Kirk. *Styling Jim Crow: African American Beauty Training during Segregation*. College Station: Texas A&M University Press, 2003.

Bland, Susan. "Henrietta the Homemaker and 'Rosie the Riveter': Images of Women in Advertising in *Maclean's* Magazine, 1939–50." *Atlantis* 8, 2 (1983): 61–86.

Bock, Michel. *A Nation beyond Borders: Lionel Groulx on French-Canadian Minorities*. Trans. Ferdinanda Van Gennip. Ottawa: University of Ottawa Press, 2014.

Bogdan, Robert. *Freak Show: Presenting Human Oddities for Amusement and Profit*. Chicago: University of Chicago Press, 1988.

Boilard, Gilberte, and Claude Lajoie. *Le Parti québécois: Bibliographie, 1991–2003*. Quebec: Bibliothèque de l'Assemblée nationale, 2004.

Bonavia, George. *Maltese in Canada*. Ottawa: Multiculturalism Directorate, Department of the Secretary of State, 1980.

Bordo, Susan. "Feminism, Foucault and the Politics of the Body." In *Feminist Theory and the Body: A Reader*, ed. Janet Price and Margrit Shildrick, 246–57. New York: Routledge, 1999.

Boyer, Kate. "'Miss Remington' Goes to Work: Gender, Space, and Technology at the Dawn of the Information Age." *Professional Geographer* 56, 2 (2004): 201–12.

–. "'Neither Forget nor Remember Your Sex': Sexual Politics in the Early Twentieth-Century Canadian Office." *Journal of Historical Geography* 29, 2 (2003): 212–29.

Brand, Dionne. "'We weren't allowed to go into factory work until Hitler started the war': The 1920s to the 1940s." In *'We're Rooted Here and They Can't Pull Us Up': Essays in African Canadian Women's History*, ed. Peggy Bristow, 171–92. Toronto: University of Toronto Press, 1994.

Brand, Peg Zeglin, ed. *Beauty Matters*. Bloomington: Indiana University Press, 2000.

Braunberger, Christine. "Revolting Bodies: The Monster Beauty of Tattooed Women." *NWSA Journal* 12, 2 (2000): 1–23.

Bridger, Bobby. *Buffalo Bill and Sitting Bull: Inventing the Wild West*. Austin: University of Texas Press, 2002.

Brookfield, Tarah. "Modelling the U.N.'s Mission in Semi-Formal Wear: Edmonton's Miss United Nations Pageants of the 1960s." In *Contesting Bodies and Nation in Canadian History*, ed. Patrizia Gentile and Jane Nicholas, 247–66. Toronto: University of Toronto Press, 2013.

Brown, Wendy. *Regulating Aversion: Tolerance in the Age of Identity and Empire*. Princeton, NJ: Princeton University Press, 2008.

Brownmiller, Susan. *Femininity*. New York: Fawcett Columbine Books, 1984.

Bruce, Jean. *Back the Attack! Canadian Women during the Second World War at Home and Abroad*. Toronto: Macmillan, 1985.

Burbick, Joan. "Romance, Rodeo Queens, and the 1950s." *Frontiers* 17, 3 (1996): 124–45.

Burr, Christina. "Gender, Sexuality, and Nationalism in J.W. Bengough's Verses and Political Cartoons." *Canadian Historical Review* 83, 4 (2002): 505–54.

Burstyn, Varda. *The Rites of Men: Manhood, Politics, and the Culture of Sport*. Toronto: University of Toronto Press, 1999.

Burwell, Barbara Peterson, and Polly Peterson Bowles. *Becoming a Beauty Queen: The Complete Guide*. New York: Prentice Hall, 1987.

Butler, Judith. *Bodies That Matter: On the Discursive Limits of "Sex."* New York: Routledge, 1993.

Bynum, Caroline. "Why All the Fuss about the Body? A Medievalist's Perspective." *Critical Inquiry* 22, 1 (1995): 1–33.

Cahn, Susan K. "From the 'Muscle Moll' to the 'Butch' Ballplayer: Mannishness, Lesbianism, and Homophobia in U.S. Women's Sport." In *The Politics of Women's Bodies: Sexuality, Appearance, and Behavior*, ed. Rose Weitz, 67–81. New York: Oxford University Press, 1998.

Cairns, Alan C. *Reconfigurations: Canadian Citizenship and Constitutional Change: Selected Essays*. Ed. Douglas E. Williams. Toronto: McClelland and Stewart, 1995.

Canning, Kathleen. "The Body as Method? Reflections on the Place of the Body in Gender History." *Gender and History* 11, 3 (1999): 499–513.

Cardin, Jean-François. *Comprendre octobre 1970: Le FLQ, la crise et le syndicalisme*. Montreal: Méridien, 1990.

Carel, Ivan. "Le Révolution tranquille en paradigmes." *Bulletin d'histoire politique* 12, 1 (2003): 201–10.

Carter, Sarah. *Capturing Women: The Manipulation of Cultural Imagery in Canada's Prairie West*. Montreal and Kingston: McGill-Queen's University Press, 1997.

–. "Categories and Terrains of Exclusion: Constructing the 'Indian Woman' in the Early Settlement Era in Western Canada." In *Out of the Background: Readings on Canadian Native History,* 2nd ed., ed. Ken Coates and Robin Fisher, 177–95. Toronto: Copp Clark, 1996.

Chenier, Elise. "Class, Gender, and the Social Standard: The Montreal Junior League, 1912–1939." *Canadian Historical Review* 90, 4 (2009): 671–710.

Chisholm, Christine. "The Curious Case of Thalidomide and the Absent Eugenic Clause in Canada's Amended Abortion Law of 1969." *Canadian Bulletin of Medical History* 33, 2 (2016): 493–516.

Clapperton, Jonathan. "Naturalizing Race Relations: Conservation, Colonialism, and Spectacle at the Banff Indian Days." *Canadian Historical Review* 94, 3 (2013): 349–79.

Cleverdon, Catherine L. *The Woman Suffrage Movement in Canada.* Toronto: University of Toronto Press, 1974.

Clowes, Lindsay. "'Are You Going to Be MISS (or MR) Africa?' Contesting Masculinity in *Drum* Magazine 1951–1953." *Gender and History* 13, 1 (2001): 1–20.

Coates, Colin M., and Cecilia Morgan. *Heroines and History: Representations of Madeleine de Verchères and Laura Secord.* Toronto: University of Toronto Press, 2001.

Cobble, Dorothy Sue. *Dishing It Out: Waitresses and Their Unions in the Twentieth Century.* Urbana: University of Illinois Press, 1992.

–. "'A Spontaneous Loss of Enthusiasm': Workplace Feminism and the Transformation of Women's Service Jobs in the 1970s." *International Labor and Working-Class History* 56 (1999): 23–44.

Coleman, Daniel. *White Civility: The Literary Project of English Canada.* Toronto: University of Toronto Press, 2006.

Comacchio, Cynthia R. *"Nations Are Built of Babies": Saving Ontario's Mothers and Children, 1900–1940.* Montreal and Kingston: McGill-Queen's University Press, 1993.

Conor, Liz. "'Blackfella Missus Too Much Proud': Techniques of Appearing, Femininity, and Race in Australian Modernity." In *The Modern Girl around the World: Consumption, Modernity, and Globalization,* ed. Alys Eve Weinbaum, Lynn M. Thomas, Priti Ramamurthy, Uta G. Poiger, Madeleine Yue Dong, and Tani E. Barlow, 220–39. Durham, NC: Duke University Press, 2008.

–. *The Spectacular Modern Woman: Feminine Visibility in the 1920s.* Bloomington: Indiana University Press, 2004.

Conrad, Margaret. "'Not a Feminist, But ... ': The Political Career of Ellen Louks Fairclough, Canada's First Female Federal Cabinet Minister." *Journal of Canadian Studies* 31, 2 (1996): 5–28.

Cook, Sharon A. *Sex, Lies, and Cigarettes: Canadian Women, Smoking, and Visual Culture, 1880–2000.* Montreal and Kingston: McGill-Queen's University Press, 2012.

Cooper, Afua. *The Hanging of Angélique: The Untold Story of Canadian Slavery and the Burning of Old Montreal.* New York: HarperCollins, 2006.

Coulthard, Glen Sean. *Red Skin, White Masks: Rejecting the Colonial Politics of Recognition.* Minneapolis: University of Minnesota Press, 2014.

Craig, Maxine Leeds. *Ain't I a Beauty Queen? Black Women, Beauty, and the Politics of Race.* New York: Oxford University Press, 2002.

Crawford, John Darrock. "The Maltese Diaspora: The Historical Development of Migration from Malta." MA thesis, University of Victoria, 1990.

Crosby, Andrew, and Jeffrey Monaghan. *Policing Indigenous Movements: Dissent and the Security State.* Winnipeg: Fernwood, 2018.

Cross, Gary. *An All-Consuming Century: Why Commercialism Won in Modern America.* New York: Columbia University Press, 2000.

Cuccioletta, Donald, and Martin Lubin. "The Quebec Quiet Revolution: A Noisy Evolution." *Quebec Studies* 36 (2003–04): 125–38.

Cumbo, Richard S., and John P. Portelli. "A Brief History of Early Maltese in Toronto and Canadian Society of Toronto, Inc." http://www.maltamigration.com/settlement/associations/ca/mcst2.shtml.

Davidson, Tina. "'A Woman's Right to Charm and Beauty': Maintaining the Feminine Ideal in the Canadian Women's Army Corps." *Atlantis* 26, 1 (2001): 45–54.

Davis, Donald F., and Barbara Lorenzkowski. "A Platform for Gender Tensions: Women Working and Riding on Canadian Urban Public Transit in the 1940s." *Canadian Historical Review* 79, 3 (1998): 431–65.

Davis, Michaela Angela, "Our Crowns, Our Glory: America's Reigning Beauty Queens Are Black, Bold and Rocking Many Crowns." *Essence,* October 3, 2019. https://www.essence.com/feature/black-beauty-queens-2019-digital-cover.

Dawson, Michael. *The Mountie from Dime Novel to Disney.* Toronto: Between the Lines, 1998.

–. *Selling British Columbia: Tourism and Consumer Culture, 1890–1970.* Vancouver: UBC Press, 2004.

Deford, Frank. *There She Is: The Life and Times of Miss America.* New York: Viking, 1971.

Deloria, Philip J. *Playing Indian.* New Haven, CT: Yale University Press, 1998.

Demczuk, Irène. "Léa Roback: De toutes les luttes." In *Ces femmes qui ont bâti Montréal,* ed. Maryse Darsigny, Francine Descarries, Lyne Kurtzman, and Évelyne Tardy, 228–30. Montreal: Éditions du remue-ménage, 1995.

D'Emilio, John, and Estelle B. Freedman. *Intimate Matters: A History of Sexuality in America.* 2nd ed. Chicago: University of Chicago Press, 1988.

Dennett, Andrea Stulman. *Weird and Wonderful: The Dime Museum in America.* New York: New York University Press, 1997.

Denning, Michael. *The Cultural Front: The Laboring of American Culture in the Twentieth Century.* London: Verso, 1997.

Dickason, Olive P. *The Myth of the Savage and the Beginning of French Colonialism in the Americas.* Edmonton: University of Alberta Press, 1997.

Dow, Bonnie J. "Feminism, Miss America, and Media Mythology." *Rhetoric and Public Affairs* 6, 1 (2003): 127–49.

Dubinsky, Karen. *Improper Advances: Rape and Heterosexual Conflict in Ontario, 1880–1929.* Chicago: University of Chicago Press, 1993.

–. *The Second Greatest Disappointment: Honeymooning and Tourism at Niagara Falls.* Toronto: Between the Lines, 1999.

Dummitt, Chris. "Finding a Place for Father: Selling the Barbecue in Postwar Canada." *Journal of the Canadian Historical Association* 9, 1 (1998): 209–23.

Dussel, Enrique. "Eurocentrism and Modernity." *boundary 2* 20, 3 (1993): 65–76.

Dyck, Erika. *Facing Eugenics: Reproduction, Sterilization, and the Politics of Choice.* Toronto: University of Toronto Press, 2013.

Echols, Alice. *Daring to Be Bad: Radical Feminism in America, 1967–1975.* Minneapolis: University of Minnesota Press, 1989.

Eco, Umberto. *Storia della bruttezza.* Milan, Italy: Bompiani, 2007.

Erickson, Bruce. "A Phantasy in White in a World That Is Dead." In *Rethinking the Great White North: Race, Nature, and the Historical Geographies of Whiteness in Canada,* ed. Andrew Baldwin, Laura Cameron, and Audrey Kobayashi, 19–38. Vancouver: UBC Press, 2011.

Erickson, Lesley. *Westward Bound: Sex, Violence, the Law, and the Making of a Settler Society.* Vancouver: UBC Press, 2012.

Evans, Caroline. *The Mechanical Smile: Modernism and the First Fashion Shows in France and America, 1900–1929.* New Haven, CT: Yale University Press, 2013.

Faludi, Susan. *Backlash: The Undeclared War against American Women.* New York: Anchor Books, 1991.

Favreau, Robert, dir. *Le soleil a pas d'chance.* Quebec: National Film Board, 1975.

Fenton Griffing, Marie. *How to Be a Beauty Pageant Winner.* New York: Simon and Schuster, 1981.

Fielding, Stephen. "The Changing Face of Little Italy: The Miss Colombo Pageant and the Making of Ethnicity in Trail, British Columbia, 1970–1977." *Urban History Review* 39, 1 (2010): 45–58.

Filey, Mike. *I Remember Sunnyside: The Rise and Fall of a Magical Era.* Toronto: Dundurn, 1996.

Fisher, Robin. "The Image of the Indian." In *Contact and Conflict: Indian-European Relations in British Columbia, 1774–1890,* 73–94. Vancouver: UBC Press, 1977.

Fiske, Jo-Anne. "Pocahontas's Granddaughters: Spiritual Transition and Tradition of Carrier Women of British Columbia." *Ethnohistory* 43, 4 (1996): 663–81.

Flandrin, Jean-Louis, and Marie-Claude Phan. "Les métamorphoses de la beauté féminine." *L'Histoire* 68 (1984): 48–57.

Forestell, Diane G. "The Necessity of Sacrifice for a Nation at War: Women's Labour Force Participation, 1939–1946." *Histoire sociale/Social History* 22, 44 (1989): 323–43.

Foucault, Michel. *Discipline and Punish: The Birth of the Prison.* Trans. Alan Sheridan. New York: Vintage Books, 1995.

–. *The History of Sexuality.* Vol. 3, *The Care of the Self.* Trans. Robert Hurley. New York: Vintage Books, 1990.

Fournier, Louis. *F.L.Q.: Histoire d'un mouvement clandestin.* Montreal: Éditions Québec/Amérique, 1982.

Francis, Daniel. *The Imaginary Indian: The Image of the Indian in Canadian Culture.* Vancouver: Arsenal Pulp, 1992.

–. *National Dreams: Myth, Memory, and Canadian History.* Vancouver: Arsenal Pulp, 1997.

Francis, Margot. *Creative Subversions: Whiteness, Indigeneity, and the National Imaginary.* Vancouver: UBC Press, 2011.

Fraser, Alistair B. "A Canadian Flag for Canada." *Journal of Canadian Studies* 25, 4 (1990–91): 64–80.

Fraser, Graham. *René Lévesque and the Parti Québécois in Power*. Montreal and Kingston: McGill-Queen's University Press, 2001.

Fretz, Eric. "P.T. Barnum's Theatrical Selfhood and the Nineteenth-Century Culture of Exhibition." In *Freakery: Cultural Spectacles of the Extraordinary Body*, ed. Rosemarie Garland Thomson, 97–107. New York: New York University Press, 1996.

Gagnon, Gemma. "Rose Pesotta: Une fine stratège syndicale." In *Ces femmes qui ont bâti Montréal*, ed. Maryse Darsigny, Francine Descarries, Lyne Kurtzman, and Évelyne Tardy, 225–27. Montreal: Éditions du remue-ménage, 1995.

Gagnon, Mona-Josée. "Les comités syndicaux de condition féminine." In *Travailleuses et féministes: Les femmes dans la société québécoise*, ed. Marie Lavigne and Yolande Pinard, 161–76. Montreal: Boréal Express, 1983.

Gaines, Kevin K. *Uplifting the Race: Black Leadership, Politics, and Culture in the Twentieth Century*. Chapel Hill: University of North Carolina Press, 1996.

Gallagher, Catherine, and Thomas Laquer, eds. *The Making of the Modern Body: Sexuality and Society in the Nineteenth Century*. Berkeley: University of California Press, 1987.

Gannagé, Charlene. *Double Day, Double Bind: Women Garment Workers*. Toronto: Women's Press, 1986.

Gatens, Moira. "Corporeal Representations in/and the Body Politic." In *Writing on the Body: Female Embodiment and Feminist Theory*, ed. Katie Conboy, Nadia Medina, and Sarah Stanbury, 80–89. New York: Columbia University, 1997.

Gentile, Patrizia. "Blair, Winnifred C." In *Oxford Companion to Canadian History*, ed. Gerald Hallowell, 74. Toronto: Oxford University Press, 2004.

–. "'Government Girls' and 'Ottawa Men': Cold War Management of Gender Relations in the Civil Service." In *Whose National Security? Canadian State Surveillance and the Creation of Enemies*, ed. Dieter K. Buse, Gary Kinsman, and Mercedes Steedman, 131–41. Toronto: Between the Lines, 2000.

–. "Queen of the Maple Leaf: A History of Beauty Contests in Twentieth Century Canada." PhD diss., Queen's University, 2006.

–. "Searching for 'Miss Civil Service' and 'Mr. Civil Service': Gender Anxiety, Beauty Contests and Fruit Machines in the Canadian Civil Service, 1950–1973." MA thesis, Carleton University, 1996.

Gentile, Patrizia, and Jane Nicholas, eds. *Contesting Bodies and Nation in Canadian History*. Toronto: University of Toronto Press, 2013.

Gill, Tiffany M. *Beauty Shop Politics: African American Women's Activism in the Beauty Industry*. Urbana: University of Illinois Press, 2010.

Gilman, Sander L. *Making the Body Beautiful: A Cultural History of Aesthetic Surgery*. Princeton, NJ: Princeton University Press, 1999.

Göle, Nilüfer. *The Forbidden Modern: Civilization and Veiling*. Ann Arbor: University of Michigan Press, 1996.

Goss, David. "The Fairest Girl." *The Beaver* 83, 1 (2003), 29–32.

Gosse, Van. *The Movements of the New Left, 1950–1975: A Brief History with Documents*. Boston: Bedford/St. Martin's, 2005.

Government of Canada. *The Criminal Code and Other Selected Statutes of Canada.* Ottawa: F.A. Acland, 1928.

Government of Ontario. "Maltese." In *Ontario Ethnocultural Profiles.* Toronto: Minister of Culture and Recreation, 1982.

Grace, Sherrill E. *Canada and the Idea of North.* Montreal and Kingston: McGill-Queen's University Press, 2001.

Gray, Charlotte. *Flint and Feather: The Life and Times of E. Pauline Johnson, Tekahionwake.* Toronto: Harper Collins, 2002.

Gray, Dorothy. "Which among Our Polish Women in Western Pennsylvania Is the Most Beautiful? Matylda Zygmunt and the Polish Beauty Contest of 1930." *Western Pennsylvania History,* Fall 2005, 9–16.

Green, Rayna. "The Pocahontas Perplex: The Image of Indian Women in American Culture." *Massachusetts Review* 16, 4 (1975): 698–714.

Grout, Holly. *The Force of Beauty: Transforming French Ideals of Femininity in the Third Republic.* Baton Rouge, LA: LSU Press, 2015.

Gundle, Stephen. "Feminine Beauty, National Identity and Political Conflict in Postwar Italy, 1945–1954." *Contemporary European History* 8, 3 (1999): 359–78.

Hall, M. Ann. *The Girl and the Game: A History of Women's Sport in Canada.* Toronto: Broadview, 2002.

–. "Toward a History of Aboriginal Women in Canadian Sport." In *Aboriginal Peoples and Sport in Canada: Historical Foundations and Contemporary Issues,* ed. Janice Forsyth and Audrey R. Giles, 64–91. Vancouver: UBC Press, 2013.

Hamblin, Jennifer. "Queen of the Stampede: 1946–1966." *Alberta History* 60, 3 (2012): 33–42.

Hamilton, Roberta. *Gendering the Vertical Mosaic: Feminist Perspectives on Canadian Society.* Toronto: Copp Clark, 1996.

Hamlin, Kimberley A. "Bathing Suits and Backlash: The First Miss America Pageants, 1921–1927." In *"There She Is, Miss America": The Politics of Sex, Beauty, and Race in America's Most Famous Pageant,* ed. Elwood Watson and Darcy Martin, 27–51. New York: Palgrave Macmillan, 2004.

Haque, Eva. *Multiculturalism within a Bilingual Framework: Language, Race, and Belonging in Canada.* Toronto: University of Toronto Press, 2012.

Harvey, Karen. "The Century of Sex? Gender, Bodies, and Sexuality in the Long Eighteenth Century." *Historical Journal* 45, 4 (2002): 899–916.

Haynes, Michaele Thurgood. *Dressing Up Debutantes: Pageantry and Glitz in Texas.* New York: Oxford University Press, 1998.

Henderson, Jennifer. *Settler Feminism and Race Making in Canada.* Toronto: University of Toronto Press, 2003.

Heron, Craig, and Steve Penfold. "The Craftsmen's Spectacle: Labour Day Parades in Canada, the Early Years." *Histoire sociale/Social History* 29, 58 (1996): 357–89.

–. *The Workers' Festival: A History of Labour Day in Canada.* Toronto: University of Toronto Press, 2005.

Higham, John. "Indian Princess and Roman Goddess: The First Female Symbols of America." *Proceedings of the American Antiquarian Society* 100, 1 (1990): 45–79.

Hillmer, Norman. *O.D. Skelton: A Portrait of Canadian Ambition*. Toronto: University of Toronto Press, 2015.

Hobbs, Margaret, and Joan Sangster, eds. *The Woman Worker, 1926–1929*. St. John's, NL: Canadian Committee on Labour History, 1999.

Horn-Miller, Kahente. "My Mom, the 'Military Mohawk Princess': kahntinetha Horn through the Lens of Indigenous Female Celebrity." In *Indigenous Celebrity*, ed. Jennifer Adese, Robert Innes, and Zoe Todd. Winnipeg: University of Manitoba Press, forthcoming.

Ingraham, Chrys. *White Weddings: Romancing Heterosexuality in Popular Culture*. New York: Routledge, 1999.

James, Patrick, Donald E. Abelson, and Michael Lusztig, eds. *The Myth of the Sacred: The Charter, the Courts, and the Politics of the Constitution of Canada*. Montreal and Kingston: McGill-Queen's University Press, 2002.

Jedwab, Jack. "To 'Bi' or Not to 'Bi': Canada's Royal Commission on Bilingualism and Biculturalism, 1960–1980." *Canadian Issues*, June 2003, 19–26.

Jewell, K. Sue. *From Mammy to Miss America and Beyond: Cultural Images and the Shaping of US Policy*. London: Routledge, 1993.

Johnson, Mark. *Beauty and Power: Transgendering and Cultural Transformation in the Southern Philippines*. Oxford: Berg, 1997.

Jones, Jacqueline. *Labor of Love, Labor of Sorrow: Black Women, Work, and the Family, from Slavery to the Present*. New York: Basic Books, 2010.

Joudrey, Susan L. "The Expectations of a Queen: Identity and Race Politics in the Calgary Stampede." In *The West and Beyond: New Perspectives on an Imagined Region*, ed. Alvin Finkel, Sarah Carter, and Peter Fortna, 133–55. Edmonton: Athabasca University Press, 2010.

Jozic, Jennifer, and Jillian Staniec. "No Ordinary Life: Remembering the Miss Roughrider and Miss Grey Cup Pageants, 1951–1991." *Saskatchewan History* 62, 2 (2010): 8–12.

Kealey, Linda, ed. *A Not Unreasonable Claim: Women and Reform in Canada, 1880s–1920s*. Toronto: Women's Press, 1979.

Kelm, Mary-Ellen. "Manly Contests: Rodeo Masculinities at the Calgary Stampede." *Canadian Historical Review* 90, 4 (2009): 711–51.

–. *A Wilder West: Rodeo in Western Canada*. Vancouver: UBC Press, 2011.

Keshen, Jeff. *Saints, Sinners, and Soldiers: Canada's Second World War*. Vancouver: UBC Press, 2004.

Kicksee, Richard G. "'Scaled Down to Size': Contested Liberal Commonsense and the Negotiation of 'Indian Participation' in the Canadian Centennial Celebrations and Expo '67, 1963–1967." MA thesis, Queen's University, 1995.

King-O'Riain, Rebecca Chiyoko. *Pure Beauty: Judging Race in Japanese American Beauty Pageants*. Minneapolis: University of Minnesota Press, 2006.

King, Tiffany. "In the Clearing: Black Female Bodies, Space and Settler Colonial Landscapes." PhD diss., University of Maryland, 2013.

–. *The Black Shoals: Offshore Formations of Black and Native Studies*. Durham, NC: Duke University Press, 2019.

Kinloch, Valerie Felita. "The Rhetoric of Black Bodies: Race, Beauty, and Representation." In *"There She Is, Miss America": The Politics of Sex, Beauty, and Race in*

America's Most Famous Pageant, ed. Elwood Watson and Darcy Martin, 93–109. New York: Palgrave Macmillan, 2004.

Kirkham, Pat. "Fashioning the Feminine: Dress, Appearance and Femininity in Wartime Britain." In *Nationalising Femininity: Culture, Sexuality, and British Cinema in the Second World War,* ed. Christine Gledhill and Gillian Swanson, 152–74. Manchester: Manchester University Press, 1996.

Kirkman, Emily. "Fashioning Identity: The Hostesses of Expo 67." MA thesis, Concordia University, 2011.

Klausen, Susanne. "The Plywood Girls: Women and Gender Ideology at the Port Alberni Plywood Plant, 1942–1991." *Labour/Le Travail* 41 (1998): 199–235.

Klein, Richard. "Fat Beauty." In *Bodies Out of Bounds: Fatness and Transgression,* ed. Jana Evans Braziel and Kathleen LeBesco, 19–38. Berkeley: University of California Press, 2001.

Korinek, Valerie J. "'Mrs. Chatelaine' vs. 'Mrs. Slob': Contestants, Correspondents and the *Chatelaine* Community in Action, 1961–1969." *Journal of the Canadian Historical Association* 7, 1 (1997): 251–75.

–. *Roughing It in the Suburbs: Reading* Chatelaine *Magazine in the Fifties and Sixties.* Toronto: University of Toronto Press, 2000.

Kozol, Wendy. "Miss Indian America: Regulatory Gazes and the Politics of Affiliation." *Feminist Studies* 31, 1 (2005): 64–94.

Labbé, Pierrick. "L'Arsenal canadien: Les politiques canadiennes et la fabrication de munitions au Canada durant la Deuxième Guerre mondiale." PhD diss., University of Ottawa, 2012.

Laegreid, Renée M. *Riding Pretty: Rodeo Royalty in the American West.* Lincoln: University of Nebraska Press, 2006.

–. "Rodeo Queens at the Pendleton Round-Up: The First Go-Round, 1910–1917." *Oregon Historical Quarterly* 104, 1 (2003): 6–23.

Lake, Marilyn. "Female Desires: The Meaning of World War II." In *Feminism and History,* ed. Joan Wallach Scott, 429–49. New York: Oxford University Press, 1996.

Latham, Angela J. "Packaging Woman: The Concurrent Rise of Beauty Pageants, Public Bathing, and Other Performances of Female 'Nudity.'" *Journal of Popular Culture* 29, 3 (1995): 149–67.

Laurendeau, André. *Journal tenu pendant la Commission royale d'enquête sur le bilinguisme et le biculturalisme.* Quebec: VLP éditeur, 1990.

Laurendeau, Marc. *Les Québécois violents: La violence politique 1962–1972.* Montreal: Boréal, 1990.

Lavenda, Robert H. "'It's Not a Beauty Pageant!': Hybrid Ideology in Minnesota Community Queen Pageants." In *Beauty Queens on the Global Stage: Gender, Contests, and Power,* ed. Colleen Ballerino Cohen, Richard Wilk, and Beverly Stoeltje, 31–46. New York: Routledge, 1996.

–. "Minnesota Queen Pageants: Play, Fun, and Dead Seriousness in a Festive Mode." *Journal of American Folklore* 101, 400 (1988): 168–75.

Lears, Jackson. *Fables of Abundance: A Cultural History of Advertising in America.* New York: Basic Books, 1994.

LeCompte, Mary Lou. *Cowgirls of the Rodeo: Pioneer Professional Athletes*. Urbana: University of Illinois Press, 1993.

Leeder, Elaine J. *The Gentle General: Rose Pesotta, Anarchist and Labor Organizer*. Albany: State University of New York Press, 1993.

Lefolii, Ken. *The Canadian Look: A Century of Sights and Styles*. Toronto: Canadian Centennial, 1965.

Léger, Marcel. *Le Parti québécois: Ce n'était qu'un début*. Montreal: Éditions Québec/Amérique, 1986.

Lévesque, Andrée. *Making and Breaking the Rules: Women in Quebec, 1919–1939*. Trans. Yvonne M. Klein. Toronto: McClelland and Stewart, 1994.

Lieu, Nhi T. "Remembering 'the Nation' through Pageantry: Femininity and the Politics of Vietnamese Womanhood in the *Hoa Hau Ao Dai* Contest." *Frontiers* 21, 1–2 (2000): 127–51.

Llewellyn, Kristina R. "Teaching June Cleaver, Being Hazel Chong: An Oral History of Gender, Race, and National 'Character.'" In *Feminist History in Canada: New Essays on Women, Gender, Work, and Nation*, ed. Catherine Carstairs and Nancy Janovicek, 178–99. Vancouver: UBC Press, 2013.

Lowe, Margaret A. *Looking Good: College Women and Body Image, 1875–1930*. Baltimore, MD: Johns Hopkins University Press, 2003.

Lugones, María. "Heterosexualism and the Colonial/Modern Gender System." *Hypatia* 22, 1 (2007): 186–219.

Macdonald, Charlotte. *Strong, Beautiful and Modern: National Fitness in Britain, New Zealand, Australia and Canada, 1935–1960*. 2011. Vancouver: UBC Press, 2013.

Mackey, Eva. *The House of Difference: Cultural Politics and National Identity in Canada*. Toronto: University of Toronto Press, 2002.

Malacrida, Claudia. *A Special Hell: Institutional Life in Alberta's Eugenic Years*. Toronto: University of Toronto Press, 2015.

Manring, M.M. *Slave in a Box: The Strange Career of Aunt Jemima*. Charlottesville: University of Virginia Press, 1998.

Manuel, Arthur, and R.M. Derrickson. *Unsettling Canada: A National Wake-Up Call*. Toronto: University of Toronto Press, 2015.

Marks, Lynne. *Revivals and Roller Rinks: Religion, Leisure, and Identity in Late-Nineteenth-Century Small-Town Ontario*. Toronto: University of Toronto Press, 1996.

Marwick, Arthur. *Beauty in History: Society, Politics and Personal Appearance, c. 1500 to the Present*. London: Thames and Hudson, 1988.

Matheson, John Ross. *Canada's Flag: A Search for a Country*. Belleville, ON: Mika, 1986.

Matthews Grieco, Sara F. "The Body, Appearance, and Sexuality." In *A History of Women in the West: Renaissance and Enlightenment Paradoxes*, ed. Natalie Zemon Davis and Arlette Farge, 46–84. Cambridge, MA: Belknap Press of Harvard University Press, 1993.

May, Elaine Tyler. *Homeward Bound: American Families in the Cold War Era*. New York: Basic Books, 1988.

McAllister, Carlota. "Authenticity and Guatemala's May Queen." In *Beauty Queens on the Global Stage: Gender, Contests, and Power*, ed. Collen Ballerino Cohen, Richard Wilk, and Beverly Stoeltje, 105–24. New York: Routledge, 1996.

McCallum, Mary Jane Logan. *Indigenous Women, Work, and History: 1940–1980.* Manitoba: University of Manitoba Press, 2014.

McClintock, Anne. *Imperial Leather: Race, Gender and Sexuality in the Colonial Contest.* New York: Routledge, 1995.

McLaren, Angus. *Our Own Master Race: Eugenics in Canada, 1885–1945.* Toronto: Oxford University Press, 1990.

McNally, David. *Bodies of Meaning: Studies in Language, Labor, and Liberation.* Albany: State University of New York Press, 2001.

McPherson, Kathryn. "Home Tales: Gender, Domesticity, and Colonialism in the Prairie West, 1870–1990." In *Finding a Way to the Heart: Feminist Writings on Aboriginal and Women's History in Canada,* ed. Robin Jarvis Brownlie and Valerie J. Korinek, 222–40. Winnipeg: University of Manitoba Press, 2012.

McRoberts, Kenneth. *Quebec: Social Change and Political Crisis.* 3rd ed. Toronto: McClelland and Stewart, 1988.

Menzies, Robert, Robert Adamoski, and Dorothy E. Chunn. "Rethinking the Citizen in Canadian Social History." In *Contesting Canadian Citizenship: Historical Readings,* ed. Robert Adamoski, Dorothy E. Chunn, and Robert J. Menzies, 11–41. Toronto: Broadview, 2002.

Meyerowitz, Joanne, ed. *Not June Cleaver: Women and Gender in Postwar America, 1945–1960.* Philadelphia: Temple University Press, 1994.

–. "Women, Cheesecake, and Borderline Material: Responses to Girlie Pictures in the Mid-Twentieth-Century U.S." *Journal of Women's History* 8, 3 (1996): 9–35.

Mignolo, Walter. *The Darker Side of Western Modernity: Global Futures, Decolonial Options.* Durham, NC: Duke University Press, 2011.

Miller, J.R. *Compact, Contract, Covenant: Aboriginal Treaty-Making in Canada.* Toronto: University of Toronto Press, 2009.

–. *Skyscrapers Hide the Heavens: A History of Indian-White Relations in Canada.* Rev. ed. Toronto: University of Toronto Press, 1991.

Mills, Sean. *The Empire Within: Postcolonial Thought and Political Activism in Sixties Montreal.* Montreal and Kingston: McGill-Queen's University Press, 2010.

Mire, Amina. "Skin-Bleaching: Poison, Beauty, Power, and the Politics of the Colour Line." *Resources for Feminist Research* 28, 3–4 (2001): 13–38.

Mohanram, Radhika. *Black Body: Women, Colonialism, and Space.* Minneapolis: University of Minnesota Press, 1999.

Morgan, Cecilia. "'A Wigwam to Westminster': Performing Mohawk Identity in Imperial Britain, 1890s–1990s." *Gender and History* 15, 2 (2003): 319–41.

Morgan, Robin, ed. *Sisterhood Is Powerful: An Anthology of Writings from the Women's Liberation Movement.* New York: Vintage Books, 1970.

Morrissey, Katherine G. "Miss Spokane and the Inland Northwest: Representations of Regions and Gender." *Frontiers* 22, 3 (2001): 6–12.

Morton, Suzanne. *Ideal Surroundings: Domestic Life in a Working-Class Suburb in the 1920s.* Toronto: University of Toronto Press, 1995.

Mullenbach, Cheryl. *Double Victory: How African American Women Broke Race and Gender Barriers to Help Win World War II.* Chicago: Chicago Review Press, 2013.

Nahoum-Grappe, Véronique. *Beauté, laideur: Un essai de phénoménologie histo-rique.* Paris: Payot, 1990.

–. "The Beautiful Woman." Trans. Arthur Goldhammer. In *A History of Women in the West: Renaissance and Enlightenment Paradoxes,* ed. Natalie Zemon Davis and Arlette Farge, 85–100. Cambridge, MA: Belknap Press of Harvard University Press, 1993.

Nakamura, Masako. "'Miss Atom Bomb' Contests in Nagasaki and Nevada: The Politics of Beauty, Memory, and the Cold War." *U.S.-Japan Women's Journal* 37 (2009): 117–43.

Newton, Esther. *Cherry Grove, Fire Island: Sixty Years in America's First Gay and Lesbian Town.* Boston: Beacon, 1993.

Nicholas, Jane. "Beauty Advice for the Canadian Modern Girl in the 1920s." In *Consuming Modernity: Changing Gendered Behaviours and Consumerism,* ed. Cheryl Krasnick Warsh and Dan Malleck, 181–99. Vancouver: UBC Press, 2013.

–. *Canadian Carnival Freaks and the Extraordinary Body, 1900–1970s.* Toronto: University of Toronto Press, 2018.

–. "Catching the Public Eye: The Body, Space, and Social Order in 1920s Canadian Visual Culture." PhD diss., University of Waterloo, 2006.

–. "A Debt to the Dead? Ethics, Photography, History, and the Study of Freakery." *Histoire sociale/Social History* 47, 93 (2014): 139–55.

–. "Gendering the Jubilee: Gender and Modernity in the Diamond Jubilee of Confederation Celebrations, 1927." *Canadian Historical Review* 90, 2 (2009): 247–74.

–. "'I Was a 555-Pound Freak': The Self, Freakery, and Sexuality in Celesta 'Dolly Dimples' Geyer's Diet or Die." *Journal of the Canadian Historical Association* 21, 1 (2010): 83–107.

–. *The Modern Girl: Feminine Modernities, the Body, and Commodities in the 1920s.* Toronto: University of Toronto Press, 2014.

–. "Representing the Modern Man: Beauty, Culture, and Masculinity in Early-Twentieth-Century Canada." In *Canadian Men and Masculinities: Historical and Contemporary Perspectives,* ed. Christopher J. Greig and Wayne J. Martino, 42–60. Toronto: Canadian Scholars' Press, 2012.

Nicholson, Ian A.M. "Gordon Allport, Character, and the 'Culture of Personality,' 1897–1937." *History of Psychology* 1, 1 (1998): 52–68.

Nielsen, Georgia Panter. *From Sky Girl to Flight Attendant: Women and the Making of a Union.* Ithaca, NY: Cornell University Press, 1982.

Nielson, Carmen J. "Caricaturing Colonial Space: Indigenized, Feminized Bodies and Anglo-Canadian Identity, 1873–94." *Canadian Historical Review* 96, 4 (2015): 473–506.

–. "Erotic Attachment, Identity Formation and the Body Politic: The Woman-as-Nation in Canadian Graphic Satire, 1867–1914." *Gender and History* 28, 1 (2016): 102–26.

Nolan, Michael. *CTV: The Network That Means Business.* Edmonton: University of Alberta Press, 2001.

Obomsawin, Alanis, dir. *Kanehsatake: 270 Years of Resistance.* Montreal: National Film Board, 1993.

Off, Carol, and Alex Shprintsen. "Of Fatwas and Beauty Queens." *CBC News: Correspondent,* November 14, 2004.

"Oh, (Miss) Canada." *Native Appropriations,* September 12, 2011. http://nativeappropriations.com/2011/09/oh-miss-canada.html.

Oliver, Michael. "The Impact of the Royal Commission on Bilingualism and Biculturalism on Constitutional Thought and Practice in Canada." *International Journal of Canadian Studies* 7–8 (1993): 315–32.

Owram, Doug. *Born at the Right Time: A History of the Baby Boom Generation.* Toronto: University of Toronto Press, 1996.

Palmer, Beth. "Choices and Compromises: The Abortion Movement in Canada, 1968–1988." PhD diss., York University, 2012.

Palmer, Bryan. *Working-Class Experience: The Rise and Reconstitution of Canadian Labour, 1800–1980.* Toronto: Butterworths, 1983.

Pang, Henry. "Miss America: An American Ideal, 1921–1969." *Journal of Popular Culture* 2, 4 (1969): 687–96.

Parr, Joy. *Domestic Goods: The Material, the Moral, and the Economic in the Postwar Years.* Toronto: University of Toronto Press, 1999.

–. *The Gender of Breadwinners: Women, Men, and Change in Two Industrial Towns, 1880–1950.* Toronto: University of Toronto Press, 1990.

Payne, Carol. *The Official Picture: The National Film Board of Canada's Still Photography Division and the Image of Canada, 1941–1971.* Montreal and Kingston: McGill-Queen's University Press, 2013.

Peers, Frank W. *The Public Eye: Television and the Politics of Canadian Broadcasting, 1952–1968.* Toronto: University of Toronto Press, 1979.

Peiss, Kathy. *Cheap Amusements: Working Women and Leisure in Turn-of-the-Century New York.* Philadelphia: Temple University Press, 1986.

–. *Hope in a Jar: The Making of America's Beauty Culture.* New York: Metropolitan Books, 1998.

Perlmutter, Dawn. "Miss America: Whose Ideal?" In *Beauty Matters,* ed. Peg Zeglin Brand, 155–68. Bloomington: University of Indiana Press, 2000.

Pesotta, Rose. *Bread upon the Waters.* 1944. Reprint. Ithaca, NY: Cornell University, 1987.

Pickles, Katie. *Female Imperialism and National Identity: Imperial Order Daughters of the Empire.* Manchester: Manchester University Press, 2002.

Pickles, Katie, and Myra Rutherdale, eds. *Contact Zones: Aboriginal and Settler Women in Canada's Colonial Past.* Vancouver: UBC Press, 2006.

Pierson, Ruth Roach. *"They're Still Women After All": The Second World War and Canadian Womanhood.* Toronto: McClelland and Stewart, 1996.

Porter, John. *The Vertical Mosaic: An Analysis of Social Class and Power in Canada.* Toronto: University of Toronto Press, 1965.

Prentice, Alison, Paula Bourne, Gail Cuthbert Brandt, Beth Light, Wendy Mitchinson, and Naomi Black. *Canadian Women: A History.* Toronto: Harcourt Brace Jovanovich, 1988.

Purdy, Sean. "Scaffolding Citizenship: Housing Reform and Nation Formation in Canada, 1900–1950." In *Contesting Canadian Citizenship: Historical Readings,* ed. Robert Adamoski, Dorothy E. Chunn, and Robert Menzies, 129–53. Toronto: Broadview, 2002.

Quijano, Aníbal. "Coloniality and Modernity/Rationality." *Cultural Studies* 21, 2–3 (2007): 168–78.

Razack, Sherene H. *Race, Space, and the Law: Unmapping a White Settler Society.* Toronto: Between the Lines, 2002.

Rebick, Judy. *Ten Thousand Roses: The Making of a Feminist Revolution.* Toronto: Penguin Canada, 2005.

Reichert, Tom. *The Erotic History of Advertising.* Amherst, NY: Prometheus Books, 2003.

Rifkin, Mark. "The Erotics of Sovereignty." In *Queer Indigenous Studies: Critical Interventions in Theory, Politics, and Literature,* ed. Qwo-Li Driskill, Chris Finley, Brian Joseph Gilley, and Scott Lauria Morgensen, 172–89. Tucson: University of Arizona Press, 2011.

Riverol, Armando. *Live from Atlantic City: A History of the Miss America Pageant.* Bowling Green, OH: Bowling Green State University Popular Press, 1992.

Roberts, Blain. "A New Cure for Brightleaf Tobacco: The Origins of the Tobacco Queen during the Great Depression." *Southern Cultures* 12, 2 (2006): 30–52.

–. *Pageants, Parlors, and Pretty Women: Race and Beauty in the Twentieth-Century South.* Chapel Hill: University of Northern Carolina Press, 2014.

Roberts, Helene E. "The Exquisite Slave: The Role of Clothes in the Making of the Victorian Woman." *Signs* 2, 3 (1977): 554–69.

Robertson, Jennifer. "Japan's First Cyborg? Miss Nippon, Eugenics and Wartime Technologies of Beauty, Body and Blood." *Body and Society* 7, 1 (2001): 1–34.

Ross, Becki. *Burlesque West: Showgirls, Sex, and Sin in Postwar Vancouver.* Toronto: University of Toronto Press, 2009.

–. *The House That Jill Built: A Lesbian Nation in Formation.* Toronto: University of Toronto Press, 1995.

Rothblum, Esther, Sondra Solovay, and Marilyn Wann, eds. *The Fat Studies Reader.* New York: New York University Press, 2009.

Rowe, Rochelle. "'Glorifying the Jamaican Girl': The 'Ten Types–One People' Beauty Contest, Racialized Femininities, and Jamaican Nationalism." *Radical History Review,* 103 (2009): 36–58.

Rush, Florence. "The Many Faces of Backlash." In *The Sexual Liberals and the Attack on Feminism,* ed. Dorchen Leidholdt and Janice G. Raymond, 165–74. New York: Pergamon, 1990.

Rutherdale, Myra, and Jim Miller. "'It's Our Country': First Nations' Participation in the Indian Pavilion at Expo 67." *Journal of the Canadian Historical Association* 17, 2 (2006): 148–73.

Rutherford, Paul. *When Television Was Young: Primetime Canada, 1952–1967.* Toronto: University of Toronto Press, 1990.

Rutledge Shields, Vickie, and Colleen Coughlin. "Performing Rodeo Queen Culture: Competition, Athleticism and Excessive Feminine Masquerade." *Text and Performance Quarterly* 20, 2 (2000): 182–202.

Sangster, Joan. *Dreams of Equality: Women on the Canadian Left, 1920–1950.* Toronto: McClelland and Stewart, 1989.

–. *Earning Respect: The Lives of Working Women in Small-Town Ontario, 1920–1960.* Toronto: University of Toronto Press, 1995.

–. "'Queen of the Picket Line': Beauty Contests in the Post–World War II Canadian Labor Movement, 1945–1970." *Labor: Studies in Working-Class History* 5, 4 (2008): 83–106.

–. *Transforming Labour: Women and Work in Post-War Canada.* Toronto: University of Toronto Press, 2010.

Savage, Candace. *Beauty Queens: A Playful History.* Vancouver: Greystone Books, 1998.

Schackt, Jon. "Mayahood through Beauty: Indian Beauty Pageants in Guatemala." *Bulletin of Latin American Research* 24, 3 (2005): 269–87.

Schofield, Ann. "The Uprising of the 20,000: The Making of a Labor Legend." In *A Needle, A Bobbin, A Strike: Women Needleworkers in America,* ed. Joan M. Jensen and Sue Davidson, 167–82. Philadelphia: Temple University Press, 1984.

Schwartz, Hillel. *Never Satisfied: A Cultural History of Diets, Fantasies, and Fat.* New York: Free Press, 1986.

Segalen, Martine, and Josselyne Chamarat. "La Rosière et la 'Miss': Les 'reines' des fêtes populaires." *L'Histoire* 53 (1983): 44–55.

Shilling, Chris. *The Body and Social Theory.* London: Sage, 1993.

Shissler, A. Holly. "Beauty Is Nothing to Be Ashamed Of: Beauty Contests as Tools of Women's Liberation in Early Republican Turkey." *Comparative Studies of South Asia, Africa and the Middle East* 24, 1 (2004): 107–22.

Shorter, Edward. *A History of Women's Bodies.* New York: Basic Books, 1982.

Simpson, Audra. *Mohawk Interruptus: Political Life across the Borders of Settler States.* Durham, NC: Duke University Press, 2014.

Simpson, Leanne Betasamosake. *As We Have Always Done: Indigenous Freedom through Radical Resistance.* Minneapolis: University of Minnesota Press, 2017.

Simpson, Leanne Betasamosake, and Kiera Ladner. *This Is an Honour Song: Twenty Years since the Blockades.* Winnipeg: ARP Books, 2010.

Smith, Andrea. "Indigeneity, Settler Colonialism, White Supremacy." In *Racial Formation in the Twenty-First Century,* ed. Daniel Martinez HoSang, Oneka LaBennet, and Laura Pulido, 66–90. Berkeley: University of California Press, 2012.

–. "Queer Theory and Native Studies: The Heteronormativity of Settler Colonialism." In *Queer Indigenous Studies: Critical Interventions in Theory, Politics, and Literature,* ed. Qwo-Li Driskill, Chris Finley, Brian Joseph Gilley, and Scott Lauria Morgensen, 43–65. Tucson: University of Arizona Press, 2011.

Smith, Helen, and Pamela Wakewich. "'Beauty and the Helldivers': Representing Women's Work and Identities in a Warplant Newspaper." *Labour/Le Travail* 44 (1999): 71–107.

–. "Trans/Forming the Citizen Body in Wartime: National and Local Public Discourse on Women's Bodies and 'Body Work' for Women during the Second World War." In *Contesting Bodies and Nation in Canadian History,* ed. Patrizia Gentile and Jane Nicholas, 305–27. Toronto: University of Toronto Press, 2013.

Sobel, David, and Susan Meurer. *Working at Inglis: The Life and Death of a Canadian Factory.* Toronto: James Lorimer, 1994.

Srigley, Katrina. *Breadwinning Daughters: Young Working Women in a Depression-Era City, 1929–1939.* Toronto: University of Toronto Press, 2010.

St-Amand, Isabelle. *Stories of Oka: Land, Film, and Literature.* Winnipeg: University of Manitoba Press, 2018.

Stearns, Peter N. *Fat History: Bodies and Beauty in the Modern West.* New York: New York University Press, 1997.

Steele, Jeffrey. "Reduced to Images: American Indians in Nineteenth-Century Advertising." In *Dressing in Feathers: The Construction of the Indian in American Popular Culture,* ed. S. Elizabeth Bird, 45–64. Boulder, CO: Westview, 1996.

Stern, Alexandra M. "Beauty Is Not Always Better: Perfect Babies and the Tyranny of Paediatric Norms." *Patterns of Prejudice* 36, 1 (2002): 68–78.

Stern, Stephen. "Ceremonies of 'Civil Judaism' among Sephardic Jews of Los Angeles." *Western Folklore* 47, 2 (1988): 103–28.

Strange, Carolyn. *Toronto's Girl Problem: The Perils and Pleasures of the City, 1880–1930.* Toronto: University of Toronto Press, 1995.

Strange, Carolyn, and Jennifer A. Stephens. "Eugenics in Canada: A Checkered History, 1850s–1990s." In *The Oxford Handbook on the History of Eugenics,* ed. Alison Bashford and Philippa Levine, 523–38. Oxford: Oxford University Press, 2010.

Strong-Boag, Veronica. "Canada's Wage-Earning Wives and the Construction of the Middle Class, 1945–60." *Journal of Canadian Studies* 29, 3 (1994): 5–25.

–. "'A Red Girl's Reasoning': E. Pauline Johnson Constructs the New Nation." In *Painting the Maple: Essays on Race, Gender, and the Construction of Canada,* ed. Veronica Strong-Boag, Sherrill Grace, Avigail Eisenberg, and Joan Anderson, 130–54. Vancouver: UBC Press, 1998.

Strong-Boag, Veronica, and Carole Gerson. *Paddling Her Own Canoe: The Times and Texts of E. Pauline Johnson (Tekahionwake).* Toronto: University of Toronto Press, 2000.

Sugiman, Pamela. *Labour's Dilemma: The Gender Politics of Auto Workers in Canada, 1937–1979.* Toronto: University of Toronto Press, 1994.

Suleiman, Susan R., ed. *The Female Body in Western Culture: Contemporary Perspectives.* Cambridge, MA: Harvard University Press, 1986.

Susman, Warren I. *Culture as History: The Transformation of American Society in the Twentieth Century.* New York: Pantheon Books, 1984.

"The Swan." *TV.com,* n.d. http://www.tv.com/swan/show/25662/summary.html.

Synnott, Anthony. "Truth and Goodness, Mirrors and Masks – Part I: A Sociology of Beauty and the Face." *British Journal of Sociology* 40, 4 (1989): 607–36.

–. "Truth and Goodness, Mirrors and Masks – Part II: A Sociology of Beauty and the Face." *British Journal of Sociology* 41, 1 (1990): 55–76.

Tertsakian, Carina. "Nigeria: The 'Miss World Riots': Continued Impunity for Killings in Kaduna." *Human Rights Watch* 15, 13 (2003): 1–32.

Theobald, Andrew. "Divided Once More: Social Memory and the Canadian Conscription Crisis of the First World War." *Past Imperfect* 12 (2006): 1–19.

Thobani, Sunera. *Exalted Subjects: Studies in the Making of Race and Nation in Canada.* Toronto: University of Toronto Press, 2007.

Thomson, Rosemarie Garland, ed. *Freakery: Cultural Spectacles of the Extraordinary Body.* New York: New York University Press, 1996.

Tice, Karen W. *Queens of Academe: Beauty Pageants and Campus Life*. London: Oxford University Press, 2012.

Todd, Jan. "Bernarr Macfadden: Reformer of Feminine Form." *Journal of Sport History* 14, 1 (1987): 61–75.

Tuck, Eve, and Rubén A. Gaztambide-Fernández. "Curriculum, Replacement, and Settler Futurity." *Journal of Curriculum Theorizing* 29, 1 (2013): 72–89.

Tuck, Eve, and K. Wayne Yang. "Decolonization Is Not a Metaphor." *Decolonization: Indigeneity, Education and Society* 1, 1 (2012): 1–40.

Turner, Dale. *This Is Not a Peace Pipe: Towards a Critical Indigenous Philosophy*. Toronto: University of Toronto Press, 2006.

Vachon, Auguste. "Choosing a National Flag." *Archivist* [Canada] 17, 1 (1990): 8–10.

Valaskakis, Gail Guthrie, and Marilyn Burgess. *Indian Princesses and Cowgirls: Stereotypes from the Frontier/Princesses indiennes et Cow-Girls: Stéréotypes de la frontière*. Montreal: Oboro, 1995.

Valverde, Mariana. *The Age of Light, Soap, and Water: Moral Reform in English Canada, 1885–1925*. Toronto: McClelland and Stewart, 1991.

–. "The Love of Finery: Fashion and the Fallen Woman in Nineteenth-Century Social Discourse." *Victorian Studies* 32, 2 (1989): 169–88.

–. "Social Purity." In *The International Encyclopedia of Human Sexuality*. Hoboken, NJ: John Wiley and Sons, 2015.

Van Kirk, Sylvia. *Many Tender Ties: Women in Fur-Trade Society, 1670–1870*. Norman: University of Oklahoma Press, 1983.

Van Vugt, Sarah. "Beauty on the Job: Visual Representation, Bodies, and Canada's Women War Workers, 1939–1945." PhD diss., University of Victoria, 2016.

Veracini, Lorenzo. *Settler Colonialism: A Theoretical Overview*. London: Palgrave, 2010.

Vertinsky, Patricia. "The Social Construction of the Gendered Body: Exercise and the Exercise of Power." *International Journal of the History of Sport* 11, 2 (1994): 147–71.

Vigarello, Georges. *Histoire de la beauté: Le corps et l'art d'embellir de la Renaissance à nos jours*. Paris: Éditions de Seuil, 2004.

–. *Le corps redressé: Histoire d'un pouvoir pédagogique*. Paris: Delarge, 1978.

–. *Le propre et le sale: L'hygiène du corps depuis le Moyen Âge*. Paris: Éditions de Seuil, 1985.

Walden, Keith. *Becoming Modern in Toronto: The Industrial Exhibition and the Shaping of a Late Victorian Culture*. Toronto: University of Toronto Press, 1997.

–. "The Road to Fat City: An Interpretation of the Development of Weight Consciousness in Western Society." *Historical Reflections* 12, 3 (1985): 331–73.

Waldinger, Roger. "Another Look at the International Ladies' Garment Workers' Union: Women, Industry Structure and Collective Action." In *Woman, Work and Protest: A Century of U.S. Women's Labor History*, ed. Ruth Milkman, 86–109. Boston: Routledge and Kegan Paul, 1985.

Walker, Susannah. "Black Is Profitable: The Commodification of the Afro, 1960–1975." In *Beauty and Business: Commerce, Gender, and Culture in Modern America*, ed. Philip Scranton, 254–77. New York: Routledge, 2001.

Wall, Sharon. "Totem Poles, Teepees, and Token Traditions: 'Playing Indian' at Ontario Summer Camps, 1920–1955." *Canadian Historical Review* 86, 3 (2005): 513–44.

Warren, Heather A. "The Shift from Character to Personality in Mainline Protestant Thought, 1935–1945." *Church History* 67, 3 (1998): 537–55.

Warsh, Cheryl Krasnick, and Dan Malleck, eds. *Consuming Modernity: Gendered Behaviour and Consumerism before the Baby Boom.* Vancouver: UBC Press, 2013.

Warsh, Cheryl Krasnick, and Greg Marquis. "Gender, Spirits, and Beer: Representing Female and Male Bodies in Canadian Alcohol Ads, 1930s–1970s." In *Contesting Bodies and Nation in Canadian History,* ed. Patrizia Gentile and Jane Nicholas, 203–25. Toronto: University of Toronto Press, 2013.

Watson, Elwood, and Darcy Martin. "The Miss America Pageant: Pluralism, Femininity, and Cinderella All in One." *Journal of Popular Culture* 34, 1 (2000): 105–26.

–, eds. *"There She Is, Miss America!" The Politics of Sex, Beauty, and Race in America's Most Famous Pageant.* New York: Palgrave Macmillan, 2004.

Watson, Graham. "The Reification of Ethnicity and Its Political Consequences in the North." *Canadian Review of Sociology and Anthropology* 18, 4 (1981): 453–69.

Weinbaum, Alys Eve, Lynn M. Thomas, Priti Ramamurthy, Uta G. Poiger, Madeleine Yue Dong, and Tani E. Barlow, eds. *The Modern Girl around the World: Consumption, Modernity, and Globalization.* Durham, NC: Duke University Press, 2008.

Welch, Georgina Paige. "'Up Against the Wall Miss America': Women's Liberation and Miss Black America in Atlantic City, 1968." *Feminist Formations* 27, 2 (2015): 70–97.

Welsh, Christine, dir. *Keepers of the Fire.* Montreal: National Film Board, 1994.

Welter, Barbara. "The Cult of True Womanhood: 1820–1960." *American Quarterly* 18, 2, part 1 (1966): 151–74.

Whitaker, Reginald. "Apprehended Insurrection? RCMP Intelligence and the October Crisis." *Queen's Quarterly* 100, 2 (1993): 383–406.

–. *Canadian Immigration Policy since Confederation.* Ottawa: Canadian Historical Association, 1991.

Winks, Robin W. *The Blacks in Canada: A History.* 2nd ed. Montreal and Kingston: McGill-Queen's University Press, 2008.

Wolfe, Patrick. "Race and the Trace of History: For Henry Reynolds." In *Studies in Settler Colonialism: Politics, Identity and Culture,* ed. Fiona Bateman and Lionel Pilkington, 272–96. New York: Palgrave Macmillan, 2011.

–. *Settler Colonialism and the Transformation of Anthropology: The Politics and Poetics of an Ethnographic Event.* London: Cassell, 1999.

Wu, Judy Tzu-Chun. "'Loveliest Daughter of Our Ancient Cathay!': Representations of Ethnic and Gender Identity in the Miss Chinatown U.S.A. Beauty Pageant." *Journal of Social History* 31, 1 (1997): 5–31.

Index

Note: "i" after a note number indicates an illustration.